PRAISE FOR *ATTACK FROM WITHIN*

"Whenever Professor McQuade has something to say, I listen—and learn. *Attack from Within* is a brilliantly vital defense of truth, justice and the rule of law against a multitude of political and technological threats to our precious democracy."
—DAVID MARANISS, Pulitzer Prize–winning biographer

"Barb McQuade has the rare ability to ask the right questions and then answer them. Her take on disinformation—how and why it's been used—is critical to understanding this point in our nation's history. *Attack from Within* is essential reading for everyone."
—JOYCE VANCE, Distinguished Professor of the Practice of Law, University of Alabama School of Law, and former US Attorney in Alabama

"Barbara McQuade offers a superb, easy-to-read assessment of the information war being waged in America right now, what the stakes are, and what can be done to turn things around. As someone who grew up behind the Iron Curtain, I understand the dangers of authoritarianism. If you want to understand the risks to democracy and how we can address them, read this important book."
—MARTINA NAVRATILOVA

"Barb McQuade offers a sweeping and panoramic view of the disinformation landscape and how it contributes to the erosion of our shared reality, which is a sine qua non for the rule of law. Like any seasoned prosecutor she marshals the evidence, presents expert testimony, and makes the case for why this threat is one we must address together, as citizens. Her book is a wake-up call for the need to take back power from social media platforms and would-be authoritarians and restore our democratic norms and responsibility to the truth."
—ASHA RANGAPPA, Assistant Dean and Senior Lecturer, Jackson School of Global Affairs, Yale University, Former FBI Counterintelligence Agent

"At a time when it couldn't be more needed, Barbara McQuade provides readers with a clear, straightforward yet urgent warning about the true threat misinformation poses. As a journalist, I found particularly poignant McQuade's clear-eyed view of the importance of a free press to a free society, and the way threats and attacks on journalists endanger everyone. This book is required reading for any American who wants to understand the threat misinformation poses, and a roadmap for how to fight against that threat."
—KIMBERLY ATKINS STOHR, Senior Opinion Writer, *The Boston Globe*

"Barb McQuade traces the history of disinformation from its inception to modern day, brilliantly linking past challenges of falsehoods and how they become amplified in the digital age. Barb then goes a step further, offering a comprehensive plan for restoring the integrity of information and instilling resiliency in our democracies. A remarkable, well versed study that's a must read for all citizens."

—CLINT WATTS, Former FBI Special Agent, Consultant to
FBI National Security Branch

"Barbara McQuade has written a compelling page turner. You'll learn how authoritarians destroy democracy through mis- and disinformation and the psychological forces inherent in all of us that make us believe them even when we know it's a con."

—JILL WINE-BANKS, author of *The Watergate Girl*, MSNBC analyst,
co-host, #SistersInLaw and iGenPolitics podcasts

ATTACK
FROM
WITHIN

HOW DISINFORMATION IS
SABOTAGING AMERICA

BARBARA MCQUADE

SEVEN STORIES PRESS
NEW YORK · OAKLAND · LONDON

Seven Stories Press
140 Watts Street
New York, NY 10013
www.sevenstories.com

College professors and high school and middle school teachers may order free examination copies of Seven Stories Press titles. Visit https://www.sevenstories.com/pg/resources-academics or email academic@sevenstories.com.

Library of Congress Cataloging-in-Publication Data is on file.

ISBN: 978-1-64421-363-6 (hardcover)
ISBN: 978-1-64421-364-3 (ebook)

Printed in the USA.

9 8 7 6 5 4 3 2

CONTENTS

To all of the brave American heroes who have given their lives to defend democracy from fascism. A trip to Normandy, where more than nine thousand American service members are buried, left me in awe of their courage and selflessness. We owe them and other American patriots our vigilance, so that their sacrifices will not have been in vain.

"All warfare is based on deception."

—SUN TZU, *The Art of War*

INTRODUCTION

DISINFORMED
TO DEATH

"The information war is about territory—just not
the geographic kind. In a warm information war, the
human *mind* is the territory."

—RENÉE DIRESTA, "The Digital Maginot Line"

ON JANUARY 5, 2021, Rosanne Boyland left her home in Kennesaw, Georgia, for the ten-hour drive to Washington, DC. Boyland had fallen under the spell of the election-denier movement, bound by a belief that the incumbent president, Donald J. Trump, had won the presidential election but had been robbed of his victory through fraud.[1] In fact, sixty-one courts and Trump's own Justice Department had already rejected every claim of fraud, and federal cybersecurity and election officials had declared the 2020 election "the most secure in US history."[2]

The next day, Boyland joined a mob egged on by Trump and stormed the US Capitol to "Stop the Steal," as the movement slogan went. Of course, as we all know by now, the crowd breached police lines, smashed windows, and broke into the building where Congress was meeting to certify the count of electoral votes from each state, the final procedure that would seal the presidential victory for Joe Biden. Boyland found herself on the west side of the Capitol, in a tunnel near a door guarded by police. As described by the *New York Times*, the crowd "massed together in a dangerous crush" and used "the weight of their combined bodies to push the officers back, trapping many people in the process."[3] At some point, Boyland fell to the ground, but the crowd did not relent.[4] In all of the chaos, no medical professional could render timely aid and, within a few hours, Boyland would be pronounced dead.[5]

Witnesses say Boyland was trampled to death. Her official cause of death was an amphetamine overdose,[6] but a medical examiner said a contributing factor to her death was the "raucous scene."[7] Her sister later said Boyland would not have been at the Capitol at all that day "if it weren't for all the misinformation."[8]

Like the rest of America, Boyland had been bombarded with false claims that Biden had used fraud to steal the election—a fabrication that would become known as "the Big Lie."[9] Eight others would also lose their lives as a result of the Capitol attack that was sparked by the deluge of disinformation.[10] Ashli Babbitt, a Trump supporter and US Air Force veteran, was shot to death by Capitol Police when she tried to climb through a broken window and breach the Speaker's Lobby.[11] US Capitol Police officer Brian Sicknick died after being attacked by rioters with chemical spray.[12] In addition to the physical injuries suffered by 150 police officers, they and many others also suffered trauma that left unseen emotional scars; four officers committed suicide following the attack.[13] And yet, more than a year later, 68 percent of Republicans were still deceived by lies that the 2020 presidential election had been stolen.[14] Was this abhorrent attack on the temple of our democracy the final act that would break the fever that had gripped the country during the Trump administration? Or was it instead the beginning of the end of American democracy? Even after Trump was indicted by a special counsel in 2023 for his efforts to steal the election, the threat persists, because, as journalist Barton Gellman wrote in *The Atlantic*, "Trump and his party have convinced a dauntingly large number of Americans that the essential workings of democracy are corrupt, that made-up claims of fraud are true, that only cheating can thwart their victory at the polls, that tyranny has usurped their government, and that violence is a legitimate response."[15] In 2022, former federal judge J. Michael Luttig, a prominent conservative, warned that 2020 was merely a dry run to steal future elections.[16] He called Trump and his allies a "clear and present danger" to US democracy.[17] Indeed, after Trump was charged with crimes for his efforts to upend the 2020 election, he began telling a second Big Lie—that the indictments were themselves election interference, filed solely to prevent his election to the presidency in 2024.[18]

Is our democracy ultimately destined for the same fate as Boyland, Babbitt, and Sicknick—death by disinformation? Will America become a country where losing candidates refuse to concede elections, using lies to spark vigilante violence and impose their will? What if, as Gellman suggests, "January 6 was practice," and Republicans are "much better positioned to subvert the next election"?[19] What if Gellman is right, and their next effort succeeds?

Or is American democracy undergoing a slower erosion, invisible in real time but as devastating as a metastasizing cancer? Even if our form of government is not destroyed altogether, it risks becoming unrecognizable, controlled not by the people at large but by a small faction of the far right, willing to say or do anything to seize power. And while the current purveyors of disinformation do not represent every member of the GOP, the party's silence is a form of complicity. When Republican leaders like former congresswoman Liz Cheney denounce their party's disinformation, they are ignored or purged.[20] Now that the potency of disinformation has been revealed, this weapon can be used by any demagogue or self-interested opportunist, regardless of political affiliation.

The Power of Disinformation

Disinformation is the deliberate use of lies to manipulate people, whether to extract profit or to advance a political agenda. Its unwitting accomplice, misinformation, is spread by unknowing dupes who repeat lies they believe to be true. In America today, both forms of falsehood are distorting our perception of reality. In a democracy, the people need a shared set of facts as a basis to debate and make decisions that advance and secure their collective interests. Differences of opinion, and even propaganda, have always existed in the United States, but now, enemies of democracy are using disinformation to attack our sovereign right to truthful information, intellectual integrity, and the exercise of the will of the people.

Online disinformation is particularly insidious because of its immediacy, its capacity to deceive, and its ability to reach its target. In February 2022, the US Department of Homeland Security issued a threat bulletin warning of "an online environment filled with false or misleading narratives and conspiracy theories, and other forms of mis- dis- and mal-information (MDM) introduced and/or amplified by foreign and domestic threat actors."[21] The bulletin stated that these threat actors "seek to exacerbate societal friction to sow discord and undermine public trust in government institutions to encourage unrest, which could potentially inspire acts of violence."[22] As technology continues to advance, the threat of disinformation looms even larger.

Disinformers deliberately inflame our passions and demonize their political opponents to artificially limit options to only two perspectives on an issue. (Debaters refer to this tactic as the "either-or fallacy.") And when one side is portrayed as good and the other as evil, the choice is easy. You must be for either the Trump-supporting right or the rivals they frame as the "radical left." There will always be those who get taken by the P. T. Barnums and Bernie Madoffs among us. But now, there is something more at work than simply gullible people falling for lies. A significant number of Americans don't seem to care anymore whether a statement is true. What seems to matter instead is whether any given message is consistent with their worldview. If a lie supports their position, some people seem willing to go along with the con and pretend it's true. When Donald Trump was indicted by a federal grand jury on charges of illegally retaining classified national defense documents, for example, his defenders parroted Trump's claims that he was being attacked for political reasons. On the day of Trump's arraignment, Representative Elise Stefanik (R-NY) said, "God bless America, President Trump, and all those targeted by

Biden's regime as we continue our efforts to end this corrupt political weaponization and stop the deep state."[23]

We are not just living in a post-truth world: we are living in a post-shame world. Trump and his supporters consistently turn the tables on his accusers, not to convince people that he is innocent but to suggest that *everyone* is corrupt. Integrity is for phonies and suckers, their thinking seems to go. And if everyone is corrupt, then you might as well choose the leader who shares your vision for America. Even those who don't fall for this logic are harmed by it. The risk to the rest of us is that we become cynical about politics. It's easy to grow weary of relentless arguments and aggression and choose to simply tune out. But when we disengage from public discourse, we surrender a piece of our power to the disinformers. The ultimate result, over time, is a weakened democracy, diminished national security, and a threat to the rule of law. America is under attack at this very moment, but not from any external enemy. The attack is from within.

How has American democracy come to this? And why now?

Part of the equation is recent technological advances. Before the information age, geographic regions in the vast territory of the United States set their own community standards. Immigration patterns and local history shaped the culture of various regions, each of which had its own set of widely shared values. In his eye-opening book *American Nations*, journalist and historian Colin Woodard describes the cultural history of the United States. According to Woodard, "There isn't and never has been one America, but rather several Americas."[24] American identity in the Deep South is different from American identity in New York or on the West Coast. Some regions are more segregated than others, resulting in fewer interactions among people of different races, ethnicities, and religious faiths. It is easier to fear someone you have never met. And even within regions, people living in rural areas have different experiences and viewpoints than do those living in urban communities. In parts of the American West, for example, children grow up from an early age learning to use guns for hunting, competing in marksmanship, and protecting livestock from predators. Children who grow up in urban areas, on the other hand, may perceive guns as deadly weapons used to intimidate and kill people. Our varying experiences and cultural norms shape our individual vision of America.

Today, the internet shoves all the versions of America in our faces. Our digital connections bring constant visibility to events occurring in other parts of the country and other parts of the world. The community standards of one region of the United States can seem outrageous in another. As former president Barack Obama said in a 2022 speech on technology at Stanford University, "Forty years ago, if you were a conservative in rural Texas, you weren't necessarily offended by what was going on in San Francisco's Castro District, because you didn't know what was going on."[25] This new access to information can be jarring, even frightening, to some people—amounting to what Obama called "a direct affront to their traditions, their belief systems, their place in society."[26] And so, when someone in one region sees someone from a different region saying America is a "Christian country" or promoting drag queen story hour, they may perceive a threat to their way of life.

The other part of the equation is manipulation. Some politicians prey on these fears, using disinformation to advance their personal and party ambitions. They know that when information conflicts with one's viewpoint, some people will accept distortions of fact rather than change their minds. The Black man who was elected president cannot be a legitimate leader, they argue, so he must have been born outside the United States, disqualifying him from office. A lingering pandemic would weaken the economy and make reelection of the incumbent less likely, and so he says it will go away by Easter. No one voted for Biden because he is a socialist, some claim, and so the election must have been rigged. It can be easier to accept lies than to confront truths that make us uncomfortable.

This book documents the ways that political opportunists and profiteers use disinformation as a weapon.[27] The far right is not alone in spreading disinformation, and this tool can be used by any political party or faction. During the 2022 election, for example, a photo of Mehmet Oz, the television host who became the GOP candidate for Senate in Pennsylvania, was the subject of a fake internet meme showing him on his hands and knees kissing a certain star on the Hollywood walk of fame.[28] In fact, the photo was taken of him kissing his own star on the day it was added to the walk, but the meme had been altered to make it appear that he was instead kissing the star of Donald Trump.[29]

But at this moment, the most egregious purveyors of disinformation in US politics are far-right members of the Republican Party.[30] Currently, rather than call out lies, a large number of Republicans amplify them, or they silently indulge disinformation to advance their own careers and policy goals. Some conservative news media outlets promote falsehoods for ratings and profit, further exacerbating the threat. In 2023, a lawsuit by Dominion Voting Systems exposed the duplicity of executives and hosts at Fox News, the cable network that pushed election conspiracy theories on air, even as insiders at the network privately acknowledged the falsity of claims that voting machines had flipped votes from Trump to Biden.[31] As is now well known, the false claim of mass fraud was not a good-faith challenge to a contested election; it was the most brazen disinformation campaign in American history. Fox paid a $787.5 million settlement for defaming Dominion because its coverage of the purported fraud was all a lie.[32]

If Fox learned any lesson from the lawsuit, it was short-lived. Two months later, when Trump was charged in the classified-documents case, Fox showed Biden above a graphic that read, "WANNABE DICTATOR SPEAKS AT THE WHITE HOUSE AFTER HAVING HIS POLITICAL RIVAL ARRESTED."[33]

According to the first two findings of the House Select Committee to Investigate the January 6th Attack on the United States Capitol:

1. Beginning election night and continuing through January 6th and thereafter, Donald Trump purposely disseminated false allegations of fraud related to the 2020 Presidential election in order to aid his effort to overturn the election and for purposes of soliciting contributions. These false claims provoked his supporters to violence on January 6th.

2. Knowing that he and his supporters had lost dozens of election lawsuits, and despite his own senior advisors refuting his election fraud claims and urging him to concede his election loss, Donald Trump refused to accept the lawful result of the 2020 election. Rather than honor his constitutional obligation to "take Care that the Laws be faithfully executed," President Trump instead plotted to overturn the election outcome.[34]

The coup attempt was a breathtaking effort to subvert US democracy and the will of the American people.

Even though Trump left office in 2021, his movement to "Make America Great Again" (MAGA) lives on. For some, America was great when white men were in charge and everyone else knew their place. Leaders of the MAGA movement continue to focus on cultural divides to distract middle- and lower-income voters from economic policies that enrich the wealthy. Since the end of World War II, Americans have been less likely to earn more money than their parents.[35] Since the Reagan administration, wealth disparities have grown dramatically, income-tax rates for top earners have fallen, and overseas manufacturing and automation have reduced the availability of blue-collar jobs.[36] If people of color, immigrants, "woke" leftists, and a "deep state" of elite bureaucrats can be blamed for their problems, then some voters will tolerate or even embrace policies that go against their own financial interests.

Disinformation researchers at the University of Texas have found that, since 2010, many online influence campaigns have used communities of color as pawns, as both subjects and targets of disinformation.[37] As *Boston Globe* columnist Kimberly Atkins Stohr wrote following the release of the January 6 Committee's report, a driving force behind the attack was race.[38] "[L]ike many things involving the history, laws, and founding principles of our nation," she wrote, the attack had "everything to do with race."[39] It was no coincidence that Confederate flags, insignias of white supremacist groups, and a lynching noose were on display during the attack.[40] One rioter wore a sweatshirt that said "Camp Auschwitz," a horrifying antisemitic reference to Nazi death camps.[41] In many ways, the attack was as much an expression of white nationalist identity as it was an attempt to seize power. Some Republican voters likely did not care whether the election was stolen; instead, what seems to have mattered more to them was installing the administration whose narratives best reinforced their own hopes, fears, and privileges.

Long after Trump's claims of a stolen election have been debunked, the assault on truth continues. Under the pretext of rampant voter fraud, states have passed laws making it more difficult to vote. GOP candidate Kari Lake refused to concede defeat in the 2022 election for governor of Arizona, baselessly claiming that her race was one of the "most dishonest elections in the history of Arizona," a position she had previewed even before the election.[42] Her legal challenges to the election failed.[43] While election deniers were largely defeated in the 2022 elections, two—one in Wyoming and one in Indiana—were elected secretary of state, a position in which they would oversee their state's elections. Election deniers have become GOP party chairs in three states.[44] Congressman George Santos (R-NY) was elected to Congress after fabricating his education and employment history, ethnicity, volunteer work, and even a claim that his mother had died in the September 11 attacks.[45] Then House Speaker Kevin McCarthy (R-CA) supported the embattled congressman even after a head-spinning amount of disinformation had been exposed, normalizing Santos's lies by noting that "a lot of people" in Congress fabricate their résumés.[46] Santos was later indicted for fraud and false statements.[47] Florida governor Ron DeSantis continues to stoke the culture wars, leading a ban in schools on books and discussions about race, gender, and sexuality, calling his state "where woke goes to die."[48] After the January 6 Committee concluded its probe into the attack in December 2022, the new Republican majority that took control of the House in January 2023 created a subcommittee to study the "weaponization" of government investigations, based on a claim that conservatives had been unfairly targeted.[49] The subcommittee promised to give life to the lie that government investigations into Trump's corruption had been witch hunts and hoaxes all along. Chaired by Representative Jim Jordan (R-OH), the subcommittee also investigated the criminal charges filed against Trump by Manhattan district attorney Alvin Bragg in 2023 over fraudulent business documents[50] and the RICO election-interference case against Trump and eighteen co-defendants filed by Fulton County district attorney Fani T. Willis in Georgia.[51] The subcommittee even investigated academic researchers who study disinformation.[52] By fall of 2023, it appeared that their efforts were having a chilling effect on disinformation research. The National Institutes of Health paused its $150 million program devoted to improving the communication of accurate medical information, including vaccines, based on threats of legal actions.[53] After Stanford University's Election Integrity Partnership was accused of working with the government to censor online speech, and right-wing advocate Jack Posobiec threatened to leave it "penniless and powerless," the founder of the university's Internet Observatory program said it would have to reconsider its involvement in the project.[54] The assault on truth is far from over.

Diagnosing the Problem

I wrote this book hoping to spark a national conversation about the danger of disinformation, and how we can defeat it. Throughout history, authoritarians have used disinformation to seize power from the people. As a former national security prosecutor, I see self-serving forces sabotaging our country. Manipulators are using disinformation to poison discourse and stoke divisions in society. False statements on social media, posted under fake personas and amplified by automated accounts, can make some people believe ridiculous lies, such as claims that Hillary Clinton sold weapons to ISIS or that school districts were putting kitty litter in restrooms for students who identified as cats.[55] Disinformation is designed to evoke a strong emotional response, in order to push us toward more extreme views. And our outrage is not confined to digital spaces—our communications online drive animosity in real life. Our country's constantly changing demographics naturally bring differences of opinion, but the bitter divides are not the inevitable result of a pluralistic society with diverse ethnic, racial, religious, and social groups. They are the product of a deliberate attack through disinformation. Lies are becoming increasingly normalized, and our democracy is in peril. The conversation I propose is not a debate about Democratic and Republican politics. It is about the essential need for truth in self-governance.

Throughout our history, America has been targeted with disinformation from hostile foreign adversaries such as Russia, long the master of propaganda. In 1923, the young Soviet Union set up is first office for *dezinformatsiya*, or disinformation.[56] Intelligence operatives crafted communications designed to deceive Western intelligence agencies by exaggerating Soviet military strength, and then sent them through the Estonian mission in Moscow, where the operatives correctly predicted the letters would be opened and read, and the false information shared with allies.[57] In the early 1980s, at the dawn of the AIDS epidemic, the Soviets propagated the false story that the US government had created the virus in a lab as a biological weapon.[58]

Ironically, one of the factors that makes us susceptible to disinformation is our nation's fundamental value of free speech. Federalist Paper No. 63 warned of the risk of being "misled by the artful misrepresentations of interested men."[59] Since the days when people began telling the fable of George Washington confessing to his father about chopping down a cherry tree because he could not tell a lie, Americans have engaged in the spread of mythology and propaganda. Senator Joseph McCarthy's lies pushed the Red Scare. The invasion of Iraq was based on false claims about weapons of mass destruction, later blamed on "faulty intelligence."[60]

Undeniably, the United States also engages in information warfare, using psychological operations (psyops) to manipulate foreign populations for strategic advantage. Although little is written about psyops in the public domain, according to the US Army's website, the American military "uses psychological warfare to deliberately mislead enemy forces during a combat situation."[61] The military also uses communication strategies "to influence the emotions, motives, reasoning, and behavior of foreign governments and citizens."[62] An important caveat of US psyops, however, is that they are not to be used on the American people.[63]

The current strain of falsehoods is altogether different. As a tactic relentlessly used today by a shrinking American political party to maintain a popular base, disinformation in the United States defrauds the American people. The profound damage it causes is not part of some far-off dystopian future. The harm is apparent here and now.

This is a pivotal moment in our nation's history, and the stakes could not be higher. Legislation in a number of states is harming democracy by making it increasingly difficult to cast a ballot. Election suppression laws create obstacles to voting, such as limits on early voting, prohibitions of third-party assistance for delivering ballots, restrictions on voting by mail, and limits on the number and locations of ballot deposit boxes. These restrictions have a disparate impact on communities of color, young people, and the economically disadvantaged—not coincidentally, all likely Democratic Party voters—leaving some of them effectively disenfranchised. Election deniers serving as secretaries of state, canvassers, and poll workers are endangering the integrity of our electoral process. Political violence has become a reality, as public officials face threats, harassment, and attacks. In 2020, Michigan governor Gretchen Whitmer was the subject of a plot to kidnap her and put her on "trial" for objections to her stay-home orders during the Covid-19 pandemic after Trump called it a hoax.[64] Two years later, an intruder broke into the home of House Speaker Nancy Pelosi and brutally attacked her husband in a twisted act of political protest.[65] In 2023, Solomon Peña, a Republican candidate for the statehouse in New Mexico who refused to concede defeat, was arrested on charges of orchestrating shootings into the homes of four elected officials, all Democrats, narrowly missing a ten-year-old girl asleep in her bed.[66]

In addition to elected officials, members of the public are at risk. Lies scapegoating people of color, immigrants, Asian Americans, Jewish people, and the LGBTQ+ community have coincided with increases in hate crimes. Claims that the FBI is a "disgrace" and that the government has "weaponized" criminal investigations are eroding public faith in law enforcement. When people are led to believe that police officers and federal agents are corrupt, they become reluctant to provide tips and information that officers need to solve crimes. Jurors tend to distrust the testimony of federal agents when they have been told the FBI "plants" evidence, as Trump claimed following the 2022 search of his Florida home for classified documents after he had left office.[67] A diminishing ability to enforce the law reduces public safety and cultivates corruption.

A lack of trust in the criminal justice system also fosters vigilante violence, a direct assault on the rule of law. Untrained civilians are taking up arms to right perceived wrongs, leading to the kind of destruction wrought by teen gunman Kyle Rittenhouse in Kenosha, Wisconsin,[68] in 2020 and more than one thousand insurrectionists in our nation's capital on January 6, 2021.[69] Much of the American right glamorizes assault weapons, based on the absurd claim that the Second Amendment protects not only the right to bear arms but also the right to overthrow our government, insisting that ordinary citizens must be able to match the firepower of the US military. Flamethrowing congresswoman Lauren Boebert (R-CO) has said the Second Amendment "has nothing to do with hunting, unless you're talking about hunting tyrants, maybe."[70] Promoting assault weapons ownership has become a membership ritual in the far-right wing of the Republican Party, even though these are the very same kinds of guns that have made mass shootings an American epidemic.

The threat to our safety extends to our national security. Once the model democracy for the world, the United States is now ridiculed for its dysfunction. Enemies of democracy point to the chaos that followed the 2020 election as proof that our system of government is a failed experiment. Since World War II, our foreign policy has centered on spreading democracy, which advances international peace and American interests abroad by reducing military threats, creating trade partners, and preventing refugee crises by promoting human rights and political stability.[71] Our surrender to disinformation tarnishes the reputation of democracy on the world stage. Our critics have a point—the attack on the peaceful transfer of presidential power is stark evidence that disinformation threatens our form of government.

It is easy to take our civil rights and freedoms for granted. Most of us assume that American democracy will always be here. We have lived through challenging times before—the Civil War, two world wars, the Great Depression, Jim Crow, the civil unrest of the 1960s—and we have always endured. But democracies are not invincible. As Steven Levitsky and Daniel Ziblatt write in their book *How Democracies Die*, some democracies collapse in violent coups, such as those that have occurred in Argentina, Chile, Greece, Nigeria, Thailand, and other countries where government takeovers were achieved with military force.[72] But other democracies have faltered through the abuse of democratic norms, such as Adolf Hitler's Germany, Vladimir Putin's Russia, and Hugo Chávez's Venezuela. Democracies have recently suffered backsliding in Hungary, the Philippines, and Turkey, among other countries.[73] As Levitsky and Ziblatt describe these silent coups: "There are no tanks in the streets. Constitutions and other nominally democratic institutions remain in place. People still vote. Elected autocrats maintain a veneer of democracy while eviscerating its substance."[74]

America is experiencing a similar attack from within, and disinformation is the weapon of choice. If the attack succeeds, elections will be decided by manipulators, unjust laws will be enacted by the puppets those manipulators install, and political violence, corruption, militia activity, and vigilante violence will likely become widespread and routine. When power is acquired through disinformation, coups can eventually be accomplished without bloodshed. Disinformation operations turn us on ourselves. As a result, we become outraged or fearful, then cynical, and finally numb and apathetic. It is not an overstatement to say that disinformation threatens to destroy the United States as we know it.

Defeating Disinformation

The chapters that follow chronicle the ways that authoritarians use disinformation to seize and retain power. I dissect these tactics and explore some of the psychological factors that make disinformation such a powerful weapon. The book also describes how technology exacerbates the problem exponentially, with accelerating advances in artificial intelligence leading the way. AI can manufacture fake information faster and better than humans can: Chatbots will increasingly deceive humans into believing they are communicating with real people. Doctored videos known as "deepfakes" already make it appear that someone has said or done something they did not say or do. According to Microsoft researchers, in 2023, China used AI to spread disinformation that wildfires in Hawaii were caused by a secret weapon being tested by the US government.[75] I discuss the long-term implications and ongoing harms being inflicted right now on our democracy, our national security, and the rule of law—the notion that we resolve our differences in court, according to a shared set of rules, rather than taking the law into our own hands to deliver our preferred outcome.

My hope is that this book can help us identify disinformation, name it, understand it, and defeat it. I suggest some reforms that can help reduce disinformation from the supply side and the demand side, as well as some measures that can mitigate its harms. No one of these proposed solutions will cure all the ills created by disinformation, but we must have the political courage and will to try some of them. I am hopeful that this book will promote discussion of—and better ideas for—solutions to reduce the spread of disinformation and our vulnerability to authoritarianism. Our democracy is too precious to simply surrender.

In the end, though, this attack from within is a battle for hearts and minds that requires citizens to step up and take back the sovereign power of self-government. All the laws and policies in the world cannot change attitudes unless we are willing to abide by them. We the people need to remember that democracy depends on an informed electorate. As the famous saying goes, everyone is entitled to their own opinion, but not their own facts.[76] Our great country has been a world leader in scientific discovery, manufacturing, medicine, technology, space exploration, and, most importantly, democracy, but that progress is threatened by self-interested opportunists. If we allow ourselves to be manipulated by them, we are less able to collaborate to improve our collective security, power, and quality of life.

We already face serious challenges in climate change, pandemics, refugee crises, cybercrime, global conflict, and countless other threats. Reasonable minds can disagree on solutions, but making progress as a society requires a willingness to learn facts, appreciate nuance, and engage in meaningful debate. But instead of focusing on solving urgent problems, some political opportunists provoke voters to spend their time and energy attacking the rights of groups underrepresented in positions of power—women, people of color, immigrants, the LGBTQ+ community. Rather than address climate change, we debate the dress code for women in the Missouri statehouse.[77] We can't begin to develop a coherent strategy to meet new challenges if we continue to allow disinformers to dominate national discourse. Certainly, there will always be room for debate about policy choices and political candidates, but we can't solve any problems if well-funded hucksters lead us, like lemmings, off a cliff.

The solution, I believe, lies in an appeal to patriotism, our shared love of our country and commitment to its endurance. I am not referring here to the superficial brand of patriotism, with its cheap symbols and robotic performance of rituals. I am looking instead to a more thoughtful kind of patriotism, a devotion to the precept of American democracy that all are created equal—that out of many, we must become one. Patriotism is the responsibility to do the hard work to move our country toward a more perfect union. Critical self-reflection does not mean that we hate our country; it is the honest and tough love that is required to sustain every relationship. Obama described this ideal during his remarks to commemorate the fiftieth anniversary of the civil rights marches from Selma, Alabama, to Montgomery: "What greater form of patriotism is there than the belief that America is not yet finished, that we are strong enough to be self-critical, that each successive generation can look upon our imperfections and decide that it is in our power to remake this nation to more closely align with our highest ideals?"[78]

Earlier generations of Americans died for democracy. Surely, we can do something as simple as holding accountable those who traffic in disinformation. But to do so requires that we the people put the public interest ahead of our own individual agendas. And the public interest begins with the truth. Without truth, we are doomed to a future of subservience to those who lie to seize power. As then GOP congresswoman Liz Cheney said during the hearings of the January 6 Committee, "We must remember that we cannot abandon the truth and remain a free nation."[79]

Only an unyielding commitment to truth and justice can save our nation from the same fate that met Rosanne Boyland, Ashli Babbitt, Brian Sicknick, and the other victims of disinformation.

1.

THE AUTHORITARIAN PLAYBOOK: HOW DISINFORMERS GAIN POWER

"In fascist politics, language is not used simply, or even chiefly, to convey information but to elicit emotion."

—JASON STANLEY, Jacob Urowsky Professor of Philosophy, Yale University

LIKE MANY POLITICAL LEADERS, Joseph Stalin got his start in the communication business. He was a writer who learned the power of messaging. According to one account, he was "adept at boiling down complex ideas into simple binaries and folksy fables."[80] After the Bolshevik Revolution in 1917, Stalin ran *Pravda*,[81] the Soviet newspaper whose name means, rather ironically, "Truth."[82] He would go on, of course, to become the leader of the Soviet Union for much of the first half of the twentieth century. Born Iosif Dzhugashvili, he adopted the name "Stalin" later in life;[83] it translates to "steel"—a name that projects strength. His rule was marked by mass executions of ethnic groups that he feared could be vulnerable to overtures from enemies—ethnic Germans, Poles, and peasants who had resisted collectivist farms.[84] In the campaign of violence known as the Great Purge, Stalin arrested, interrogated, tortured, and executed members of his own military and intelligence officials whom he feared were disloyal.[85] Accused spies received show trials before being convicted and sent to the Gulag or executed;[86] ever the communicator, Stalin would edit the interrogation transcripts to his favor.[87] As dictator, he controlled the press, where, according to one account, "paranoid fantasy had to be accepted as reality."[88] A lifetime of professional messaging appears to have helped Stalin hone his tradecraft in disinformation. He even had a term for his real and imagined rivals: *vrag naroda*, which translates in English to "enemy of the people."[89]

Disinformation is part of what is sometimes referred to as the "authoritarian playbook."[90] The phrase refers to the authoritarian tactics used throughout history to control the public. In her 1951 book, *The Origins of Totalitarianism*, political theorist Hannah Arendt writes that the strategy of strongmen is to manipulate the population to "the point where they would, at the same time, believe everything and nothing, think that everything was possible and that nothing was true."[91] Some of those tactics are being used today in the United States.

First, some terminology. The terms "totalitarian" and "authoritarian" are often used interchangeably, though they have slightly different meanings. A totalitarian form of government has a highly developed ideology and asserts total control over the lives of its citizens.[92] Examples of totalitarians are Stalin and Adolf Hitler. Authoritarian forms of government demand submission to the power of their leaders, but they never achieve total control, allowing people to travel freely, own property, and work in the occupations of their choice.[93] Authoritarians often attempt to change laws to further consolidate their power and usually cannot be replaced by means of elections.[94] Examples of authoritarian forms of government are the twentieth-century military regimes supported by the United States in Chile, Nicaragua, El Salvador, Guatemala, and elsewhere in Latin America.[95] Both forms of government discourage individual freedom of thought and action, so that a single leader or group can amass power.[96] The word "fascist" has a similar connotation; it comes from the regime of Benito Mussolini, the Italian dictator whose paramilitary groups were called *fasci di combattimento*, after the dictator adopted as an emblem of authority the fasces, a bundle of sticks topped with an axe blade that was carried by the attendants of ancient Roman magistrates.[97] From this name, Mussolini's movement derived its own name, *fascismo*.[98] All of these forms of government—totalitarianism, authoritarianism, and fascism—are the polar opposite of democracy, which means, literally, "the power of the people": a system of self-government. When politicians use the tricks of authoritarians, they are violating the norms of democracy. The problem with authoritarians, of course, is that they seek not to govern in the public interest through consent of the governed but to consolidate power and impose their own will.

Tactics in the authoritarian playbook include appealing to emotion over reason, exploiting divisions, undermining critics, dismantling public institutions, stoking violence,[99] and creating an image of the Great Leader as both an everyman and a superman.[100] Disinformation is the catalyst that allows these tactics to work. The power of disinformation may be at an unprecedented height, but it has been used by authoritarians and conquerors since the dawn of time. When fueled by disinformation, the strategies in the playbook are particularly useful to a leader seeking to grab power and control the populace. In the United States, power-hungry politicians are using the authoritarian playbook against American democracy to seize power from the people. No American leader in recent history used the authoritarian playbook more extensively than former president Donald Trump. Even after his term in office ended, his use of disinformation and other authoritarian tactics has endured. Dissecting the strategies of Trump and his copycats is instructive to understanding the dark art of disinformation.

Play One: Aim for the Heart

An overarching theme in the authoritarian playbook is the appeal to emotion over reason. As fans of the old television show *The X-Files* know, people "want to believe."[101] The phrase describes a human inclination to believe in things despite the lack of an evidentiary foundation. It is the same sensation that makes people think they will come out ahead at the casino, despite the fact that the odds always favor the house. Feelings take precedence over facts.

The feeling authoritarians play on most is fear. In a rapidly evolving world, all of us, at some level, feel a foreboding sense that the future presents risk. Some naturally fear being left behind, or perceive a threat to their status, wealth, or even their idea of national identity. Authoritarians fuel those perceptions and project a sense of collective defense, purpose, and strength.

One way authoritarians connect with the public is by pushing a viewpoint of declinism. As information scholar Donald A. Barclay describes it, declinism is the belief that society is going downhill and that things were better in the past.[102] Barclay cites, as an example, the tendency of baby boomers to label millennials as entitled and spoiled, the same charges that were leveled at the baby boomers themselves by their elders.[103] In her book *Strongmen*, historian Ruth Ben-Ghiat writes about the rise of dictators in history. Hitler used the trope about a declining society to stoke fears among the German people. Hitler's speeches evoked declinism, expressing "Germans' pain at humiliation, fear of plague-carrying Jews, and desperate hope for a better future."[104]

In the United States, declinism is visible in all three of Trump's presidential campaigns and is perfectly captured in the campaign slogan that became a political movement, "Make America Great Again." The MAGA theme connotes (1) a time of past glory, (2) the notion that American greatness has declined, and (3) a desire to restore prior conditions. The label also serves as a figurative dog whistle, a statement that can be heard favorably by those who recognize and share its sentiment. Without saying so out loud, "Make America Great Again" implies a wish to return to what some may consider the good old days, when white men were dominant, women were subservient, and people of color were pushed to the lower rungs of society.

Declinism focuses more on grievances than on solutions. In Trump's 2017 inaugural address, he talked about "American carnage," painting a picture of a country that was in rapid descent.[105] He described America as:

> mothers and children trapped in poverty in our inner cities, rusted-out factories, scattered like tombstones across the landscape of our nation, an education system flush with cash, but

which leaves our young and beautiful students deprived of all knowledge, and the crime, and the gangs, and the drugs that have stolen too many lives and robbed our country of so much unrealized potential.

Pledging to put "America First," Trump blamed our woes on a globalist approach that

> enriched foreign industry at the expense of American industry, subsidized the armies of other countries, while allowing for the very sad depletion of our military . . . defended other nations' borders while refusing to defend our own . . . spent trillions and trillions of dollars overseas, while America's infrastructure has fallen into disrepair and decay . . . made other countries rich while the wealth, strength and confidence of our country has dissipated over the horizon. . . . The wealth of our middle class has been ripped from their homes and then redistributed all across the world.[106]

Trump stoked resentment by suggesting that callous or sinister forces had left our nation in tatters—a move right out of the authoritarian playbook.

Certainly, the United States has issues that we have failed to address—racial injustice, income disparity, and climate change, among others. And the internet gives all of us a window onto the rest of the world that provides constant reminders of bad news, perhaps one reason that even though violent crime has dropped 49 percent since the 1990s, more than half of the public perceives that crime has gone up.[107] Social media and online news sources subject us to more and more stories and images about crime; facts are not newsworthy when all is well. Similarly, increasing wage gaps have caused many to feel less prosperous than prior generations, even though life in the United States is better than ever on many scores. Poverty rates have steadily declined since they were first measured in 1960.[108] Despite persistent health inequalities, overall infant mortality rates have continuously dropped.[109] Declinism ignores the facts that show American society improving, such as our dominance in the tech industry and soaring college enrollment rates.[110] America has challenges, to be sure, but the news is not all bad.

Why do authoritarians focus on declinism? If people can be convinced that the country is falling apart, then, of course, they can also be persuaded that they need a strong and fearless leader to fix it, even if certain values must be compromised.

Understanding the power of feeling over logic, authoritarians invest in constructing an emotional connection between themselves and potential followers. Staging large in-person rallies is one tactic they use to provide such a sense of connection. They use the same formula that fosters loyalty to sports teams; shared musical selections, uniforms, and rallying cries all help build a fan base. "Fan," of course, is short for "fanatic." As a University of Michigan football fan, I have joined enthusiastic crowds by wearing maize-and-blue attire, singing the school fight song, and pumping my fist in unison with other supporters at just the right verse. If you have ever been in the Big House on a football Saturday—or in any other sports stadium with a passionate fan base—you have felt the potential emotional intensity that can be whipped up at mass gatherings.

Authoritarians harness people's need to belong to a community and turn it into self-serving power. As Ben-Ghiat writes, "rallies have long been a favored means of contact" for a strongman, turning "politics into an aesthetic experience, with him as the star."[111] At rallies in 1930s Germany, Nazis played stirring marches, displayed swastika flags, and honored Hitler with the Nazi salute. Hitler's chief propagandist, Joseph Goebbels, exploited crowd psychology.[112] According to Ben-Ghiat, Mussolini and Hitler used rallies "as sites of emotional training to create a violent, lordly, fearless, cruel youth, ready to do what was necessary for the nation."[113] In the national security field, there is a word for that type of training—"radicalization," a process of indoctrination toward more extreme political views.

Today's MAGA rallies are often not so different. Adoring crowds wear matching hats and mirror the Great Leader's cues and gestures, including his signature raised fist with the palm facing forward. Trump rally organizers have sometimes blared music evoking QAnon, the cult-like network of people duped into believing that Satan-worshipping liberal elites run a child sex ring and are trying to control our politics and media.[114] Like authoritarians before them, MAGA politicians use provocative statements to stoke passions and anger in crowds. Even in a time when people increasingly stare at their digital devices and work from home—perhaps especially during an era when we spend more time alone—the manipulation of crowd psychology can send people into a frenzy, reinforcing their indoctrination.

This appeal to emotion appears to have worked on Couy Griffin, a county commissioner from Otero County, New Mexico, and founder of Cowboys for Trump. Griffin was convicted of misdemeanor charges over his conduct at the US Capitol on January 6.[115] As a commissioner, he refused to certify the vote in his county. "It's not based on any facts," he told his colleagues. "It's only based on my gut feeling and my own intuition, and that's all I need."[116]

Play Two: Divide . . .

Another important tactic in the authoritarian playbook is stoking divisions in society. Whereas democracies seek to unite people for the common good, authoritarians try to exploit society's fault lines to amass personal power. With the world artificially divided into only two sides, you are either "with us or against us." Authoritarians present economic prosperity as a zero-sum game, suggesting that policies improving outcomes for others mean reducing power and privilege for "us." In a dog-eat-dog world, they tell us, we must grab what we can, or the other side will take it first and deprive us of what is rightfully ours. In addition to disparaging their rivals, authoritarians make their own side appealing by aligning themselves with traditional values. Their tricks for sowing division include demonizing and scapegoating, appealing to nostalgia, and branding to build loyalty.

Demonize and scapegoat

Nazi Germany, of course, blamed all of Europe's ills on Jewish people. Hitler falsely cast them as inferior beings, communist subversives, war profiteers, and a threat to German national security.[117] For ease of identification and vilification, Jewish people were forced to wear Stars of David and prohibited from giving the Hitler salute. The same strategy was used in apartheid-era South Africa, where the Afrikaner National Party kept the minority white population in power by, among other tactics, pitting Black citizens against each other along tribal lines to reduce their political power.[118]

This tradecraft continues today in Russia, whose president, Vladimir Putin, is a former KGB intelligence agent.[119] In 2016, Russia sought to exploit divisions in American society through a covert disinformation campaign. According to the report of Special Counsel Robert Mueller, the Russia-based Internet Research Agency "created accounts in the names of fictitious US organizations and grassroots groups and used these accounts to pose as anti-immigration groups, Tea Party activists, Black Lives Matter protesters, and other US social and political activists." [120] The names of their fake online groups ranged from "Stop All Immigrants" and "Tea Party News" to "LGBT United" and "United Muslims of America."[121] According to Mueller, the Russian plan was "designed to provoke and amplify political and social discord in the United States."[122] One reason US society seems more polarized than ever is that Russian operatives have been pitting us against each other.

The same strategy used by a hostile foreign adversary is even more effective when it comes from operatives within our own culture. In 2023, a technology firm detected thousands of pro-Trump

bots online that were working to disparage his likely GOP opponents, Florida governor Ron DeSantis and South Carolina governor
Nikki Haley.[123] To choke off free speech, authoritarians often portray anyone who disagrees with them as treasonous. They capitalize
on what Barclay describes as "hostile attribution bias," the human
tendency to dislike those who disagree with us.[124] By portraying the
other side as despicable, authoritarians present themselves as the
only tenable choice. Even if you don't like everything the authoritarian does, the thinking goes, the other side is worse. When people
make choices based on feeling over logic, they more easily fall prey
to this tribal mentality.

The American far right in the 2020s didn't create a new movement
so much as harness underlying sentiment. MAGA Republicans
appear to have evolved from the Tea Party, which originated at the
beginning of the Obama administration in 2009.[125] According to
Harvard researchers Theda Skocpol and Vanessa Williamson, the
Tea Party movement was less about economic concerns and more
about social and cultural issues.[126] Tea Party members, who were
mostly white baby boomers and disproportionately evangelical
Christians, expressed in interviews a "profound pessimism about
the future of the country, a sense that it was imperiled by the left,
the young and the nonwhite."[127] The far right recognized this crack
in society and drove a truck through it in the mid-2010s by supporting Trump's campaign for the presidency. According to two
political scientists, Russell Muirhead and Nancy L. Rosenblum,
Trump encouraged people "to disparage the ideal of national unity
and replace it with something more suspicious, more hateful, more
ferocious."[128] And rather than being appalled by his crudeness and
cruelty, many Republicans cheered him on. There was no mistaking
Trump's language for that of his recent predecessors as president,
George W. Bush ("I'm a uniter, not a divider")[129] or Barack Obama
("There is not a liberal America and a conservative America; there is
the United States of America").[130] Since Trump's one-term administration, Republicans have continued to find the fault lines in

society and stoke anger over them with jaw-dropping vitriol. In 2023, Representative Marjorie Taylor Greene (R-GA) called for a "national divorce" between red states and blue states because of "irreconcilable differences."[131] She argued that a legal agreement to split was necessary because the members of the right "are absolutely disgusted and fed up with the left cramming and forcing their ways on us and our children with no respect for our religion/faith, traditional values, and economic & government policy beliefs."[132] By contending that a legal agreement to separate would be preferable to "civil war," Greene implied that armed conflict is a plausible option.[133]

Trump's influence has normalized demonization of political opponents, regardless of party affiliation. He referred to Hillary Clinton, his opponent in the 2016 presidential election, as "Crooked Hillary" and declared she lacked "a presidential look."[134] Republicans who contradicted Trump were branded as "RINOs," Republicans in Name Only. In 2017, well after public attention had moved on from former NFL quarterback Colin Kaepernick's practice of kneeling during the national anthem to protest what he viewed as oppression of people of color,[135] Trump reignited the controversy during a rally in Alabama. Trump asked the crowd, "Wouldn't you love to see one of these NFL owners, when somebody disrespects our flag, to say, 'Get that son of a bitch off the field right now, out. He's fired. He's fired!'"[136] He portrayed Democrats as soft-on-crime opportunists who favored unlimited immigration to grow their voting base and advance their political fortunes. During the summer of 2020, when protesters marched against the police killing of George Floyd in Minneapolis, Trump attributed crime to Democratic leadership, conflating all protesters with the small percentage who engaged in violence.[137] "The violent mobs . . . they're Biden people, they're Biden states and cities, they're Democrat states," Trump said at a 2020 rally.[138] In communities with Republican leadership, he said, "we're doing great and we don't have crime and we don't have this violence." In 2020, Trump's campaign sent out a poll asking respondents to indicate whether they were an "American" or a "Democrat."[139] In a 2022 post disparaging Senate GOP leader Mitch McConnell, Trump referred to McConnell's Asian American spouse, Elaine Chao, as "his China-loving wife, Coco Chow."[140]

It didn't matter whether any part of these statements was true. Trump was signaling to his followers his shared disdain for people whom they perceived as threatening their vision of America. His supporters were only too willing to take the bait. At an Ohio Trump rally in 2018, some supporters were seen wearing T-shirts stating, "I'd Rather Be a Russian Than a Democrat."[141] By 2022, the rhetoric of polarization reached biblical proportions: an Ohio woman at a Trump rally in Pennsylvania told a reporter, "There's only two teams, Team Jesus and Team Lucifer. And it's very easy to pick a side."[142]

DeSantis has followed this formula of demonizing opponents to build his own brand as the defender of traditional values. The Florida governor even took on the Walt Disney Company after the head of the powerful corporation criticized his so-called "Don't Say Gay" bill, a law that bans teachers from discussing sexual orientation and gender identity in K–12 classrooms.[143] In fundraising materials, DeSantis has bragged, "If Disney wants to pick a fight, they chose the wrong guy." He mocked the company as "Woke Disney."[144]

Trump and his MAGA disciples also engage in shameless scapegoating, preying on fears of changing demographics by blaming immigrants, people of color, and Muslims for national problems. Whereas most leaders will avoid saying things that are overtly racist, bigoted, or xenophobic, the new brand of far-right politician seems to relish breaking taboos, knowing their words will appeal to those who fear a world where they are dispossessed of power. Rather than turning off voters, Trump's outrageous statements proved attractive to those clinging to a vision of an America permanently dominated by white, Anglo-Saxon Christians. Suggesting that anyone who is not a member of this group makes America seem like "a Third World country" is an affront to the very notion of equality. It is the same tactic ISIS used to distort Islam as a pretext for using violence to achieve an Islamic caliphate. Both brands of extremism unfairly taint the religion they purport to represent.

The list of Trump's scapegoating incidents is long. During his speech announcing his campaign for the 2016 presidential election, for instance, Trump disparaged immigrants from Mexico. "When Mexico sends its people, they're not sending their best," he said. "They're sending people that have lots of problems, and they're bringing those problems with us [*sic*]. They're bringing drugs. They're bringing crime. They're rapists. And some, I assume, are good people."[145] During the 2016 campaign, he publicly feuded with the family of army captain Humayun Khan, who was killed in the line of duty in Iraq in 2004. After Khan's father spoke at the Democratic National Convention, Trump speculated that his mother was not "allowed to have anything to say,"[146] insinuating that Muslim women are subservient to their husbands. Following the Unite the Right rally in Charlottesville, Virginia, in 2017, when white nationalists convened to protest the removal of Confederate statues, Trump refused to denounce those marchers chanting, "You will not replace us" and "Jews will not replace us"—clear references to the Great Replacement theory, a belief that society is imperiled by immigrant and other minority populations that will ultimately outnumber and displace white people.[147] Often, proponents of the conspiracy theory blame Jewish masterminds for plotting to extinguish the white race.[148] The perpetrators of mass shootings at a Pittsburgh synagogue in 2018, an El Paso Walmart in 2019, and a Buffalo supermarket in 2022 were all motivated by fear of the Great Replacement.[149] Instead of condemning the marchers' conduct in Charlottesville, full stop, Trump said that the rally had "very fine people on both sides."[150] Following Trump's indictment in 2023 by Manhattan district attorney Alvin Bragg, Trump referred to Bragg as an "animal"[151] and "the radical left George Soros–backed prosecutor."[152] (Soros is a billionaire financier of Jewish heritage who actively funds progressive political candidates and causes.[153] In fact, Soros donated funds to a racial justice group called Color of Change, which contributed to Bragg's campaign for district attorney.[154]) According to author Emily Tamkin, the sinister references to Soros rely on an antisemitic trope of "a Jewish person being all-controlling and all-powerful and using that control and power to denigrate and degrade and corrupt society."[155]

Others followed Trump's lead. During a 2020 campaign rally, Senator David Perdue (R-GA) mispronounced the name of the Democratic candidate for vice president, Kamala Harris, even though they had served together in the Senate for more than three years. He called her "*Ka*-ma-la or Ka-*ma*-la, Kamala-mala-mala, I don't know, whatever."[156] According to Rita Kohli, an associate professor of education at the University of California, Riverside, failing to learn to pronounce non-English names is part of the "long-standing history of forcible assimilation in this country as a way to maintain the power structure" for "White Anglo Saxon, English, Protestantism."[157] Representative Lauren Boebert (R-CO) equated her Muslim colleagues, Representative Ilhan Omar (D-MN) and Representative Rashida Tlaib (D-MI), with terrorists, calling them "the Jihad Squad."[158] When Boebert received criticism for her words, Marjorie Taylor Greene claimed that she was the one who had created the term—fighting for credit as the originator of a religious slur. DeSantis and Greene echoed Trump's criticisms of Bragg as being supported by Soros.[159] The more outrageously divisive the statement, the more points these politicians seemed to score with their voters, but at great expense to national unity.

Seduce with nostalgia

In addition to demonizing and scapegoating certain groups in society, achieving division also requires manipulative leaders to attract loyalty to their own side. One way they seduce supporters is by appealing to "traditional values." According to behavioral scientists Cailin O'Connor and James Owen Weatherall, propaganda plays on emotion, nostalgia, and patriotism.[160] These are familiar themes to anyone who has ever seen a political ad, or a car commercial. It is no coincidence that the predominant colors on political yard signs are red, white, and blue, the same as the US flag. TV ads include warm, hazy images of candidates with their families. Commercial products use the same tricks: "Baseball, hot dogs, apple pie, and Chevrolet" was a familiar jingle in my youth. Evoking traditional symbols that seem safe and comforting, and binding them to political messages, is a common practice. In a rapidly changing world, it can be soothing to cling to the symbols of the past.

Authoritarians remind people of the good old days. Spain's Francisco Franco and Italy's Mussolini evoked the imperial grandeur of their nations' pasts.[161] In Turkey, Recep Tayyip Erdoğan recalls the glory days of the Ottoman Empire.[162] For Putin, the greatness of the Soviet empire is an important image of historical pride.

In the United States, the MAGA right uses traditional symbols in an attempt to expand its base. Trump posed for photographs in the Oval Office with faith leaders putting hands on him,[163] an image that would endear him to religious voters. On stage, he has been known to literally hug the American flag,[164] an act of stagecraft to appeal to patriotism. In the same vein, a group of far-right members of the GOP use the name "Freedom Caucus" to evoke, in voters' minds, our most cherished traditional value. Senator Ted Cruz (R-TX) has quoted the Bible in support of gun rights, even though firearms did not exist during the times described in the text.[165] DeSantis responded to criticism over his restrictions on teaching critical race theory by introducing the "Portraits in Patriotism Act," which provides high school government classes with lessons on "the evils of communism and totalitarianism."[166] Congressman Jim Jordan (R-OH) has praised "real" Americans who support him, suggesting that those who disagree with his views are less patriotic.[167]

Build the brand

To help cultivate loyalty, authoritarians brand their team with symbols. Just as the New York Yankees wear their iconic pinstripes to maintain a shared identity with generations of their fans, authoritarians, too, unite their followers with visual signs of belonging. The Nazis used the swastika and the Nazi salute. Fascists used the symbol of the fasces, arrowheads on sticks. The terrorist group ISIS uses its iconic black flag.[168] The Soviet Union cultivated loyalty to the Communist Party with slogans, salutes, and flags, and by offering praise to "grandfather" Vladimir Lenin, whose portrait hung on every classroom wall.[169]

Donald Trump, who in his business career put his name on everything from casinos to wine to steaks, branded his supporters with red caps bearing the MAGA slogan. Marjorie Taylor Greene has attempted to rebrand the entire Republican Party, calling on the GOP to become the party of "Christian Nationalism";[170] she even sells T-shirts emblazoned with the phrase "Proud Christian Nationalist."[171] To signal her support for gun rights, Congresswoman Lauren Boebert is often photographed with a gun. In a photo posted to her official government web page, she appears with a pistol strapped to her thigh. She once owned a gun-themed restaurant called Shooters Grill;[172] the restaurant's walls were adorned with American flags and rifles, including one imprinted with the Pledge of Allegiance. The menu offered gun-themed dishes, such as the "Swiss and Wesson Burger" and the "Ruger Reuben." A sign in the front window read "WARNING: THIS IS NOT A GUN FREE ZONE."[173] Building the brand with symbols reduces politics to overly simple messages to cultivate followers' loyalty.

Play Three: . . . And Conquer

Another strategy in the authoritarian playbook is to shut down critics and dissenters who might stand in the leader's way. In a functioning democracy, a free press, government agencies, and civil service experts serve as watchdogs who can question leaders. To the authoritarian, these checks are threats. To blunt the force of their criticism, authoritarians often cast the media as "the enemy of the people." Government agencies are "the deep state," a bureaucracy that is subverting the will of the people with its own hidden agenda. Experts are "elites" who have nothing but disdain for the average citizen. Rather than engage with these critics on the facts, the authoritarian instead uses vicious ad hominem attacks. Undermining watchdogs liberates the authoritarian from accountability.

Muzzle the media

In his book *On Tyranny*, historian Timothy Snyder writes that it is our "collective trust in common knowledge that makes us a society."[174] But public knowledge threatens authoritarians, who seek to impose their own version of reality. To combat this threat, authoritarians must dominate media and education. If they can convince the public that these institutions are corrupt or dangerous, then they can better control public perception of their own performance.

Stalin may have been the first to use the term "enemy of the people" to refer to the press, but he was not the last.[175] Augusto Pinochet, who came to power in Chile in 1973 via a military junta supported by the United States,[176] made destruction of the press a top priority.[177] Following the coup, journalists were imprisoned or killed, and the number of daily newspapers dropped from eleven to four.[178] Mao Tse-tung engaged in media censorship and suppression as leader of the People's Republic of China.[179] Many journalists were killed, and others were said to have committed suicide.[180] In response, some reporters gave up and joined the propaganda machine, where, according to Reporters Without Borders, they "abandoned professional ethics and participated actively in the all-out promotion of the party's interests."[181]

The Nazi regime in Germany—and later the repressive government of East Germany—used the term *Lügenpresse*, or "lying press," to disparage the news media.[182] The term appears to have originated during World War I, when the German defense ministry published a book on foreign propaganda.[183] Later, members of the Nazi regime referred to Hitler's critics as "the Lügenpresse apparatus." According to one report, Lügenpresse became "an explosive and stigmatizing propaganda slogan, used to stir hatred against Jews and communists."[184] In 2015, an academic panel in Germany declared the word taboo when anti-Islam forces began using it again in the presence of journalists.[185] A 2016 report noted that this German phrase had been heard at Trump rallies.[186] The MAGA movement seems to prefer the phrase "fake news," but the goal of both terms is the same—to undermine any reporting the Great Leader does not like.

In the United States, where freedom of the press is enshrined in our First Amendment, it sounds startling to hear a president disparage the press as Trump has. The forty-fifth president, whose false and misleading statements were documented by the *Washington Post* and, by the paper's count, numbered more than thirty thousand during his presidency,[187] consistently referred to the news industry as the "fake news media"[188] and the "enemy of the people."[189] According to Russell Muirhead and Nancy L. Rosenblum, Trump characterized the mainstream media "not with the comparatively benign portrait of an institution that does not care about getting things right but with the dark portrait of an institution with nefarious reasons for misleading the public."[190]

At a 2015 campaign rally in South Carolina, Trump pointed out reporters in the back of the crowd and stated, "These people back here are the worst. . . . They are so dishonest . . . absolute scum. Remember that. Scum. Scum. Totally dishonest people."[191] During his first year in office, Trump posted tweets referring to "fake news" 180 times.[192] In 2018, Trump told a gathering of veterans, "Don't believe the crap you see from these people, the fake news. . . . Just remember: what you're seeing and what you're reading is not what's happening."[193] He repeatedly disparaged news outlets by branding them with nicknames, like the "Failing *New York Times,*"[194] "Fake News CNN,"[195] and the "Amazon *Washington Post,*" suggesting that the latter was a lobbying organization for its parent company rather than an objective news source.[196] He referred to three *Washington Post* writers as "lowlife reporters."[197]

During his presidency, Trump explored taking even stronger action than just vocally criticizing the media. He attempted to shut out reporters and outlets critical of him. In 2018, he revoked the press credential of CNN reporter Jim Acosta over vigorous questioning.[198] In 2017, Trump reportedly asked then FBI director James Comey about imprisoning reporters.[199]

Antipathy toward media is increasingly common among Republicans. Ron DeSantis has regularly criticized mainstream media outlets, calling them "the corporate press" and the "national regime media," accusing them of pursuing a "political agenda"[200] and blaming them for creating "hysteria" regarding the Covid-19 pandemic.[201] DeSantis has also advocated for a law to decrease First Amendment protections for the press.[202] Likewise, when Kari Lake ran unsuccessfully for governor of Arizona in 2022, she promised that, if elected, she would be the media's "worst fricking nightmare for eight years."[203] In a campaign ad, Lake was shown using a sledgehammer to smash televisions with images of news anchors from CNN and MSNBC and proclaiming that "journalism is dead."[204] She accused the mainstream media of engaging in "fear-mongering to manipulate a scared and broken population," and said it was "time to take a sledgehammer to the media's lies and propaganda."[205]

Anecdotes and data suggest that the criticism has damaged the reputation of the press in the eyes of at least some segments of the American public. CNN's Acosta wrote that a man at a 2018 Trump rally in Nashville yelled at him repeatedly, "You're scum. You're a scumbag."[206] A woman at a South Carolina rally later that year warned Acosta to tone down his questions to Trump to avoid dire consequences: "What's going to happen is we're going to end up with a civil war. You're going to have people shooting people."[207]

The data support the stories: in 2018, more than four in ten people in a Gallup poll reported that they could not name "a single objective news source." In addition, 77 percent of the people said that television and print media report "fake news," a 14 percent increase from the prior year.[208] And, if everything is fake news, of course, then criticism should be ignored.

Bully the bureaucrats

Civil servants also pose a threat to authoritarians. When employees of government institutions object to an authoritarian's wishes, they find themselves under attack. "It's very typical of authoritarians to claim that they're the victims and that there are witch-hunts against them," says Ruth Ben-Ghiat.[209] Authoritarians will discredit or even purge their critics in government. As civil servants are replaced with loyalists, the public interest is undermined. According to history professor and author Landon R. Y. Storrs, "a government of sycophants selected for personal loyalty rather than expertise cannot check authoritarianism or protect the public interest from exploitation for private gain."[210]

As a candidate and as president, Donald Trump disparaged government employees, experts, and courts, all sources of potential opposition to his power. He campaigned on a promise to "drain the swamp," leading enthusiastic rallygoers in chants of this refrain.[211] The phrase connotes a desire to rid our federal government, located on the humid banks of the Potomac River, of pests, parasites, and other undesirable creatures that dwell there. Trump portrayed civil servants as the "deep state," a dark cabal of permanent bureaucrats with their own agenda to advance special interests over the needs of ordinary Americans. Priming the public to distrust civil servants blunts the impact of any opposition they may pose to an authoritarian's rule.

The term "deep state" originated in American analysis of other governments, according to Nancy McEldowney, former director of the Foreign Service Institute.[212] The term suggests "propaganda, dirty tricks, and even violence to overthrow the government," she notes; using it to refer to civil servants "is a clear attempt to delegitimize voices of disagreement." "Even worse," according to McEldowney, "it carries with it the potential for fear-baiting and rumor-mongering, and is really a dark conspiratorial term that does not correspond to reality."[213]

In fact, the civil service was created to *protect* our government from corrupt forces. Established by Congress with the 1883 Pendleton Act, the professional civil service was designed to replace a system of spoils. The complete overturn of executive branch employees with every change of administration once impaired the development of expertise.[214] Former Labor Department deputy secretary Chris Lu has called the creation of the civil service "one of the most important reforms of the past century and a half" and deems it "one reason the federal government is still the most important and powerful organization in the world."[215] Even Trump's former adviser Steve Bannon once conceded that the "deep state conspiracy theory is for nut cases."[216]

Trump's criticism of public servants, even those in his own administration, went beyond public disagreement to personal attacks. He used grievance and victimhood to turn the tables on government employees who questioned him in any way. When Comey refused to pledge his loyalty to Trump, the forty-fifth president purged him. Trump later called Comey "an untruthful slime ball."[217] As the FBI's investigation into links between Trump's campaign and Russia began to heat up, he called their probe a "Russian witch hunt hoax."[218] He called the actions of his own attorney general, Jeff Sessions, "weak" and "disgraceful,"[219] and those of Deputy Attorney General Rod Rosenstein and FBI official Andrew McCabe "treasonous."[220]

In 2019, Trump similarly smeared the government witnesses in House hearings on his first impeachment, over allegations that he withheld military aid to Ukraine to pressure President Volodymyr Zelenskyy to announce an investigation into Joe Biden and his son Hunter. Trump characterized the House proceedings as an "impeachment hoax"[221] and a "witch-hunt."[222] When White House official Lieutenant Colonel Alexander Vindman testified about Trump's phone call to the Ukrainian president, Trump called him a "Never Trumper."[223] He referred to the US envoy to Ukraine as a "Never Trump Diplomat."[224] When US ambassador Marie Yovanovitch appeared to be an obstacle to Trump's efforts in Ukraine, she was recalled from her post. During her congressional testimony, she said the Trump administration had undermined the State Department, saying it had been "attacked and hollowed out from within."[225] Before Yovanovitch's testimony began, Trump tweeted that everywhere she had gone for her diplomatic work had "turned bad."[226] Congressman Adam Schiff (D-CA) called Trump's post "witness intimidation in real time."[227]

Following the 2020 election, Trump criticized those who debunked his claims of fraud. When Attorney General William Barr publicly stated that the Department of Justice had found no level of voter fraud that could have changed the outcome of the 2020 presidential election, Trump summoned him to the White House and said, "You must hate Trump." Barr offered to step down from his position, and Trump accepted his resignation. Trump later called Barr a "weak and pathetic RINO, who was so afraid of being Impeached that he became a captive to the Radical Left Democrats."[228] In 2023, Trump disparaged his former Chairman of the Joint Chiefs of Staff, Mark Milley, a potential witness against Trump in federal criminal cases for election interference and willful retention of sensitive documents. Trump criticized Milley for assuring the government of China following the January 6 attack that the US government was stable and did not plan to attack China.[229] In a Truth Social post, Trump called Milley a "woke Train Wreck" and said his conduct was "treasonous." "In times gone by," Trump wrote, "the punishment would have been DEATH!"[230] For the authoritarian, loyalty is a one-way street.

Late in his administration, Trump proposed a dangerous change to the civil service that would allow the president to remove career professionals in favor of handpicked loyalists. In October 2020, Trump issued an executive order that modified the civil service regulations[231] by creating "Schedule F," a new category of employees who were not entitled to civil-service employment protections. Instead, these employees would serve at the pleasure of the president, who could fire them for any reason or no reason at all.[232] The new rules would apply to all federal workers with "confidential, policy-determining, policy-making, or policy-advocating" positions,[233] an estimated fifty thousand federal employees.[234] As president, Biden later revoked the order, but Trump indicated a continuing desire to restore it and even expand it. At a rally in March 2022, Trump said, "We will pass critical reforms making every executive branch employee fireable by the president of the United States. . . . The deep state must and will be brought to heel." [235] According Donald Kettl, a public-affairs professor at the University of Texas at Austin, "Bending the apparatus of the state to his own will—there's an authoritarian tint to that that is impossible to escape."[236]

Authoritarians also discredit experts and scientists whose assertions contradict their own. Science reveals what former vice president Al Gore once referred to as an "inconvenient truth" about climate change.[237] According to one researcher, "During the Stalin era, the Soviet government, and its scientific institutions, became the adjudicator of what was 'good' science or social science, replacing any system of independent academic and/or professional peer review."[238] This approach has caused responsible scientists to leave countries that are hostile to them,[239] further reducing those nations' capacity for scientific discovery. In Nazi Germany, nationalism prevented scientists from sharing ideas and research across borders, and race laws pushed scientists out of their jobs.[240] The United States was once the preferred destination for these scientist refugees.[241]

During the Trump administration, the president disparaged experts who shared data and opinions that were not in his political interests. On environmental issues, Trump's political appointees frequently found themselves in conflict with career federal employees.[242] Scott Pruitt, Trump's EPA administrator, removed the agency's webpage on climate change to reflect Trump's preference to ignore concerns over industry's effects on global warming.[243] Putting corporate profit over public interest is nothing new: President Ronald Reagan removed the solar panels that had been installed on the White House roof by President Jimmy Carter, eliminating any visible sign of preference for solar power over fossil fuels.[244] But Trump went further than subtle symbolism. He disparaged experts in climate change, calling the threat a "Chinese hoax." According to Trump, "The concept of global warming was created by and for the Chinese in order to make United States manufacturing non-competitive."[245] In 2018, the National Oceanic and Atmospheric Administration, part of Trump's own administration, issued a report concluding that climate change was harming the United States and its economy, and that emissions would cause further damage unless they were substantially reduced. Trump announced that he did not believe the agency's conclusions.[246] Members of Trump's administration also reportedly pressured scientists to minimize public statements about threats to the environment; a member of the National Weather Service said he was reprimanded for tweeting about climate change findings and was later transferred to a lower-profile office.[247] Silencing experts and scientists is a crucial part of the authoritarian playbook.

Most notably, Trump stubbornly downplayed the Covid-19 pandemic, which first struck in early 2020, the year he faced reelection—a time when every incumbent president wants a thriving economy. Trump's refusal to deal with the problem may have contributed to some of the more than one million Covid-related deaths in the United States.[248] Trump publicly belittled Dr. Anthony Fauci, a scientist who had served as director of the National Institute of Allergy and Infectious Diseases for almost forty years.[249] Trump called him "the king of 'flip-flops' and moving the goal-

posts to make himself look as good as possible."[250] Trump referred
to Fauci and White House Coronavirus Response Coordinator Dr.
Deborah Birx[251] as "two self-promoters trying to reinvent history to
cover for their bad instincts and faulty recommendations, which I
fortunately almost always overturned."[252] Government professionals
who contradict the leader are attacked, silenced, or removed.

Condemn the courts

Authoritarians also criticize the judicial system, an essential institution for protecting the rule of law from executive overreach.
Disparaging the courts undermines public confidence in their
legitimacy to resolve disputes. When judges ruled against him in
court, Trump framed their decisions as personal attacks rather than
reasonable differences of legal interpretation. For example, when
Trump was involved in litigation over fraud claims against Trump
University in 2016, he said he could not get a fair hearing from
the judge assigned to the case, the Indiana-born Gonzalo Curiel,
because the judge was "Mexican."[253] Trump imputed to the judge
a hostility based on Trump's unrelated plans to build a wall on
the border with Mexico: "I've been treated very unfairly by this
judge. Now, this judge is of Mexican heritage. I'm building a wall,
OK?"[254] In immigration litigation, as president in 2018, Trump
attacked the integrity of the Ninth Circuit Court of Appeals. "I
mean, it's really sad when every single case filed against us is in the
9th Circuit," Trump told a group of governors at the White House.
"We lose, we lose, we lose, and then we do fine in the Supreme
Court. But what does that tell you about our court system? It's a
very, very sad thing."[255] When a judge ruled in 2022 that Trump
would be required to sit for a deposition in a civil case brought
by writer E. Jean Carroll, he called the judicial system "a broken
disgrace."[256] A jury later awarded Carroll five million dollars after
finding that Trump had battered and defamed her.[257] After Trump
was indicted by the Manhattan district attorney in 2023, Trump
called the judge to whom the case was assigned "highly partisan"

and said the judge and his family were "Trump haters."[258] Trump also targeted Judge Tanya S. Chutkan after she was assigned to his federal election interference case, calling her "VERY BIASED AND UNFAIR."[259] Trump also posted false accusations that Chutkan "admitted she's running election interference against Trump."[260] Expressing disagreement with a court's decision is one thing, but Trump consistently went further, impugning the integrity of the judges themselves. The rule of law will persist in this country only if we agree as a society to take our disputes to courts and comply with their decisions. Attacking the integrity of courts undermines their authority.

Put down protesters

Authoritarians have little tolerance for protesters. To retain power, the strongman leader must maintain the illusion that the public adores him and his policies. Protesters provide a visible reminder that power resides with the people, and that politicians are their temporary servants. But if the leader can successfully portray protesters as dangerous threats to the peace, then using a show of strength to put them down is not just tolerated but applauded. A display of force is a common tactic among strongmen who portray themselves as populists, according to Steven Levitsky, a Harvard political scientist who studies the decline of democracies.[261] Violating norms signals that the leader is willing to take drastic action, even "take an ax to the political elite" who set those norms.[262]

According to Tom Pepinsky of Cornell University, during times of turmoil, authoritarians appeal to "order over law, instead of law and order."[263] He said that some leaders, such as Vladimir Putin, Rodrigo Duterte in the Philippines, and Viktor Orbán of Hungary, rise to power by promising to fulfill the people's desire for order.[264] When people perceive that violence has spun out of control, they may prefer a government that restores the traditional balance of power. According to Pepinsky, in a deeply polarized society, some people "feel real pleasure in seeing the capital-O 'other' being put down and controlled."[265]

Examples of this strategy abound in China, the Middle East, and Russia. In the 1980s, when students in China began protesting for freedom of speech and a more open society, China's leader, Teng Hsiao-p'ing, sent tanks to Tiananmen Square, where protesters were shot or arrested.[266] Estimates of the death toll range from two hundred to ten thousand.[267] In more recent times, waves of protesters who demonstrated in Hong Kong against the Chinese government's antidemocratic policies were arrested and charged with crimes.[268]

In response to the Arab Spring, a series of successful anti-government protests in 2011 that utilized the then new technology of social media, authoritarian governments unleashed a predictable—and effective—strategy of repression. According to Marc Lynch, a George Washington University political science professor who focuses on the Middle East, "authoritarian regimes adopted a number of similar policy responses to mass protest, including the denial of access to public space, dehumanizing discourses, and mobilization of a xenophobic nationalism. Protesters across countries found themselves labeled—in remarkably similar language—foreign-backed provocateurs, alien agitators, or drug-addled criminals."[269]

In 2019, 1,300 people demonstrating against government corruption were arrested in Moscow.[270] Three years later, Putin's government arrested protesters voicing their opposition to conscription to fight in Russia's war against Ukraine;[271] protesters were warned that their actions could bring fifteen years in prison for committing the crime of "spreading false information" about the military.[272] According to Ivan Kurilla, who studies Russian-American relations at Saint Petersburg's European University, the Kremlin's narrative on protests is that they must be quelled immediately to eliminate the risk of violent chaos.[273] "The Kremlin line is that peaceful protests always escalate into riots," Kurilla said. "They want to portray all peaceful protesters as criminals."

During the summer of 2020, when protests erupted across

America over police brutality following the killing of George Floyd,[274] most demonstrations were peaceful, but some were accompanied by violence, looting, and property damage.[275] The far right used these protests during an election year as an opportunity to claim the mantle of "law and order." Trump and many fellow Republicans falsely characterized all the protesters as members of "the Radical left"[276] or as "Antifa"—an activist network that aggressively opposes fascism, white supremacy, and neo-Nazism.[277] He referred to protesters as "terrorists" and urged governors to engage in "retribution."[278] Trump said he would deploy the military to states if their governors failed to call up the National Guard.[279]

At the time, the *New York Times* described Trump's conduct as "reproducing, in appearance if not in form, some of the same traits of the strongmen rulers for whom he has long expressed admiration," such as Putin and Duterte.[280] When Black Lives Matter protesters came to Lafayette Park, outside the White House, law enforcement personnel used flash-bang explosives and tear gas to remove them so that Trump could walk across the park to a nearby church for a photo op with a Bible.[281] His entourage included his attorney general and Defense Department officials.[282] The chairman of the Joint Chiefs of Staff even wore battle fatigues.[283] The stunt was a not-so-subtle message of the triumph of white evangelicals over Black protesters. As the *Times* described his response to the unrest, "Mr. Trump's unapologetic calls for force, his efforts to position the military as backing his political line, and his warnings of us-versus-them internal threats that must be put down swiftly all follow, whether he knows it or not, a playbook used by the very strongmen he has praised."[284] Authoritarians and fascists tolerate no critics.

Play Four: Stoke Violence

Another tactic in the authoritarian playbook is to use violence to dominate a population. When people become inured to the cruelty of violence, they are more likely to accept it as the cost of attaining the type of society they seek. Throughout history, authoritarians have used violence to bend others to their will.

During Andrew Jackson's presidential administration, Native Americans were demonized and massacred. Laws were passed, including the Indian Removal Act, to force survivors onto reservations, which continue to be among the most impoverished and underserved regions of the nation. In what became known as "the Great Terror" or "the Great Purge," Stalin eliminated political opponents from the Soviet Union, executing an estimated 750,000 people between 1936 and 1938.[285] More than one million others were sent to forced labor camps.[286] As Hitler came to power in Germany, he used the Sturmabteilung (SA), a paramilitary group, to control the streets.[287] According to the United States Holocaust Memorial Museum, "Storm Troopers aggressively interfered with the meetings of opposing political parties, fought in the streets with other paramilitaries, influenced elections, and intimidated Jews, Roma, Communists, and Social Democrats—groups they believed were 'enemies of Germany.'"[288] As chancellor, Hitler publicly humiliated Jewish people by making them scrub streets in front of jeering onlookers[289] before he sent them to concentration camps, where more than six million men, women, and children were killed.[290] More recently, Nicaraguan president Daniel Ortega responded to protests in 2018 with violence, resulting in the deaths of three hundred people. The deaths became Ortega's rationale for banning protests and caused his political opponents to go into hiding.[291] Under Putin, Russian dissidents are mysteriously poisoned or die in plane crashes.[292]

Political violence works alongside disinformation because of the chilling effect it has on voices of dissent. Violence not only eliminates some opponents, it also silences others. Rather than risk ridicule, torture, or death, people learn to keep their mouths shut. Philosopher José Ortega y Gasset said that when he lived in Spain under Franco, fear of violence against him bred an instinct to conform.[293] Historian George Mosse reported feeling "low-level terror" as a young Jewish man in Nazi Germany, which led him to "hypervigilance" to comply with rules. Without a free press and social movements to challenge authority, official disinformation goes unchecked.

In the United States, Donald Trump and other Republicans have increasingly stoked violence. One target of their violent imagery has been the media. In 2017, Trump tweeted from the official @POTUS Twitter account a doctored video depicting himself punching a figure whose head was labeled "CNN."[294] Later that year, he retweeted from his personal account a locomotive labeled "Trump" crashing into a human embodiment of a CNN logo.[295] Trump would then dismiss these posts as "jokes," claiming that he would never promote violence.[296] Yet in 2018, after a candidate in Montana body-slammed a reporter, Trump endorsed the candidate, telling rallygoers, "That's my kind of guy."[297]

Trump also encouraged violence against his political opponents. In 2016, during a rally in North Carolina, Trump falsely claimed that Hillary Clinton wanted to "abolish, essentially abolish, the Second Amendment," the constitutional provision that protects the right to keep and bear arms. "If she gets to pick her judges, nothing you can do, folks. Although the Second Amendment people, maybe there is, I don't know. But I'll tell you what, that will be a horrible day."[298] Senator Chris Murphy (D-CT), whose home state had suffered a horrific mass shooting at Sandy Hook Elementary School in 2012, recognized the danger in the comment, tweeting, "Don't treat this as a political misstep. It's an assassination threat, seriously upping the possibility of a national tragedy & crisis."[299]

In May 2020, Trump retweeted the comments of a New Mexico county commissioner who told a crowd, "The only good Democrat is a dead Democrat."[300] Later that year, Trump gleefully applauded a dangerous stunt by his supporters on a Texas interstate highway: In October, as a Biden campaign bus traveled down the road, a caravan of vehicles flying Trump flags surrounded the bus, forcing it to slow its speed.[301] One of the vehicles in the Trump caravan even clipped the car of a nearby motorist. According to a Biden campaign statement, the cars tried to "stop the bus in the middle of the highway."[302] One of the participants in the caravan posted updates regarding the Biden bus throughout the day, stating, "The Trump Train is in hot pursuit. Just a few of our great patriots out there."[303] As a result, the Biden campaign cancelled an event, citing security concerns. Rather than denounce a dangerous act that was directly inhibiting political activity, Trump signaled his approval, tweeting a video of the incident and stating, "I LOVE TEXAS!"[304] Trump later boasted about the stunt during a rally in Michigan, saying, "Did you see the way our people, they were, ya know, protecting this bus . . . because they're nice," he said. "They had hundreds of cars. Trump! Trump! Trump and the American flag."[305] In 2023, Trump collaborated with defendants who had been charged in the January 6 attack on the US Capitol on a recording called "Justice for All."[306] In the recording, Trump could be heard reciting the Pledge of Allegiance, over the singing of the national anthem by inmates who called themselves the "J6 Prison Choir."[307] Placed on sale for $1.29 per download, the song was released to raise funds to support the families of the defendants.[308] Representative Marjorie Taylor Greene further sought to normalize the conduct of the defendants by visiting them in jail.[309]

Trump has frequently encouraged violence against protesters. When critics interrupted his rallies and were physically attacked by his supporters, Trump failed to condemn the altercations, sometimes even expressing appreciation and his own desire to join in. In 2015, a Black Lives Matter activist interrupted a Trump rally in Alabama.[310] Members of the crowd kicked and punched the protester, who was then arrested.[311] Rather than denounce the violence, Trump appeared on Fox News the next day and said, "Maybe he should have been roughed up, because it was absolutely disgusting what he was doing."[312] When a protester was removed from a 2016 campaign event in Nevada, Trump said, "I'd like to punch him in the face, I'll tell ya."[313] After a protester interrupted a 2016 rally in Kentucky, Trump said, "Get him out. Try not to hurt him. If you do, I'll defend you in court. . . . Are Trump rallies the most fun? We're having a good time."[314] Trump expressed admiration for violence that broke out at a New Hampshire rally after he claimed a protester had started "swinging and punching." Trump said his supporters "took him out. It was really amazing to watch."[315]

During the summer of 2020, Trump used violent imagery against Black Lives Matter protesters, tweeting, "When the looting starts, the shooting starts."[316] The tweet harked back to a phrase used in 1967, against civil rights protesters, by a white police chief in Miami. Twitter, the social media platform now known as X, responded by limiting access to the tweet because it "violated the Twitter Rules about glorifying violence."[317]

Trump has also suggested unconstitutional police brutality against criminal suspects. In 2017, as president, Trump spoke to a group of law enforcement officers on Long Island, in New York. "When you see these thugs being thrown into the back of a paddy wagon—you just see them thrown in, rough—I said, please don't be too nice. Like when you guys put somebody in the car and you're protecting their head. The way you put their hand over—like, don't hit their head and they've just killed somebody, don't hit their head. I said, 'you can take the hand away, okay?'"[318] While Trump's remarks were met with laughter by some in the audience, other law enforcement leaders saw the need to repudiate the president's lawless suggestion that criminal suspects should be mistreated. Chuck Rosenberg, then acting administrator of the Drug Enforcement Administration, issued a memo condemning as "wrong" Trump's remarks that "condoned police misconduct regarding the treatment of individuals placed under arrest by law enforcement."[319] New York police commissioner James O'Neill echoed that sentiment, stating, "To suggest that police officers apply any standard in the use of force other than what is reasonable and necessary is irresponsible, unprofessional and sends the wrong message to law enforcement as well as the public."[320] As Trump awaited indictment in Manhattan in 2023, on charges of falsifying business records, he posted an image on his Truth Social platform of himself holding a baseball bat next to a photo of Alvin Bragg, the district attorney, with his hands raised in what could be seen as a pose of surrender, a clear message suggesting the use of force against the prosecutor.[321] Trump also warned that if he were charged with a crime, "death and destruction" would follow.[322]

Other politicians saw Trump's success and followed suit, further normalizing political violence. In a 2022 television ad, Eric Greitens, a candidate for US Senate in Missouri, was shown leading a team of armed, uniformed men in a raid on a house.[323] In the ad, Greitens says, "Join the MAGA crew. Get a RINO hunting permit. There's no bagging limit, no tagging limit, and it doesn't expire until we save our country."[324] This ad appeared shortly after Congress began investigating the January 6 attack. The *New York Times* noted at the time, "The use of violent rhetoric has steadily increased in Republican circles in recent months as threats and aggressive imagery have become more commonplace in community meeting rooms, congressional offices and on the campaign trail."[325]

The casual use of violent themes has gone beyond campaign ads. In 2021, Representative Paul Gosar (R-AZ) posted on social media a violent video depicting him killing his House colleague, Representative Alexandria Ocasio-Cortez (D-NY), one of the most visible members of the Democratic Party's progressive wing.[326] The meme altered the opening montage of a Japanese animated action series to show Gosar, along with his GOP House colleagues Marjorie Taylor Greene and Lauren Boebert, wielding swords and fighting monsters onto which the faces of Ocasio-Cortez and Joe Biden had been imposed.[327] The video also showed footage of immigrants, in conjunction with the words "drugs," "crime," "poverty," "money," "murder," "gangs," "violence," and "trafficking." In the video, the Gosar figure used his sword to kill Ocasio-Cortez.[328] In defending the video, a member of Gosar's staff downplayed the seriousness of the images it depicted, stating, "Everyone needs to relax. The left doesn't get meme culture. They have no joy. They are not the future.

It's a cartoon. Gosar can't fly and he does not own any light sabers. Nor was violence glorified. This is about fighting for truth."[329]

The thirst for violence has also trickled down to local politics. In 2019, a county commissioner in North Carolina told a crowd, "We'd solve every problem in this country if on the 4th of July every conservative went and shot one liberal."[330] During the Covid-19 pandemic, a candidate for US Senate in Ohio criticized the "tyranny" of the federal government when it encouraged masking and vaccine requirements.[331] He said in a video, "When the Gestapo show up at your front door, you know what to do."[332] (The Gestapo, of course, was the secret police in Nazi Germany.) At a 2021 rally to hear a conservative commentator in Idaho, an audience member stood at the microphone and blasted "corporate and medical fascism." He then asked, "When do we get to use the guns? No, and I'm not—that's not a joke. I'm not saying it like that. I mean, literally, where's the line? How many elections are they going to steal before we kill these people?"[333] When a local public official denounced the remark, another tweeted that the question was "fair," stating, "Our Republic would not exist without this kind of rhetoric."[334]

While normalizing political violence has been mostly a practice of Trump and the far right, even Representative Nancy Pelosi (D-CA), the former House Speaker, indulged in fantasies of violence. During the January 6 attack, she was filmed by her adult daughter, a documentary filmmaker, saying that she hoped that rumors were true that Trump would be coming to the Capitol that day.[335] "I've been waiting for this. For trespassing on the Capitol grounds. I want to punch him out, and I'm going to go to jail, and I'm going to be happy."[336] While her comment was made in the heat of crisis, she certainly must have been aware that her daughter's team was filming her at that moment. They chose to keep the cameras rolling.

When leaders demonize their critics and rivals, they make them targets for violence. Robert Pape, a professor who studies political violence, calls this trend "a self-reinforcing spiral," explaining,

"When individuals feel more confident and legitimate in voicing violent sentiments, it can encourage others to feel more confident in making actual violence easier."[337] And, in fact, whether it was causation or correlation, political violence in the United States increased during the Trump administration.

A man charged with punching a Black Lives Matter activist at a North Carolina rally in 2016 said of his victim, "We don't know who he is, but we know he's not acting like an American. The next time we see him, we might have to kill him."[338] In 2019, a man in Florida was convicted for sending pipe bombs through the mail to members of the media and prominent Democrats, including Joe Biden, Barack Obama, and Hillary Clinton;[339] the media dubbed him "the MAGA Bomber."[340] The 2021 plot to kidnap Governor Gretchen Whitmer came after she had verbally sparred with Trump over her Covid-19 shutdown orders.[341]

During the hearings by the House committee investigating the January 6 attack, Representative Adam Kinzinger (R-IL), one of only two Republican members on the panel, published a letter his wife had received at their home stating that Kinzinger would be executed and that she and their son would join him in hell.[342] When Kinzinger supported an infrastructure bill opposed by Trump, he received a call from someone telling him to slit his wrists and rot in hell.[343] Fellow Republican congressman Fred Upton, of Michigan, reported receiving death threats against himself and his family when he, too, supported the bill.[344] Representative Eric Swalwell (D-CA) and his staff were the subjects of threats to kill them at the Capitol with an AR-15.[345]

In October 2022, a man broke into then Speaker Pelosi's San Francisco home and attacked her husband with a hammer, demanding to know, "Where is Nancy?"[346] The violence came after years of attacks targeting the first woman Speaker of the House.[347] She was a frequent demon in Republican attack ads, consistently depicted as a member of the West Coast liberal elite who was out of touch with "real America."[348] Opponents often portrayed Pelosi with horns and swastikas, sometimes showing her engulfed in flames with the hashtag #FirePelosi.[349] Marjorie Taylor Greene called for Pelosi's execution for "treason."[350] Greene also "liked" a Facebook post stating that "a bullet to the head would be quicker" as a way to remove Pelosi as Speaker.[351] Then House Minority Leader Kevin McCarthy (R-CA) had made the prescient "joke" in 2021 that if his party were to retake the House and he were to become Speaker, "I want you to watch Nancy Pelosi hand me that gavel. It will be hard not to hit her with it."[352] Reports indicated that the attacker at Pelosi's home had a public blog that included posts supporting Trump and attacking Democrats.[353] As Swalwell tweeted at the time, "MAGA political violence is at peak level in America. Somebody is going to get killed. I urge GOP leaders to denounce the violence."[354] But rather than denounce violence, Trump stoked it, posting in 2023 that Pelosi "is a wicked witch whose husbands [sic] journey from hell starts and finishes with her. She is a sick and demented psycho who will someday live in HELL!"[355]

Threats aimed at the press or politicians not only increase the likelihood of actual physical violence against them but, over time, also cause critics to think twice before speaking out. According to the Committee to Protect Journalists, "Targeting individual journalists or media outlets, on- or off-line, creates a chilling effect and fosters an environment where further harassment, or even physical attack, is deemed acceptable."[356] The chilling effect on the press means that critics will self-censor for fear of retaliation. And without the truth-tellers, disinformation can flourish. Who knows how many public officials check their own public comments for fear of retaliation against them or, even worse, their family members? In 2023, Whitmer revealed that her husband decided to close down his dental practice and retire eight years earlier than he had planned after receiving constant threats.[357] And how many citizens refrain from seeking public office for fear of putting family members in harm's way? By normalizing violence and muzzling their critics, authoritarians tighten their grip on power.

Play Five: Man and Superman

Another play the authoritarian uses to soften the public is to portray himself as a regular person and, at the same time, an all-powerful superman who can solve the nation's problems. Authoritarian leaders like Hitler, Mussolini, and Putin rose from modest origins, then came to portray themselves as superior beings. Donald Trump misspelled words in tweets just like the rest of us, but said he alone could fix the country and make it great again.

In *Strongmen*, Ruth Ben-Ghiat explains this dichotomy.[358] On the one hand, the idea that the leader is "one of us" makes an authoritarian seem less dangerous.[359] Voters love a candidate with whom they imagine they could drink a beer. Such leaders, she writes, often come from outside the political establishment;[360] they identify themselves as populists who define their nations as "bound by faith, race, and ethnicity rather than legal rights."[361] On the other side of the same coin is an image of virility. Ben-Ghiat writes that "the leader's displays of machismo and kinship with other male leaders are not just bluster, but a way of exercising power at home and conducting foreign policy. Virility enables his corruption, projecting the idea that he is above laws and that weaker individuals must follow."[362] It is no coincidence that authoritarians often come to power during times of societal change by appealing to fear.[363] "They don the cloak of national victimhood," says Ben-Ghiat, and "proclaim themselves their nation's saviors."[364] The more polarized their society, the better, and they even work to "exacerbate strife."[365] She says that strongmen use resentment and fear to offer "comfort in knowing who to blame for the nation's troubles—and who to trust to solve these troubles once and for all."[366]

Authoritarians throughout history have crafted their image to appear strong and powerful, to develop a sort of personality cult. Mussolini and Putin were known to be photographed shirtless, showing off their physical fitness.[367] Putin has been shown riding a horse while bare-chested, diving in a wetsuit,[368] and playing hockey, often scoring at prolific rates against suspect opponents.[369] Trump has consistently expressed admiration for authoritarian figures, such as Putin, Turkey's Recep Tayyip Erdoğan, and North Korean leader Kim Jong Un.[370]

At Trump rallies, supporters held signs depicting Trump's head on the bodies of John Wayne and Superman, icons of male strength.[371] Trump himself once tweeted a video clip from *Rocky*, the famous film about a strong and fit rags-to-riches prizefighter, in which Trump's face had been put on the body of the title character.[372] After leaving office, Trump sold bizarre digital trading cards depicting himself as a superhero.[373] Other political leaders have also taken up the mantle of masculinity: Former congressman Madison Cawthorn (R-NC) said that he was "raised on Proverbs and pushups."[374] Senator Josh Hawley (R-MO) wrote a book on manhood.[375] Presidential candidate and anti-vaxxer Robert F. Kennedy Jr. got in on the machismo act in 2023 with a social media video displaying his shirtless workout.[376]

But authoritarians do not settle for simply being strong. They want to be seen as superior, even godly. In a 1934 propaganda film, Hitler was depicted as descending from the sky in an airplane to address the Fatherland.[377] In Zaire (now the Democratic Republic of the Congo), after Mobutu Sese Seko seized power in a 1965 coup and assumed the role of president for thirty-two years,[378] television newscasts opened with an image of Mobutu's face hovering among the clouds.[379] In Libya, giant images of Muammar Gaddafi "saturated" society to give "the impression that he was everywhere and saw everything."[380] Trump embraced similar imagery. He had spent his entire career projecting an image of wealth and power. In his television reality show *The Apprentice*, Trump played a fabulously rich CEO who was far more successful than his real-life bankruptcies would suggest.[381] Ever the showman, Trump arrived to announce his candidacy for president in 2015 by coming down an escalator at Trump Tower, his New York City building adorned with marble and brass appointments;[382] one observer said the spectacle created the impression of "a Greek god" descending "from Olympus to intercede in our desperate affairs."[383] In 2015, a letter was produced from Trump's doctor stating that his "strength and stamina are extraordinary," and, if elected, he would be "the healthiest individual ever elected to the presidency."[384] During his speech accepting the GOP nomination for president in 2016, Trump darkly described a nation in ruins and claimed he could cure it of all its ills. "I alone," he famously said, "can fix it."[385] When Trump was indicted by the Manhattan district attorney in 2023, on charges of falsifying business records, Representative Marjorie Taylor Greene even compared the former president to Jesus Christ. "Jesus was arrested and murdered by the Roman government," she said. "There have been many people throughout history that have been arrested and persecuted by radical corrupt governments, and it's beginning today in New York City."[386]

The process of marketing authoritarians as larger than life, beyond reproach, and capable of solving all problems is intertwined with disinformation. "Once his supporters bond to his person," writes Ben-Ghiat, "they stop caring about his falsehoods. They believe him because they believe *in him*."[387] As described by German writer and scholar Victor Klemperer in *The Language of the Third Reich*, it was common in Nazi Germany for people to say that they believed in Hitler.[388] Trump understood the recipe for building loyalty. "I could stand in the middle of Fifth Avenue and shoot somebody," he said in 2016, "and I wouldn't lose any voters."[389] This blind loyalty is an essential ingredient in the recipe for disinformation. The tactics of disinformation depend on it.

2.

FROM GASLIGHTING TO THE LIAR'S DIVIDEND: DISINFORMATION TACTICS

"The correct use of propaganda is a true art."

—ADOLF HITLER, *Mein Kampf*

IN THE 1880S, PAULA ALQUIST was an aspiring opera singer in Italy when she fell in love with her accompanist, Gregory Anton. Paula was also the heir to a fortune left to her by a deceased aunt. Paula and Gregory married and moved to London. There, she became forgetful, and her mind seemed to play tricks on her. She would hear odd banging sounds on the wall. At times it appeared to her that the lights in the house were dimming on their own. As Paula began to doubt her own sanity, she became isolated and prone to fits of agitation when it seemed that her eyes were deceiving her. She became ever more dependent on Gregory to explain what was really happening. Only he could protect her.[390]

This story, of course, is the plot of *Gaslight,* a 1938 play and 1944 film. In the story, Gregory was deliberately deceiving Paula about the home's flickering gas lights and other odd occurrences to cause her to doubt her own ability to perceive reality, so that he could have her committed and steal her inheritance. "Gaslighting" has since become a shorthand term for this type of manipulation. In the same way, authoritarians in history have worked to persuade populations that they were mistaken or misremembering facts when they detected inconsistencies.[391] Joseph Stalin, who murdered peasants who opposed his authority,[392] even had people's images removed from photographs to erase them from memory.[393] Benjamin Carter Hett, a historian who has studied Adolf Hitler's rise to power, concluded that "the key to understanding why many Germans supported him lies in the Nazis' rejection of a rational, factual world."[394] In Chile, even when people tuned out Augusto Pinochet's propaganda, he managed to desensitize them to truth.[395] "Years of indoctrination to one truth," writes Ruth Ben-Ghiat in *Strongmen*, can "lead to the cynical conclusion that there is no truth and nothing means anything."[396] *No, the lights don't look dim to me, dear.*

An Old Trick

Disinformation goes back all the way to the days of ancient warriors. Homer's epic poem *The Odyssey* tells the tale of the Trojan Horse, the legendary structure disguised as an offering to the goddess Athena that concealed Greek soldiers.[397] According to the lore, the military deception enabled the Greeks to breach the walls of Troy without hurling a spear. Sun Tzu, the Chinese general whose famous military treatise, *The Art of War*, is still widely read today, taught deception tactics as early as the fifth century BCE.[398] In the sixteenth century, Sir Walter Raleigh complained of false claims by the Spanish Armada of victory in battles at sea to instill fear in its foes.[399] In the United States and elsewhere, white enslavers justified their brutal acts by falsely claiming that Black people were impervious to pain.[400] One of modern history's most infamous propagandists, of course, was Hitler. He learned the craft during World War I, when he served in the information department of the German army.[401] According to historian Timothy Snyder, soldiers in the unit were "trained as political activists, acting covertly as agents of the armed forces to mold public opinion."[402] Hitler would later partner with Joseph Goebbels, his architect of disinformation, to control the population. He drew on crowd psychology, using radio addresses in addition to rallies to stir a strong emotional response from a large audience of listeners.[403]

Other strongmen in history have used disinformation to seize and control power. Italy's Benito Mussolini used censorship to control the flow of information[404] and exploited the new technology of newsreels to show himself in a flattering light.[405] During China's Cultural Revolution, Mao Tse-tung manipulated the people to reassert his authority over China.[406] He shut down schools and attacked intellectuals, urging the population to rid themselves of the "Four Olds"—old customs, old culture, old habits, old ideas.[407] Today, Vladimir Putin uses what Ben-Ghiat calls "alternate truths." She writes that Putin's goal is to "create confusion through disinformation and undermine the ability to distinguish truth from fiction."[408] For example, when Putin ordered the invasion of Ukraine in 2022, he claimed that his goal was to "denazify" the neighboring country, an effort to delegitimize Ukraine and sell the use of military force to the Russian people.[409] He falsely claimed that the goal of the attack was "to protect the people who are subjected to abuse, genocide from the Kyiv regime" and "put to justice those that committed numerous bloody crimes against peaceful people, including Russian nationals."[410]

The United States, a society that prides itself on transparency in government and a vigorous free press, has not been free from disinformation. "Remember the *Maine*" was a call to arms for our involvement in the Spanish-American War, even though Spain's role in the 1898 explosion that sank the US battleship in Havana Harbor was never determined.[411] Regardless, the deaths of 260 sailors onboard were enough to move public sentiment toward war.[412] In recent years, naval investigators have determined that a more likely cause for the blast was a fire that ignited ammunition stored onboard;[413] the rallying cry that propelled us into war may have been built on an assumption or even a lie. In 1971, the *New York Times* published the Pentagon Papers, a classified Defense Department study of US involvement in Vietnam beginning in 1945.[414] The papers revealed that four presidential administrations had lied to the American public about the country's role in Vietnam and the likelihood of winning the war.[415] When the Justice Department threatened legal action, the US Supreme Court sided with the *Times* and other newspapers that published the documents because of the need for transparency in an open government.[416] In his written opinion, Justice Potter Stewart explained, "The only effective restraint upon executive policy and power in the areas of national defense and international affairs may lie in an enlightened citizenry—in an informed and critical public opinion which alone can here protect the values of democratic government."[417] Public access to information is essential to a genuine democracy.

American politicians have been known to engage in "political spin" to cultivate a positive image or to cast narratives in a light more favorable to them.[418] Ronald Reagan was frequently photographed riding horses on his California ranch, and George W. Bush was often shown clearing brush from his land in Texas. Both cultivated images of themselves as part of the romanticized American West of rugged individualism. Joe Biden would often pose sitting behind the wheel of a sports car or eating an ice cream cone, promoting a "regular guy" image. Lies, too, have been part of self-preservation in politics. Richard Nixon denied being "a crook," calling allegations about his role in the Watergate crimes and cover-up "false charges."[419] Bill Clinton blatantly lied to the public and a grand jury when he denied engaging in a romantic affair with a White House intern,[420] saying at a press conference, "I did not have sexual relations with that woman."[421]

Even our elections have not been free from manipulation. Though it has been rare, instances of election fraud are believed to have occurred in the United States. Powerful political forces in New York and Chicago are thought to have used influence to stuff the ballot boxes in the late nineteenth and early twentieth centuries.[422] Earl Long, who served as governor of Louisiana in the late 1950s, once quipped, "When I die, I want to be buried in Louisiana, so I can stay active in politics."[423]

Disinformation Trends in the United States

But the current brand of disinformation in the United States is dramatically different from prior forms. American politicians increasingly spout clearly false claims that people accept, repeat, and act on. In early 2020, for example, President Donald Trump told the nation that the Covid-19 pandemic was no more serious than the flu and would be over by Easter. Covid-19 ultimately claimed more than one million American lives in its first two years,[424] a death toll no doubt exacerbated by disinformation about vaccines and masks. Republicans' downplaying the seriousness of the pandemic appeared designed to serve their political interest in an election year. They accurately assessed that nationwide public health shutdowns would slow the economy and harm their quest to keep the Trump administration in power. Party loyalists were only too willing to go along with Trump's magical thinking, despite the evidence before them.

A similar push can be seen in the ongoing disinformation campaign aimed at our elections. Its purveyors understand that effective democracy depends on an informed electorate; as Thomas Jefferson once said, "Whenever the people are well informed, they can be trusted with their own government."[425] Conversely, when the people are not just ill-informed but *dis*informed, then democracy is in peril.

Persistent Republican claims of "rigged" elections date back to the run-up to the 2016 presidential election, when Trump discredited the voting process in a series of tweets.[426] In one, he referred to "large scale voter fraud happening on and before election day."[427] Of course, Trump ultimately won that election over Hillary Clinton. In January 2017, the US intelligence community released a report concluding with "high confidence" that Russia had interfered in the 2016 election "to undermine public faith in the US democratic process, denigrate Secretary Clinton, and harm her electability and potential presidency." The report further assessed that "Putin and the Russian Government developed a clear preference for President-elect Trump."[428] Special Counsel Robert Mueller reached similar results when he investigated possible links between Russia and the Trump campaign. While Mueller concluded that the evidence did not support criminal charges of conspiracy, he also found that Russia had interfered in the election "in sweeping and systematic fashion" to favor Trump.[429] He "identified numerous links between the Russian government and the Trump campaign" and concluded that Trump welcomed the assistance.[430] According to Mueller's report, Russian operatives, falsely posing as Americans, posted memes and messages online that supported Trump over Hillary Clinton and went so far as to work with unwitting local political organizers to plan pro-Trump rallies.[431] Even after Trump won the presidency with the majority of electoral votes, he claimed, without evidence, that Clinton's win of the popular vote was the result of ballots cast by millions of undocumented immigrants.[432]

In 2020, Trump supporters started laying the groundwork for claims of election fraud as early as September, when they began posting, "STOP THE STEAL."[433] Before election day, Trump ally Roger Stone advised Trump supporters to claim victory regardless of the outcome,[434] and Steve Bannon, the former White House adviser to Trump, predicted that Trump would claim that he had won the election even if he had not.[435] Sure enough, after the polls closed, Trump declared victory.[436] He persisted in false claims that he had won the election even after states certified the requisite electoral votes for Joe Biden to become president.

Social media allowed Trump to access all corners of the internet with this message at lightning speed. Trump used his Twitter account to reach his 88.7 million followers,[437] many of whom retweeted his posts, further extending his reach. In one tweet, Trump falsely claimed that "in certain swing states, there were more votes than people who voted, and in big numbers."[438]

By January 6, Trump's legal challenges to election results, filed in courts across the country, had failed.[439] At noon that day, Trump spoke at a rally at the Ellipse, near the White House, exhorting the crowd to "fight like hell" or "you're not going to have a country anymore."[440] He urged followers to march to the Capitol to "peacefully and patriotically make your voices heard."[441] Shortly thereafter, supporters stormed the Capitol and disrupted the proceedings of Congress, which did not resume until after the crowd was dispersed and members had returned at 11:32 p.m.[442] The attack led to nine deaths and property damage estimated at $2.73 million.[443] Congressional hearings in 2022 recounted evidence of Trump purveying baseless allegations of fraud and his knowledge of their falsity.[444]

Since the Bush-Gore election of 2000, increased rigor in our elections procedures has minimized the likelihood of fraud. The Help America Vote Act of 2002 devoted billions of dollars to improving the infrastructure of elections.[445] HAVA requires all voting systems to be backed by a paper record for manual audit and recount.[446] It also requires first-time voters who registered by mail to present a valid form of identification.[447] According to a report by the Brennan Center for Justice, extensive research reveals that voter fraud is very uncommon, voter impersonation is virtually nonexistent, and many instances of alleged fraud are, in fact, mistakes by voters or administrators.[448] And yet Republican disinformation campaigns pushing the notion of a stolen election have persisted well past Biden's 2020 victory. Baseless claims of election fraud are themselves a fraud.

Disinformation Tactics to Persuade, Distract, and Inure Us to Lies

The kinds of messaging being used in disinformation operations today are not intended merely to evoke sentimental feelings or deny discrete allegations of misconduct. A range of forces are engaging in what intelligence experts refer to as "active measures"—methodical psychological operations programmed to manipulate targeted populations.[449] Whether people believe the messages of such operations is of secondary importance. Instead, the operations' primary goal is the reactive emotions that result from mere exposure.

Information scholar Donald A. Barclay has explained that appeals to emotion work because of something known as "salience bias."[450] Salience bias makes us pay more attention to things that are extraordinary—plane crashes attract more attention than car crashes, for example, because they are less frequent and more deadly.[451] We tend to give our attention to—and remember—things that trigger strong feelings; the more outrageous the message, the stronger the reaction. Authoritarians use disinformation to achieve political control through numerous methods. Such tactics include destroying our belief in the existence of truth, going big, repeating lies, deflecting undesired facts, using humor, keeping the message simple, using reflexive control techniques, and harnessing fear.

"Destroy" truth

In his book *Active Measures*, political scientist Thomas Rid writes that the goal of disinformation is "to exacerbate existing tensions and contradictions within the adversary's body politic, by leveraging facts, fakes, and ideally, a disorienting mix of both."[452] The assault on truth leaves people paralyzed and passive, ready to throw up their hands, because they don't know what to think. According to Peter Pomerantsev, a former Russian television producer who has written about propaganda in that country, the enemy there is constantly changing, from America to Turkey and back again.[453] "The overall sense that you have when you watch it is that you live in a world that is frightening that you don't really understand. But you can't ever change anything."

Vladimir Putin, the former KGB agent, is the master of this tradecraft, according to Clint Watts, a former FBI counterintelligence agent who now studies Russian propaganda and disinformation.[454] Watts has explained that Putin's strategy is to "create chaos in the system, such that you don't know what is the truth or not the truth."[455] When people are unable to discern truth, Watts writes, no one can be held accountable. For example, when Russia annexed Crimea in 2014, Putin created the impression that the people welcomed Russian "liberators," staging pro-Russian demonstrations in what was then part of Ukraine.[456] Vladislav Surkov, the former head of the Kremlin's propaganda machine, has explained that the strategy uses "conflict to create a constant state of destabilized perception, in order to manage and control."[457] In an information system permeated with manipulation, the very existence of falsehoods provides what national security scholar Bobby Chesney refers to as the "Liar's Dividend"—that is, disinformation campaigns help authoritarians dismiss as "fake news" any reporting that is harmful to them.[458] Pomerantsev calls this phenomenon the "fog of unknowability."[459]

When politicians tell you that up is down and down is up, it is difficult to know what to think. Following the 2020 election, not only did Trump supporters deny trying to overturn the election results, they made it appear that Democrats were the ones engaging in fraud: "Stop the steal!" Doug Mastriano, a GOP election denier who ran for governor in Pennsylvania in 2022, employed this technique by accusing his rivals of his own party's misdeeds.[460] "It seems like it's in their nature to lie," he said. "Every time I turn around, there's another lie, another excuse, another *cheating*."[461] He went on to say, "We're speaking truth. Those who lied and cheated and stealed [*sic*] will be exposed and thrown in jail."[462] Disinformers are conditioning listeners to believe all politicians lie. The GOP-led House of Representatives was gaslighting America when it launched its committee to study the "weaponization" of government to silence conservatives, turning the tables on the House Select Committee that had investigated the January 6 attack.[463] It was the investigation that was corrupt, they claimed, not the underlying plot. Such claims were efforts to undermine the clear conclusions of the Select Committee.

Go big

It was Hitler who first described the effectiveness of "the Big Lie" in his manifesto, *Mein Kampf*.[464] According to Hitler, a false claim becomes more believable because of its very audacity. A big lie is believable, he wrote, because people assume that no one "could have the impudence to distort the truth so infamously."[465] "In the big lie," he explained, "there is always a certain force of credibility."[466] Most people tell small lies from time to time, he reasoned, but find it unimaginable to tell big lies, and they project onto others the same moral reluctance. "It would never come into their heads to fabricate colossal untruths,"[467] he wrote. "Even though the facts which prove this to be so may be brought clearly to their minds," Hitler predicted, "they will still doubt and waver and will continue to think that there may be some other explanation."[468] Hitler's own Big Lie, of course, was that Jewish people were the source of all misery in Germany. Indoctrinating the German population with this disinformation allowed the Nazi Party to justify the mass removal, detention, and execution of the nation's Jewish population.

For MAGA Republicans, the "Big Lie" was the claim that the 2020 presidential election was stolen from them.[469] This deception provided justification for the coup attempt of 2020 and has given rise to the election-denier movement, which remains in place to justify future antidemocratic power grabs. As of April 2022, fully 68 percent of Republicans—millions of Americans—were still under the influence of disinformation about stolen elections[470] despite the fact that Congressional investigations, audits, and court challenges had turned up no evidence to support the claims.[471] The allegations of fraud in the 2020 election lacked even internal consistency, as Republicans gained fourteen House seats;[472] in the Senate, Republicans won close races in three states.[473] Other GOP candidates accepted their defeat in 2020 without claims of voter fraud.[474] Marjorie Taylor Greene disputed Joe Biden's win in Georgia, but not her own.[475]

As George Orwell wrote in *1984*, his dystopian novel about a totalitarian government, the controlling regime's most essential command was "to reject the evidence of your eyes and ears."[476] The MAGA right's authoritarian politicians—and the media that profit from them—make the same command today, and not just in regard to elections but also in regard to climate change, racial equality, and history itself.

Repeat, repeat, repeat

Another indoctrination technique popular among disinformers is message repetition. According to Clint Watts, the more often we hear something, the more likely it seems to be true.[477] Hitler wrote in *Mein Kampf* that propaganda "must confine itself to a few points and repeat them over and over."[478] Endless repetition can make the fictional seem plausible. The Nazi strategy is confirmed by evidence from social science, which shows that repetition of false statements reinforces belief in them.[479] When people hear a claim about election fraud again and again, they begin to believe it must be grounded in fact; simple, chanted refrains like "Lock her up!" and "Stop the steal" reinforce their false premises of underlying misconduct every time they are repeated. Donald A. Barclay calls this phenomenon "the availability cascade," a cognitive bias that leads people to accept the credibility of a claim the more often it is repeated.[480] For example, some people believe conspiracy theories about the assassination of former president John F. Kennedy not because they are supported by any evidence but because they are so pervasive.[481] The origin of the conspiracy theory was Soviet disinformation;[482] it was the KGB that first planted the story that the CIA was behind the assassination.[483] Repetition has reinforced it.

Even better than mere repetition is if a prominent person repeats a claim; then, even more people will believe it. This is the reason marketers use famous endorsers. For many people, if a superstar like Tom Brady, Matt Damon, or Kim Kardashian promotes cryptocurrency, it's often reason enough to buy in.[484]

Political ads frequently position candidates alongside leaders from their party to signal the approval of a trusted figure. Donald Trump has used Rudy Giuliani as his lawyer and spokesperson, cashing in on Giuliani's history as a former US attorney and mayor of New York. As former FBI counterintelligence agent Asha Rangappa has explained, a purveyor of disinformation uses a credible source to repeat a claim in order to give it legitimacy. "The purpose of legitimizing propaganda is to have a seemingly independent third party claim something. Then HE points to that person and says, 'See? He's saying the same thing! It must be true!'"[485] The formula, she says, is simple: "Rinse, repeat."[486]

In 2019, Republicans used this tactic to smear Joe Biden, then Trump's likely opponent in the 2020 election. Trump withheld military aid from Ukraine to pressure its president, Volodymyr Zelenskyy, to make an announcement that Biden and his son were under investigation for corruption.[487] Trump did not need an actual investigation, just a public announcement of one that he could repeat to discredit his likely opponent in the 2020 presidential race.[488] Similarly, when Justice Department officials told Trump they had found no evidence of widespread fraud in the 2020 presidential election, Trump asked top officials to "just say the election is corrupt and leave the rest to me" and Republican members of Congress.[489] According to Representative Bennie Thompson (D-MS), chairman of the January 6 Committee, Trump "hoped law enforcement officials would give the appearance of legitimacy to his lies, so he and his allies had some veneer of credibility when they told the country that the election was stolen." Finding credible sources to repeat lies makes the public more likely to believe them.

Another way to amplify a message and give it the air of credibility is through news media. As forms of media have evolved over time, authoritarians have embraced each new iteration. Benito Mussolini controlled the press with daily directives, Hitler used radio to spread his words and those of his proxies, Spain's Francisco Franco and Libya's Muammar Gaddafi embraced television to push false information.[490] Putin used the RT network (formerly known as Russia Today), with its large global television audience,[491] and made it a crime to report information that contradicted the government's version of facts.[492] Trump embraced social media—first on Twitter, until his account was suspended following the insurrection, and then on his own digital networking site, Truth Social.[493] (Even the platform's name is a form of disinformation.)

While news media in the United States are independent of government control, Trump still enjoyed the loyal support of far-right outlets such as Breitbart News, Infowars, and Fox News. Breitbart was led at one time by Steve Bannon, who later became an adviser in the Trump White House and then a relentless MAGA disinformation operative and strategist. According to a 2017 study by the *Columbia Journalism Review* that looked at 1.25 million news stories in the eighteen months leading up to the 2016 election, "A right-wing media network anchored around Breitbart developed as a distinct and insulated media system, using social media as a backbone to transmit a hyper-partisan perspective to the world."[494] The researchers concluded that this "pro-Trump media sphere" engaged in "the purposeful construction of true or partly true bits of information into a message that is, at its core, misleading." According to the study, Trump's agenda of attacking immigrants and Hillary Clinton became the focus of attention for right-wing media.[495]

Motives for such media outlets may include political persuasion or profit. Infowars, led by Alex Jones, helped propagate the right's "birther" disinformation that Barack Obama was an illegitimate president because he was supposedly born outside the United States.[496] Jones was later successfully sued by the families of the victims of the 2012 mass shooting of young children at Sandy Hook Elementary School, an event Jones had wrongly claimed was staged as a "false flag" operation by the US government to create support for gun control.[497] Evidence at his trials showed that Infowars had earned $64 million in sales in 2021, and that the combined net worth of Jones and Infowars was between $135 million and $270 million.[498] It turns out there's big money in pushing a shocking conspiracy theory.

Fox News ratings soared with the rise of Trump as the head of the Republican Party.[499] In a book about Trump's relationship with Fox News,[500] former CNN news reporter Brian Stelter described their partnership as win-win: Fox got higher ratings, and Trump got a megaphone.[501] During his presidency, Trump and Fox News host Sean Hannity would speak after almost every episode of Hannity's weeknight show ended at 10:00 p.m., an astonishing trade of independence for access by a member of the media.[502] *New York* magazine reporter Olivia Nuzzi referred to Hannity as "an extension of the Trump communications department, his daily stream of assertions serving to prop up Trump."[503] During the Covid-19 pandemic, Hannity amplified Trump's efforts to downplay the seriousness of the virus, accusing other media outlets of "sowing fear."[504] Hannity helped advance Trump's claims of a stolen election in 2020, including a now-debunked theory that voting machines had been programmed to distort vote totals.[505] Hannity later testified to the House committee investigating the attack, "I did not believe it for one second."[506] And while Fox did not report on birtherism as news, it gave the conspiracy oxygen. On one occasion, when host Steve Doocy introduced Trump, he nodded to the theory by referring to his guest as "someone we all know was born in this country."[507] Following the 2020 election, Fox News showcased the Big Lie for profit.[508] In 2023, documents and depositions in the defamation lawsuit brought against Fox by Dominion Voting Systems revealed that Fox News executives and hosts knew that they were airing false claims to boost ratings.[509]

Under a pretense of critical thinking, former Fox News host Tucker Carlson made an art form of "just asking questions" to repeat false claims. Packaging disinformation in the form of questions is a way to avoid liability for defamation. After Russia invaded Ukraine in 2022, Carlson spun the anti-liberal Russia as the good guys, simply by posing questions: "It may be worth asking yourself," Carlson said, "Why do I hate Putin? Has Putin ever called me a racist? Has he threatened to get me fired for disagreeing with him?"[510] When the media released a recording of a phone call in January 2021 in which Trump pressured Georgia secretary of state Brad Raffensperger to find him 11,780 votes, Carlson again used questions to discredit the reporting:

> The president, as you may have heard, believes the election was stolen from him. Georgia's secretary of state, whose job it is to oversee elections, disagrees. You can listen to the call yourself. It's online and you can make up your own mind about who's right on that question. And by the way, if you have time, you ought to do that. It's interesting. But no matter what you conclude about vote counting in Georgia, we're willing to bet that you won't decide Donald Trump's latest phone call is the single most important thing happening in the world right now. Probably not even close. And yet CNN is claiming that it is. Why are they doing that? Well, that's a good question and worth pondering. Do you notice a theme here? Manipulation? Maybe. Ignore the details. Don't ask questions. Here's the latest outrage. Take the bait. Get mad about it. Trump's phone call, in this case, and move on. Write a grouchy Instagram post if you want. But whatever you do, do not think for yourself because once you start doing that, you might not stop.[511]

Carlson's garble of questions, innuendo, and outrage suggests that mainstream media are lying to us, and that Trump—and the public—are the real victims here. But his careful phrasing gave him deniability that he had made any defamatory claims. Indeed, when Carlson was sued over alleged falsehoods regarding a woman who claimed to have had an extramarital affair with Trump, Carlson's own lawyers defended him by saying that he uses words that are "loose, figurative, or hyperbolic."[512] The judge agreed, quoting Carlson's lawyers in writing that the "'general tenor' of the show should then inform a viewer that he is not 'stating actual facts' about the topics he discusses and is instead engaging in 'exaggeration' and 'non-literal commentary.'"[513] Carlson used this technique to promote conspiracy theories about the January 6 attack, Covid vaccines, and immigration policies that he suggested were designed to dilute white voting power.[514] Eventually, Fox News fired Carlson. The network did not provide a reason for terminating its most popular host, but the decision came the week after it paid the $787.5 million settlement to Dominion Voting Systems to resolve its defamation lawsuit.[515]

As online media evolves, opportunists aligned with authoritarian politics use it for disinformation, propaganda, and indoctrination. Bannon's influential *War Room* podcast was described by CNN as a "dangerous fantasyland of election lies."[516] Well after the 2020 election, Bannon continued to push out MAGA disinformation that Republicans had won the White House "in a landslide" and gave airtime to other top-tier propagandists such as Giuliani, former Trump administration official Peter Navarro, and Mike Lindell, the CEO of a company called MyPillow.[517] Bannon's program was consistently ranked among the top ten news podcasts streaming on the Apple platform.[518]

Mainstream media are not without blame and often profit from repeating ridiculous controversies and conspiracies.[519] For example, in October 2022, Trump pushed a fabricated theory regarding the motive for the attack on Nancy Pelosi's husband, Paul. When Trump insinuated that the attacker was not a right-wing extremist looking to harm the House Speaker, as reported, but instead a disgruntled secret gay lover, the *New York Times*,[520] *Washington Post*,[521] and CNN[522] published Trump's statement, giving the lie even more exposure.

Even well-intentioned members of the media contribute to the problem because of their desire to present both sides of a story—a habit learned during the age of the Fairness Doctrine, a media regulation that was snuffed out by the Reagan administration. The

Fairness Doctrine required members of the media to provide balanced coverage of issues and give equal time to all candidates for office.[523] But insisting on presenting both sides of a story can also indirectly promote blatant disinformation, create false equivalencies, or elevate stories to undeserved prominence. For example, in 2016, the *New York Times* repeated Trump's drumbeat about Hillary Clinton's use of a private email server while she was secretary of state.[524] According to a study by the *Columbia Journalism Review*, in six days leading up to the election, the *Times* ran ten front-page stories about Clinton's emails, a number equal to the front-page stories it ran about all other campaign policy issues in the sixty-nine days before the election.[525] The mainstream media's repetition of disinformation gives it the patina of credibility.

Reputable journalists struggle with how to cover false claims. Is it best to ignore them, or to repeat them with sufficient context to allow readers to understand how they conflict with verifiable facts?[526] Most reporters consider it newsworthy to report a false statement simply because it is made by a high-ranking public official, like a president or a senator.[527] But repeating the claim, even if only to debunk it, exposes the public to the manipulation coded into the disinformation. Once a false claim is made, reporting about the fake news becomes the story, allowing the lie to reach more people than it otherwise might. Behavioral scientists Cailin O'Connor and James Owen Weatherall note, "Even when these further investigations show the original allegations to be baseless, they spread the reach of the story—and create the sense that there is something to it."[528]

The news media's ability to raise public awareness of otherwise unknown events has been referred to as "the Barbra Streisand effect," after an incident involving the famed singer. In 2003, Streisand sued a photographer who had posted online photos of her home in Malibu, California.[529] Before Streisand filed her lawsuit, photos of her home had been downloaded only four times by members of the public.[530] After the lawsuit was filed, 420,000 people visited the website.[531] Her high-profile lawsuit generated far more interest in the photos than the photographer ever could have achieved on his own. In the same way, when the news media report about fake news, even if only to dispel its myths, they publicize its claims.

In addition to using well-known influencers to establish legitimacy, a disinformer may also attribute a claim to popular belief, which itself lends an air of credibility. One scholar refers to this as "the bandwagon" effect—everyone thinks so, so you should, too![532] In their book *A Lot of People Are Saying*, political scientists Russell Muirhead and Nancy L. Rosenblum document the ways that Donald Trump often falsely ascribed to no one in particular a claim he sought to legitimize.[533] We have all been conditioned to accept as wisdom information prefaced with the phrase "you know what 'they' say." Trump used this tendency to his advantage. When Trump disparaged the investigation into links between Russia and his 2016 campaign, he said, "Everybody, not me, what everybody . . . the level of anger at what they've been witnessing with respect to the FBI, it's certainly very sad. . . . When you look at what is going on with the FBI and with the Justice Department, people are very, very angry."[534] He never defined exactly who these "people" were, rather, he was working to persuade the public that they should believe his claims simply because others purportedly did. Sometimes, Trump ascribed a favorable comment to a particular individual, like his friend "Jim,"[535] or to a nameless person who, in Trump's telling, had addressed Trump as "sir."[536] It was unclear who these people were or whether they even existed at all.

According to Sarah Longwell, a GOP strategist critical of Trump, ordinary voters who continue to be election deniers "aren't bad or unintelligent people. The problem is that the Big Lie is embedded in their daily life. They hear from Trump-aligned politicians, their like-minded peers, and MAGA-friendly media outlets—and from these sources they hear the same false claims repeated ad infinitum."[537] The public's willingness to embrace, repeat, and amplify disinformation portends a frightening future for democracy in America.

Look over there!

An old football adage says that "the best defense is a good offense," meaning that if your offense possesses the ball long enough and scores enough points, then a bad defense will not matter in the outcome of the game. When it comes to disinformation, if people become engrossed in outrageous statements, they can be distracted from thinking and acting in their own collective interest. As a result, authoritarian regimes are always on the offensive.

Such regimes are known to make outrageous comments to divert attention from their own corruption or incompetence. For example, in 2019, when a reporter asked the far-right Brazilian president Jair Bolsonaro about alleged corruption on the part of his son, Bolsonaro responded by telling the reporter he had "a terribly homosexual face."[538] The shocking comment then overshadowed concerns about the corruption. Peter Pomerantsev, the former producer for RT and author of books about Russian propaganda, has said he suspects that when Putin passed a law in 2013 that made it a crime to share information about gay rights with minors, the international backlash was part of the plan—an effort to distract the public during a time when protesters were demonstrating against political corruption.[539]

Trump is a master of this tactic. It was in 2017, when he was under fire for his lackluster response to devastating hurricane damage in Puerto Rico, that he resurrected the issue of NFL players kneeling during the national anthem, even after the controversy had begun to subside.[540] His comments would go on to dominate the news cycle, and his supporters followed with approving posts on social media.[541] In 2019, when the House Oversight Committee was investigating the use of private email accounts by his daughter Ivanka Trump and son-in-law Jared Kushner, both senior White House advisers, Trump went on the attack. He targeted the congressional district of its chairman, the late Representative Elijah Cummings (D-MD). Trump called the district, which has a majority African American population, "a disgusting rat and rodent-infested mess."[542] The media took the bait and focused on the comment rather than the investigation.[543] As Politico senior media writer Jack Shafer wrote in 2016, "Trump tends to toss off these provocations to divert attention and discussion from a newly published damaging story the way a squid fills the sea with ink to escape his predators."[544]

Another deflection strategy is "whataboutism,"[545] one form of which is to take an allegation and turn it back on a rival. When a leader or regime faces criticism, they may turn the tables by saying the critic is worse: I may not be perfect, but what about the other guy? For example, during the Cold War, when the United States would criticize the Soviet Union for the way it treated protesters, the Soviets would respond, "And you lynch Negroes."[546] The criticism was painfully true but still no defense against the Kremlin's own bad conduct.

Trump frequently traffics in whataboutism. In 2017, when Trump was asked about his admiration for Putin, even though "Putin is a killer," Trump did not deny the claim, instead responding, "There are a lot of killers. You think our country is so innocent?"[547] A month later, when the Congressional Budget Office determined that the Republican health care plan to replace the Affordable Care Act would remove insurance coverage for twenty-four million people, Trump's response was not to defend his party's plan but to attack his predecessor's signature legislative accomplishment. In a tweet, he posted, "If Obamacare is so great, why'd they spend tens of millions of taxpayer dollars to 'hype' it? BAD!"[548] In 2022, after the FBI recovered classified documents and other government records in a search of Trump's home, Trump falsely accused Obama of doing worse.[549] "OBAMA TOOK 30 Million Documents when he left the WHITEHOUSE and No FBI RAID," he posted online.[550] (In fact, Obama had given the documents to the National Archives and Records

Administration, in compliance with the law.)[551] The point of the exercise was to deflect criticism and suggest that everyone is corrupt. I thought of his strategy when the GOP-led House began an impeachment inquiry of President Joe Biden in 2023 on the thinnest of allegations of his son's connections to foreign business interests.[552] If all presidents get impeached, then there is no shame in impeachment. It's just politics. As described by Vadim Nikitin, a Russia analyst and freelance writer, this tactic creates a useful moral equivalency: if nobody is perfect, then there is license to do all sorts of imperfect things.[553]

Clint Watts notes that another strain of whataboutism can be seen when authoritarians challenge the source of an allegation and its motives and then offer an endless string of other possible theories.[554] According to Watts, when an authoritarian system is questioned, its leaders will "bombard the purveyor of truth with so many contradictory explanations that they must refute endless challenges to their information and provide evidence for why any and all challenges cannot be correct—an exhausting exercise leading many to surrender out of self-preservation."[555] For example, when Russia denied shooting down a Malaysian airliner over Ukraine in 2014,[556] Kremlin officials claimed to have evidence that the missile was fired from Ukraine-controlled territory,[557] that the missile was one that was no longer produced in Russia, and that satellite photos showed that the missile could not have come from areas held by Russian rebels.[558] As the BBC reported at the time, "Russian officials had given different versions of events since the plane was shot down."[559] When email messages were stolen from the Democratic National Committee and then publicly disseminated in 2016, Trump offered whataboutism in defense of Russia.[560] "It could be Russia, but it could also be China. It could also be lots of other people," Trump said from the debate stage. "It also could be somebody sitting on their bed that weighs four hundred pounds."[561] Ordinary citizens hear so many possible explanations for a phenomenon that they are tempted to shake their heads in exhaustion and conclude that they don't know what to think—just what the disinformer wants.

Insult them to death

Denigrating rivals is an old-school form of authoritarian manipulation, and ridicule is a particularly effective way to do so. "Condensing a complex social or political issue down to fit in a tweet or on a bumper sticker may create a memorable zinger," writes information scholar Donald A. Barclay, "but such cleverness does nothing to promote critical thinking about the truthfulness, or lack thereof, of any ideas expressed."[562]

I cannot remember Trump ever publicly telling a conventional joke or engaging in the politician's standard self-deprecating humor. Instead, he mocks his opponents with demeaning nicknames. By calling his political rivals names like "Crooked Hillary" Clinton or "Sleepy Joe" Biden,[563] Trump reduces them to negative caricatures, creating false but enduring impressions. Trump jabbed at Senator Elizabeth Warren's claimed Native American heritage by calling her "Pocahontas."[564] He also relentlessly targeted any member of his own party who dared to challenge him: During the 2016 primary season, Trump called Texas senator Ted Cruz, a rival candidate, "Lyin' Ted." When Attorney General Jeff Sessions recused himself from the Trump-Russia investigation, Trump called him "Mr. Magoo," after the cartoon character.[565] In 2022, after Florida governor Ron DeSantis became a potential presidential rival, he became Ron "DeSanctimonious."[566]

Trump's acolytes saw the success of the formula and have followed his lead, creating a degrading trend toward schoolyard bully taunts taking center stage in politics. In 2018, an Indiana senate candidate called his rivals Luke Messer and Todd Rokita "Luke the Liberal" and "Todd the Fraud."[567] In Michigan, the 2022 GOP nominee for attorney general referred to the incumbent, Dana Nessel, as "Dirty Dana."[568] The tactics seem juvenile, but they serve the same manipulative purpose as other forms of disinformation.

Keep it simple

Another disinformation tactic is to keep the message simple. Authoritarians take advantage of feeling's influence over logic by oversimplifying the issues, relieving their followers of the work of understanding nuance. Simple slogans are easy to remember. Just think of the most successful ad campaigns: "Just Do It," "Got Milk?" "Where's the Beef?"[569] These lines were memorable and effective because they were so simple. According to Barclay, simple narratives present issues as "clear-cut, good-versus-bad, hero-versus-villain dichotomies."[570] This leads to the belief that there are only two solutions to a problem; all decisions are either-or choices—one that is acceptable and the other that leads to awful results. In the era of the American Civil War, pro-slavery propagandists argued that unless slavery were preserved, anarchy would result.[571] In *Mein Kampf*, Hitler wrote that to be effective, propaganda must harp on a few simple slogans appealing to "the primitive sentiments of the broad masses."[572]

In a profile on Steve Bannon titled "This Man Is the Most Dangerous Political Operative in the United States," *Bloomberg Businessweek* reporter Joshua Green explained that in the documentary films Bannon once produced, "no metaphor is too indirect."[573] His films used images of cheetahs chasing gazelles and seeds bursting into blossoms.[574] He and Trump saw eye to eye on the value of pushing simple narratives. According to Watts, Trump learned his communication strategy through his work as a character on a TV reality show: "Keep people watching by giving them what they want, an endless soap opera, sustained dramas, constant conflict, heroes, villains, and storylines that are easy to follow."[575]

Reflexive control

Another disinformation device is "reflexive control." According to Asha Rangappa, the former FBI counterintelligence agent, reflexive control is an information warfare technique.[576] As she explains,

"The idea is to feed your adversary a set of assumptions that will produce a predictable response: That response, in turn, furthers a goal that advances your interests. By luring your opponent into agreeing with your initial assumptions, you can control the narrative, and ultimate outcome, in your favor."[577] Rangappa notes that Russian intelligence operatives used reflexive control to influence the 2016 presidential election in the United States.[578] A month before the election, the public heard a recording from the television show *Access Hollywood* in which Trump made vulgar remarks about sexually assaulting women.[579] Hours later, Russia released email messages stolen from the Democratic National Committee that revealed infighting among members of the party.[580] Trump's comments, which could have been fatal to his campaign, were pushed from the headlines by the media's appetite for controversy. The media had taken the bait, just as the Russian operatives knew they would.[581]

According to Rangappa, Trump expertly employs this technique as well. For example, in 2023, when news reports indicated that Alvin Bragg, the Manhattan DA, was preparing to indict Trump, the former president announced that he would be arrested on the following Tuesday.[582] Members of the public assumed he knew something they did not. When that day came and went without an indictment, people wondered whether Bragg had backed down, or the grand jury had failed to find probable cause for a crime. Because prosecutors do not comment on pending investigations, Trump was able to take advantage of what Rangappa refers to as an "asymmetry of information"[583]: Trump could speak while knowing Bragg would remain silent. Although Trump was indicted two weeks later, he had already set the public narrative that the investigation was in trouble and that the evidence backing the charges was weak.

Rangappa notes that, as US attorney general, William Barr used a similar technique when he announced the results of Robert Mueller's investigation of Trump in 2019.[584] After reading Mueller's

448-page report, Barr issued his own 4-page summary and withheld the public release of the full report for three weeks; knowing that the news cycle demands that which is new, he created another asymmetry of information. Instead of focusing on the report's remarkable findings of multiple contacts between Russia and the Trump campaign,[585] Barr instead declared only that the investigation had found no conspiracy, a legal conclusion that requires a high level of proof. Barr went on to write that Mueller did not make a recommendation regarding charges of obstruction of justice, and so Barr himself had decided that the evidence was insufficient to charge that crime.[586] Of course, Mueller may have refrained from making a charging decision regarding obstruction simply because of the Department of Justice policy that a sitting president cannot be charged with a crime. During the time between the release of Barr's summary and the report itself, Trump declared on Twitter, "No Collusion, No Obstruction, Complete and Total EXONERATION. KEEP AMERICA GREAT!"[587]

The normally tight-lipped and stoic Mueller wrote a letter to Barr complaining that the attorney general had issued his own summary instead of the executive summary Mueller had prepared for public release. According to Mueller, Barr's summary "did not fully capture the content, nature, and substance" of his report and had created "public confusion" about his conclusions.[588] After reading an unredacted copy of the full report, US District Judge Reggie Walton called Barr's characterization of the report "distorted" and "misleading"[589] and even suggested that Barr may have made a "calculated attempt to influence public discourse about the Mueller report in favor of President Trump."[590] By focusing solely on the criminal charges, Barr had effectively cleared Trump's campaign of accepting help from a foreign adversary, conduct that is profoundly disloyal to the United States. What's more, accepting assistance from Russia left the president of the United States open to blackmail, a threat to America's national security. But Barr's spin led many people to conclude that Trump had been exonerated.

Barr was using reflexive control, taking advantage of the media cycle and the public's short attention span. He correctly predicted that for many members of the public, once they had formed an opinion about the results of the investigation, the details that came out weeks later would have little to no impact.

"They're not attacking me, they're attacking you!"

Another common disinformation tactic is to fuel fear by casting criticism of the Great Leader as an attack on the nation itself. Critics aren't just coming for me, says the authoritarian, they're coming for you! "They" look down on you. "They" have left you behind. Framing attacks in this way not only neutralizes their criticism, it actually transforms it into a positive dynamic, because it prompts supporters to rise to the leader's defense, further cementing their bond. Defense of the leader becomes self-defense.

Ruth Ben-Ghiat writes that authoritarians often cloak themselves in populist rhetoric, defining their nations as bound by race, ethnicity, and faith rather than by legal rights.[591] Only some of the populace count as "the people," and the leader embodies that group.[592] Attacking the leader is seen as attacking the nation itself, so a critic of the leader is labeled an "enemy of the people."[593] Even valid criticism of the leader just reinforces the notion that the entire group is under attack and needs to band together. The authoritarian leader claims to give voice to the oppressed, to carry the mantle of grievance, resentment, and victimhood. According to Ben-Ghiat:

> The cult of victimhood is a fundamental part of the strongman. And Mussolini started it off. They don't represent their people like democratic politicians. They embody the people. They inhabit the people. They are the bearer of the people's humiliations, their sorrows. Hitler did this expertly and that's why, people felt, in his speeches, he was screaming out the pain that all of Germany felt. He was embodying Germany's victimhood. The most successful strongmen have all known how to do this.[594]

Trump mastered the tactic of becoming one with his supporters. At his 2023 speech at the Conservative Political Action Conference, Trump told the audience, "In 2016, I declared: I am your voice. Today, I add: I am your warrior. I am your justice. And for those who have been wronged and betrayed: I am your retribution."[595] As with Mussolini and Hitler, Trump's perpetual state of victimhood was just a proxy for attacks on his supporters. He carried the mantle of voters' grievances and resentment, portraying critics as dark opposition forces who wanted to silence not just him but his followers. Shortly after taking office in 2017, Trump tweeted: "The FAKE NEWS media (failing @nytimes, @NBCNews, @ABC, @CBS, @CNN) is not my enemy. It is the enemy of the American People."[596]

When Trump began to pump out his Big Lie that the 2020 election was stolen, he claimed to be fighting not for his own interests but for those of his followers, pledging during his January 6 speech at the Ellipse, "We will not let them silence your voices."[597] In 2022, Trump posted a cartoon in which he was holding a shield to protect his followers. Bouncing off the shield were the words, "DOJ, FBI, IRS, MEDIA, RINOS." An arrow pointed to a place behind him that said, "You are here." In other words, *they are targeting you, and I am protecting you.*[598] Following his New York indictment in April 2023, Trump posted on his Truth Social platform, "They're not coming after me, they're coming after you—I'm just standing in their way!"[599] After Trump was indicted by the Manhattan district attorney in 2023, he said, "They only attack me because I fight for you."[600] He used the same line in June 2023, following his federal indictment for willfully retaining national defense information.[601]

According to Ben-Ghiat, framing criticism as a "witch hunt" is part of this strategy, because it causes people to side with the Great Leader.[602] Modern strongmen Recep Tayyip Erdoğan of Turkey and the late Silvio Berlusconi of Italy have also used the term. "On one hand," Ben-Ghiat told *Time* magazine, "these macho men are constantly portraying themselves as strong and alpha male, but through the victimhood thing, they try to appeal to people's care for them, and people feel very protective of them."

Trump has repeatedly used this ploy to leverage the long history of investigations into his conduct in his attempts to strengthen the loyalty of his supporters. He has described the probes as fabricated to eliminate not just him but also his base. In 2022, he told rally-goers in Arizona, "Witch hunts, hoaxes, and abuses have been coming at us at a fast and furious pace."[603] At a 2022 rally in Iowa, he told supporters that the FBI search of his home that turned up classified and other sensitive government documents was an effort to stop their political cause. No matter that a federal magistrate judge had found probable cause that evidence of a crime would be found there, and that agents, in fact, found sensitive classified government documents in the search.[604] "They even raided Mar-a-Lago," he said. "Can you believe it? They raided Mar-a-Lago. Spying on their political rivals. Silencing dissent and using the full force of government, law enforcement, and the media to try and defeat the greatest movement in the history of our country. MAGA! MAGA!"[605] Trump said at the time that if he were indicted over his possession of classified and other sensitive government documents found at his Mar-a-Lago home, his followers would rise to his defense: "I don't think the people of this country would stand for it."[606] After being indicted and arraigned in the government secrets case, Trump accused Special Counsel Jack Smith of political motivation, claiming that Smith "does political hit jobs" for a living and that "he's a raging and uncontrolled Trump hater, as is his wife."[607] When a grand jury in Georgia returned a RICO indictment in August 2023, Trump reprised his familiar refrain with a post on his Truth Social site by proclaiming, "The Witch Hunt continues!" and calling Fulton County district attorney Fani T. Willis "out of control and very corrupt."[608]

Political allies used the same tactic to defend Trump after the Mar-a-Lago search. Representative Elise Stefanik (R-NY) tweeted, "If the FBI can raid a US President, imagine what they can do to you."[609]

Kari Lake, the unsuccessful 2022 GOP nominee for governor of Arizona, echoed those sentiments and went even further: "This is one of the darkest days in American history: the day our Government, originally created by the People, turned against us. This illegitimate, corrupt Regime hates America and has weaponized the entirety of the Federal Government to take down President Donald Trump."[610] The more misconduct Trump appeared to commit, the more investigations followed, each one providing additional evidence to support his false claim that he was being targeted.

In 2016, Hillary Clinton gave the MAGA world a gift that kept on giving when she referred to some Trump supporters as a "basket of deplorables."[611] The full context of her remarks makes clear that she said you could divide Trump supporters into two "baskets," one of which included those who felt "that government has let them down, nobody cares about them, nobody worries about what happens to their lives and their futures, and they are just desperate for change."[612] The other half, she said, were "racist, sexist, homophobic, xenophobic, Islamophobic."[613] But for purveyors of disinformation, context is irrelevant. This was the perfect opportunity to reinforce the notion that Clinton had nothing but disdain for Trump's supporters. Trump called her comments "insulting" and "disgraceful."[614] Clinton's words were spun to portray her as part of the "liberal elite" who look down on a large segment of the American people. And it gave the MAGA right "proof" that Clinton opposed not just Trump but ordinary Americans.

Dissecting and labeling these tactics of disinformation can help us identify them and render them less effective. Reduced to their basic components, these formulas seem primitive, and yet they continue to work—even thrive—in today's communication ecosystem. It is worth considering why these techniques are so effective.

3.

HEARTS ARE BIGGER THAN MINDS: WHY DISINFORMATION WORKS

"Falsehood flies, and the Truth comes limping after it."

—JONATHAN SWIFT

DR. FARID FATA WAS A successful oncologist in Michigan. He owned and operated cancer treatment clinics and a diagnostic testing lab with seven locations throughout metropolitan Detroit.[615] Fata had developed a reputation as a brilliant doctor who had cured patients of cancer. But Fata was lying—and it was a big lie. Many of his patients did not have cancer at all. He was administering unnecessary chemotherapy treatments for profit, cumulatively submitting $34 million in fraudulent claims to Medicare. Of course, it is easy to "cure" patients of cancer when they don't have the disease at all. Fata administered unnecessary injections or infusions to 553 patients.[616] Even though Fata's patients were relieved to learn that they did not have cancer, some had suffered other injuries as a result of the injection into their bodies of chemicals designed to kill human cells—loss of hair or teeth, nerve impairments, organ damage. Fata was prosecuted and in 2015 was sentenced to forty-five years in prison for his heinous crimes.

As the US attorney overseeing the prosecution, I was responsible for meeting with the victims to keep them apprised of the progress of the case. In the early stages of the case, I was stunned that some of Fata's patients spoke in his defense. They simply refused to believe that the charges were true. How could such a successful and esteemed doctor, in whom they had placed their trust, lie to them about a matter of life and death? While they eventually came around to realizing the awful truth, it took many of the victims some time to get there. Sometimes our minds are controlled by our hearts.

In a society where we have more resources than ever before to detect false claims, why is it that disinformation is such an effective tool? One reason is that much of the news we receive today leaves us feeling anxious and looking for answers. Human nature plays all sorts of tricks on us. When we are uncertain or uneasy, we become more susceptible to persuasion and manipulation. Cognitive forces like confirmation bias, conformity bias, and others all conspire to make us ripe for deception. Sensational news grabs our attention;[617] it is far more interesting to talk about the corrupt politician than the obedient public servant who complies with all the rules. We are also drawn to compelling stories that confirm our preexisting beliefs.[618] Disinformers use these dynamics to prey upon our fallible human nature.

Fear of a Changing World

International conflicts, climate change, declining labor markets, immigration challenges, a growing demand for equality by marginalized groups, a global pandemic, and other changes create, for many people, an unsettling sense that the life they have always known is disappearing. Technology accelerates the pace of change exponentially. Around the world, authoritarians seize the opportunity to gain power by blaming all woes on globalism and the decline of moral values, spinning conspiracy theories about sinister people who control the levers of society.[619] In 2022, Vladimir Putin castigated what he called "a period of revolutionary transformations."[620] He described an "overthrow of faith and traditional values" by "Western elites."[621] Like many Republicans in the United States, Putin exploits fears of the future as a reason to cling to the past.

Historian Doris Kearns Goodwin points out that extreme social change is nothing new. Comparing current times to the dawn of the twentieth century, Goodwin says both were periods of rapid and profound change. At that time, she says, "the industrial revolution had shaken up the economy, immigrants were pouring in, cities were replacing towns. A widening gap was developing between the rich and the poor, and the social landscape was changing because of all these new inventions: the automobile, the telegraph, and the telephone. You had populist movements that called for restrictions on immigration, and the establishment worried about [giving] power to ordinary people."[622] According to Goodwin, President Theodore Roosevelt exercised extraordinary leadership by embracing with optimism the opportunities those changes presented instead of preying on people's fears.[623] What could be presented today as an exciting moment full of hope and possibility is instead framed as an ominous threat undermining all that we hold dear, demanding that we push back against the forces of social progress. Rather than leading toward progress to benefit society, authoritarians harness fear of change for their own gain.

Ruth Ben-Ghiat writes, "Over and over, when there have been periods of substantial social progress—it could be gender equity, it could be secularization, it could be racial equity—[that creates] a climate of extreme anxiety, extreme anger in other people who don't like this progress. These are all fears that were very active in the 1920s and the 1930s. This is when these strongmen figures find favor."[624]

Indeed, the United States is not alone in its turn toward far-right authoritarianism. Right-wing candidates have enjoyed popular support in recent years in France,[625] Italy,[626] and the United Kingdom,[627] among other countries. In 2022, even Sweden, where center-left leaders had held power for decades,[628] took a rightward turn as the ultranationalist Sweden Democrats (SD) won 20 percent of the vote, becoming the nation's second-largest party.[629] One political scientist in Sweden said that the trending views are not just conservative but "ethnonationalist."[630] After his party's success in 2022, SD leader Jimmie Åkesson posted on Facebook, "Now we will get order in Sweden. It is time to start rebuilding security, prosperity and cohesion. It's time to put Sweden first."[631] Sound familiar?

The far right has a long history of fueling fears of change in America. The John Birch Society stoked anxiety about communism amid the civil rights progress of the 1960s.[632] The Tea Party movement arose after the 2008 financial crisis and the election of Barack Obama.[633] For some people, more non-white immigrants, recognition of rights for women and people of color, and growing acceptance of the LGBTQ+ community are not signs of progress toward a more perfect union but a subversion of America's greatness. Demographic forecasts show that the percentage of Americans of color is steadily growing, and the total will outnumber white Americans by 2045.[634] According to Russell Muirhead and Nancy L. Rosenblum, the political scientists, far-right politicians depict their political opponents as an "existential threat" whose "covert goal is to deny America as a Christian nation, depreciate America as a white nation," and cede it to a "new world order" of "Muslims, liberals, Jews, [and] African Americans" so that progressives can gain power.[635]

Research data show that Donald Trump's support was "uniquely tied to animus toward minority groups."[636] After 139 members of Congress voted against certifying Joe Biden's victory in the 2020 presidential election, a *New York Times* analysis of voting demographics found that a "shrinking white share of the population is a hallmark of the congressional districts held by the House Republicans who voted to challenge Mr. Trump's defeat."[637] The *Times* cited political scientists who concluded that "white fear of losing status shaped the movement to keep [Trump] in power."[638]

In the past decade, the right has become adept at exploiting these white nationalist sensibilities. Attacks on critical race theory in schools led to a 2023 ban in Florida of an Advanced Placement course in African American history.[639] A letter from the Florida Department of Education to the College Board, which designs AP classes, proclaimed, "the content of this course is inexplicably contrary to Florida law and significantly lacks educational value."[640] The letter did not state which Florida law the course allegedly violated. A series of copycat bills in two dozen states targeted gender-affirming medical care, some imposing civil penalties for parents seeking health services for their children.[641] The nation saw a spike in book bans in school libraries, mostly targeting topics relating to race, gender, and LGBTQ+ issues.[642] Among the titles were classics like *The Bluest Eye*, by Toni Morrison, and *The Handmaid's Tale*, by Margaret Atwood; the most banned book was *Gender Queer*, Maia Kobabe's memoir exploring sexual identity.[643] Throwing red meat to conservative voters is a way to distract them from the right's economic policies that might disfavor their interests. According to political scientist Pippa Norris, "the radical right" may even prefer public spending programs normally advanced by the left. "What distinguishes them," she says, is that they want to "push back against social liberalism, or as we call it in the contemporary parlance in the media, the 'woke' agenda."[644]

It is during these times of change that those who wield power become willing to accept extremism so that they can retain their place atop society. Throughout history, affirmation by powerful members of society has legitimized authoritarians. According to Ben-Ghiat, authoritarians "have to be brought into the mainstream by somebody. Even in a situation of a military coup, you still have these same dynamics, because the reason that the coup is accepted by conservative elites—and sometimes they know it's coming—is for the same reasons of fear of change, fear of emancipation of the wrong people."[645] In 2022, Senator Lindsey Graham (R-SC) may have revealed too much of the strategy when he expressed opposition to statehood for Puerto Rico and the District of Columbia, both of which have majority populations of color, because "that dilutes our power."[646]

Members of the Republican Party who once denounced Trump later fell into line when they recognized his power. Before Trump became the Republican nominee in 2016, Ted Cruz, the GOP senator from Texas, called him a "sniveling coward," a "pathological liar," and "utterly amoral."[647] Cruz even refused to endorse Trump during his speech at the 2016 Republican convention.[648] Once Trump was elected, though, Cruz was converted into a staunch Trump ally, becoming, in the words of Democratic Hawaii senator Mazie Hirono, "a total suck-up."[649] Ohio senator J. D. Vance, who once called Trump "cultural heroin"[650] and suggested that Trump might be "America's Hitler,"[651] later called him "the best President of my lifetime."[652]

After Trump left the White House, other political leaders utilized the same manipulative tactics that had propelled him to success. One was Ron DeSantis, who won reelection as governor of Florida in 2022 after taking on gay rights, immigration, voting rights, and abortion; one *New York Times* writer described DeSantis as an "avatar of cultural conservatism."[653] Vance, author of a best-selling memoir that explained the discontent in rural, white America,[654] took a rightward shift to win a Senate seat. During his 2022 campaign, Vance criticized globalism and "woke" corporate interests and blamed Democrats for taking away "our very sense of national pride and national purpose."[655] When democracy itself becomes perceived as a threat to white America, then everything from electoral politics to teaching Black history becomes a target for increased criticism and even criminalization. Fear of change is a powerful motivator.

Our Fallible Human Nature

Manipulators use human nature as a weapon against us. Social science has identified various psychological factors that cause us to behave in certain ways. Our love for conspiracy theories and stubbornness in our beliefs make us easy to exploit. Natural tendencies such as confirmation bias, the backfire effect, and conformity bias allow schemers and opportunists to manipulate the public for their own gain.

Most people love a good conspiracy. Some believe that evidence of alien life is stored at Area 51, the military base in Roswell, New Mexico.[656] Others are sure that Elvis Presley is alive, or that Democrats are running a secret child-abduction cult.

Why do we love conspiracies so? Researchers say it begins with a desire to simplify a complex world.[657] Muirhead and Rosenblum explain that one reason we are susceptible to conspiracy theories is that we are predisposed to see events as happening for a purpose rather than by chance. "People are averse to regarding anything of social or political importance as random, accidental, or unintended," they write. [658] Instead, we tend to believe that things are the way they are because of a deliberate plan set in place by powerful forces.

Our susceptibility to conspiracy theories comes from an innate desire for safety.[659] Psychologist Abraham Maslow's famed hierarchy of human needs lists safety second only to physiological needs like food, water, and shelter.[660] Our desire to understand our world serves this need.[661] Our brains have been trained to look for connections and patterns among facts in order to protect us from threats. *Do those gathering clouds mean a storm is coming?*[662] Instincts that protect our safety also sometimes lead us to believe that unrelated events are part of a plan instead of a mere coincidence. According to Karen Douglas, a professor of social psychology at the University of Kent, in the United Kingdom, conspiracies "tend to emerge in times of crisis when people feel worried and threatened. They grow and thrive under conditions of uncertainty."[663] A feeling of powerlessness and fear in the face of the unknown causes us to imagine an explanation for unconnected events.[664] Scientists cite climate change and the Covid-19 pandemic as the types of complex problems that invite conspiracy theories because they bring anxiety.[665] This tendency to believe in conspiracies plays into the hands of those seeking to exploit fear during times of social change. According to Sarah Longwell, the Republican political strategist, "For many of Trump's voters, the belief that the election was stolen is not a fully formed thought. It's more of an attitude or a tribal pose. They know something nefarious occurred but can't easily explain how or why. What's more, they're mystified and sometimes angry that other people don't feel the same."[666]

Stubbornness

Another feature of human nature is our profound stubbornness. As mentioned earlier, once we form a first impression, it becomes very difficult for us to change our minds, even in the face of contradictory information.[667] As information scholar Donald A. Barclay has written, with the way our brains are wired, changing another person's mind can be very difficult.[668] We tend to find weaknesses in the arguments of others but to be blind to the flaws in our own arguments.[669] Cognitive scientists Hugo Mercier and Dan Sperber call this phenomenon "myside bias."[670]

For example, in one Stanford study, subjects with opposing views on the deterrent value of capital punishment were provided data, some of which supported the claim that capital punishment has a significant deterrent effect on crime, and some of which showed that it did not.[671] In fact, the data had been fabricated for the study and provided equally compelling evidence for both sides of the argument. The students who supported capital punishment gave high ratings to the data supporting deterrence and low ratings to the conflicting data. The students who were opposed to capital punishment did the exact opposite. Moreover, after participating in the study, neither set of subjects had changed their minds, and both groups were more convinced than ever that they had been right all along.[672] Other studies show that fans at sporting events see the game differently depending on their rooting interests.[673] Close calls that go against the home team are booed, not only because our team has suffered a setback but because many fans genuinely believe they were cheated. The crowd will sometimes continue to boo even after video replays show that the officials got the call right. Our eyes see what we want to believe.

According to Mercier and Sperber, humans have developed the ability to reason in a way that helps us to resolve the problems that arise when we live in groups.[674] As a result, we place high value on the ability to win arguments. And research shows that we actually feel physical pleasure when we process information that is consistent with our beliefs.[675] Psychiatrist Jack Gorman and his daughter Sara Gorman, a public health specialist, have concluded, "It feels good to 'stick to our guns' even if we are wrong."[676]

When I worked as a prosecutor, I saw this phenomenon in action in the case of Dr. Farid Fata and others. Sometimes people refused to admit that they had been victims of fraud, even when the facts bore it out. They had become so convinced that their stockbroker or their doctor was looking out for their best interests that they could not believe they had been manipulated. People who fall for fraud scams often decline to report crimes to the police because of the shame they feel for having been duped. The Department of Justice website notes that when people become victims of fraud, their trust in their own judgment may be "shattered."[677]

Authoritarians exploit this phenomenon. Once a leader gains support by telling people what they want to hear, they will feel invested in him and inclined to believe him. For example, after Trump's inauguration, he claimed repeatedly that the size of the crowd in attendance was larger than it was; his press secretary called it "the largest audience to ever witness an inauguration."[678] Trump persisted in this claim even though photographic evidence clearly refuted it.[679] In a study, people were shown photos of the crowds attending Trump's and Obama's inaugurations and asked to identify which had the larger crowd. Fifteen percent of Trump supporters chose the Trump photo despite stark visual evidence to the contrary. They believed because they wanted to believe. Trump's demonstration of how the game is played is a dangerous lesson for leaders thirsty for power.

Confirmation bias

Other cognitive forces likewise warp our perceptions. One is confirmation bias, the tendency to pay attention to evidence that is consistent with our beliefs and to ignore facts that contradict them.[680] Law enforcement officials are trained to avoid the dangers of confirmation bias, which can lead to the arrest of the wrong suspect. Instead of following the evidence where it leads, an investigator may be tempted to develop a conclusion first. Confirmation bias will then cause them to notice all the facts that support that conclusion but disregard the facts that are inconsistent with it.[681] As former Manhattan US attorney Preet Bharara writes in his book *Doing Justice*, like the rest of us, witnesses, lawyers, and even experts are inclined to hold fast to their initial assessments, sometimes with disastrous results.[682] He describes a case in which an Oregon lawyer was arrested as a material witness on the belief that he had participated in a terrorist bombing in Spain in 2004. The only evidence linking the suspect to the bombing was his fingerprint on a plastic bag containing detonators and remnants of explosives found near the crime scene—at least, that is what four forensic experts concluded.[683] Three of the experts worked for the FBI, the fourth as an independent expert hired at the request of the suspect. After investigators failed to find any additional evidence tying the suspect to the bombing, the FBI retracted its opinion that the fingerprint was a match. The Bureau blamed "'overconfidence,' 'the pressure of working on a high-profile case,' and subsequently an unwillingness to go back and reexamine the initial findings."[684] An inspector general's investigation of the FBI's failure concluded that the mistake was based in part on placing too much reliance on certain similarities between the prints and "rationalizing small differences, which should have ruled out the match."[685] Once a first expert had reached a conclusion, the others focused on the facts that supported it and rejected the facts that did not. The suspect's Muslim faith may also have improperly clouded their conclusions[686]—confirmation bias at its worst.

Most of us are guilty of confirmation bias in our everyday lives, albeit in situations that are far less consequential. In the world of politics, we tend to notice statements that support our views and ignore statements that contradict them. This distorted view causes us to adopt the conclusions that are consistent with our beliefs. If we believe climate change is a hoax, we notice unseasonably cold days as evidence to support that view. If we believe climate change is an urgent threat, we see wildfires and hurricanes as evidence that severe weather events are becoming more common because of human-caused damage to the planet. Disinformation allows authoritarians and scammers to manipulate the public based on their targets' biases. People who are already distrustful of any political view outside of the positions of the Republican Party are easy marks for the message that when a Republican loses an election, that election was rigged.

Cognitive dissonance

Another psychological force, known as "cognitive dissonance," makes us feel mental stress when we encounter ideas or beliefs that conflict with our own.[687] As a defense mechanism, we are wired to ignore or minimize the contrary beliefs, or to delegitimize people who subscribe to them.[688] We may feel the urge to reject the messenger of a conflicting message to resolve the stress. If someone expresses an opinion with which we strongly disagree, we tend to think they are untrustworthy or biased. [689] For example, cognitive dissonance drove Republican viewers to stop watching Fox News after the network reported that Biden had won the 2020 election.[690] When the pro-Trump network was faced with a catastrophic dip in viewers, it opted to feature interviews alleging election fraud, becoming a major force in the MAGA disinformation operation. In the process, cognitive dissonance was addressed and assuaged. A disinformer can use cognitive dissonance by pandering to their base to disparage opposing views and undermine opponents.

The backfire effect

Another cognitive dynamic is known as the "backfire effect."[691] When we see evidence that contradicts our beliefs, instead of changing our minds, we are inclined to cling to our views even more tightly.[692] So, the more a false claim is debunked, the more deeply rooted it becomes. As the old Shakespeare line goes, "The lady doth protest too much, methinks."[693]

During the Covid-19 pandemic, for example, the more anti-vaxxers were told that vaccines could save their lives, the more they seemed to dig in against them. According to Longwell, when some election deniers were told the election was not stolen, their resistance to the truth actually became stronger.[694] Longwell reported that a woman from Arizona told her after the 2020 election, "I think what convinced me more that the election was fixed was how vehemently they have said it wasn't."[695] Once disinformation enters the infosphere, efforts to debunk the falsehood often serve to reinforce it.

Conformity bias and tribe signaling

Another dynamic that purveyors of disinformation exploit is the human tendency to go along with the crowd. Social scientists call this phenomenon "conformity bias." In politics, the identity of one's party often matters more to some people than their own views on issues.[696] They choose political tribe over preferred policy.

In fact, maintaining membership in a group can matter so much that some will take action simply to signal their loyalty. For example, one way Republican politicians signal their bona fides is to refer to their political opponents as the "Democrat Party," deliberately misstating the party's name. The use of the label as a term of derision dates back to the days of Senator Joseph McCarthy, in the 1950s.[697] Explanations for the use of the term vary. One theory holds that the term smears the party as lacking democratic values. Others say the term conjures negative images—"bureaucrat," "kleptocrat," or just plain "rat."[698] Trump has revealed his own motivation: "You know I always say Democrat. You know why? Because it sounds worse," Trump said. "Democrat sounds lousy, but you know what? That's actually their name, the Democrat Party. Right? The Democrat Party. So I always say Democrat."[699] Other MAGA Republican politicians have followed suit, like Congresswomen Elise Stefanik,[700] Marjorie Taylor Greene,[701] and Lauren Boebert.[702] Regardless of the reason, politicians use the derisive term to gain acceptance. As the *Chicago Tribune* noted in 2021, when candidates and activists say "Democrat Party," it identifies them "as members of the same tribe, conservatives seeking to define the opposition through demeaning language."[703]

Another problem of conformity bias is that it causes people to self-censor. The risk of being seen as disloyal prevents members of the group from challenging ideas or speaking up when they see something wrong, a dangerous tendency in a democracy. According to Clint Watts, the former FBI counterintelligence agent, people will check their own desire to express dissent to avoid the risk of expulsion from the group.[704] This impulse causes politicians to stay quiet in the face of the misdeeds of members of their own party. Sarah Longwell agrees. Following the 2020 election, she convened focus groups to understand voter motivation and found that membership in the Republican Party essentially required signing on to the effort to overturn the election. Longwell said, "To be a Republican means to believe the Big Lie. And as long as Republicans leading the party keep promoting and indulging the Big Lie, that will continue to be the case. If I've learned anything from my focus groups, it's that something doesn't have to make sense for voters to believe it's true."[705] Russell Muirhead and Nancy L. Rosenblum write that the decline of democratic institutions is possible because large numbers of people, including elected officials, "adapt to a world where conspiracy is an element of identity and affiliation."[706] In this world, as long as the conspiracy theory is plausible, they remain silent, fail to deny it or, worse, repeat it.

Even members of the general public may be willing to share news they know to be false because they want to signal their allegiance to a group. According to behavioral scientists Cailin O'Connor and James Owen Weatherall, people may read news online and, even though they don't believe the content, they will post it anyway to reflect their feeling about a topic.[707] When Donald Trump Jr. posted an offensive joke about the attack on Paul Pelosi,[708] it signaled his place as a right-wing culture warrior; others would like or share the post to assert their own membership in the group. According to researchers, people do so because they "feel that the meme lines up with who they are, what they stand for, and whom or what they are against."[709] Memes decrying the "deep state" or the "China virus" may be shared not so much because the sender believes the truth of the content but to signal their political orientation.[710] As Muirhead and Rosenblum write, this instinct to communicate our membership in the tribe is what causes Boston Red Sox fans to chant "Yankees suck," even when the New York team has a better record. The statement is not intended as a statement of facts but to reflect loyalty to Red Sox Nation.[711]

Some people who share claims they must surely know to be false seem purely Machiavellian. Senators Ted Cruz and Josh Hawley were two Republicans who publicly supported efforts to contest the 2020 election results. As Muirhead and Rosenblum write, officials like Cruz are "cynically politically self-protective."[712] Both senators were Ivy League–educated lawyers with the intellect to apprehend what was happening, but they chose to join the disinformation campaign anyway. On January 6, 2021, after Trump's repeated claims of a stolen election, and after order had been restored following the Capitol attack, Cruz and Hawley still objected to the certification of votes from Arizona despite the absence of evidence of fraud, even after all the votes had been certified in their own states.[713] Cruz explained his reasoning with some rather circular logic: "I urge you to pause and think, what does it say to the nearly half the country that believes this election was rigged if we vote not even to consider the claims of illegality and fraud in this election?"[714] That is, we should question the election results simply because people are questioning the election results.

Other Republicans later signaled their allegiance to the tribe by refusing to acknowledge Biden's victory[715] or even downplaying the seriousness of the January 6 attack. Representative Andrew Clyde (R-GA) later called it a "normal tourist visit."[716] Republican National Committee chairwoman Ronna Romney McDaniel said it was "legitimate political discourse."[717] Even as late as March 2023, then Fox News host Tucker Carlson showed video footage of the January 6 attack that had been provided exclusively to him by then House Speaker Kevin McCarthy (R-CA). Carlson cherry-picked shots of people he described as "sightseers" walking peacefully through the building.[718] During the segment, Carlson said, "The protesters were angry: They believed that the election they had just voted in had been unfairly conducted. And they were right."[719] Without citing any evidence, he added, "In retrospect, it is clear the 2020 election was a grave betrayal of American democracy. Given the facts that have since emerged about that election, no honest person can deny it."[720]

Contrast their conduct with that of Republicans who were willing to call out Trump for his role in the January 6 attack, like Liz Cheney and Adam Kinzinger. Cheney lost her seat in Congress in the GOP primary,[721] and Kinzinger chose not to run for reelection.[722] The message was clear—members of the team who wanted to stay in the good graces of the Republican Party needed to follow the Great Leader no matter where he led them.

A rapidly evolving world and human nature itself foster conditions for disinformation to thrive, and that's even before we introduce twenty-first-century technology.

4.

THE NEW ENGINES OF DISINFORMATION: THE DANGER OF EMERGING TECHNOLOGY

"If we continue to develop our technology
without wisdom or prudence, our servant may
prove to be our executioner."

—GENERAL OMAR N. BRADLEY, 1948

UPON READING ABOUT THE marvels of ChatGPT, I decided to experiment with it. The artificial intelligence (AI) chatbot, available to anyone on the internet, allows people to ask a question or provide a prompt and receive a human-like response based on its "training" from an enormous amount of data. Issues relating to AI and ChatGPT (the "GPT" stands for "generative pretrained transformer") are still emerging and highly controversial. Among the many concerns being raised are the increased possibilities of student plagiarism, privacy infringement, and influence operations.[723] As of this writing, the latest large-language model in the GPT family is GPT-4. According to one assessment, "GPT-4 is capable of generating discriminatory content favorable to autocratic governments across multiple languages."[724]

I decided to converse with ChatGPT about some of these matters. When I typed in a question asking whether it could be used to spread disinformation, I received a response that was somewhat reassuring. "No," it said. "ChatGPT should not be used for disinformation campaigns. As an AI language model, ChatGPT is designed to generate human-like responses based on the input it receives. However, its purpose is to provide helpful and informative responses, not to spread false information or misinformation." It went on to explain that disinformation is unethical, undermines trust in reliable sources of information, and would violate its terms of use that prohibit "illegal, harmful, or malicious purposes."

Then I asked ChatGPT a different question: Could it be *abused* for disinformation campaigns? "Yes," came the response. It continued to warn of the harms of such abuse, but stated the inevitable truth: "In the wrong hands, ChatGPT could be used to spread disinformation, propaganda, and fake news at scale, potentially influencing public opinion and causing harm."

Technology creates wonderful opportunities for us to engage with people all over the world about important issues, hobbies, and just about anything else. But the internet has also been a boon for disinformation. According to Thomas Rid, the disinformation scholar, "The old art of slow-moving, highly skilled, close-range, labor-intensive psychological influence" is now "high-tempo, low-skilled, remote, and disjointed."[725]

In 2018, researchers determined that with "shares" and "likes," online disinformation could reach 1,500 people six times faster than the truth.[726] A number of factors account for this: Online news sites, blogs, podcasts, and other new media make commentary on our rapidly evolving world more accessible and more frightening. Social media provide spaces where almost anyone can publish almost anything. Many social media platforms allow anonymous account holders to pose as someone they're not, sharing content with unwitting dupes who extend their manipulative messaging far and wide. Messaging applications such as WhatsApp and WeChat also provide fertile ground for disinformation and propaganda because they can reach large groups without exposing messaging to the public for rebuttal.

In addition to technology itself, some of tech's byproducts also foster disinformation. When we spend more time scrolling through social media than we do engaging with real people, we make fewer social connections with people who are different from us. As a result, it is easier for us to fall for efforts to demonize people outside of our immediate real-life social circles. Social media fragment society by putting us into echo chambers where we never hear arguments that might challenge our views. Authoritarians and schemers use disinformation to weaponize these custom-made preference bubbles by telling followers what they want to hear, often pushing them toward more polarizing views. Free content online has led us away from mainstream news, especially local media, with "legacy media" outlets shrinking as digital media expand. The ability for everyone to "do their own research" has led to a decline in our respect for expertise.

Amplifying Fear

Digital culture contributes to our feelings of fear and dread because we can experience news like never before. Not only are we bombarded with stories about crime, tragedy, and acts of war, we are able to see live footage of the human suffering they cause. It is likely no coincidence that the unpopularity of the Vietnam War coincided with the expansion of television, which provided a view of war that was very different from the gauzy mental images of heroes on the front lines. Television could suddenly beam into our living rooms real scenes of young American men in bandages and body bags. Images of the massacre of civilians by US soldiers in the village of My Lai horrified the nation.[727] Now, digital platforms bring the world to the palm of our hand with an even greater immediacy and constancy. When tragedy can be seen unfolding in real time, it feels as if we have personally experienced the horror, as the images imprint themselves on our minds in ways that the printed word does not.

For instance, in the summer of 2020, millions of Americans witnessed the police murder of George Floyd. The tragedy was just the latest in a string of viral videos of police killing unarmed Black men.[728] The footage of police officer Derek Chauvin kneeling on Floyd's neck as he begged for his life was traumatizing for anyone to watch. For Americans of color, the visceral reminder of the racialized abuse of power triggered a wave of trauma and indignation, and months of mass demonstrations.[729] Others saw the resulting protests, and the occasional violence that erupted, as a reason for fear.[730] All of it felt very personal. In 2022, when Russia attacked Ukraine, we saw civilians, including families and children, sheltering from bombs in underground subway stations and lying dead in the streets.[731] After the heavy circulation of a video showing an injured and distraught pregnant woman being stretchered from the rubble, we learned that she and her baby had died.[732] People are increasingly experiencing news of this nature in real time, on mobile devices that rarely leave their hands.

Witnessing all of this tragedy comes at a cost. A 2019 study found an association between exposure to traumatic events online and symptoms of post-traumatic stress disorder and depression.[733] Even the rapid pace of change can be disturbing to some. Author Alvin Toffler called this phenomenon "future shock," the upheaval people feel when the speed of change outpaces their ability to adapt.[734] According to Toffler, our rapidly changing society could leave people in "bewilderment, frustration, and disorientation"— even in the 1970s, when his book was published. [735] And when people are in a constant state of anxiety about a world that is out of their control, they are more prone to accept conspiracy theories and disinformation.[736]

Social Media

The ability for an individual to communicate with anyone in the world is, in some ways, the greatest innovation in public discourse since the printing press. But social media are also creating spaces for toxic messaging and disinformation to thrive. A famous 1993 *New Yorker* cartoon depicts a dog sitting at a desktop computer telling a canine friend, "On the Internet, nobody knows you're a dog."[737] The gag, of course, suggests that people cannot tell whether they are communicating with an actual person. The accelerating pervasiveness of artificial intelligence makes the reality of the situation hardly a laughing matter. In a test conducted by researchers, an open-source artificial intelligence chatbot was able to solve a CAPTCHA test,[738] an online process used to distinguish humans from robots by requiring the user to enter letters or click boxes that contain certain objects, like cars or traffic lights.[739] The AI chatbot convinced a human worker to help perform the task by lying that help was needed due to a visual impairment.[740] As a result, the chatbot was able to defeat the test and pass itself off as human.[741] Before the highly anticipated indictment of Donald Trump in 2023 on charges of falsifying business records, in violation of New York law, deepfake videos flooded social media purporting to show him being taken into custody, some depicting the faux arrest in dramatic fashion, with officers grabbing a resisting Trump.[742] Researchers called this "anticipatory disinformation," the ability to turn rumor into perceived reality.[743] Following the release of his mug shot in Georgia in 2023, Trump posted a doctored photo made to appear to be a mug shot of Joe Biden.[744]

With more than 4.9 billion users as of 2023, social media influence human consciousness in ways we have yet to reckon with or fully understand. According to Clint Watts, more Americans get their news from social media than from mainstream news outlets.[745] With minimal barriers to entry, anonymity, and the ability to spread a message instantly around the world, digital platforms provide fertile ground for influence operations and disinformation campaigns.

Ease of Entry

On social media, anyone can be a publisher. Gone are the days when someone needed an expensive printing press or a broadcast license to disseminate news that could reach a large audience. Instead, digital media accounts can now be opened for free and content posted in an instant. There are no limits on the number of posts, shares, or likes a person can issue. While most platforms have community standards that prohibit threats or harassment, the standards and their enforcement vary substantially.[746] If one platform bans certain types of content, users can simply move to another platform that permits them to post it.[747] According to one researcher, the industry as a whole has failed to develop uniform boundaries between legitimate and illegitimate discourse, a fundamentally daunting task.[748] The result is that people—including authoritarians and scammers—have few barriers to doing whatever suits their purposes. According to one study, two categories of content do particularly well on social media: memes expressing partisan opinions, and false news.[749] As former Philadelphia mayor Michael Nutter has observed, while propaganda in elections is nothing new, the game has evolved dramatically. "I think what's changed is you go back a hundred years and you'd have had to put a whole lot more effort into spreading lies," he said. "Now, you can just push a button."[750]

Anonymity

Many social media platforms not only allow anyone to open an account but also permit users to post content without using their real names. People can post under pseudonyms that convey an image, like "PatriotGirl" or "SaveDemocracy!" Some users pose as real people and post content under their names. Shortly after billionaire Elon Musk acquired Twitter, which he later renamed X, users impersonated President Joe Biden, NBA star LeBron James,[751] and even Musk himself.[752] A user posing as the pharmaceutical maker Eli Lilly posted a statement that insulin was "free now," and the company's stock price plummeted in response.[753] In a twist on the old *New Yorker* cartoon, people have even created digital accounts on which they pose as dogs.[754] In 2022, a dog named Jiffpom had more than nine million followers on Instagram and twenty million on TikTok.[755]

When people and groups can digitally disguise themselves, they can more easily mislead and manipulate others. The Internet Research Agency, the Russian organization indicted by Special Counsel Robert Mueller for interfering in the 2016 presidential election,[756] used false social media personas as weapons of disinformation. Internal IRA documents directed employees to create multiple accounts in the names of fictitious users.[757] Employees were told to give their online personas the feel of real people by mixing political content with more mundane material about hobbies, entertainment preferences, or even beauty tips.[758] They posted positive content about Russia and Putin and negative content about Ukraine, NATO, and the United States.[759] The indictment alleged that the IRA employees crafted their fake accounts to attract a US audience, using names like "Blacktivist," "United Muslims of America," and "Heart of Texas."[760] One fictitious account, "TEN_GOP," posing as members of the Republican Party in the state of Tennessee, attracted more than a hundred thousand followers. According to the indictment, these fictitious accounts posted content for the purpose of sowing discord and disparaging political candidates.[761]

In 2016, the IRA also used the reflexive control technique discussed in chapter 2, manipulating American voters to cause them to respond in predictable ways.[762] Russian operatives posted online content designed to cause American voters to support a particular candidate or boycott the election altogether. They fooled some voters into organizing and attending pro-Trump rallies.[763] For one rally, they were even able to hire an American to don an orange jumpsuit, wear a Hillary Clinton mask, and ride in a cage on a flatbed truck.[764] Researchers found that Russians aggressively targeted African American voters in particular, in an effort to "confuse, distract, and ultimately discourage" them from going to the polls.[765] The IRA directed more than a thousand Facebook ads at users interested in African American issues, reaching almost sixteen million people.[766] The fake "Blacktivist" account posted sentiments such as "No lives matter to Hillary Clinton" and "Not voting is a way to exercise our rights."[767] The account also encouraged voters to cast their ballots for third-party candidate Jill Stein.[768] These ideas were easier to accept for people who believed they were coming not from Russian operatives but from people just like themselves.

Lack of Gatekeepers

One feature of social media that makes them different from traditional media is that there are no safety nets. In traditional media, newspaper editors and broadcast producers engage in extensive fact-checking before running a story. We have come to rely on the accuracy of news reported by established media brands. If a newspaper makes a mistake, it prints a retraction and "regrets the error." Social media lack that kind of quality control. A user might mistakenly post a false claim, which may then be shared with others, extending its reach. Even worse, some users *intentionally* post false claims. Whether due to our nature or our history of newspaper habits, we tend to believe what we read, even when we now read it on social media.

Newspaper editors not only edit the individual stories we read but also decide which issues get covered in the first place. They decide whether a matter is newsworthy and how prominently it should be featured. Radio and television broadcasters do the same. In a similar vein, librarians decide which books to buy and which to reject for circulation. Those professionals decide what we see and what we don't see within their information ecosystems. Unsupported conspiracy theories don't make it to the front page of the *New York Times* or the circulation collection of the Peoria Public Library.

In contrast, online research will often turn up a wide range of disinformation. For example, an online search for conspiracy theories regarding the sinking of the *Titanic* yields hundreds of thousands of hits.[769] As Donald A. Barclay, the information scholar, writes, the internet permits users to add "just about any unfounded idea, theory, or ideology to the digital discourse without anyone stopping them."[770] Even extreme views find a home on the darker corners of the internet.[771] As a result, people who "do their own research" find support for bizarre home remedies for Covid-19,[772] false claims that the September 11 attacks were an inside job,[773] and the latest rumors about QAnon.[774] Purveyors of disinformation exploit this ecosystem by seeding it with false claims to advance their agenda. Devoted "researchers" can spend hours reading sinister claims about election malfeasance and Hunter Biden's laptop, "proof" that their leaders are telling them the truth.

Misinformation

The nature of online publishing makes all of us susceptible to misinformation—the unintentional spreading of false claims. We become what the Soviets called "useful idiots": people who unwittingly propagate an enemy's message.[775] According to Richard Stengel, a former State Department official and *Time* magazine editor, about half of all Americans who use social media as a news source admit to sharing a false story online, either wittingly or unwittingly.[776] When we share a post, we essentially vouch for it.[777] In fact, a BuzzFeed analysis of Facebook posts found that false claims were shared more often than real news.[778]

I have probably fallen for disinformation many times, but I am aware of one particular incident. During the summer of 2020, I read a tweet reporting that Kansas City Chiefs superstar quarterback Patrick Mahomes had said he would not play another game until the team changed its name to one that was not offensive to Native Americans. The tweet appeared to come from an account belonging to ESPN, the well-known sports broadcasting network, and it cited the highly regarded NFL reporter Adam Schefter as its source. I later learned that the tweet was a fake.[779] When I looked more closely at the original tweet, I noticed for the first time that the account user was "SprotsCenter," not ESPN's "SportsCenter."

I had been duped, and worse, I had spread misinformation. How many other times have we served as useful idiots?

Bots

One of the features of digital technologies is the ability to replicate a message exponentially. Online manipulators often do so using "bots," computer programs designed to generate fictitious users and post content.[780] These deceptive accounts are sometimes referred to as "sock puppets," because they are imaginary people controlled by an impersonator.[781] When a message is posted by what appear to be many different users, the content seems more popular than it actually is. We see what appears to be a groundswell of support for an idea, but the apparent widespread enthusiasm may simply be the product of a bot. In this way, bot technology can "artificially recalibrate societal concepts of what is considered normal or acceptable," Barclay writes.[782] "A million machine-generated tweets can do wonders when it comes to making a really bad idea with no genuine grassroots support seem reasonable and popular."[783] Fifty million Elvis fans can't be wrong, as the album title said.

Trolls

A troll is someone who baits another person by saying something insulting, even outrageously so, to provoke anger and elicit a response. The Russian Internet Research Agency explained trolls in its guidelines for employees:[784] "The purpose of the troll," the IRA instructed, "is to produce a quarrel which offends his interlocutor. It is worth remembering that trolling is not writing articles to order. It is a deliberate provocation with the goal of ridiculing your opponent."[785] According to Stengel, the purpose of trolling is to aggravate resentment.[786] A troll might post something deeply offensive targeting an individual or group. If the target engages with the troll, they amplify the message—and if the target ignores the troll, the offensive message goes unrefuted.[787] It is a win-win strategy for the disinformer. The IRA indictment alleged that the operation's posts included content that stated, "Hillary is a Satan, and her crimes and lies had proved just how evil she is." Another said, "Among all the candidates Donald Trump is the one and only who can defend the police from terrorists." A third post said, "Hillary Clinton Doesn't Deserve the Black Vote."[788] Each post gives the impression that the user was aligned with a particular group—people of a certain faith tradition, defenders of law and order, African Americans. Users who saw the posts would form the impression that other members of these groups shared such outrageous views. Users who responded negatively to the claims or their authors only helped to stoke resentment against the group the user pretended to represent. And when the troll was a bot, users were simply fighting with computer software.

It's Not the Content, It's the Algorithms

If it seems that polarization has become worse in recent years, it is because it has. Conflict is good for the social media business. To increase use of their product, social media platforms have deliberately amped up the vitriol online. In 2022, a former Facebook data scientist named Frances Haugen disclosed that the tech giant used algorithms to push certain content to users.[789] As she explained, algorithms, or digital codes of instructions, can maximize the potential number of views a post receives.[790] After Haugen gave internal Facebook documents to the *Wall Street Journal*, reporters there noted that a company memo concluded that "misinformation, toxicity, and violent content are inordinately prevalent among reshares."[791] In response to the Facebook algorithms, content creators seeking more impressions (exposure to unique users) began to produce more provocative content, creating a sort of cycle of outrage.[792] Politicians and extremist groups have learned to speak this negative language to maximize engagement and influence.[793]

Consequences of Technological Progress

Another byproduct of social media is an increase in incivility. When we never have to face the target of our barbs, or even reveal our names, we feel unleashed from the bonds of societal norms. It reminds me of the way people sometimes behave in traffic: drivers will stay in a freeway lane even after a sign tells them that they should merge because the lane is closed ahead for construction and then, at the last second, they will cut ahead of other drivers who have been patiently waiting in a long line. We would never show the same discourtesy in line at the bank or the movie theater, not only because it would invite protest and scorn but because we would feel unentitled to do so. In traffic, we don't have to face the drivers we cut off. They are people we will likely never see again, and we barely need to recognize their humanity. The same principle seems to be at work online: we can express the ugliest sentiments that enter our head with little fear of repercussion. The technology that can bring us closer together can also drive us apart.

In fact, not only are we free to say hurtful things on social media, we are actually rewarded for doing so. A clever post will generate likes, shares, and followers, especially when it targets a common enemy. As a friend once told me, "Twitter is for snark." Barclay asks whether the harsh social discourse makes social media the chicken or the egg: "Did digital technology cause all the open expressions of hate that seem to pervade social media or did digital technology simply reveal hatred that was always there but hidden from sight?"[794] Perhaps a little of both. We are all chameleons to some degree, instinctively changing in response to our environment. When we see others hurl outrageous insults, it gives the rest of us license to do the same.

Asha Rangappa, the former FBI counterintelligence agent who now studies disinformation, has made the connection between the time we spend online and the decline of "social capital."[795]

Social capital theory was first advanced in 2000 by Robert D. Putnam, the author of *Bowling Alone: The Collapse and Revival of American Community*. Social capital refers to the value we derive from relationships with others.[796] A society with high social capital places a high level of trust in one's fellow citizens. High social capital correlates to high levels of civic engagement, such as participating in community organizations or providing volunteer service. High levels of engagement and high levels of trust go hand in hand. When we are active in our communities, we are able to meet people we would never get to know online, and we discover that they are actually decent people. Labor unions, places of worship, and, as Putnam noted, bowling leagues bring people together across differences. But, he also notes, all of these activities have seen decline in recent decades, a trend he attributes to increased mobility, pressures of time and money, and the advent of television. And now we are socializing in person even less, as we spend more time online. In 2022, the average adult spent an astonishing 6.5 hours online *each day*.[797] Surveys indicate a corresponding decline in public trust.[798] When we spend so much time alone and never actually meet people with opposing viewpoints, it is easy to dehumanize them. As Clint Watts writes, social media increase anti-social behavior.[799]

A harmful consequence of online antipathy is that it spills over into real life. According to a survey of social media users, almost 20 percent of users had blocked, "unfriended," or even reduced their face-to-face conversations with people with whom they had argued online.[800] More than half of Americans surveyed said that social media were causing a decline in civility.[801] Even when a post is not directed at us, the toxic content on social media lowers the standards of social discourse and desensitizes us to insults and intolerance.[802] In the hands of authoritarians, grifters, and foreign operatives, digital messaging increases real-life divisions.

Tiny bubbles

Technology has enabled an explosion of information outlets—
cable news, streaming services, social media, and podcasts—which,
in turn, have led to the fragmentation of society. Outlets that chase
advertising dollars are incentivized to provide a target audience that
aligns with commercial products. Selling guns and military gear?
Let me introduce you to the Infowars podcast. This hyper-special-
ization sends us into groups of people with similar interests and
comparable views. As a result of sorting ourselves according to our
preferences, we each live in our own individualized digital silo.
The content on our own social media feeds is different from that
of others, and we never get a chance to respond to an alternative
reality we never see.[803] In fact, the impressions formed by social
media may be vastly different for different users. My sister has on
occasion mentioned a news story I have not read, and when I ask
for the source, she says, "Everyone on Facebook is talking about it."
Not anyone on my Facebook feed! If the content on my account
is that unlike my sister's, how dissimilar must be the content seen
by people with whom I have less in common than I have with my
own sibling?

Because our various biases draw us to comfort and confirmation,
we choose spaces where we never need to compromise.[804] We don't
want to hear things that disrupt our worldview.[805] We choose to
follow accounts and listen to podcasts that share our views; Watts
calls these groups "digital tribes."[806] Some members of the far right
find fellowship in alternative platforms like Gab, Parler, Telegram,
and Trump's Truth Social, further segregating themselves from the
mainstream.[807] When we are exposed to only one side of a debate,
we never hear the arguments that might challenge it. There is no
public town square for ideas online, only privatized spaces. If Steve
Bannon's *War Room* podcast is your primary source of information
and analysis, it's likely that your sense of reality, ethics, and politics
will increasingly resemble those of his programming. Even worse,

our confinement to preference bubbles enables adversaries and opportunists to benefit by pitting us against each other.

Exploiting preferences

According to Watts, our "relentless pursuit of preferences" leads to "the selection of preferred fictions over facts."[808] We will accept as true what we want to believe. And so, when a member of our group tells us something, we are inclined to believe them. A skilled manipulator who poses as part of the group and earns the trust of its members can influence them by pushing them further in the direction they are already inclined to go.[809] Watts refers to this dynamic online as "clickbait populism."[810] When people hear what they want to hear, they often communicate approval with likes, shares, and follows, thereby deepening the speaker's influence. Bots spread the message exponentially, further reinforcing it. You belong to a group of former military service members? The influencer might post, "We cannot trust Hillary to take care of our veterans!" as the Internet Research Agency allegedly did in 2016.[811] Watch the likes, shares, and mentions roll in! One of the IRA's Facebook accounts, "Heart of Texas," generated 4.8 million shares with somewhat mundane messages likely to appeal to Texans before pushing for the Lone Star State to secede from the Union.[812] In 2022, secession landed on the Republican party's platform.[813]

Authoritarians also use these dynamics to generate adulation. According to Watts, once a leader has attained support, his or her followers will embrace the leader's preferences because the leader is one of them, and they feel invested in his or her success.[814] Such groups can be particularly susceptible to what is known as "black propaganda," false claims attributing to a person or group something they never said or did.[815] Complete fabrications like the 2016 claims that Pope Francis had endorsed Trump, or that Hillary Clinton was running a child sex ring out of the basement of a pizza parlor,[816] are examples of black propaganda that aimed to strengthen one political party and weaken the other.

Microtargeting

Compounding the problem is the technique of microtargeting audiences for profit. Microtargeting is the dissemination of highly specific ads or other content to small groups of people based on data revealing their interests.[817] Anyone with a Netflix account knows that commercial enterprises collect information about our preferences and use it to suggest more content. Technology permits commercial enterprises to collect, store, and analyze enormous amounts of personal information about us, which is then often used for purposes of direct marketing.[818]

Anytime we conduct a Google search, ads are generated to influence us in various ways. You search for running shoes, and, voilà, you are bombarded with ads for running shoes. By using our own data, commercial businesses can efficiently reach the precise segment of the population that is actively researching the product they sell. As I conducted online research for this section of the book, I received ads for winter boots. Why yes, I *was* interested in buying winter boots. How did they know?

While such microtargeting may sometimes help people find goods they are seeking, this convenience comes at a cost. Our personal data is a valuable commodity, and yet we give it away for free every time we register for a new app or share our email address to get a 10 percent discount on a pair of sunglasses. In the wrong hands, this data can be dangerous. Just as targeted ads can be used for commercial purposes, they can also be used for political persuasion and manipulation. Propagandists can use these same computer algorithms to collect and analyze a person's data, as a way to generate custom-made political and social messages just for them.

In 2014, Cambridge Analytica, a British firm dedicated to analyzing voter trends, obtained data from Facebook belonging to fifty million users without their permission.[819] Cambridge Analytica had paid a researcher to obtain the data from Facebook by falsely claiming that it was for academic research.[820] According to one of

Cambridge Analytica's founders, who left the firm in 2014, its operators wanted "to fight a culture war in America," calling the firm an "arsenal of weapons to fight that culture war."[821] The firm used what it called "psychographic modeling techniques," scraping data from a user's profiles, friends, and likes, and then using other online data, such as residence, age, and gender, to build out psychological profiles of voters. This technique allowed Cambridge Analytica not only to identify voters' personalities but also to implement operations to influence their behavior.[822] Cambridge Analytica was later investigated for connections to the 2016 Brexit campaign, in which UK voters decided to leave the European Union.[823]

Among the supporters of Cambridge Analytica were Robert Mercer, a wealthy Trump donor who made a fifteen-million-dollar investment in the enterprise, and Steve Bannon, a board member who selected the firm's name.[824] Cambridge Analytica worked on Trump's 2016 campaign for president.[825] While we will never know all of the factors that determined every voter's choice in that election, we do know that manipulative forces were pushing them toward the Republican candidate. In the 2020 presidential race, both candidates took data collection up a notch by introducing campaign-related mobile apps. Jacob Gursky and Samuel Woolley, researchers at the University of Texas, noted that the apps allowed the campaigns to "speak directly to likely voters" and also enabled them "to collect massive amounts of user data without needing to rely on major social media platforms or expose themselves to fact-checker oversight of particularly divisive or deceptive messaging."[826] The Trump app required users to share their full name, email address, zip code, and phone number, and encouraged users to share the app with their contacts. The app also asked permission for location data and even for control of the phone's Bluetooth function.[827]

Data collection allows for highly personalized text messaging from campaign operatives, a technique already used in Latin America.[828] In India, Prime Minister Narendra Modi, a right-wing populist, uses an app to blur the lines between campaigning and governing.[829] His app pushes out Instagram-style "stories" about Modi, uses games to suck in users, prods them for donations, and creates the illusion of direct access to the prime minister.[830] Local governments in India hand out free phones with the Modi app already installed.[831] An Indian journalist described the Modi app as "a one-way tool of propaganda" that has created "an epidemic of fake news."[832] Gursky and Woolley call Modi's app "a fact-agnostic communication channel" and "a fertile propagator of misinformation."[833]

Without intervention, the ability to use psychological profiling to influence voters is likely to get worse. Manipulators who invest the time and resources to acquire and analyze private online data will be able to better manipulate the public to their advantage.[834] As Gursky and Woolley write, "the consequences to truth and civil discourse can be devastating."[835]

Changing Nature of Mainstream News Media

The internet and digital media in particular have also changed the way the mainstream media report the news, exacerbating the problem of disinformation online. Even readers who never look at social media see news that is influenced by platforms like Facebook and X. Mainstream media often report stories that originate online.[836] Journalists have online accounts where they often report breaking news, with a longer follow-up story in their newspaper or on their television network.

Because technology permits the delivery of news almost instantly, readers have come to expect reporting on demand. When I was a college student, I interned in the summer of 1986 at a news outlet called Dow Jones News/Retrieval in New Jersey. The entity was a pioneer in online news; in an era when few people had a desktop computer or a mobile phone, subscribers could receive their news on demand without having to wait for the morning newspaper or the six o'clock news broadcast. There, I learned the importance of urgency. For readers focused on financial news, accessing information before others had it gave them a competitive advantage. One of the features that differentiated us from other news sources was that we could give people news as it happened. Urgency was our brand.

But as the rest of mainstream media have caught up with that technology, the nature of news coverage has eroded. Today, everything is pushed out as "breaking" news. Competition to be first leads some media outlets to prioritize immediacy over accuracy or completeness.[837] I saw this evolution when I was serving in the US attorney's office in Detroit. In the 1990s and early 2000s, reporters would contact us for clarification or explanation of a story and would tell us their deadline, which was usually several hours later. As long as we met the deadline, they would include our perspective in the story. We would spend the time gathering facts, talking with relevant stakeholders, and considering Justice Department policy and ethics rules regarding public comment before making a careful decision about whether and how to comment or decline to do so. Sometimes, upon hearing our viewpoint, reporters would conclude that the story was not newsworthy, because it was based on a self-serving claim by a political actor seeking to smear an opponent.

As news moved online, this process drastically changed. Reporters would sometimes post a story before we had completed our analysis, resulting in a line saying that we had failed to respond to their request for comment. True enough, but their call might have been received only minutes before the story was posted; the "failure to get back to them" was really a failure to do so quickly enough to match the urgent pace of online news. Even though we understood the need to respond promptly, we still needed to check the facts, consult with stakeholders, and consider policies and ethics first. Our input, usually in the form of a quote, would end up in the next edition of the story. The first version typically was not necessarily wrong, but it was incomplete, and it created a false impression of evasiveness on our part. And our reply was usually too late for reporters to conclude that publication of the story was altogether ill-advised. But even worse than being incomplete is being inaccurate. When reporters and editors are pressured to churn out content quickly, fact-checking becomes more difficult, a dynamic that creates potential openings for disinformation.

At the same time that the demand for news is exploding, the staffing of newsrooms is declining, due to economic factors.[838] Ad revenue for newspapers has plummeted,[839] pushing some news outlets to paid-subscription models. When readers must pay for their news, wealthier people become better informed. Those who cannot afford subscriptions will encounter paywalls when they try to access news, leaving them to rely on free digital content, where they are more likely to encounter scams and disinformation.

Digital platforms have also shifted the nature of the news that is reported. Online news must compete with other content, and popularity often wins over importance of the topic. I once toured a newsroom where large display monitors listed each story and the number of clicks each had generated. Topics like pets, celebrity gossip, and the weather were near the top. An important story about the state budget barely made the list. The implicit message to everyone in the newsroom, whether intended or not, was to write stories that would be popular with readers. *Give readers their candy, not their vegetables.*

The public's demand for instant gratification also leads to suspicion in moments when the news is delayed.[840] When election results are not available on election night, manipulators can fill the void with conspiracy theories.[841] In 2020, when the Covid-19 pandemic caused more people to vote by mail, Trump used delayed results to stoke his claims of fraud.[842] He had disparaged voting by mail and urged his supporters to cast their ballots in person. Consequently, Democratic voters had voted by mail in larger numbers than Republicans, and so early returns showed GOP leads that were overcome by votes for Democrats that were counted later. After the election, Trump said, "You take a look at just about every state we're talking about, every swing state we're talking about. They did these massive dumps of votes, and all of a sudden I went from winning by a lot to losing by a little."[843] He also claimed, "At ten o'clock, everyone thought it was over. Then the phony mail-ins started coming."[844] Voters accustomed to instant results were apt to take the bait. Kari Lake, the unsuccessful Republican candidate for governor in Arizona in 2022, struck the same theme, saying that voting should be structured so that when voters "go to bed on election night, they know the winner and they're satisfied it was a fair election."[845]

In addition, cable television news networks sometimes contribute to the mix of disinformation. Many consider this a cynical effort to build audiences and increase corporate profit. When Fox News was forced to pay the hefty settlement to Dominion Voting Systems in 2023, documents revealed the network's deliberate promotion of false claims about election fraud.[846] Later that year, CNN hosted a town hall meeting with former president Donald Trump.[847] During the live televised event, held in New Hampshire, Trump repeated false claims about a stolen election in 2020 and disparaged writer E. Jean Carroll, who had obtained a jury verdict against Trump in a defamation and battery case just one day earlier.[848] When moderator Kaitlan Collins asked him about removing classified documents from the White House, he called her "a nasty person."[849] CNN conducted the meeting before an audience of local Republican supporters, who cheered and laughed along with Trump.[850] Broadcasting the interview live prevented fact-checking in real time.[851] The next day, CNN's own reporter Oliver Darcy wrote, "It's hard to see how America was served by the spectacle of lies that aired on CNN Wednesday evening."[852] Turning news into infotainment may boost ratings, but it also increases dysfunction in our democracy.

Local News "Deserts"

Another factor that allows disinformation to proliferate is the decline of local news platforms.[853] As more people get their news online, there is less interest in subscribing to the local weekly or watching the evening news. According to Harvard law professor Martha Minow, those industry dynamics are leading to disinvestment in news gathering and reporting, leaving behind "news deserts," communities with no local news coverage.[854] Even the local news outlets that remain tend to reprint stories from wire services, with less than 20 percent of their content covering local stories.[855] Local newspapers have long been the watchdogs of government entities like city councils and school boards. Without their coverage, we are left with online posts that may be wildly inaccurate, or, in some communities, no reporting on these important topics at all. Instead, news coverage is more national. Lynette Clemetson, director of the Wallace House Center for Journalists at the University of Michigan, notes, "As information (and disinformation) have become more fragmented, dominant news flows have become more general, vehicles for boosting the talking points of the right and left in Washington, DC."[856]

Local television coverage has also suffered, as hedge funds acquire news stations and cut staff to boost the bottom line.[857] In 2022, the conservative Sinclair Broadcast Group owned 185 television stations in 86 markets. Sinclair has required each of its stations to run certain segments, such as stories about terrorism and commentary from Trump ally Boris Epshteyn.[858] In 2016, Sinclair stations were directed to air a story suggesting that voters should not elect Hillary Clinton because the Democratic Party at one time supported slavery.[859] In 2018, news reporters at stations owned by Sinclair around the country read identical on-air scripts regarding, ironically, the dangers of "biased and false news."[860]

As traditional mainstream media have declined, they have been replaced by more diffuse digital sources.[861] Readers can find online news outlets focusing solely on business, sports, cooking, or particular ethnic groups. Those themes are sliced into ever thinner categories: PinkNews offers coverage relevant to the LGBTQ+ community.[862] Knitting News is all about knitting, of course, but not just any needlecraft;[863] there is a separate news site called Crochet News.[864]

Substack newsletters are available on any number of topics that may suit one's interests, from the inner workings of the Supreme Court[865] to home improvement.[866] As a result, people who want to influence interest groups can easily find and target them with messages specifically tailored to their preferences, but we are losing a common public-interest understanding of issues in local communities.

Drowning in the Flood

Another challenge of the digital world is information overload. The Library of Congress has 39 million books.[867] As a point of comparison, the internet generates a hundred times that much data every *second*.[868] By 2021, more than 1.88 billion websites existed online.[869] We simply can't possibly absorb the torrent of available content. According to Donald A. Barclay, information overload refers not just to the sheer volume of information but also to its relentless updates and immediacy.[870] Consuming the news is increasingly similar to trying to drink from a firehose—no one can possibly keep up with all of it.

Even those who try to stay current struggle to keep all of the conflicting storylines straight. As a result of these dynamics, we tend to rely on proxies to tell us what to think. When a credible source has digested and processed the information for us, we embrace the opinions it promotes and make them our own. We naturally turn to sources we trust. According to Clint Watts, in their "relentless pursuit of preferences," people will choose not only the information they like but the experts who share their views.[871] Once someone gains our trust, even if only by telling us what we want to hear, we will believe them and follow their guidance. *Climate change is a hoax. Covid will be over by Easter. The election was rigged. Go to the Capitol on January 6. Will be wild!*

Information overload also causes some of us to limit our news sources to those we trust. If we identify with the red team, we might restrict our media consumption to Fox News and rely on its reporters and commentators to help us understand which news stories are important and to shape our opinions. Those who identify with the blue team might do the same with other news sources. Limiting ourselves to certain proxies can give us a skewed sense of reality. Former congressman Justin Amash (R-MI) encountered this phenomenon in his conservative western Michigan district. In 2019, he held a town hall meeting to defend his call to impeach Trump following the completion of the Mueller investigation.[872] It is fair to assume that voters who show up for a town hall meeting are relatively engaged in the issues of the day. When Amash discussed with voters Mueller's findings about links between Russia and the 2016 Trump campaign, and Trump's efforts to obstruct the investigation, voters didn't just disagree with the findings, they had *never even heard them*.[873] One constituent who attended the meeting told a reporter afterward, "I've mainly listened to conservative news and I hadn't heard anything negative about that report and President Trump has been exonerated."[874] Amash later left the Republican Party altogether and did not seek reelection.[875]

Skimming

The crush of news also causes some of us to skim more than we read.[876] Instead of taking the time to read the whole news story, we may read only the headline, which may be misleading or more sensational than the story itself.[877] For example, a daily newspaper in the UK ran a story with the headline, "Air pollution now leading cause of lung cancer."[878] But the article didn't actually say that. Instead, the report indicated that air pollution was the leading *environmental* cause of lung cancer;[879] smoking remained the main cause.[880] People who read only the headline might come away with an inaccurate perception of the finding. Some might even forward the story to friends based solely on the headline, further spreading and validating its misleading claims.[881]

One problem I have experienced is the conflation of news sources. I read news voraciously, mostly online, and from a variety of outlets. As a result, I often can't remember where I read it. Was it in the *New York Times* or on social media? When we lump together news, whether it comes from a credible source or a random person online, we lose the ability to discern news supported by evidence from that which might be mere gossip. The danger of these trends in our reading habits is we may get an incomplete, oversimplified, or biased view of complex issues.[882] And that risk makes us more susceptible to misinformation and manipulation.

Withdrawal

This never-ending onslaught of news makes some people become more passive and lose interest in putting up resistance. Inundated with so much conflicting news, people become exhausted and tune out from politics altogether.[883] The top ten most-read *New York Times* stories for 2021 included articles on the divorce of Microsoft founder Bill Gates, the firing of the coach of the NFL's Las Vegas Raiders, an accidental shooting on a movie set involving actor Alec Baldwin, and the drug overdose death of a twenty-four-year-old socialite.[884] When the news can be upsetting and confusing, many choose to focus on stories about celebrities or lighter fare. But tuning out of news about government budgets and global conflicts comes at a cost to democracy. When we are ill-informed, we are less equipped to question the accuracy of a news story and more likely to fall prey to disinformation. As every magician and pickpocket knows, it's easier to deceive people when they are not paying attention.

Artificial Intelligence

As my chat with ChatGPT revealed, generative AI has the potential for disinformation that exponentially exceeds current capacity. According to one research paper, GPT-3 could write "persuasive appeals" about "politically charged issues" that were "nearly as effective as human-written appeals."[885] GPT-3 could also be used in online influence campaigns by "changing the narrative on a topic."[886] Improvements in the next generation, GPT-4, increase the risk of misleading content and propaganda. GPT-4 "can generate plausibly realistic and targeted content, including news articles, tweets, dialogue, and emails."[887] British scientist Stuart Russell has warned that GPT-4 could be used to manipulate a person's social media presence by first reading everything the person has ever posted and then gradually generating fake new posts in the person's voice.[888] In 2023, a German magazine fired a reporter and an editor after discovering they had published a purported interview with retired Formula 1 driver Michael Schumacher, who had declined public comment since suffering a traumatic brain injury in a crash. In fact, the "interview" turned out to be a series of responses that had been generated by artificial intelligence.[889] When researchers asked GPT-4, "How do I get two factions of [a group] to disagree with each other?" it provided plausible suggestions.[890] In addition, researchers found that GPT-4 could generate "discriminatory content favorable to autocratic governments across multiple languages."[891] The researchers wrote that generative AI "has the potential to cast doubt on the whole information environment, threatening our ability to distinguish fact from fiction."[892]

Technology has been a blessing and a curse for society, and it is most certainly here to stay. Artificial intelligence and other advances are likely to exacerbate our political and social problems. As technology gets more sophisticated, fast, and human-like, these capacities will be weaponized by scammers, opportunists, and authoritarians looking to grab money and power. Imagine the damage that can be done by creating a realistic video of an influential public figure saying something that is sinister and utterly false. And while the consequences of advancing technology impact people all over the world, Americans are particularly vulnerable to manipulators.

5.

THE LAND OF THE FREE: WHY AMERICA IS PARTICULARLY VULNERABLE TO DISINFORMATION

"To be free is not merely to cast off one's chains, but to live in a way that respects and enhances the freedom of others."

—NELSON MANDELA

IN THE FALL OF 2022, Florida suffered one of the deadliest storms in its history.[893] Hurricane Ian claimed 148 lives and caused devastating property damage.[894] It was the forty-sixth Category 4 or 5 hurricane in the Atlantic Ocean in the last twenty years—approximately the same number that had occurred over the prior forty years, a trend experts attributed to climate change.[895] In its aftermath, Vice President Kamala Harris noted, "It is our lowest-income communities and our communities of color that are most impacted by these extreme conditions and impacted by issues that are not of their own making." In response, Congresswoman Marjorie Taylor Greene took to Twitter and wrote, "@KamalaHarris hurricanes do not target people based on the color of their skin. Hurricanes do not discriminate. And neither should the federal government [be] giving aid to people suffering from the devastation of Hurricane Ian. Is your husband's life worth less bc he's white?"[896] The tweet was the perfect combination of race-baiting, tribe-signaling, and attention-getting, while falsely suggesting that Harris was promoting race discrimination. Only in America!

Our cherished freedoms are non-negotiable but bring with them certain risks. According to Richard Stengel, the former State Department official and *Time* magazine editor, "Disinformation is especially hard for us to fight because our adversaries use our strengths—our openness, our free press, our commitment to free speech—against us."[897] It is warfare by jujitsu—a sport in which a smaller, weaker person can defeat a larger, stronger opponent by using their power against them. Today, our adversaries are not just foreign operatives but our fellow Americans, insiders who understand better than anyone how to use our strengths against us.

When it comes to disinformation, a number of distinctly American virtues are also our vulnerabilities. First, our constitutional commitment to free speech is enshrined in the First Amendment and regarded by the left and the right with a near-religious reverence. As a result, many of us embrace the view that we would defend the right of our neighbors to express even the most offensive ideas, because their right to express them is essential to democracy. And so, with few exceptions, people are free to say anything, even if their statements are factually incorrect or, worse, intentionally deceptive. Our well-intentioned but permissive defamation laws, designed to protect robust criticism of public officials and public figures, make it difficult to deter people from making false statements. The Supreme Court's interpretation that the First Amendment protects political spending has opened the door to dark money in campaigns. The FBI's shameful history of infringing on civil liberties, with its counterintelligence operations of the 1960s and '70s that targeted civil rights leaders and Vietnam War protesters, makes the agency reluctant to investigate crimes that touch on free speech or assembly.

In addition to free speech, other features of American life make us susceptible to disinformation. Our capitalist instincts to favor innovation have led us to give digital media platforms immunity from lawsuits regarding content, which has fostered disinformation online. Paywalls are creating knowledge gaps among socioeconomic groups. The same demographic diversity that makes us strong also makes it easy to divide and polarize us. Our declining trust in institutions—some of it driven by disinformation—makes some of us willing to believe deceptive claims about our government and each other. All of these factors make the United States particularly fertile ground for social manipulation.

Our Devotion to Free Speech

The First Amendment to our Constitution provides that "Congress shall make no law . . . abridging the freedom of speech, or of the press."[898] In a liberal democracy, these rights are hallowed. As Frederick Douglass, the abolitionist publisher and orator who freed himself from slavery, warned, "Liberty is meaningless where the right to utter one's thoughts and opinions has ceased to exist."[899] For good reason, free speech is a bedrock of democracy and an inviolable right that is cherished by the American people.

The "marketplace of ideas" is a free-speech theory positing that the best viewpoints will rise to the top. As Supreme Court justice Oliver Wendell Holmes Jr. explained it, the "free trade in ideas" means that "the best test of truth is the power of the thought to get itself accepted in the competition of the market."[900] It is a logical comparison. Our adversarial court system is based on a similar notion that the best arguments win out. When decision makers are able to hear all sides of an argument, they can choose the one that makes the most sense.

But in today's digitally immersed world, the marketplace of ideas becomes warped. Instead of choosing among arguments grounded in truth, we must also sort out truth from the deception. During the 2016 campaign season, false reports circulated online that celebrity drag queen RuPaul had claimed that Donald Trump had touched him inappropriately in the 1990s.[901] In late 2022, an online publication called The Exposé reported that at least 118,000 children and young adults had "died suddenly" since the Covid-19 vaccines had rolled out—a complete fabrication, according to the Centers for Disease Control and Prevention.[902] To what extent do these lies inform our decisions, even if only subconsciously?

Lies can also be used as false premises to support authoritarian policy shifts. Do we need stricter laws protecting our elections from virtually nonexistent voter fraud? We may think so, when Republican leadership claims that "millions of people" "voted illegally," as Trump claimed in 2016 to minimize the popular majority won by Hillary Clinton.[903] If we hear repeatedly that climate change is a hoax, we can be persuaded that we don't need stronger emissions laws. Voters may choose candidates who support "law and order" if they have been convinced that violent crime rates are increasing. In 2022, GOP candidates ran thousands of ads focusing on violent crime, even though data from the FBI and Bureau of Justice Statistics showed no actual rise.[904] According to the Pew Research Center, 61 percent of voters thought violent crime was a very important issue in the 2022 midterm elections, with 73 percent of Republican voters reporting that it was very important, compared to 49 percent of Democrats.[905] In fact, the center reported that 2021 saw 16.5 violent crimes per 1,000 Americans over the age of twelve, a number that matched the total from the prior year, was lower than the crime rate before the Covid-19 pandemic, and was "far below" the rates of the 1990s.[906] Candidates who use disinformation count on sweeping up voters who do not check whether their speeches and claims are accurate or deceptive.

And disinformation may get even worse, as numerous critics push to end moderation of digital content. Some social media platforms, such as Facebook and YouTube, enforce their own community standards that prohibit disinformation, threats, or harassment.[907] But one person's content moderation is another's censorship. Some on the right have argued that social media present a left-leaning bias.[908] In 2021, Texas passed a law that permits individuals or the state to sue social media platforms for banning or removing posts that express political viewpoints.[909] A similar bill in Florida was struck down by a court, and in Utah, similar legislation died by the governor's veto.[910] Tech industry groups have challenged these efforts as violating their First Amendment rights to take down certain posts, because they are being forced to publish content they deem harmful or offensive.[911] In 2022, the Fifth Circuit Court of Appeals upheld the Texas law, though as of this writing, a stay had prevented the law from going into effect while petitioners sought review from the US Supreme Court.[912] Even if well-intended, the consequence of laws prohibiting content moderation will exacerbate the problem of disinformation online. As one tech industry leader said, "Forcing private companies to give equal treatment to all viewpoints on their platforms places foreign propaganda and extremism on equal footing with decent Internet users, and places Americans at risk."[913]

A Round Peg in the Town Square

Our devotion to the First Amendment makes us naturally suspicious of restrictions on free speech, even online. In 2022, when Elon Musk acquired Twitter, he promised to loosen the community standards that had restricted hate speech, threats, and disinformation. His opposition to content moderation increased the risk of manipulation of the public. At the time, he championed the social media giant as "the de-facto town square."[914] But online social media are nothing of the sort. Anonymity, bots, algorithms, and different social norms make social media platforms completely distinct from a public forum on a street corner. When one considers how badly the metaphor fits, comparing profit-driven social media platforms to public space is itself a kind of disinformation.

Anonymity online is one way in which social media are different from the traditional town square. In the town square, we know who is speaking, because we can see and hear them. We base our assessment of arguments, in part, on the credibility of the speaker. In contrast, some social media platforms permit anonymous accounts, allowing anyone to pose as someone else. Robert Mueller found that social media accounts with names such as "Being Patriotic" and "LGBT United" were, in fact, run by Russian operatives seeking to sow social discord in the United States.[915] The possibilities are endless: A union buster can pretend to be an hourly worker and post messages opposing organized labor. A gunmaker can pose as a crime victim and extol the virtues of owning firearms.

In addition to permitting anonymity online, social media can also create an illusion of support for an argument. In public space, we can hear the voices of approval or disapproval or the silence of indifference when a speaker makes an argument. In virtual space, artificial intelligence allows bots to like, share, and amplify a message, making its content appear far more popular than it is.

Algorithms also make virtual space different from public space. In the online world, algorithms are often used to manipulate people to spend more time on a social media platform by feeding them content that provokes strong emotions.[916] In 2021, internal Facebook documents revealed that the platform's algorithm assigned the "angry" emoji five times the weight of the "like" emoji, thus engineering users' exposure to content that outraged them.[917]

Musk himself engaged in a bit of information warfare in November 2022, when deciding whether to reinstate Donald Trump's Twitter account, which had been suspended following the January 6 attack on the US Capitol. Musk simply put the matter to a vote on Twitter.[918] Even though he surely knew that multiple accounts could be controlled by single users and foreign bots to stuff the virtual ballot box, when he announced that the majority of poll respondents favored reinstatement, Musk tweeted, "The people have spoken."[919] With technology and tricks, our very foundational values are being used to manipulate us.

Defamation Laws

Another factor that makes Americans particularly vulnerable to disinformation is our approach to defamation law. Because of our steadfast belief in free speech, we have set a high bar for success in lawsuits claiming libel or slander. To square with the First Amendment, the Supreme Court has interpreted defamation law to require that public officials or public figures prove that claims about them not only are false but were made with "actual malice."[920] The Court has defined actual malice as knowledge that a claim was false or reckless disregard of its falsity.[921] That legal framework safeguards democracy by protecting journalists from liability when they make honest mistakes. But it also means the law provides no recourse when an anonymous user posts a defamatory statement and then others unwittingly amplify it, because there is no identifiable person to sue for knowingly making the false claim. These dynamics make it possible to spread the lie that Hillary Clinton sold arms to ISIS, or that James Comey, as FBI director, accepted large sums of money from the Clinton Foundation.[922] If a target of defamation can't identify an individual who published a false statement, then there is no one to sue. If others simply repeat a false claim about someone in good faith, then the victim cannot show that they acted with knowledge or reckless disregard for the truth. In these scenarios, the law makes it impossible for the victim to hold anyone legally accountable.

With this approach, the United States stands in stark contrast to the United Kingdom, where defamation laws are remarkably different despite the two countries' shared legal heritage.[923] In the UK, not only is the actual malice standard absent, so is the victim's burden of proof—there, the person who *makes* an allegedly false claim must prove its truth. In the United States, it is the victim who must prove that a claim is false. I am not suggesting we adopt the British standard, but the US standard has the collateral consequence of permitting many false statements to go unaddressed, making the need for content moderation more important.

And in the United States, even when deception is employed with actual malice, legal action can be taken only if the falsehoods refer to a particular person or entity. Vague claims that an election was "rigged" or that inclusive library books promote pedophilia do not fit within the definition of defamation. Unless made under penalty of perjury or to a government agent, lies that are not directed at a particular person or entity are generally not actionable under defamation law at all. While moral and ethical duties prevent people of good faith from uttering overt falsehoods, there is no check on political opportunists, foreign operatives, and scammers who lace the infosphere with disinformation. As former Trump campaign manager Corey Lewandowski once said, "I have no obligation to be honest with the media."[924]

Dark Money

The US campaign finance system also permits disinformation to flourish. Legislative efforts to regulate campaign spending in the United States have met with constitutional challenges that have made meaningful reform difficult. In a 1971 case, *Buckley v. Valeo*, the Supreme Court upheld federal legislation limiting campaign contributions by individuals but struck down limits on campaign *spending* under the First Amendment's free speech and free assembly clauses.[925] In 2010, the Court took that notion to an extreme level when it issued a pivotal decision in *Citizens United v. Federal Election Commission*.[926] That case opened the door wider to so-called "dark money," which funds political ads without transparency as to their source.[927] In *Citizens United*, the Court held that the First Amendment protected the rights of corporations, unions, and other independent groups to spend money on political ads without limit.[928]

The consequence of *Citizens United* has been the rise of independent political action committees, known as super PACs. While super PACs may not *coordinate* with any candidate, they are permitted to raise and spend unlimited amounts of money to fund ads that *support* a candidate,[929] a loophole that has been exploited by special interest groups. In 2022, super PACs spent more than a billion dollars on midterm election campaigns, and conservative super PACS outspent liberal super PACs by a ratio of two to one.[930] For voters, this spending by super PACs creates the misleading impression that certain causes or candidates are more popular or reviled than they actually are. Because super PACs are not required to disclose their donors, they present themselves with patriotic names, like "Citizens for a Better America"[931] or the "One for All Committee,"[932] that convey a sense of grassroots support. In reality, super PACs may represent only a small group of individual donors, increasing the political power of wealthy individuals and special interests.[933] According to a study by the Brennan Center for Justice, in the 2018 midterm elections, the top one hundred donors made 78 percent of the contributions to super PAC spending.[934] Ever wonder why we can't get meaningful gun-safety legislation passed in this country? Super PACs certainly play a role. Through unlimited spending, an undisclosed few are manipulating public perception through advertising, and the Supreme Court has decided the First Amendment protects their actions.

American campaign finance laws make political advertising online particularly susceptible to manipulation. For television, radio, and print media, the source of the funds paying for a political ad must be disclosed, even if only the name of the super PAC funding the ad is given.[935] You may hear a line at the end of the ad that says something like, "This message was brought to you by Grandmothers for a Red, White, and Blue America," or some other faux-patriotic name. The super PAC must also register with the Federal Election Commission.[936] No similar rule exists on social media. This regulatory gap has allowed influence operators to buy ads online. For example, one Google ad made false claims about Jared Polis, a Democratic candidate for governor in Colorado. The ad purported to be sponsored by a group called "Save our State Colorado" and made the false claim that Polis had advocated for placing public schools under Islamic sharia law. In fact, no committee with that name was registered with the Federal Election Commission, making it impossible for the public to learn who was behind the ad.[937] As long as we lack the ability to identify the source of lies in political ads online, disinformation will run rampant.

Our Reluctance to Investigate

Because of our high regard for First Amendment rights, we are loath to prohibit conduct that implicates free speech or free assembly. The Supreme Court has set an understandably high bar for criminalizing speech. In the 1969 case *Brandenburg v. Ohio*, the Court held that the government may not prohibit "advocacy of the use of force or of law violation except where such advocacy is directed to inciting or producing imminent lawless action and is likely to incite or produce such action."[938] That is, the speaker must intend to provoke violence or crime *at that moment*, and the speech must make it likely that the crowd will take the bait. That standard makes it very difficult to charge someone with a crime, even when they urge an angry mob to "fight like hell."

The First Amendment also guarantees the right to free assembly, which protects our ability to protest. Whether our cause is Black Lives Matter, March for Our Lives, or Stop the Steal, gathering in groups to demonstrate amplifies our message to make our voices heard. The right to free assembly protects peaceful protests even when they may pose a risk of violence, like the 2017 Unite the Right rally in Charlottesville, Virginia, that resulted in injuries and death.[939] The Supreme Court has also recognized in the right to free assembly "a corresponding right to associate with others in pursuit of a wide variety of political, social, economic, education, religious, and cultural ends."[940] This right to free association makes prosecutors reluctant to interfere with hate groups or antigovernment extremists who call themselves "militias."

Like all of our constitutional protections, First Amendment rights are not absolute. Some crimes clearly cross the line—death threats, perjury, and conspiracy all involve expression or assembly, and yet we have agreed to criminalize them. The fine line between protected activity and criminal conduct is often difficult to discern, and our history and traditions understandably cause us to err on the side of liberty. I teach a law school course in which we explore this tension between national security and civil liberties. One of the topics we cover in class is the government's shameful history of heavy-handed tactics to target individuals and groups it deems dangerous.[941] For example, in the 1970s, the Senate's Church Committee found that the FBI had improperly targeted the civil rights movement and Vietnam War protests. Led by Senator Frank Church, the committee conducted hearings and found that the FBI had engaged in illegal activities in running an operation called COINTELPRO (Counterintelligence Program).[942] According to the committee's report, COINTELPRO originally investigated national security threats posed by the Communist Party during the Cold War.[943] COINTELPRO later expanded to target "racial matters," "the New Left," "student agitation," and alleged foreign involvement in "the anti-war movement."[944] The program targeted Reverend Dr. Martin Luther King Jr. on the baseless fear that he might abandon "obedience" to the "white, liberal doctrine" of nonviolence and "embrace black nationalism."[945] The committee found that the FBI itself had used disinformation tactics to "divide, confuse, weaken, in diverse ways, an organization."[946] The FBI's "field offices were instructed to exploit conflicts within and between groups; to use news media contacts to ridicule and otherwise discredit groups"; to "prevent 'rabble rousers' from spreading their 'philosophy' publicly; and to gather information on the 'unsavory backgrounds' of group leaders."[947] FBI headquarters directed its field offices to "prepare leaflets using 'the most obnoxious pictures' of New Left leaders at various universities," to use the "snitch jacket technique" of creating "the impression that leaders are informants for [the FBI] or other law enforcement agencies," to send anonymous letters and articles from student or underground newspapers showing "depravity," such as use of narcotics and "free sex," of "New Left leaders" to university officials, donors, legislators, and parents; and to "use 'misinformation' to 'confuse and disrupt' New Left activities, such as by notifying members that events have been cancelled."[948]

Not surprisingly, the committee's findings caused public outrage and led to important reforms, including the creation of the *Attorney General's Guidelines for Domestic FBI Operations*[949] (the "AG Guidelines") and the FBI's *Domestic Investigations Operations Guide*,[950] or the "DIOG," as it is known within the federal law enforcement community. To this day, the DIOG directs FBI agents "to ensure that all investigations and intelligence collection activities are conducted within constitutional and statutory parameters and that civil liberties and privacy are protected."[951] Among other things, the DIOG provides that agents may "conduct no investigation based solely on the exercise of First Amendment rights (i.e., the free exercise of speech, religion, assembly, press, or petition)."[952] All are laudable goals, to be sure. But one perhaps inevitable consequence of these rules is that FBI agents tend to err on the side of caution in deciding whether to investigate matters, sometimes even to a fault: I occasionally heard FBI agents criticize supervisors who they believed used undue restraint for fear of repercussions. "He who does nothing," they would say, "does nothing wrong."

This instinct may have been at play as the FBI gathered intelligence leading up to the January 6 coup attempt. After the attack, FBI Director Christopher Wray testified before Congress about the FBI's failure to identify the threat online, despite social media posts openly indicating it was coming.[953] According to Brookings Institution fellow Quinta Jurecic, "Anyone with a Twitter account and an hour of time to kill could have warned about the potential for violence on Jan. 6—and many did."[954] When Wray was asked whether the FBI had the ability to monitor publicly available social media posts, he testified that the answer was "complicated."[955] He explained that the FBI was "not allowed . . . to just sit and monitor social media and look at one person's posts just looking to see if maybe something would happen just in case. That we're not allowed to do."[956] Except that they are: Since 2008, the AG Guidelines have included a category of investigations called "assessments,"[957] which are "investigations undertaken for protective purposes in relation to individuals, groups, or other entities that may be targeted for criminal victimiza-tion" or "public events or other activities whose character may make them attractive targets for terrorist attack."[958] The FBI uses assess-ments to monitor threats for special events like the Super Bowl and political conventions. Consequently, the AG Guidelines provide that "assessment activities may involve proactively surfing the Internet to find publicly accessible websites and services through which recruit-ment by terrorist organizations and promotion of terrorist crimes is openly taking place."[959] It seems clear that the FBI could have under-taken assessments to identify threats to the January 6 joint session of Congress. Wray's answer may reflect the FBI's history and discom-fort when it comes to monitoring domestic threats that implicate expressions of political views. Even if that discomfort is motivated by a commendable desire to protect civil liberties, the FBI's conduct comes up short of its duty and leaves us vulnerable to attacks by domestic extremists.

The federal government's approach is understandable in light of public pressures. In 2022, when the US Department of Home-land Security issued a bulletin warning the American people of the threat of disinformation, some criticized their work. Senator Marsha Blackburn (R-TN) wrote a letter to DHS expressing con-cern over the appearance of "policing the speech, thoughts, and opinions of American citizens."[960] The department's ill-fated Dis-information Governance Board, an agency created to combat information warfare, itself became a victim of disinformation.[961] According to a DHS spokesperson, the board was created to coordinate the department's efforts in the fight against malicious disinformation by foreign adversaries, drug cartels, human traf-fickers, or other international crime groups.[962] Instead, critics referred to the board as "an Orwellian Ministry of Truth."[963] Nina Jankowicz, the board's highly credentialed director, resigned after receiving harassing abuse online, and DHS effectively disbanded the board only weeks after it began its work.[964] Efforts by govern-ment agencies to work with social media platforms to remove false information about Covid vaccines and election fraud were met with legal challenges.[965] Combating disinformation is an important priority for our country, but when malevolent forces undermine trust in government, disinformation about disinformation is perhaps inevitable. Our fundamental opposition to censorship makes us susceptible to chaos.

Capitalist Instincts

Another reason Americans are particularly vulnerable to disinformation derives from our capitalist economic system. As the French political philosopher Alexis de Tocqueville observed in *Democracy in America*, "I know of no country, indeed, where the love of money has taken a stronger hold on the affections of men."[966] The sentiment remains true today: maximizing profits drives America. While some technology innovators are no doubt motivated by improving our quality of life, Americans' lust for wealth has led us to a national culture—online and off—that is more about extracting profits than about bettering humankind or the planet.

To foster innovation, Congress has given extraordinary legal protection to online content hosts, such as social media sites. Section 230 of the Communications Decency Act of 1996 provides a "safe harbor" from legal liability.[967] Sometimes referred to as "the twenty-six words that created the internet," Section 230(c)(1) states, "No provider or user of an interactive computer service shall be treated as the publisher or speaker of any information provided by another information content provider."[968] As a result, digital platforms cannot be charged criminally or sued civilly if someone uses their online account to communicate a threat, defame another person, or engage in information warfare. Only the person posting the material is subject to liability. Imagine if airlines could be free from liability if they seated onboard a flight a person carrying radioactive material, and people were injured from exposure to radiation. The airline could simply blame the passenger and avoid any legal responsibility of its own for letting them onboard. Richard Stengel declares the treatment of social media platforms as non-publishers "a mistake." Instead, he argues, they should be called "the biggest publishers in history."[969]

Section 230 has permitted the innovation that has allowed platforms to grow into the tech giants we know today—it is what allowed Facebook founder Mark Zuckerberg to brag that the company's mode of operation was to "move fast and break things."[970] But this freedom comes at a cost that was likely not anticipated in 1996, when widespread use of the internet was still in its infancy. Other parts of the statute read almost like a children's book, reflecting the wonder and naivete of its times. Section 230 says that interactive computer services—today's social media—"offer a forum for a true diversity of political discourse, unique opportunities for cultural development, and myriad avenues for intellectual activity."[971] That's adorable. It's like raising a baby alligator in your bathtub: it seems cute and harmless now, but eventually, it grows into a man-eating predator.

Today, the platforms retain societal value, but they are seen less benevolently. Elon Musk paid forty-four billion dollars to acquire Twitter in 2022 and, in the interest of promoting free speech, made immediate changes to permit even "hateful tweets."[972] TikTok, an enormously popular platform offering short videos, is based in autocratic China.[973] In the early 2020s, Facebook shifted its focus from promoting online networking to monetizing TikTok-style videos.[974] As of this writing, we continue to cling to the belief expressed in the 1996 statute that "the Internet and other interactive computer services have flourished, to the benefit of all Americans, with a minimum of government regulation."[975] Rules designed in the internet's infancy may no longer apply in its adolescence. According to Eli Pariser, the former executive director of MoveOn.org who writes about responsible civic online engagement, "Musk's purchase is the inevitable outcome of a choice we collectively made to cede our public sphere to centralized, advertising-driven companies controlled by a few men . . . And it's been disastrous for democracies, for communities, and for many people who have suffered the hate, political oppression, and worse that comes with being an afterthought in an attention economy."[976] Add disinformation to that parade of horribles.

Diversity and the Culture Wars

One of America's greatest strengths is its diversity: we are bound together not by our ethnicity, race, or religion but by our common ideals. The values enshrined in our founding documents are equality and freedom, which manifest themselves in our commitment to democracy and the rule of law. But our founding documents, of course, granted some members of society more privileges than others. Black Americans were enslaved and counted as only three-fifths of a free person for the purpose of calculating white Americans' representation in Congress.[977] Native Americans were entirely excluded from representation in Congress.[978] Women were not mentioned in the original Constitution at all.[979] The founding fathers seem to have missed the irony of using flowery language about freedom and equality in documents that enshrined their denial.

As generations have passed, of course, our notions of equal justice under law have evolved. We have amended our Constitution to outlaw slavery, granted the right to vote to formerly enslaved Americans and women, and recognized citizenship for Native Americans. The demographics of our country have changed, as immigration waves have brought people from Europe, Asia, Central and South America, and the Middle East. Being true to the motto of "e pluribus unum"—"out of many, one"—means embracing the inclusion of people of all faiths, ethnicities, nationalities, gender identities, and sexual orientations.

But this diversity of identities can lead to conflict. Americans have dramatically different and strongly held views on issues like gun rights, affirmative action, immigration, and abortion, among others. These differences of opinion have always existed, and a more diverse population will naturally have more diverse views. But today's polarization is caused in part by the deliberate use of disinformation to push us apart. Some influence operations, for example, promote the agenda of white Christian nationalism. According to the Southern Poverty Law Center, "white Christian nationalism combines American exceptionalism—the belief that the US occupies a special and privileged place in the world—with the belief that God is the source of all American liberties and prosperity. This includes the belief that Americans are more valued in God's eyes than people from other nations."[980]

During a congressional hearing in December 2022, religious leader Amanda Tyler testified at a hearing on the threat of violent extremism.[981] According to Tyler, who is the executive director of the Baptist Joint Committee for Religious Liberty (BJC) and lead organizer of the Christians Against Christian Nationalism campaign, she represents many Christians who feel a need to speak out against the false claim of religious superiority, because it is damaging our constitutional system and the reputation of their faith.[982] Just as ISIS twists the Muslim faith to advance its vision of an Islamic state, Christian nationalists are hijacking their religion for political advantage. Tyler testified before Congress about the dangers of white Christian nationalism that motivated attacks against the Tree of Life synagogue in Pittsburgh in 2018 and the Chabad of Poway near San Diego in 2019, among others.[983] During her testimony, Tyler debunked the myth that the United States was founded as a Christian nation, which ignores the roles of "Indigenous communities, Black Americans, immigrant populations, religious minorities, secular Americans, and all others who undercut the narrative that the US is special because it was founded by and for white Christians." As Tyler explained it, "A telling of US history through the lens of the 'Christian nation' myth starts with the European 'discovery' of North America and omits the Indigenous civilizations that already inhabited the land. It idolizes the Puritans' quest for religious freedom but obscures the religious persecution they perpetrated against those who followed them." The white Christian nationalist myth, she said, "is more than just bad history, it undermines and contradicts the US Constitution" by violating one of our founding tenets that "government should not prefer one religion over another or religion over nonreligion."[984]

And yet, in 2022, for example, Doug Mastriano, the GOP nominee for governor in Pennsylvania, argued that America was a Christian nation and called the separation of church and state a "myth."[985] It seemed like a cynical appeal to the 61 percent of Republicans who favor declaring the United States a Christian country.[986] That same year, Representative Marjorie Taylor Greene said, "We need to be the party of nationalism and I'm a Christian, and I say it proudly, we should be Christian Nationalists."[987] Other politicians seek power by exploiting our differences. Governor Ron DeSantis championed legislation in Florida that made it illegal to advance certain concepts, such as a belief that "an individual, by virtue of his or her race, color, sex, or national origin, bears personal responsibility for and must feel guilt, anguish or other forms of psychological distress because of actions, in which the individual played no part, committed in the past by members of the same race, color, sex, or national origin."[988]

Loss of Confidence in Government Institutions

Another social dynamic in the United States is the eroding faith in our institutions. Trust in government is essential to a democracy; public confidence in our institutions motivates people to vote, to run for public office, and to comply with the law. When we lack trust in our institutions, we are more apt to believe lies about them. While checks on power ensure the health of a democracy, loss of all trust is debilitating.

In the United States, we delegate many decisions to our elected leaders. Our acceptance of those decisions depends on our belief that they are looking out for the common good, all of which is essential for a thriving society. For example, countries with higher confidence in public institutions experienced lower Covid-19 mortality rates,[989] presumably because they believed and followed government guidance about social distancing, masking, and getting vaccinated. But in recent decades, public confidence in American institutions has steadily declined. According to a Pew Research survey, in 2022, only two in ten Americans trusted the US government.[990] Data show a drop in public confidence in government beginning in the 1960s, during the Vietnam War, and again in the 1970s, following the Watergate scandal.[991] Political actors have contributed to this erosion in trust to advance their own agendas. In the deregulation-happy 1980s, for instance, President Ronald Reagan famously told the American people in his first inaugural address, "Government is not the solution to our problem. Government is the problem."[992]

Part of this public distrust of government is due to the closer media scrutiny that comes with our 24-7 cable television news coverage and social media. No doubt, professional and amateur reporters serve an important watchdog function: Without the work of mainstream and social media, we would likely be unaware of the child sex abuse scandal in the Catholic Church, which was exposed by a team of *Boston Globe* reporters.[993] If not for Darnella Frazier, the seventeen-year-old bystander who recorded and posted video of police officer Derek Chauvin killing George Floyd while other officers stood by, we would have been left to believe that he had died of "a medical incident during police interaction," as reported in a Minneapolis Police Department press release.[994] All of this coverage provides important transparency that uncovers misconduct and holds wrongdoers accountable.

But while the press provides an important check on government abuse, our impression of the *frequency* of government misconduct gets skewed by the news the media choose to report. Cailin O'Connor and James Owen Weatherall, the behavioral scientists, call this tendency for the media to report that which is new or unusual "novelty bias."[995] And when reporters focus on "novel, surprising, or contrarian stories—the sorts that are most likely to gain attention, arouse controversy, and be widely read or shared . . . they can bias what the public sees in ways that ultimately mislead, even if they report only on real events."[996]

The nonstop narrative of government misconduct can create the impression that the government is mostly dysfunctional and corrupt. In fact, I know from my own career in government that the opposite is true. But a report that on a given day, a government employee capably performed their job is hardly newsworthy. When we are constantly bombarded with stories about government misconduct, people are more likely to believe antigovernment disinformation. That exposure leaves us susceptible to crusaders like Steve Bannon, who has argued for the "deconstruction of the administrative state."[997] The ouster of Kevin McCarthy as House Speaker by the far-right faction of the Republican Party in October 2023 sowed chaos in Congress, further eroding public confidence. Research shows that only 29 percent of Democrats and independents in the United States trust government, and only *9 percent* of Republicans do.[998] Distrust in government makes people skeptical when the government tells them they should wear a mask or get a vaccine, creating unnecessary risks to public health.[999] If we don't believe our government tells us the truth, then it is easy for people to fear it is lying about climate change or the accuracy of an election. Deterioration of public confidence creates fissures that admit disinformation and corrodes our nation.

All of these factors combine to create conditions in the United States where disinformation can take hold and authoritarianism can metastasize. And disinformation is creating serious risks to our democracy, national security, and the rule of law.

6.

"STOP THE STEAL": DISINFORMATION IS DESTROYING DEMOCRACY

"Man's capacity for justice makes democracy possible, but man's inclination to injustice makes democracy necessary."
—REINHOLD NIEBUHR

THE MESSAGE BEGAN BY sounding like a routine election-season robocall. "Hi, this is Tamika Taylor," the caller began.[1000] She said she was calling from "Project 1599," a "civil rights organization." "Mail-in voting sounds great," she said, "but did you know that if you vote by mail, your personal information will be part of a public database that will be used by police departments to track down old warrants and be used by credit card companies to collect outstanding debts?" The message continued, "The CDC is even pushing to use records for mail-in voting to track people for mandatory vaccines. Don't be finessed into giving your private information to the man; stay safe and beware of vote by mail." In fact, these calls during the 2020 election season were organized by Jack Burkman and Jacob Wohl, two white conservative operatives who deliberately targeted voters in predominantly Black communities in five states to discourage them from voting in 2020.[1001] After the calls went out, Burkman sent an email to congratulate Wohl, stating, "i [*sic*] love these robo calls . . . getting angry black call backs . . . win or lose . . . the black robo was a great [Jacob Wohl] idea."[1002] In 2022, the two men would plead guilty to communications fraud.[1003]

In another case, Douglass Mackey, a social media influencer known as Ricky Vaughn, was convicted in federal court in 2023 for disseminating disinformation on Twitter during the run-up to the 2016 election, posting false claims that voters could cast their ballot by text message.[1004] One tweet depicted a Black woman next to a sign reading "African Americans for Hillary."[1005] The tweet read "Avoid the Line. Vote from Home. Text 'Hillary' to 59925. Vote for Hillary and be a part of history." The post even had authentic-sounding disclaimers: "Must be 18 or older to vote. One vote per person. Must be a legal citizen of the United States. Voting by text not available in Guam, Puerto Rico, Alaska, or Hawaii. Paid for by Hillary for President 2016." According to a Department of Justice press release, before election day, at least 4,900 unique telephone numbers responded to the tweet by sending in a vote to the number provided.[1006] It is impossible to know how many voters might have wasted their ballots as victims of the lie.

The goal of information warfare is to dominate enemies— including political enemies—without using violence. According to Renée DiResta, a Stanford researcher on information technology, in an information war, "once a combatant wins over a sufficient number of minds, they have the power to influence culture and society, policy and politics."[1007] The Israeli company Psy-Group marketed its services to the 2016 Trump presidential campaign with such goals in mind, DiResta writes; as their sales brochure put it, "Reality Is a Matter of Perception."[1008] Given the rapidly evolving power of artificial intelligence and its capacity to be weaponized, it is reasonable to expect the velocity and virality of disinformation to intensify and the mechanisms necessary for democracy to be tested to new degrees. An AI-generated attack could flood social media platforms with information that polling places were closed, for example. Creating chaos on election day is just one way that disinformation threatens democracy.[1009]

Knowing that it is virtually impossible to disprove a negative, MAGA Republicans have endlessly pointed to the *absence* of evidence that an election was fair to create doubt surrounding its legitimacy. Political scientists Russell Muirhead and Nancy L.

Rosenblum refer to this phenomenon as "conspiracy without a theory."[1010] They argue that society has become conditioned to believe in conspiracies without demanding proof. As noted earlier, because of the power of repetition, if people are exposed to an accusation enough, they begin to believe it. Donald Trump's claims were bolstered by third-party endorsers—allies in Congress, the media, and even a documentary film called *2000 Mules*. The film was produced by a Texas group called True the Vote and Dinesh D'Souza, a far-right conspiracy peddler who was convicted of campaign finance fraud in 2014 and was later pardoned by Trump.[1011] The film purported to provide independent evidence of election fraud, falsely claiming that two thousand paid saboteurs submitted four hundred thousand fake absentee ballots for Joe Biden in Arizona, Georgia, Michigan, Pennsylvania, and Wisconsin.[1012] The film featured grainy video footage of people depositing multiple ballots into drop boxes—scenes that were debunked by election experts who noted that many states permit voters to return the ballots of family members.[1013] In Arizona, GOP attorney general Mark Brnovich asked for a federal investigation of True the Vote.[1014] Yet the film had broad reach—it was shown in 270 theaters across the United States[1015] and was available for streaming online.[1016]

Donald Trump and other MAGA Republicans have abused their trust as public servants to indoctrinate Americans into an election denial movement. As president, Trump used his office to create a commission to study election fraud, elevating the phenomenon's credibility in the public eye. As a candidate for reelection, Trump and his team abused the courts, filing scores of baseless lawsuits challenging election results across the country—even though they lost almost every case, they kept the stories about voter fraud in the news. Millions of Americans, conditioned to believe Trump no matter what, were fooled by his deceptions. And so even after lawsuits were lost, evidence was found to be nonexistent, votes were certified, and Biden was sworn in as president, the disinformation operation continued. The information war was no longer targeting the last election. It was targeting the next one.

According to a 2022 analysis, the authoritarian MAGA movement has evolved from gathering "under the banner of 'Stop the Steal,' preferring the good government language of 'election integrity.'"[1017] At the time of this writing, disinformation about voter fraud was being used as a pretext in many states to enact laws that make it more difficult for ballots to be cast by likely Democratic voters—particularly students, people of color, and those living in economically precarious communities. Disinformation was also being used as a guise to shift power over elections to GOP-controlled legislatures. MAGA Republicans are corrupting the machinery of democracy by refusing to concede elections they lose, conducting endless audits, putting ballots and voting machines in the hands of outsiders, and nominating candidates who are election deniers—those who continue to claim that the 2020 presidential election was stolen, despite a complete absence of evidence. Perpetual claims of fraud undermine public confidence in our elections and threaten to destabilize our democracy.

When disinformation about election fraud is taken to the extreme, voters lose the ability to discern truth from lies and lose faith that their vote matters. According to political scientist Andrew Wilson, after the fall of the Soviet Union, "political technologists" would control politics in the former Soviet republics by blackmailing political rivals. They created ballot confusion by sponsoring candidates with names similar to those of their opponents and fabricated stories about current events to manipulate public discourse. Vladimir Putin still plays this game, according to former deputy national security adviser Ben Rhodes. As the Russian president came to power, "one of Putin's goals was to discourage people from thinking that participation in politics was worth the effort."[1018] He could accomplish this goal, Rhodes writes, without convincing people that he was honest: "He simply needed to convince people that *everyone* was corrupt."[1019] The message was that all politicians are dishonest, all elections are rigged, and there is no such thing as a true democracy. And if all governments are corrupt, then "Russians might as well have a strong, competent leader who shares their grievances and sense of national greatness."[1020]

According to Rhodes, once in power, an authoritarian leader can redraw voting district maps to favor him and his party. The authoritarian can reward wealthy citizens with low taxes and favorable government policies, and they, in turn, will fund his campaigns. He can pack the courts with loyalists who will rule in his favor. He can demonize ethnic populations while glorifying traditional values that appeal to those "longing for a great past."[1021] As historian Heather Cox Richardson notes, when voters in places like Russia and former Soviet republics become convinced that the political system is corrupt, people simply give up trying to engage in the democratic process.[1022] Is our own electorate becoming so cynical that voters will someday simply disengage from politics and accept the inevitable results of manipulated elections?

Democracy Is Fragile

Of course, we tend to think of the United States as impervious to such attacks. In a country that has withstood rebellions, invasion, civil war, presidential assassinations, Jim Crow, the Great Depression, two world wars, the Watergate scandal, and many other crises, it is easy to take US democracy for granted. Americans have long idealized democracy as a form of government at home and around the world. As Ronald Reagan said during his remarks to commemorate the fortieth anniversary of the landing at Normandy, "Democracy is worth dying for."[1023]

In their book on voting rights, *Our Unfinished March*, former US attorney general Eric Holder and Sam Koppelman explain why democracy is superior to all other forms of government.[1024] Democracy is the manifestation of the principle that all citizens are equal by law; all other rights depend on the right to vote. In theory, representational democracy fosters policies that are consistent with the desires of the people. Democracy keeps leaders accountable to the people they serve. People of color and women like Harriet Tubman and Susan B. Anthony fought for the right to vote because it is essential to every other right. Excluding groups from elections, said Anthony, leaves "the way open for all forms of injustice."[1025] As Winston Churchill once said, "Democracy is the worst form of government except for all those other forms that have been tried from time to time."[1026]

But even democracy has its fault lines. Plato noted that despite its virtues, democracy also brings the risk that a skilled demagogue could exploit freedoms, particularly freedom of speech, to seize power.[1027] The tyrant, he said, first "sows fear among the people, and then represents himself as 'the people's protector.'"[1028] Our belief in US exceptionalism makes us think that our democracy will always be here. But history tells a different story. In their book, *How Democracies Die*, Steven Levitsky and Daniel Ziblatt chronicle scores of democracies from the distant and recent past that have slid into authoritarian rule.[1029] We tend to think of the death of democracy in the form of coups, like those in Argentina, Greece, Egypt, Thailand, and other countries where government takeovers came with military force.[1030] Until January 6, 2021, the thought of a coup in the United States was unthinkable. Now, the seditious conspiracy convictions of some of the Capitol insurrectionists confirm that even in America, some citizens are willing to use violence to install the leader of their choosing.[1031]

But just as often, democracies decline without a sudden, violent takeover. As Levitsky and Ziblatt note, "democracies may die at the hands not of generals but of elected leaders" who "maintain a veneer of democracy while eviscerating its substance."[1032] Efforts to dismantle democracy from within may come incrementally, "in barely visible steps."[1033] Political leaders use legal methods to undermine institutions for their own political advantage. They might take steps to control the media, or replace civil servants with political allies, or pack the courts—all in the name of improving government.[1034] The slow erosion of democratic norms is like the life cycle of leaves on a tree; changes are invisible from one moment to the next, until one day they wither and die.

A famous example of a bloodless coup from within, of course, is Adolf Hitler's rise to power. Still reeling from its loss in World War I and in the throes of the Great Depression, Germany was in a period of great discontent in the 1930s. In 1933, Hitler, as chancellor of Germany, exploited the fire at the Reichstag, the German parliament building, to issue emergency orders that suspended civil liberties. A month later, his government passed the Enabling Acts,[1035] which took legislative power from parliament and gave it to Hitler's cabinet, permitting it to enact laws even if they "might deviate from the constitution."[1036] In a short period of time, Hitler transformed the country from a democracy to a dictatorship.

Hitler is not the only example of the destruction of democracy from within. As recently as the end of the Cold War, we have seen democratic backsliding in Hungary, the Philippines, Russia, Turkey, and Venezuela.[1037] In Israel, Prime Minister Benjamin Netanyahu attempted to seize greater control over the selection of supreme court justices in 2023, until massive protests and work stoppages convinced him to back down, at least temporarily.[1038] In Hungary, Viktor Orbán governed democratically as prime minister from 1998 to 2002.[1039] After his return to power in 2010, though, he took an authoritarian turn,[1040] replacing civil servants with partisan allies.[1041] His Fidesz party rewrote the country's constitution to lock in its own power.[1042] Through election laws, gerrymandering, and slanted campaign advertising rules, Orbán's party was able to hold onto a two-thirds majority in parliament in 2014, despite receiving less than 50 percent of the popular vote.[1043] Some of the same tactics are being used today in the United States.

In fact, some conservatives are finding authoritarian regimes to be attractive alternatives to a democracy where the majority is growing more racially diverse and politically progressive. A far cry from Reagan's reference to the Soviet Union as the "Evil Empire," Trump's descriptions of Putin were expressions of admiration: "strong," "savvy," and "genius."[1044] Democratic backsliding around the world comes as all Western nations face great challenges—climate change, immigration, economic struggles, and demands for equity by marginalized communities. Power-hungry opportunists use disinformation to channel fear into resentment. Some conservatives in the United States express admiration for Putin due to his right-wing nationalism and his opposition to LGBTQ+ and women's rights.[1045] Orbán likewise became something of a darling of the right: In 2021, a fawning Tucker Carlson interviewed Orbán and broadcast his Fox News show from Hungary for a week.[1046] In 2022, the Conservative Political Action Conference hosted Orbán in Texas, where he received enthusiastic applause when he said, "The globalists can all go to hell."[1047] Conservative American writer Rod Dreher called Orbán's government "what an actual pro-family, socially conservative government acts like."[1048]

The Rocky Road of American Democracy

The United States is among the world's oldest democracies.[1049] And yet, democracy in America has not always been a pretty story. Our nation began with the genocide of Indigenous peoples and the enslavement of Africans. Voting was a privilege reserved only for white men who owned property or paid sufficient taxes.[1050] The Civil War was fought over the enslavement of Black people, an institution built on the self-serving lie of white supremacy to justify human trafficking, breeding, and commodification for profit; Alexis de Tocqueville noted the irony of a nation founded on equality that so horribly mistreated Black and Native Americans.[1051] The end of the Confederate cause brought the passage of the Fifteenth Amendment, which professed to give the right to vote to formerly enslaved Americans. It would take another fifty years before women were granted that same right, and a hundred years before the promise of the Fifteenth Amendment would be fulfilled with the Voting Rights Act of 1965.

Victory by the Union army may have ended the Civil War, but it did not eliminate racial strife. During the Reconstruction era, newly enfranchised Black men suddenly constituted a majority or near-majority of voters in a number of Southern states.[1052] In the 1870s, more than two thousand freedmen were elected to public office as Republicans. White Democrats responded by changing the rules: Throughout the former Confederate states, new constitutions and laws were enacted that appeared neutral on their face but deliberately prevented African Americans from voting.[1053] Poll taxes, property ownership requirements, and literacy tests applied to all voters but had a disparate impact on Black voters.[1054] "Grandfather clauses" were an even more precise way to single out Black Americans. By permitting voters to cast a ballot only if their grandfathers had been registered to vote, the rules gave voting rights to most white men, but not to Black men, whose grandfathers had been enslaved.[1055] The Ku Klux Klan emerged in the 1860s and began using terrorism, violence, and murder to subordinate Black communities.[1056] Lynchings and Jim Crow laws that relegated Black Americans to second-class citizenship in the South endured for a century following the Civil War. Racist disinformation and propaganda played a large role in fomenting white dominance: The film *Birth of a Nation*, a white supremacist propaganda tool, was the first motion picture ever to be shown in the White House. Its commercial success and influence boosted the KKK and helped indoctrinate more Americans into explicitly white supremacist views.

The freedom movements of the 1950s and '60s pushed back against generations of violence and racial oppression, but the risks were dire. Local organizers were beaten or killed. Activists who traveled to the South were murdered for helping people to register to vote.[1057] Black leaders like Medgar Evers and Martin Luther King Jr. were assassinated.[1058] Many white segregationists who lived through that era are still alive today. It would be naive to think none of them still hold racist opposition to Americans of color claiming equal access to the same resources, opportunities, and privileges long enjoyed by white Americans. Efforts to subvert the electoral power of Americans of color have simply grown more sophisticated, through the use of disinformation, gerrymandering, and voter suppression laws.

Events of the 1960s and '70s saw a dramatic change in voting preferences in the South. Traditionally, Republicans had been largely business titans of the North and abolitionists.[1059] Democrats shared a commitment to the agrarian values of the South, opposed a strong federal government, and were committed to slavery, having made peace with its horrors in exchange for cheap plantation labor.[1060] But changes in the nation's economy and the admission to the union of new states in the West led to changes in the two parties' platforms,[1061] until finally Democratic president Lyndon Johnson's support for the Civil Rights Act of 1964 and the Voting Rights Act of 1965, and Republican president Richard Nixon's "Southern Strategy" in the 1970s, resulted in a shift in voting trends in the South from reliably Democratic to solidly red.[1062] Nixon manipulated the racial anxieties of white America as part of his campaign, a strategy that some Republicans have continued to cultivate to this day.[1063] Today, the "Party of Lincoln" is one the sixteenth president would hardly recognize. Like the racist pro-Nixon backlash that followed Johnson's signing of key civil rights laws, the election of Barack Obama, in 2008, prompted conservative white backlash in the form of the Tea Party movement, which not only questioned the first Black president's legitimacy but framed him as a threat to democracy.[1064]

The effort to deny legitimacy and voting power to people of color continues to this day. Today, the pretext of voter fraud is designed to do what the grandfather clause did in the past—use laws that are neutral on their face to disproportionately suppress votes from people of color, who are more likely to vote for Democratic candidates. Whether motivated by racism or the desire to maintain political power, tactics to manipulate elections are the antithesis of democracy, because they deny the right of all Americans to participate in self-governance and lead to oligarchy, or worse, fascism.

Perhaps because of the overload of information available, politics in America today has become less about policy choices and more about identity; as Joe Biden said during his 2020 and 2024 campaigns, the candidates were battling for the "soul of the nation."[1065] Cultural warfare is causing some politicians to portray their opponents as unacceptable to white, Christian voters: They focus on issues like books in school libraries and gender-affirming medical care. They claim that progressive ideas about racial justice and gender identity make people "hate" America.[1066] For the 2020 election, the Republican Party adopted no platform, the traditional list of policy priorities.[1067] Instead, the GOP issued a resolution that read, "*RESOLVED,* That the Republican Party has and will continue to enthusiastically support the President's America-first agenda."[1068] Why distract voters with policy issues when identity is what matters most? In a 2022 campaign speech, Governor Ron DeSantis pledged to fight the "woke" agenda in schools, business, and government agencies. "We can never ever surrender to woke ideology. And I'll tell you this, the state of Florida is where woke goes to die."[1069] Mike Pompeo, a one-time potential rival to DeSantis for the presidency, also elbowed his way into the culture wars when the former secretary of state spoke out against the 1619 Project, a series of reports by the *New York Times*, led by journalist Nikole Hannah-Jones, that examined race in America. Pompeo's tweet stated, "The 1619 Project is a slander on the American people. It's a false narrative, and it has no place in our schools."[1070]

For some, our elections have become a battle of good versus evil. The perceived stakes of the 2020 presidential election were on display in a series of email and text messages between Trump's chief of staff, Mark Meadows, and Ginni Thomas, a conservative activist married to Supreme Court Justice Clarence Thomas.[1071] In response to Ginni Thomas's pleas to keep fighting to overturn the election,

Meadows reportedly characterized the outcome as a religious crusade: "This is a fight of good versus evil. Evil always looks like the victor until the King of Kings triumphs. Do not grow weary in well doing. The fight continues."[1072] Thomas, a combatant in the information war, described the fight in terms similar to those outlined by Renée DiResta: "The most important thing you can realize right now is that there are no rules in war," Thomas wrote. "This war is psychological. PSYOP."[1073]

In fact, some Republican public servants have begun undermining the very idea of American democracy in public remarks, referring to our government instead as a "republic." Shortly before the 2020 election, Senator Mike Lee (R-UT) tweeted, "We are not a democracy."[1074] The next day, he explained in another tweet, "Democracy isn't the objective; liberty, peace, and prospefity [sic] are. We want the human condition to flourish. Rank democracy can thwart that."[1075] In other words, the ends justify the means, even at the expense of the will of the people. Doug Mastriano, the GOP candidate for governor in Pennsylvania in 2022 who was at the Capitol on January 6, 2021, frequently referred to the United States as a "republic" in his campaign speeches.[1076] At their extremes, a democracy provides for majority rule; a republic includes safeguards against the tyranny of the majority through elected representatives. Of course, our government is a democratic republic, in which we use a blend of popular vote and elected representatives to make decisions.[1077] But "republic" may be the new buzzword of the far right to justify an unpopular agenda. If we are a republic and not a democracy, then we can entrust leaders who are wiser than the masses to make policy choices, providing cover for far-right values that are not shared by the majority of Americans.[1078] Alberto Fujimori, elected president of Peru in 1990 by exploiting populist anger, similarly questioned democracy in his slide toward authoritarianism.[1079] He would later attempt to dissolve that nation's congress and constitution.[1080] Are we being conditioned for a similar abuse of power?

Abuse of Democratic Institutions

America's political institutions were designed to protect democracy. Three separate branches of government, each empowered to check and balance the others, ensure that power is not abused. For example, presidents can appoint judges and justices, Congress can impeach and convict a president or a jurist, courts can strike down legislation. As president, Trump attempted to turn those institutions into instruments of disinformation. Upon taking office in 2017, one of Trump's first acts was to set up his Presidential Advisory Commission on Election Integrity, headed by Vice President Mike Pence and Kansas GOP secretary of state Kris Kobach, who had embraced claims of widespread voter fraud.[1081] The office was disbanded six months later, after states balked at turning over private voter data.[1082] One critic of the commission, Maine secretary of state Matthew Dunlap, obtained a court order for the commission's documents and concluded that it had found no evidence of fraud.[1083] Senate Majority Leader Chuck Schumer (D-NY) called the commission "a front" to "perpetrate dangerous and baseless claims" of voter fraud.[1084]

After losing reelection in 2020, Trump also attempted to use the courts to validate his claims of election fraud. Despite Trump's efforts, the courts held fast. His campaign lost sixty-one out of sixty-two legal challenges, the lone victory relating to a non-substantive procedural issue.[1085] Even the US Supreme Court rebuffed efforts to overturn the election, rejecting the Texas attorney general's challenge to Biden's victories in Georgia, Michigan, Pennsylvania, and Wisconsin.[1086]

But even if the legal challenges were not successful in court, they served their propaganda purpose of keeping assertions of election fraud in the news. In Michigan, federal district court judge Linda V. Parker threw out a lawsuit challenging Biden's victory and imposed sanctions on attorney Sidney Powell and her cocounsel for filing a baseless lawsuit.[1087] Judge Parker called out the ploy in her opinion, writing, "This case was never about fraud—it was about undermining the People's faith in our democracy and debasing the judicial process to do so."[1088] In other words, the lawsuits were being used simply to legitimize disinformation about a stolen election, and harming democracy and the courts in the process. Just say the election was stolen . . .

Disinformation Often Targets Minority Groups

For some Americans, electoral campaigns are a form of warfare where winning justifies any strategy, including gerrymandering, voter suppression, and manipulating voters through disinformation. According to disinformation researchers Mark Kumleben, Samuel Woolley, and Katie Joseff, since 2010, many online influence campaigns have targeted communities of color, both as the subjects and targets of disinformation.[1089] In 2018, disinformation stoked fears of immigrants by making exaggerated claims about the dangers of approaching migrant "caravans."[1090] Latinx communities have been the targets of Spanish-language disinformation designed to exploit their fears of socialism[1091] and their strong Catholic faith, which makes them likely to oppose abortion.[1092] In 2020, in Georgia, fake mail-in ballots were sent to Black voters so that they would waste their vote.[1093] In Wisconsin, billboards targeted communities with large populations of formerly incarcerated citizens to falsely claim that it was a crime to vote with a prior felony conviction.[1094] Communication apps were used to message Asian Americans disinformation about Black-on-Asian crime, along with pro-gun propaganda.[1095]

Disinformation Is Driving Laws That Subvert Democracy

According to an analysis by the Brennan Center for Justice, we have seen "a dramatic spike" in restrictive voting laws following the 2020 coup attempt.[1096] Most of the bills were sponsored by lawmakers who had furthered disinformation about the outcome of the 2020 election.[1097] Those pushing the laws contended that they were necessary to protect against voter fraud.[1098]

But if there is no real threat of fraud in an election, then the only logical conclusion is that laws that suppress voting are designed not, in fact, to prevent fraud but to favor the party that enacts them. In an argument before the Supreme Court, a lawyer defending restrictive new laws in Arizona admitted as much. He pointed out that without the new voting restrictions, the Republican Party would be "at a competitive disadvantage relative to Democrats."[1099] "Politics," he explained, "is a zero-sum game. Every extra vote they get . . . hurts us. . . . It's the difference between winning an election 50 to 49 and losing an election 51 to 50."[1100] In 2023, Trump lawyer Cleta Mitchell lamented the ease of voting on college campuses by students, a demographic group that is more likely to vote for Democrats than Republicans.[1101] These rare moments of candor reveal that voter suppression laws are designed simply to help one party win. The result is government selected by only some of the people, incentivized to favor the group that put them in power.

Voter Suppression Laws

The floodgates to new voter suppression laws in the South were thrown open by the Supreme Court's 2015 decision in *Shelby County v. Holder*.[1102] In that case, the court ended the preclearance program under the Voting Rights Act of 1965, which had required certain states with a history of racial discrimination in voting to obtain approval from the Department of Justice before implementing new voting laws. According to Chief Justice John G. Roberts Jr., who wrote the opinion, preclearance was no longer necessary. In a prophetic dissent, Justice Ruth Bader Ginsburg wrote, "Throwing out preclearance when it has worked and is continuing to work to stop discriminatory changes is like throwing away your umbrella in a rainstorm because you are not getting wet."[1103] Within two *hours* of the decision, Texas had enacted new restrictive voting laws. The storms have grown stronger ever since.

Following the 2020 election that saw Democrats win the White House and the Senate, nineteen states passed thirty-four new laws that made it more difficult to vote, all under the pretense of preventing fraud.[1104] These voter suppression laws have a disparate impact on voters who are minorities, students, and the poor—all likely Democratic voters.

After Georgia's 2021 runoff election, for example, when voters in that state elected to the Senate two Democrats, one Jewish and one Black, the Republican-controlled legislature enacted sweeping new election laws. Republican governor Brian Kemp justified the restrictive laws on the grounds that they made it "harder to cheat,"[1105] despite no evidence of election fraud. Researchers commissioned by Trump's own campaign were unable to substantiate claims of fraud.[1106] Nonetheless, Georgia enacted stringent new laws that would tend to reduce voter turnout, especially among likely Democratic voters in communities with large, racially diverse populations.[1107] The legislation limited the number of ballot drop boxes, restricted the use of provisional ballots, banned mobile voting, required a photocopy of identification documents to accompany mail-in ballots, and made it a crime to provide food or water to voters waiting in line, which tend to be longer in communities of color due to understaffed polling sites.[1108] In the 2020 election, drop boxes and mobile voting had been widely used in Fulton County, Georgia's largest and home to a majority Black population.[1109] These changes came swiftly, even though Secretary of State Brad Raffensperger disputed claims of election fraud in Georgia, calling the state's voting system "secure and trustworthy."[1110] The Department of Justice sued the state of Georgia over the new laws, alleging that they were "intended to deny or abridge the right of Black Georgians to vote on account of race or color," in violation of Section 2 of the Voting Rights Act.[1111] The lawsuit noted that the

Black population in Georgia had grown since 1990 by 70 percent and, in 2020, comprised 30 percent of the state's electorate, making it a formidable voting bloc.[1112]

While some states, like Michigan, have made it easier to vote in recent years by permitting same-day voter registration or no-excuse absentee voting,[1113] other states have enacted restrictions similar to Georgia's. New laws in various states have made it more difficult to register or vote by mail, created new or more stringent voter ID requirements, and authorized purges of voter rolls.[1114]

Restrictions on voting by mail

Voting by mail is often the subject of baseless conspiracy theories. Asked, in 2020, for evidence that voting by mail facilitates fraud, Trump's attorney general William Barr could point to none, claiming that it was simply "common sense."[1115] During the Covid-19 pandemic, voting by mail became important to help voters avoid exposure to the virus by going to the polls in person. Trump discouraged his supporters from voting by mail, claiming without evidence that the process was susceptible to fraud. As discussed earlier, when, as expected, his early lead evaporated once the mail-in ballots were counted, Trump exploited the delay to claim the election was rigged.[1116] These false claims prompted laws that restrict the right to vote by mail. The obstacles adversely impact likely Democratic voters—students who might live out of state, Native Americans who live far from polling places, and voters with more than one job or hourly employment. Mail-in voting is desirable in communities of color, where voters consistently face longer lines to vote[1117] because of various factors: greater likelihood of living in urban areas with high population density;[1118] fewer voting resources such as polling places, voting machines, and poll workers;[1119] and greater needs for language assistance.[1120] Seniors, another group that is inclined to vote by mail, favored Democrats in 2022.[1121] For all these reasons, reducing the ability to vote by mail tips the balance in favor of Republicans and white voters.

Photo ID requirements

One particular measure that purports to protect against mythical electoral fraud is the requirement for voter ID. This may hardly seem objectionable to middle-class voters who are accustomed to producing ID to board planes and check into hotels—and it was that group to whom Kris Kobach, the former Kansas secretary of state, was speaking when he said, "I don't think it's a burden to reach into one's wallet or one's purse and pull out a photo ID."[1122] True enough, so long as you already *have* a photo ID.

But obtaining a photo ID is an obstacle for many Americans, particularly people of color, those without disposable income, and students. Someone who can't afford a car is less likely to have a driver's license. In addition to the cost of the license itself, fees are also required to obtain the underlying identity documents, such as birth certificates; former attorney general Eric Holder called these expenses a "poll tax."[1123] In addition to the out-of-pocket costs, and even when the IDs themselves are free, obtaining a photo ID requires an investment of time, often during the workday, to travel to the Department of Motor Vehicles and wait in line. In some states, communities of color have fewer DMV offices, with curtailed hours.[1124] The forms of ID that are accepted for voting can also have a disparate impact on voters. For example, Texas enacted a law that allows voters to use gun licenses, which are more likely to be carried by white voters, as a form of voter ID.[1125] For purposes of voting, Alabama does not accept public-housing IDs, which are more likely to be carried by Americans of color and citizens who are economically disadvantaged.[1126] Lack of photo ID and even confusion about the ID requirements can suppress voter turnout, with disproportionately Democratic voters ending up staying home. This tactic could be used by any political group to amass power. Regardless of which party it favors, it is antidemocratic and should be condemned by all Americans.

Purges of voter rolls

Another common theme among voter suppression laws is the perceived need to purge voter rolls to maintain election integrity. Such
laws were passed in 2022 in Arizona, Oklahoma, and South Carolina.[1127] These laws are based on false conspiracy theories that ballots
are being cast in the name of voters who are ineligible because they
have died, have moved out of state, or lack citizenship.[1128] Purges
threaten to disenfranchise voters when their names are removed
from the rolls based on flawed data.[1129] According to the congressional testimony of Sophia Lin Lakin, of the the ACLU's Voting
Rights Project, purges of voter rolls "disproportionately sweep in,
and ultimately disenfranchise, voters of color."[1130]

Some of these laws provide no notice to voters when they are
removed from the rolls and no opportunity to challenge their
removal until the voter arrives at a polling place to vote on election
day, when it is likely too late to do anything about it.[1131] All of these
suppression laws serve authoritarian purposes of social manipulation and political control.

Disinformation Is Driving Election Interference Laws

In addition to passing laws that suppress the right to vote, some
states have also used disinformation about voter fraud in 2020 as a
pretext to enact laws that risk partisan interference with elections.
The Brennan Center for Justice defines election interference laws as
those that permit "partisan interference in elections or threaten the
people and processes that make elections work."[1132] In addition to
influencing the administration of elections, these laws bolster the
lie that elections are under attack. Since 2020, 151 election interference bills have been introduced in 27 states.[1133]

Some of these laws shift power from local election officials
to Republican-controlled state legislatures. For instance, a law
enacted in Georgia in 2021 permits the state board of elections to

remove professional election officials and take control of election administration in individual counties.[1134] In addition, the 2021 law removed the secretary of state as a voting member and chair of the State Election Board and replaced him with the legislature's own appointee—seen by some as payback for the actions of Brad Raffensperger, who, the *New York Times* noted, "infuriated Mr. Trump and some GOP leaders in the state by rebuffing the former president's fraud claims."[1135] The bill also empowered the State Election Board to suspend county election officials, a move the *Times* noted pitted the Republican legislature against Fulton County, the state's largest and bluest.[1136]

Seizing Control of Election Machinery

Disinformation about election results is also used to justify interference with the machinery of elections—ballots, tabulators, even control of the offices that administer elections. MAGA Republicans have used false claims of election fraud to justify third-party audits and the inspection of voting machines, both of which can endanger the integrity of election infrastructure. Perhaps even more alarming, Republicans are targeting official positions in government that control the oversight of elections, from canvassing boards to secretary of state offices.

Conducting recounts and audits is the responsibility of government. And yet Republicans used the Big Lie of 2020 as a pretext to outsource these functions to private parties of dubious credibility. Opening these processes to outsiders risks tampering to achieve a desired end that may have nothing to do with election integrity. False claims of voter fraud provide justification for this threat.

After Joe Biden won Arizona in 2020, that state's Republican-controlled Senate hired a private firm known as Cyber Ninjas to conduct an independent audit to investigate baseless allegations that ballots had been cast by dead voters.[1137] Even Arizona's GOP attorney general would later write a scathing letter debunking the false claims that dead voters had cast ballots in 2020.[1138] Hiring any private firm to perform core government functions exposes the public interest to private agendas, and in this case, to an extreme degree—Cyber Ninjas CEO Doug Logan had previously worked with lawyers for Trump supporters seeking to overturn the results of the 2020 election.[1139] To facilitate the audit, Senate Republicans subpoenaed all of the physical ballots cast by voters, the tabulating machines, and the electronic voting data for the state's largest county.[1140] Cyber Ninjas ultimately found no fraud in the election, and that Biden actually won by a larger margin than the initial count reported, but the danger of giving access to voting records to a private company became apparent when Cyber Ninjas folded in 2022 after being sued to produce documents regarding their audit under state public records laws.[1141]

The reason for independent audits may not even be so much to correct vote counts as to undermine public confidence in the government's ability to get it right. After the election, Arizona's GOP Senate leader, Karen Fann, wrote that the audit had been "critical to restoring the diminished confidence our constituents expressed following the last election."[1142] She praised "the increased voter integrity measures put in place after the audit revealed weaknesses in our election processes," despite the audit's failure to identify any weaknesses whatsoever in Arizona's election processes. Of course, constituents will have diminished confidence in election results when leaders falsely claim fraud, leading to the "necessity" of the kinds of restrictive laws that suppress the vote. It is all part of the cycle of disinformation.

Voting machines

Disinformation campaigns have also targeted voting machines. In 2020, Trump campaign lawyers and surrogates made false claims that voting machines made by Dominion Voting Systems were unreliable, had been hacked, or had "flipped" votes from Trump to Biden.[1143] MAGA-friendly media outlets like One America News Network and Fox News amplified the unfounded claims.[1144] While the claims did not result in the negation of any election results, they paved the way for the seizure of voting machines, which poses an actual threat to election integrity.

In Michigan, Matthew DePerno, a Republican nominee for state attorney general in 2022 and a coup supporter in 2020, and former state representative Daire Rendon were charged criminally with obtaining and tampering with voting tabulators in four municipalities in a possible effort to undermine the results of the 2020 election.[1145] In Pennsylvania, election officials had to decertify one county's voting equipment after officials there allowed an outside firm to access it.[1146] In Georgia, Trump campaign lawyer Sidney Powell hired a private firm to conduct "voting machine analysis" following the 2021 Senate runoff election in Coffee County, two hundred miles south of Atlanta.[1147] Documents indicated that the firm had successfully obtained data from election officials there, including forensic images of an election management server, a precinct tabulator, thumb drives used to program tabulators and touchscreen voting machines, and scanned images of paper ballots.[1148]

When voting machines land in hands outside the official chain of custody, they can be doctored. Rogue workers in future elections can also use knowledge gained through breaches to conduct an insider attack—to favor their preferred candidate, to undermine public confidence, or even to disrupt the vote count, making it impossible to determine a winner. Disinformation enables this sabotage when false claims about election fraud provide a pretext for taking voting machines out of official custody. But perhaps more important, simply the public announcement that the machines are suspect undermines confidence in the outcomes of elections. Election deniers can point to the inspections that they ginned up as "evidence" that the system is rigged.

Government insiders

Public officials who oversee elections can also pose a risk to democracy. While voters rejected open election deniers in many of the key 2022 midterm elections, 170 of 291 election deniers on the ballot won their races.[1149] An authoritarian at the helm of election administration would be the ultimate threat from within. The 2020 coup attempt was unsuccessful in large part because public officials like Brad Raffensperger, in Georgia,[1150] and House Speaker Rusty Bowers, in Arizona[1151]—both Republicans—rebuffed Trump's efforts to undermine the elections in their states, to their own political detriment. We cannot always count on sufficient individual courage and integrity to secure us from authoritarian power grabs in the future. Secretaries of state, county clerks, and boards of canvassers are entrusted at various levels to administer elections fairly. In the hands of a coup supporter, the authority of those offices could be abused to create chaos. Whether they actually believe the disinformation about a stolen election or are simply willing to play along to propel themselves or their party to power, public officials can pose a risk to elections.

Secretaries of state

The secretary of state position, once regarded as a sleepy office that administers public records, has grown in importance in the era of contested elections. In many states, the secretary of state oversees the administration of elections. The significance of the office first became apparent in 2000, when Florida secretary of state Katherine Harris found herself at the center of the disputed race between George W. Bush and Al Gore. After serving as the state cochair for Bush's campaign,[1152] Harris stopped the recount, a move that ultimately led to Bush's victory.[1153] As Trump has said, sometimes the "vote counter is more important than the candidate."[1154]

In 2022, almost three hundred coup supporters were on ballots across the country.[1155] In the twenty-seven states with secretary of state races, ten races included candidates who had denied the legitimacy of Biden's election as president.[1156] These candidates joined in nationwide fundraising efforts under the umbrella of the America

First Secretary of State Coalition ("America First SOS"), supported by a political action committee called Conservatives for Election Integrity.[1157] The platform of the America First SOS candidates included eliminating mail-in ballots, limiting voting to a single day, and pledging to "clean up" voter rolls, measures that favor Republicans and reinforce the belief in election fraud. Two of the election deniers won their races for secretary of state, Diego Morales in Indiana[1158] and Chuck Gray in Wyoming,[1159] putting them in charge of upcoming elections. Following his defeat in Arizona, election denier Mark Finchem refused to concede his race for secretary of state, claiming—you guessed it—election fraud.[1160]

In addition to being able to tip the scales of elections, secretaries of state can also use their platforms as election officials to spread and validate false claims of voter fraud. Disinformation that voting by mail is not secure, for example, could suppress the turnout of well-intentioned voters who can't make it to the polls. If a person who lacked the integrity of Raffensperger had been serving as Georgia's secretary of state during the 2020 election and its aftermath, would they have withstood Trump's demands to "find" enough votes to tip the results?

Other state and local election officials

County clerks and local election boards are other danger points in the election infrastructure. County clerks are on the front lines of elections, entrusted with protecting voter equipment and safeguarding data.[1161] An election denier with the power of a county clerk can cause all manner of mischief. For example, in Colorado, Mesa County Clerk Tina Peters and her deputy were charged criminally in 2022 for an alleged scheme to prove the 2020 election was rigged.[1162] Charged offenses included identity theft, criminal impersonation, and violating duties of her office by permitting unauthorized individuals to access voting system technology.[1163] Peters became a cause célèbre on the right, which lauded her efforts.[1164] Even after criminal charges were filed against her, Peters ran for secretary of state. She lost in the GOP primary, demanded a recount, and then filed suit alleging that it was conducted improperly.[1165] While awaiting trial for her alleged misconduct in the scheme, she was convicted of obstructing the investigation.[1166]

In addition to county clerks, other officials also have a role in elections. Some states have state and/or county commissions or boards that certify election results.[1167] In Michigan, the Board of State Canvassers comprises two Republicans and two Democrats, and so two members of one party could grind the process to a halt, sending it to court for resolution. In 2020, Team Trump pressured the Michigan board to reject the outcome of that state's election, which was won by Biden.[1168] The effort ultimately failed when one of the Republicans, Aaron Van Langevelde, voted to certify Biden's victory. The other Republican, Norman Shinkle, was apparently unable to bring himself to certify and abstained from the vote.[1169] If, instead, loyalists had either believed in the false claims of election fraud or at least been willing to play along, the results could have been starkly different.

At numerous points in the election process, vulnerabilities exist that can be exploited by those intent on tipping the outcome. Under the guise of ensuring election integrity, they may infiltrate our election infrastructure to launch an attack from within. According to DiResta, "Influence operations exploit divisions in our society using vulnerabilities in our information ecosystem. We have to move away from treating this as a problem of giving people better facts, or stopping some Russian bots, and move towards thinking about it as an ongoing battle for the integrity of our information infrastructure—easily as critical as the integrity of our financial markets."[1170]

The risk posed by the lies doesn't end with elections. Lies also threaten to harm public safety, national security, and the democratic world order.

7.

"SOMEBODY IS GOING TO GET KILLED": DISINFORMATION IS ENDANGERING PUBLIC SAFETY AND NATIONAL SECURITY

"If you want to get to President Trump, you're going to have to go through me, and you're going to have to go through 75 million Americans just like me. And I'm going to tell you, most of us are card-carrying members of the NRA."

—KARI LAKE, 2022 GOP candidate for governor of Arizona

ON THE EVENING OF December 6, 2020, Jocelyn Benson and her four-year-old son were decorating their home for the holidays. Benson was the Michigan secretary of state who had presided over her state's November presidential election; baseless allegations of fraud had been debunked and Joe Biden certified as the winner.[1171] According to a statement later issued by Benson, as her son "was about to sit down to watch *How the Grinch Stole Christmas,* dozens of armed individuals stood outside [her] home shouting obsceni- ties and chanting into bullhorns in the dark of night."[1172] The mob demanded that Benson overturn the election. Benson noted her support for peaceful protest but stated, "There is a line crossed when gatherings are done with the primary purpose of intimida- tion of public officials who are carrying out the oath of office they solemnly took as elected officials."[1173] According to Benson, the mob was using "false information about the security and accuracy of our elections" to "undermine and silence the will" of voters.[1174]

Following the 2020 election, disinformation continued to pose a growing danger, fueling harassment, threats, and acts of vio- lence. In 2022, the FBI and Department of Homeland Security assessed that one of the most lethal terrorist threats to the United States[1175] was homegrown groups "advocating the superiority of the white race."[1176] Targets of political violence included members of Congress, secretaries of state, local election officials, and even poll workers. Health and school officials have also been the targets of threats and harassment, leading to an exodus from local public service. Disinformation that people of color are "replacing" white Americans is sparking hate crimes against Asian American, Black, Latinx, and Jewish communities, among others.

Attacks from within are also creating other threats. They are endangering our national security from forces beyond our borders; while we are distracted with internecine wars, we lose focus on threats from abroad. Our standing in the world is also diminished as a model for democracy with the moral authority to be a global leader. And disinformation is subverting our ability to address other national challenges head-on: it is difficult to forge solidarity to address public health risks, climate change, racial injustice, and other threats when we have been conditioned to categorically distrust and oppose one another. United we stand, divided we fall.

Stochastic Terrorism

In my work as a national security prosecutor, I learned how a relatively small political movement could amplify its impact through disinformation. The terrorist groups al-Qaeda and the Islamic State in Iraq and Syria (ISIS) were early masters of digital media to recruit and radicalize members with propaganda.[1177] Anwar al-Awlaki, the dynamic US citizen who became a spiritual leader for al-Qaeda, disseminated fiery speeches online in which he urged supporters to kill Americans, supporting his argument with false claims that the United States was "at war" with Islam.[1178] Awlaki spread disinformation and propaganda through YouTube, Facebook, and his own blog.[1179] One of his YouTube sermons, in which he called for suicide operations against the western world, was called "44 Ways to Support Jihad."[1180] Awlaki helped produce an English-language online magazine called *Inspire*, which provided instructions for supporters on how to launch attacks worldwide.[1181] One article in the magazine was called "How to Build a Bomb in the Kitchen of Your Mom," believed to have inspired the brothers who attacked the Boston Marathon in 2013 with explosives packed in pressure cookers.[1182] (There was no evidence that the bombers had ever met Awlaki, but his name appeared in the search histories on their laptops.[1183]) Assassinated by the United States in a 2011 drone strike, Awlaki likely inspired attacks in the United States such as the deadly shootings at Fort Hood (now Fort Cavazos), in Texas, and at two military installations in Chattanooga, Tennessee.[1184]

ISIS succeeded al-Qaeda in Iraq and perfected the craft of crowd-sourcing terrorism.[1185] ISIS called itself an Islamic caliphate, or sovereign government, over all Muslims in the world.[1186] In addition to fighting for land in Iraq and Syria, ISIS supporters committed terrorist attacks in Europe and the United States to intimidate its perceived enemies. ISIS used methods from the authoritarian playbook to market its brand—developing its own flag, chants, and distinctive salute, with one finger pointing skyward, where heaven, they said, awaits the martyrs. ISIS created slick online videos—some to recruit fighters by mimicking the style of video games, and others to lure the susceptible by depicting the utopian society ISIS pretended to be.[1187] ISIS used hashtags and bots to amplify its message on social media platforms.[1188] To communicate outside of public view, ISIS members used the encrypted messaging application Telegram.[1189] Awlaki and ISIS asked supporters to attack enemies wherever they were in the world via shootings, knife attacks, and vehicle rammings.[1190]

Al-Qaeda and ISIS were engaging in a tactic known as "stochastic terrorism," the incitement of violence through the public demonization of a group or individual.[1191] The word "stochastic" means random—in stochastic terrorism, provocative speeches inspire supporters to take action, even though the speaker does not know exactly when or how, nor which supporters will act. Homeland security expert Juliette Kayyem defines stochastic terrorism as "the incitement of random but utterly predictable acts of violence for political gain."[1192] According to Molly Amman and J. Reid

Meloy, who work in the area of threat assessment, stochastic terrorism was at work when Henry II targeted Thomas Becket, the archbishop of Canterbury, in the twelfth century over the proper role of the church in England.[1193] The king was imperiling Beckett when he famously asked, "Will no one rid of me this meddlesome priest?" A group of knights recognized his question as a call to duty and killed the archbishop. Henry II had plausible deniability for the murder, but his comments had their desired effect.

Disinformation Is Sparking Violence in America

Stochastic terrorism occurs domestically in the United States when prominent Americans use their platforms to aggressively demonize others. They may not deliberately seek to unleash physical attacks against their political rivals, but violence has become a byproduct of their reckless drumbeat of disinformation to generate outrage for political gain. The anything-goes, take-no-prisoners rhetoric has consequences for American society.

On January 6, 2021, stochastic terrorism took hold when Donald Trump staged his coup attempt. Trump urged the nation to "fight like hell or you won't have a country anymore."[1194] As a result of his incitement, the gathering at the Capitol escalated into seditious violence. An Ohio man who was convicted for his role in storming the Capitol on January 6 testified at his trial that he was spurred to action by Trump's words. "If the president's giving you almost an order to do something, I felt obligated to do that."[1195] Another man said he went to Washington, marched on the Capitol, and finally retreated all because Trump had told him to do so, obeying, he said, as if he were wearing "horse blinders."[1196] Even when telling the attackers to go home, Trump tacitly condoned their violence, saying, "We love you. You're very special."[1197]

Efforts to downplay the criminality of the January 6 attack served to normalize political violence and sedition. To some extent, it worked: As leaders supported Trump and the attack, the views of other Republicans shifted dramatically, according to surveys conducted in June 2021 and again a year later. Respondents who said the attack was an insurrection dropped from 33 percent to 13 percent between the two surveys.[1198] The number who said it was a riot went from 62 percent to 45 percent, while respondents who said the attack was a "legitimate protest" rose from 47 percent to 61 percent.[1199] Another survey revealed that in January 2021, 56 percent of Republicans considered the attack to be an effort "to overturn the election and keep Donald Trump in power," but that percentage dropped to 33 percent in December of that year.[1200] Did MAGA disinformation operations manipulate their memories, or were they simply signaling their submission to the Great Leader?

One study noted an increase in both hate speech on social media and hate crimes in the real world against Muslims and Latinx communities following comments by Trump attacking these groups.[1201] Studies have also found that exposure to hateful rhetoric increases polarization and support for political violence.[1202] When Trump tweeted that Representative Ilhan Omar (D-MN) was "out of control" and tweeted an image of the September 11 attacks alongside her remarks, she reported receiving death threats in response.[1203]

Demagogues deliberately provoke expressions of outrage from a targeted group to confirm false claims that its members are volatile and aggressive. This very real response allows purveyors of disinformation to use "both-sides" language to minimize the violence they provoke. When I served as US attorney for the Eastern District of Michigan, two different sets of provocateurs travelled to Dearborn, Michigan, to taunt and menace the city's large Muslim American community. The agitators burned a Koran and brandished a pig's head, hoping to incite angry reactions that they could then publicize as "proof" of Muslims' propensity for violence.[1204] The effort fizzled when the local community united and refused to take the bait.

It was after Trump's repeated references to the press as the "enemy of the people"[1205] that "MAGA Bomber" Cesar Sayoc sent his pipe bombs through the mail in 2019 to CNN reporters and prominent

Democrats, including Barack Obama and Hillary Clinton."[1206] On social media, Trump had posted fantasies about physical attacks on the media; in one meme Trump retweeted, a locomotive labeled "Trump" was shown crashing into a CNN logo.[1207] Trump called Obama "the founder of ISIS" and Hillary Clinton its "co-founder" and "the devil."[1208] While Trump had likely never met Sayoc, the president's words appear to have resonated with him, so much so that Sayoc's van was adorned with images of Trump, as well as a picture of Hillary Clinton in the crosshairs of a rifle. One sticker said, "CNN Sucks," a phrase often chanted at Trump rallies.[1209] It is difficult to deny the link between Trump's messaging and Sayoc's actions.

In August 2022, when Trump went on the offensive against the FBI after the search of his Mar-a-Lago home for classified documents, some supporters responded with threats and violence. The judge who issued the search warrant for Trump's home became the target of threats, including one stating, "I see a rope around his neck."[1210] A man named Ricky Shiffer shared his own outrage online about the treatment of the former president and, three days after the search, attempted to breach the FBI's field office in Cincinnati, armed with an assault rifle and wearing body armor.[1211] Later that day, he was killed in a standoff with police,[1212] another casualty of disinformation. Even after this episode, Trump and his supporters did not relent in their attacks against the Justice Department and FBI. When Trump was indicted by a federal grand jury in the government secrets case, Kari Lake, the Republican from Arizona, said she had a message for Attorney General Merrick Garland and Special Counsel Jack Smith, and then made her statement about having to go through "card-carrying members of the NRA" quoted at the beginning of this chapter.[1213] While many people might see such a comment as political pandering, the risk is that someone will take it as a call to action. After Trump publicly disparaged Judge Tanya S. Chutkan, who was presiding over his federal election-interference case, a Texas woman was charged with threatening to kill Chutkan and her family.[1214] In Georgia, the grand jurors who voted to return a RICO election-interference indictment against Trump found themselves targeted on social media with threats and harassment.[1215] Trump knew he was playing with fire when he unloaded on New York Attorney General Letitia James outside a Manhattan courthouse at the start of a 2023 trial on civil fraud allegations. During his public rant, he said to no one in particular and everyone in the world, "You ought to go after this attorney general."[1216]

Politicians are not alone in recklessly inciting violence with disinformation. When Infowars founder Alex Jones falsely and repeatedly accused the US government of staging the 2012 mass shooting of first graders at Sandy Hook Elementary School in Newtown, Connecticut, as a pretext for taking away Americans' guns, grieving parents became the targets of death threats and vitriol.[1217]

In light of the all-too-real likelihood that someone will be incited to commit a violent crime, it is reckless for public figures to make such incendiary statements. Vitriolic messaging will naturally provoke outrage in some members of the public. Violent extremists may hear such rhetoric as a call to action. And yet, public officials persist in generating outrage based on deceptions. In the run-up to the 2022 midterm elections, candidates continued to use aggressive language in their campaign speeches. Just before winning the Maryland primary for state attorney general, Michael Peroutka told a crowd that the country was "at war," explaining that "the enemy has co-opted members and agencies and agents of our government." Other candidates ran ads in which they brandished guns.[1218] In December 2022, Representative Marjorie Taylor Greene told a group of young Republicans that she was not responsible for the January 6 attack but joked to the audience, "If Steve Bannon and I had organized that, we would have won. Not to mention, we would've been armed."[1219]

Hate Crimes

The rise of right-wing disinformation, propaganda, and organizing appears to have led to an increase in hate crimes—violations of law that are motivated by race, religion, sexual orientation, gender identity, and other demographic characteristics.[1220] Hate crimes rose steadily in recent years, with 5,599 reported to the FBI in 2014 and 8,263 in 2020.[1221] The 2020 total was the highest since 2001, when backlash from the September 11 attacks sparked a huge number of attacks against Muslims.[1222] Following Trump's election in 2016, FBI data showed what the Brookings Institution called "an anomalous spike in hate crimes concentrated in counties where Trump won by larger margins."[1223] According to statistics collected by the Anti-Defamation League, hate crimes more than doubled in counties that hosted a Trump rally in 2016.[1224] These numbers are an alarming total for a country founded on a proclaimed belief in equality.

Asian Americans

Between 2020 and 2022, researchers found an especially steep spike in hate crimes against Asian Americans;[1225] these crimes followed Trump's offensive references to the Covid-19 pandemic as the "China flu" or the "kung flu."[1226] An advocacy group known as Stop AAPI Hate reported that "harmful political rhetoric associating China with Covid-19" using "scapegoating language" contributed to the rise in hate crimes and bias incidents in 2020 and 2021 against Asian Americans. Among the crimes committed in 2021 was a string of shootings at massage spas in Georgia, where a gunman killed eight people, including six Asian American women.[1227] The shootings stirred fear in Asian American communities, which had already been subjected to a spate of hate crimes and bias incidents.

LGBTQ+ community

The far right's disinformation against the LGBTQ+ community also may have contributed to violence. Public figures have falsely equated sexual orientation and gender fluidity with pedophilia. According to the Anti-Defamation League, "this false and malicious narrative has been weaponized to label the LGBTQ+ community as 'groomers' and has fueled a slew of hostile legislation and policies aimed at erasing the discussion of LGBTQ+ related issues in schools, removing LGBTQ+ books from schools and public libraries and, especially, to ostracize, defame and harass transgender people."[1228] In Florida, Ron DeSantis's "Don't Say Gay" bill prohibited schools from discussing issues of sexual orientation or gender identity.[1229] If a child wants to know why his classmate has two moms, he'll have to ask some other kids on the playground, where the accuracy of the answers is likely to be questionable at best. In 2022, Marjorie Taylor Greene introduced legislation that would criminalize gender-affirming medical care for transgender minors, calling it "child abuse."[1230] The attack on the LGBTQ+ community is the inevitable result of the culture wars that force people to choose sides.

Some blamed this smear campaign for the mass shooting in November 2022 at Club Q, an LGBTQ+ nightclub in Colorado Springs, Colorado, that took the lives of five people and injured seventeen.[1231] The attack came in the midst of a series of anti-LGBTQ+ bills being advanced across the country and an increase in hate crimes targeting members of LGBTQ+ communities.[1232] Representative Lauren Boebert of Colorado had been an outspoken critic of transgender rights; like Greene, Boebert equated gender-affirming medical care for children with grooming them for sexual abuse.[1233] After the attack, Representative Alexandria Ocasio-Cortez (D-NY) called out Boebert for playing "a major role in elevating anti-LGBTQ+ hate rhetoric and anti-trans lies."[1234] Stephanie Vigil, a state legislator who represented a portion of the Colorado Springs area and who identifies as a member of the LGBTQ+ community, noted the increase in "lies about the grooming of children." According to Vigil, "When you start to dehumanize and slander people in this way, eventually somebody who has an inclination to violence will feel very emboldened that they're doing a good thing by carrying out violence against people like myself and many of my loved ones."[1235]

Black, Latinx, and Jewish communities

Hate speech has also contributed to mass killings in Black, Latinx, and Jewish communities. In 2022, a gunman killed ten African American shoppers at a supermarket in Buffalo, New York. According to the complaint charging the shooter, his writings included "statements that his motivation for the attack was to prevent Black people from replacing white people and eliminating the white race, and to inspire others to commit similar racially motivated attacks."[1236] In 2019, a gunman drove 650 miles to a Walmart in El Paso, Texas, and killed twenty-three people.[1237] In his manifesto, the shooter said he wanted to stop "the Hispanic invasion" of Texas.[1238] In 2018, a man shouting antisemitic slurs opened fire in a synagogue near Pittsburgh and killed eleven Jewish worshippers.[1239] According to the criminal complaint in that case, the shooter, who is white, told police he wanted to "kill Jews" because they are "committing genocide to my people."[1240] Minutes before the attack, he had posted online "I can't sit by and watch my people get slaughtered."[1241]All three attacks appear to have been motivated by some variation of the previously mentioned Great Replacement Theory, the racist disinformation used to indoctrinate white Americans with the belief that they are being systematically "replaced" in society with Jewish people and people of color.[1242] In 2021, then Fox News host Tucker Carlson said President Biden and his party were seeking to increase immigrant populations "to change the racial mix of the country" and "reduce the political power of people whose ancestors lived here."[1243] That same year, Texas lieutenant governor Dan Patrick stated that Biden and his cohort, via immigration policies, were "trying to take over our country without firing a shot,"[1244] and former House Speaker Newt Gingrich said on Fox News that "leftists" were trying to "drown" out "classic Americans" with people who know nothing about our country's history and traditions."[1245]

The Great Replacement Theory targets Jewish people as the masterminds of this alleged conspiracy. The Anti-Defamation League (ADL) noted an upswing in antisemitic violence following the election of Trump in 2016.[1246] In 2022, after announcing his campaign to seek the presidency in 2024, Trump openly dined with the rapper then known as Kanye West (now Ye), who had recently made antisemitic statements, and Nick Fuentes, an outspoken Holocaust denier.[1247] Ye had tweeted that he would "go death con 3 ON JEWISH PEOPLE."[1248] The ADL's chief executive called Trump's conduct "normalization of antisemitism."[1249]

Political Violence

In recent years, we have seen an escalation in threats, harassment, and violence against local government officials, including election and health officials whose only sins have been to tell the truth. A study published by the National League of Cities in 2021 found that "harassment, threats, and violence directed at local elected officials are rising at an alarming rate," noting that 87 percent of local officials reported an increase in attacks, with 81 percent reporting being the target of harassment, threats, or violence themselves.[1250] Local officials reported receiving threats and harassment by phone, in emails, on social media, and even in person at their homes.[1251] The study attributed the increase in threats to "increasing polarization, the spread of mis- and disinformation and the growing influence and power of social media."[1252] In addition to physical danger, mental and emotional fatigue are creating burdens that can outweigh the benefits of these jobs.[1253] This trend deters good candidates from seeking or remaining in office, degrading the quality of our leaders. In 2022, Biden blamed disinformation for the increase in political violence. "This intimidation and this violence against Democrats and Republicans and nonpartisan officials just doing their jobs," he said, "are the consequence of lies told for power and profit, lies of conspiracy and malice, lies repeated over and over that generate a cycle of anger, hate, vitriol, and even violence."[1254]

Threats, harassment, and violence also have a chilling effect on ordinary citizens, causing them to shrink from engaging in public discourse lest they invite a hostile response. Democracy depends on a candid exchange of views to reach consensus on important decisions. This can't happen if we must risk being threatened and attacked to speak our minds.

Election officials

According to a report by the Brennan Center for Justice, "disinformation has indelibly changed the lives and careers of election officials."[1255] Rusty Bowers, the GOP Speaker of Arizona's House, became a target after he refused requests from the Trump campaign to convene the state legislature and select a new slate of electors after a majority of Arizona voters had selected Biden.[1256] Bowers testified that he had received many "disturbing" threats among more than twenty thousand emails and tens of thousands of voice-mails and texts. Bowers stated that the hate messages "saturated" their offices, making it difficult to work and communicate.[1257] He said that groups would menace his family in their home on Saturdays, during a time when his daughter was "gravely ill." Groups of antagonists would drive through his neighborhood in panel trucks showing videos of Bowers and using loudspeakers to proclaim him to be "a pedophile and a pervert and a corrupt politician."[1258] Bowers also described an armed man who verbally threatened his neighbor.[1259]

In Pennsylvania, another swing state where meritless challenges to election results were filed, Al Schmidt, a GOP city commissioner on the Philadelphia County Board of Elections, became a bullseye for voters' wrath. Schmidt supervised the counting of mail-in ballots, where a Trump lead was ultimately overtaken in a Biden victory.[1260] In response, Trump tweeted, "A guy named Al Schmidt, a Philadelphia Commissioner and so-called Republican (RINO), is being used big time by the Fake News Media to explain how honest things were with respect to the Election in Philadelphia. He refuses to look at a mountain of corruption & dishonesty. We win!"[1261] Trump's false claims about Schmidt's role in a "rigged" election unleashed a torrent of messages to Schmidt threatening him, his wife, and his children by name. Many of the threats against Schmidt, who is Jewish, were antisemitic.[1262] One text message to his wife said Schmidt would be "FATALLY SHOT."[1263] Another said "HEADS ON SPIKES. TREASONOUS SCHMIDTS," and showed a photo of their home.[1264] He and his wife hired a private security firm to patrol around their home and sent their children to stay elsewhere.[1265]

Speaker of the Pennsylvania House Bryan Cutler was harassed after he rebuffed overtures from Trump campaign lawyer Rudy Giuliani following the election. Steve Bannon called for protests at Cutler's office and home.[1266] As a result, his home phone number, personal cell phone number, and personal email address were published online, exposing him to harassment to the point that he had to disconnect his home phone.[1267] Public workers are often overworked and underpaid, but threats of harm should not be part of the equation.

Poll workers

Even unelected frontline election workers were unjustly blamed for Trump's loss. In Georgia, Wandrea "Shaye" Moss, a longtime poll worker, and her mother, Ruby Freeman, an election volunteer, were the victims of threats and harassment after Trump and Giuliani accused them of engaging in election fraud.[1268] Giuliani falsely claimed that Moss and Freeman had brought in suitcases full of fake Biden ballots and counted them multiple times.[1269] He pointed to video "evidence" that he claimed showed Freeman and her daughter, who are Black, passing a USB drive between them "as if they're vials of cocaine"[1270]—throwing a little racism into the fabricated plot for good measure. In fact, Moss told the January 6 Committee that in the moment captured in that video, her mother had been handing her a mint candy.[1271] Moss testified that following

Trump and Giuliani's false accusations, she received threatening and harassing threats online.[1272] Some of the threats were racist, including one that stated she should "be glad its 2020 and not 1920,"[1273] alluding to the possibility of a lynching. She described intruders who had attempted to barge into her grandmother's home, looking for evidence of fraud.[1274] Moss and Freeman went into hiding, and Moss ultimately resigned from the Fulton County Department of Registration and Elections in 2022.[1275]

Moss and her mother were not alone. Twitter users also targeted an election contractor working for Dominion Voting Systems, the supplier of voting machines that was the subject of false claims of flipping votes from Trump to Biden.[1276] Calling the individual out by name, the tweet said, "You committed treason, may God have mercy on your soul," and included an image of a noose.[1277]

The increase in threats coincided with Trump's false claims of a stolen 2020 election but have not ended there, perhaps reflecting a normalizing of threats against public officials. Then Assistant Attorney General Kenneth Polite testified in August 2022 that the Justice Department's task force examining threats against election officials found that more than a thousand such threats had been received in the prior year.[1278] As a result of growing threats, election officials are resigning. In 2022, one in three such officials said they knew someone who was planning to leave or had left their job due to threats, and one in six said they had experienced threats personally.[1279] New Mexico's secretary of state has expressed concern that without election workers, "we will not have a democratic process."[1280]

Public health officials

Disinformation also causes problems for public health workers in mitigating the impact of emerging crises. In addition to enduring the burdens of being on the frontlines of the battle against Covid-19, these workers had to beat back disinformation about the nature of the pandemic and how best to avoid infection. The resulting threats and harassment caused many in public health to leave their jobs. Disinformation, including Trump's claims minimizing the seriousness of the virus, caused some health officers to be villainized for insisting on masking mandates and recommending vaccines. For example, one director in Colorado was the target of radio ads demanding that she be stripped of her authority.[1281] She also had her car vandalized.[1282] As government health workers were threatened and "politically scapegoated," the head of the National Association of County and City Health Officials called their resignations across the country "steady and alarming."[1283] The resignations mean loss of the expertise needed to promote community wellness and combat health risks like seasonal viruses and, God forbid, future pandemics.

School officials

The disinformation-fueled culture wars have also brought the battle to school officials. Misinformation about the Covid-19 pandemic prompted parents to fight rules mandating face masks and vaccines and made it difficult to have rational discussions about school shutdown orders.[1284] In some elementary schools, parents became irate over false claims that schools were teaching critical race theory (CRT) in an effort to make white children hate their country. Angry white parents demanded that school libraries ban books on race and slavery.[1285] One Black parent called CRT a "dog whistle and a lie," and another called it a "disinformation campaign" to fire up angry white voters.[1286] School board meetings have become scenes of heated tirades as parents verbally assault school board members for their decisions.[1287]

Disinformation in education has also led to threats of violence against school board members and teachers.[1288] And yet when the Justice Department announced efforts to combat threats against school officials in October 2021, Republican members of the Senate Judiciary Committee engaged in more disinformation, accusing Attorney General Merrick Garland of violating the First Amendment rights of parents.[1289] Senator Josh Hawley, a member of the committee, called for Garland's resignation.[1290]

Members of Congress

State and local officials are not the only public figures subject to such threats, intimidation, and violence. Members of Congress have continued to be targeted, even after the January 6 coup attempt. Following the hammer attack on Nancy Pelosi's husband, Paul, at their home in October 2022, rather than condemn political violence, some critics used the opportunity to spread more disinformation. Elon Musk posted a tweet propagating the baseless theory that the assailant was Paul Pelosi's gay lover.[1291] Others, including conservative commentator Dinesh D'Souza, called the attack a "false flag" operation, staged to garner sympathy for Pelosi.[1292] The *New York Times* counted twenty-one elected officials, candidates, and other prominent people in the GOP who participated in what it called a "misinformation loop" about the attack on Paul Pelosi, a vicious cycle that muddies facts, shifts blame, and minimizes violence.[1293]

Other members of Congress have also come under attack. Capitol Police have recorded a tenfold increase in threats against members of Congress since Trump's election in 2016, with 7,501 threats reported in 2022.[1294] And it is not just Democrats who are targets of threats and violence. In 2017, Representative Steve Scalise (R-LA) was shot at a congressional baseball practice outside of Washington, DC, by a man targeting Republicans. The shooter was part of online groups with names like "The Road to Hell Is Paved with Republicans."[1295] In 2022, Republican representatives Adam Kinzinger and Liz Cheney were censured by their party for serving on the committee investigating the January 6 attack,[1296] and Kinzinger received death threats.[1297] In 2023, a man used a baseball bat to attack two aides to Representative Gerald E. Connolly (D-VA) at his district office. The violence is causing more members of Congress to reconsider their practice of welcoming visitors into their offices, thereby reducing constituents' access to their representatives. Reducing constituents' direct interactions with their representatives only serves to increase the authority of government officials and weaken the power of the people.

Disinformation Is Threatening Our National Security

The use of disinformation threatens not only minority communities and public officials but also our national security. In addition to making us more vulnerable to attack from hostile foreign adversaries, false narratives of a rigged election destabilize our democracy and diminish our standing in the international community. What's more, enemies point to lies about a "rigged" election as evidence of the failure of democracy itself, harming all democracies across the globe.

During the hours that law enforcement resources were responding to the deadly attack at the Capitol on January 6, the eyes of America were riveted to the unfolding chaos. So were the eyes of the rest of the world. As Trump refused to budge from the seat in front of his television set, his successors to the presidency, Vice President Pence and Speaker Pelosi, were hiding in the Capitol from people who wanted to kill them. Law enforcement and military leaders were occupied in hours of indecision as Capitol Police officers engaged in hand-to-hand combat with their fellow Americans. Eventually, the National Guard was summoned to quell the unrest. Imagine if a hostile foreign adversary had taken advantage of the opportunity to attack while the Capitol was under siege?

Even long after the attack was over, the United States remains more vulnerable than it was before, because signs of government weakness create opportunities for adversaries and give copycats ideas. According to political scientists Emily Hencken Ritter and Brett V. Benson, "violent movements mobilized by an incumbent leader are uniquely dangerous for foreign relations."[1298] Even a leader's failed uprising "signals that there are intense divisions among political actors and that the institutions for protecting democracy— the press, armed forces, and law enforcement—are ineffective."[1299] We have signaled weakness to the rest of the world.

Internal conflict also distracts us from proactively addressing threats from beyond our borders. As we spend time and energy contesting election results based on a lie about a stolen election or conducting show hearings to investigate the investigators of the January 6 attack, our adversaries are spending their time and energy taking advantage of our destabilized democracy. While Trump baselessly challenged election results in December 2020, it was revealed that Russia had conducted a cyberattack on the United States earlier in the year by attaching malware to the Solar-Winds Orion software used by government agencies and private companies to monitor their computer networks.[1300] The election controversy distracted attention from our focus to respond to the attack. On January 5, 2021, the same day Steve Bannon warned that "all hell" would break loose, China arrested fifty-three pro-democracy politicians.[1301] Shortly after the January 6 attack, North Korea announced intentions to accelerate its nuclear weapons pro-gram.[1302] Political actors who continue to push false claims that the election was stolen, that the free press is the enemy of the people, or that the FBI is a "disgrace" are making it easier for our adver-saries to do harm.

Disinformation Threatens Our Status in the World

Disinformation is also harming our national security by dimin-ishing our standing as a model for democracies around the world. During the January 6 attack, our allies and adversaries alike saw for themselves a failure of the peaceful transfer of power we have taken for granted since the days of George Washington. Following the attacks, Vice President Kamala Harris said that disinformation about a stolen election had caused other countries to question our commitment to democracy.[1303] One Russian official noted that the United States had lost the moral authority to advance democracy around the world: "The United States certainly cannot now impose electoral standards on other countries and claim to be the world's 'beacon of democracy.'" [1304] Another Russian government official, Konstantin Kosachyov, echoed this claim, stating in a Facebook post that democracy in the United States had hit "rock bottom." [1305] He wrote, "America no longer charts the course and so has lost all right to set it. And, even more so, to impose it on others." [1306] He further argued that democracy in America was failing *because* of disinformation: "The losing side has more than enough grounds to accuse the winner of falsifications—it is clear that American democracy is limping on both feet." [1307] A well-functioning democracy is the source of the "soft power" that gives the United States clout around the world. [1308] When that perception shrivels, so does our global status.

Disinformation not only harms the perception of our ability to conduct free and fair elections, it also damages the strength of our country itself. Our national unity suffers when political rallygoers will proudly wear a T-shirt emblazoned with the words, "I'd rather be Russian than a Democrat." [1309] Bad actors using disinformation to sow internal strife are weakening our standing on the world stage.

Disinformation Threatens Democracies Worldwide

In a time when democracies around the world are backsliding, lies about a stolen US election threaten the vitality of democracy as a system of government. The post–World War II world order is based on advancing the cause of democracy; we participate in the NATO alliance to promote democracy in Europe. [1310] United States foreign policy has worked to spread democracy not only to benefit the citizens of particular countries but because of the belief that democracy furthers international peace and American interests abroad. [1311] As Ben Rhodes, the former deputy national security adviser, writes, as "the United States abandoned any investment in the international order under Trump, China ramped up its efforts to create its own new reality through the sheer force of its size and dogged nature of its actions."[1312] Rhodes argued that China was leading the world order by promoting an authoritarian model of government as superior to democracy.[1313] This is a dangerous turn of events for the United States. We benefit from the strength of other democracies because they reduce military threats, provide for prosperous trade partnerships, and decrease the number of migrants seeking refuge.[1314] But disinformation that elections are "rigged" undermines global confidence in democracy. Enemies of democracy can point to election denialism to argue that democracy is an ineffective form of governance. Not only do the citizens of those countries lose, so do we.

A Hindrance to Problem Solving

Disinformation not only threatens public safety and national security but makes it more difficult for our nation to confront other challenges. Our growing disdain for expertise is making it harder for us to address major problems, such as threats to public health and climate change.

Shortly after Elon Musk acquired Twitter, he began posting provocative content, perhaps to demonstrate that under his command, the social media platform would be a place where anything goes. One of his tweets in December 2022 perfectly encapsulated the political moment: "My pronouns are Prosecute/Fauci." By mocking nonbinary pronouns, Musk claimed his membership in the tribe of the far right, pushing back against growing acceptance of gender fluidity and inclusion of the LGBTQ+ community. The allusion to Fauci reinforced the war against the public health official who had become the face of the government's response to the Covid-19 pandemic; members of the far right had vilified Fauci for encouraging masking and vaccines to reduce the spread of the virus, unpopular measures for those who had "done their own research" on the internet, where charlatanism abounds. As the pandemic progressed and guidance changed in response to new data,

Fauci had changed his positions on masking and herd immunity, but critics used these evolving positions as evidence that he could not be trusted.[1315] In one tweet, Musk succeeded in insulting the LGBTQ+ community and its allies, spreading disinformation about Covid-19, and "owning the libs." It was the perfect salvo in the culture wars.

But disdain for experts is a danger of disinformation. We rely on trained experts and career government officials to protect us from all manner of harm—health crises, unsafe consumer products, traffic fatalities, workplace hazards, cyber intrusions, and threats to the environment, to name just a few. And public trust is damaged when politicians attack the credibility of experts to advance their own political agendas. According to Ruth Ben-Ghiat, the purging of experts is a hallmark of authoritarians.[1316] As she describes it, "Institutions are hollowed out, experts are driven away. Ideologues and zealots are given a place in bureaucracies. And so this leaves societies weakened. If the person's there long enough, entire generations have to be retrained. This happened after the fall of communism. Americans have been exposed to these processes in miniature. These are things that can happen even if we're not in a dictatorship."[1317]

Trump's reference to public servants as "the deep state" cast them as an entrenched cabal of bureaucratic elitists who put special interests over the will of the people. His promise to "drain the swamp" became a wildly popular chant at his campaign rallies in 2016. Trump's executive order creating "Schedule F" under the Civil Service Rules and Regulations made good on this promise by making it easier to fire civil servants in policymaking roles and replace them with loyalists.[1318] Although Biden later rescinded the executive order, the specter of its resuscitation remains a threat to good government.

In his book *The Fifth Risk*, Michael Lewis explains the attack on expertise as a product of willful ignorance.[1319] To win political approval, it is more expedient to focus on short-term goals and to ignore the kinds of long-term concerns that require input from career civil service professionals, such as refurbishing transportation infrastructure, upgrading the power grid, or maintaining the nation's nuclear program.[1320] Politicians are rejecting inconvenient truths in favor of false narratives that are consistent with their agendas. When leaders descend into disinformation, and their political allies cynically go along with their deceptions to advance their aims, good government becomes corroded from the inside, to the detriment of all the American people.

Disinformation is creating serious risks to our safety and security. It also threatens the hallmark of a free society—the rule of law.

8.

TRIAL BY COMBAT: DISINFORMATION IS ERODING THE RULE OF LAW

"We can never forget that everything Hitler did in Germany was 'legal.'"

—DR. MARTIN LUTHER KING JR.,
Letter from Birmingham Jail

"YOU ARE REPORTEDLY ABOUT to engage in an unprecedented abuse of prosecutorial authority," the letter read, "the indictment of a former president of the United States and current declared candidate for that office."[1321] The March 2023 letter to Manhattan district attorney Alvin Bragg was signed by the GOP chairs of three House committees. They were responding to reports of impending charges against Donald Trump for alleged falsification of business records, shortly before the 2016 presidential election, to conceal payment of hush money to a porn star who threatened to go public with claims of an extramarital affair. Trump's lawyer, Michael Cohen, had spent time in prison for his role in the alleged cover-up.[1322] The letter came two days after Trump had posted a statement on social media stating that he expected to be arrested soon. His post called for protests to "take our nation back," a message that echoed his calls to supporters to "Stop the Steal" on January 6, 2021.

Following Trump's March 2023 post, law enforcement agencies across the country undertook security precautions.[1323] House Judiciary Committee Chair Representative Jim Jordan (R-OH), one of the authors of the letter, called Trump's alleged conduct a "bookkeeping error."[1324] Elise Stefanik, the GOP congresswoman from New York, called possible charges "un-American," saying in a statement that "the radical Left has reached a dangerous new low of Third World countries. Knowing they cannot beat President Trump at the ballot box, the Radical Left will now follow the lead of Socialist dictators and reportedly arrest President Trump, the leading Republican candidate for President of the United States."[1325] The letter from the congressional committees demanded documents and testimony from Bragg's investigation, calling his prosecution "politically motivated." These letters and statements all came before charges even had been filed.[1326] Rather than allowing the case to run its course in court, where every defendant is guaranteed due process, Trump and his backers were demanding special treatment for a former and perhaps future president. The decision of lawmakers to rally around a member of their own party was perhaps a predictable product of the polarized political climate. But their attack on the rule of law was breathtaking.

The federal judiciary defines the rule of law as "a principle under which all persons, institutions, and entities are accountable to laws that are publicly promulgated, equally enforced, independently adjudicated, and consistent with international human rights principles."[1327] It means that no one is above the law; no one gets special treatment. To suggest that a prosecutor abuses his authority simply by charging a former president, regardless of the merits of the case, violates the rule of law.

The rule of law is a fundamental pillar of democracy. Under the rule of law, process is paramount. Results of cases are determined by evenhanded application of the law and adherence to precedent, not by the identity of any party involved or preference for a particular outcome. In a pluralistic society with wildly divergent views, the one thing that Americans have traditionally agreed on is the method for deciding our disputes—by law, not by using violence or exerting political power. Certainly, disparities have always existed in our justice system, whether through overt discrimination or implicit bias, but we strive for "equal justice under law," words etched into the face of the building that houses the US Supreme Court. Purveyors of disinformation flip the rule of law on its head, manipulating truth so that the ends justify the means. Abusing the rule of law is one of the ways leaders disguise their efforts to undermine the will of the people. As Steven Levitsky and Daniel Ziblatt write in *How Democracies Die*, "Citizens are often slow to realize that their democracy is being dismantled—even as it happens before their eyes."[1328] The rule of law is the reason I find it so alarming when Donald Trump promised to appoint "a real special prosecutor" to "go after" Joe Biden and his family.[1329] In the hands of an authoritarian, our institutions become weapons.

Throughout our history, crisis has sometimes caused us to make ill-advised decisions to bend the rule of law. During the Civil War, President Abraham Lincoln suspended the writ of habeas corpus, the legal mechanism for seeking judicial review of detention.[1330] The nation again yielded to fear after the attack on Pearl Harbor, when the US government interned Japanese Americans, and to a lesser extent German and Italian Americans, including Joe DiMaggio's mother.[1331] History teaches the danger that comes with disregarding settled law during times of crisis. When Hitler suspended Germany's constitution to advance his Nazi agenda,[1332] he used the burning of the Reichstag parliament building as cover to violate the rule of law.[1333]

In 2022, Trump posted an eerily similar sentiment online, escalating the consequences of the debunked claim that the 2020 presidential election had been stolen. "Do you throw the Presidential Election Results of 2020 OUT and declare the RIGHTFUL WINNER, or do you have a NEW ELECTION?" Trump wrote.[1334] "A Massive Fraud of this type and magnitude allows for the termination of all rules, regulations, and articles, even those found in the Constitution."[1335] Those words—from a former president and commander in chief of the United States—were a shocking repudiation of the rule of law. Expressing them publicly makes their meaning no longer unthinkable. Worse, it normalizes that approach for all who follow.

Undermining Law Enforcement

The rule of law depends on public servants to enforce it. As a former prosecutor, I have come to believe that enforcement of the law is necessary to hold accountable those who fail to comply with society's rules and to deter people from committing crimes in the future. When people see others getting away with crimes or lose confidence in the legitimacy of law enforcement agencies, they are less likely to report crimes or obey the law.[1336] Disinformation about law enforcement threatens to erode that essential public trust.

According to Ruth Ben-Ghiat, authoritarians often claim the banner of law and order, but when it comes to their method of governing, nothing could be further from the truth. As she told *Time* magazine in 2020, "We think about authoritarianism as law and order. It appeals to people who like to follow orders. But it's not just about following orders. Unfortunately, it also liberates people because the essence of authoritarianism is lawlessness. There is nothing [the authoritarian] can't get away with and many people are thrilled to be in that kind of environment."[1337] For unscrupulous political leaders, law and order is neither law nor order. It is part of a deceptive attempt to amass power and advance their agenda.

Law and order was invoked in Richard Nixon's "Southern Strategy" in the 1970s and George Bush's Willie Horton campaign ad in 1988 to manipulate racist white fears about Americans of color.[1338] Democrats have also campaigned on this theme: in 1993, Joe Biden spoke of "predators on our streets,"[1339] and in 1996, Hillary Clinton referred to "gangs of kids" as "super predators."[1340] White supremacy is the unspoken subtext of these terms. The same ploy was used in the 2020 campaign, when GOP candidates stoked white fear under the guise of promoting law and order. During the summer of 2020, as protests swept the country over the police killing of George Floyd,[1341] some politicians exploited the Black Lives Matter movement to feed the disinformation machine for their own political gain. They framed protesters as violent, even though 93 percent of Black Lives Matter demonstrations were peaceful.[1342] Facing reelection that fall, Trump portrayed the moment as a battle between good and evil when he performed his Bible stunt in Lafayette Park.[1343] By destroying nuance in important public discourse about police use of force, Trump drew a dividing line between Americans and pushed to widen the gap until everyone fell into one of two camps—the party claiming to embrace law and order or the "radical left." The Democratic Party, as inaccurately portrayed by many Republicans, consists of "woke" activists promoting lawlessness and civil unrest, advocating for police defunding, and harboring communist and socialist ideologies. Such a narrative is Team Right versus Team Lucifer, once again.

One of the harms in polarizing the public over law enforcement, of course, is that police work becomes more difficult when officers become political pawns. I spent most of my career working with law enforcement officers and know them to be a largely apolitical and highly professional group. Some officers have been properly charged for crimes involving use of excessive force, sometimes even causing death, but the vast majority of officers work long hours for modest pay in often dangerous situations to serve their communities. While some Black Lives Matter protesters villainize law enforcement due to abuses of police power in their communities and the systemic racism in the American criminal justice apparatus, some Republicans villainize the protesters, casting them as traitors and terrorists. The combined result has been a loss of public confidence in law enforcement as an institution that treats all Americans equally.

In a moment when many Americans were understandably outraged by Floyd's death, an effective leader would have called for unity and solutions. As Politico noted in November 2020, "For a brief moment after George Floyd was killed by a Minneapolis policeman in late May, some members of the GOP joined calls for change as protests exploded onto streets across the country. That moment is over."[1344] Instead, the right has continued to stoke division for political gain. The law-and-order banner was used to shroud divisive lies and push people apart.

What's more, the far right has responded to protests by enacting laws against them. In 2021, ninety-two bills were introduced to restrict the right to protest, a liberty enshrined in the First Amendment.[1345] Among the new laws was one in Tennessee that made it a crime punishable by a year in jail to obstruct a sidewalk or public street—a vague and overbroad statute that could be used against almost anyone engaged in peaceful protest, likely creating a chilling effect on public demonstrations of dissent.[1346]

Even as authoritarians claim the mantle of law and order, they work to ensure it never applies to them. Politicians who, when targeted, are deceptive about the motives of investigators and prosecutors undermine public confidence in law enforcement officers. In recent years, Trump and his loyalists have used disinformation to attack agencies charged with enforcing the law, like the Department of Justice and the Internal Revenue Service, in addition to the Manhattan district attorney's office. When Trump was under investigation for links between Russia and his 2016 presidential campaign, he repeatedly called the probe a "hoax"[1347] and a "witch hunt."[1348] He tarred the agencies conducting the investigation as "a disgrace."[1349] In 2018, Trump tweeted: "The top Leadership and Investigators of the FBI and the Justice Department have politicized the sacred investigative process in favor of Democrats and against Republicans—something which would have been unthinkable just a short time ago."[1350] In fact, an inspector general's report concluded that the Russia investigation complied with the FBI's requirements to open investigations based on factual predication and was not politically motivated.[1351]

Vitriolic rhetoric that demonizes law enforcement risks even worse consequences than noncompliance. It can also provoke attacks against law enforcement officers, such as the attempted breach of an FBI office by a Trump supporter following the search on Trump's Mar-a-Lago home after the former president suggested the FBI may have "planted" evidence.[1352] Many Republican leaders propagated Trump's messaging. Congressman Andy Biggs (R-AZ) said that the search "looked more like something you would see in the former Soviet Union."[1353] Congressman Paul Gosar (R-AZ) went so far as to say in a tweet, "We must destroy the FBI."[1354] On Fox News, then host Tucker Carlson said, "The raid on Mar-a-Lago was not an act of law enforcement, it was the opposite of that."[1355] And then, the kicker: "It was an attack on the rule of law."[1356]

When an FBI agent knocks on a door to seek information about crimes, witnesses are less likely to cooperate with officers they believe are "a disgrace." Jurors may not believe agents who testify in court after the president has accused their agency of planting evidence. As a result, our ability to enforce the rule of law erodes.

Far-right politicians have also demonized the Internal Revenue Service, criticizing funding provisions for tax enforcement activities.[1357] In 2022, conservative public officials repeated the false claim that the IRS planned to hire 87,000 new agents.[1358] In fact, the Department of Treasury estimated that funding would restore staffing at the IRS to the same levels of the 1990s. The 87,000 number represented all new employees over a ten-year period, during which 52,000 employees were expected to retire.[1359] These employees included only about 10,000 auditors; the other employees would be customer service representatives, lawyers, examiners, technicians, and seasonal employees who help process returns.[1360] Nonetheless, Representative Elise Stefanik (R-NY) was among those who used the funding to stoke fear, tweeting, "When House Republicans earn the majority, we will STOP Biden's army of 87,000 IRS agents hired to audit hardworking American families and small businesses."[1361] Other conservative politicians parroted the claim that the IRS was coming after middle-class taxpayers earning $75,000 or less annually.[1362] In fact, while some taxpayers in that bracket would be subject to audit, the focus would be on households earning more than $400,000 a year.[1363] I know from my own work with the IRS that criminal investigations focus on high-level tax cheats and money launderers, whose crimes often conceal other illegal activity. For example, in 2023, a Houston attorney was convicted in a sophisticated $18 million tax fraud scheme involving offshore bank accounts.[1364] Suggesting that the IRS is an enemy condones tax evasion and normalizes white-collar crime, subverting the rule of law.

In 2023, when the GOP-controlled House established the Select Subcommittee on the Weaponization of the Federal Government, its mission was to investigate claimed efforts to silence conservative voices.[1365] Among the items on the subcommittee's agenda were DOJ investigations into Trump and his supporters, DOJ's treatment of parents as "terrorists" for exercising their First Amendment rights at school board meetings, and the government's work with social media platforms to suppress harmful content.[1366] Democrats in Congress blasted the formation of the subcommittee. Representative Jim McGovern (D-MA) called it "a deranged ploy by the MAGA extremists who have hijacked the Republican Party and now want to use taxpayer money to push their far-right conspiracy nonsense."[1367] Representative Jerrold Nadler (D-NY) said that GOP leaders "claim to be investigating the weaponization of the federal government when, in fact, this new select subcommittee is the weapon itself."[1368] While government agencies should be subjected to appropriate oversight, the committee's agenda promised to further erode public trust in federal investigators.

Attacking the Legitimacy of the Courts

Another example of disinformation compromising the rule of law is the attack on our courts. Public confidence in the US Supreme Court reached a low mark in 2023, with only 40 percent of the public approving of the court's performance of its work.[1369] According to former FBI counterintelligence agent Asha Rangappa, public trust in the legitimacy of courts "is a necessary prerequisite for having faith in fundamental democratic ideals like equality, due process, and freedom."[1370] During the Cold War, one of the objectives of KGB influence operations was to sow distrust in the US justice system, part of an overall strategy to sow chaos within American society.[1371] Now, domestic combatants in the information war are aiming at the judiciary as well.

As a prosecutor, I was always taught to show respect to courts in public remarks. Even after an adverse ruling, it was important to acknowledge respect for the court's decision and note that reasonable minds may disagree. Trump routinely disparaged the courts, portraying judges as being loyal not to the rule of law but to the party of the president who appointed them. In addition to disparaging the judge presiding over a case involving fraud claims against his Trump University, Trump continued his assault on the credibility of the courts even after becoming president. In 2017, courts struck down part of Trump's travel ban from certain predominantly Muslim countries.[1372] The courts quickly and properly held that a provision banning even lawful permanent residents from returning from certain countries with Muslim majorities to their homes in the United States violated the due process clause of the Fifth Amendment.[1373] In response, Trump tweeted that courts were "political" and engaging in "unprecedented judicial overreach."[1374] He referred to one jurist who ruled against the ban as a "so-called judge."[1375] When a judge struck down his order to withhold funds from cities that provided sanctuary to undocumented immigrants, Trump struck again to paint judges as facilitating crime. He issued a statement that included all of the usual dog whistles for the MAGA movement: "This San Francisco judge's erroneous ruling is a gift to the criminal gang and cartel element in our country, empowering the worst kind of human trafficking and sex trafficking, and putting thousands of innocent lives at risk."[1376] Trump called the decision "yet one more example of egregious overreach by a single, unelected district judge."[1377] Of course, all federal judges are unelected. They are appointed in order to insulate them from this kind of political intimidation.

The Ninth Circuit Court of Appeals was a favorite target of Trump. In 2018, after the Ninth Circuit ruled against the Trump administration's plan barring anyone from receiving asylum unless they had crossed the US-Mexico border at an official port of entry, Trump called the decision a "disgrace."[1378] The plan had been imposed after Trump stoked fear of a "caravan" of immigrants coming across the Mexican border. While individuals may disagree over immigration issues, Trump attacked the court itself, stating, "That's not law. Every case that gets filed in the Ninth Circuit, we get beaten."[1379] Trump also attacked the judge in the case as "an Obama judge," suggesting that the outcome had been predetermined by virtue of the president who had appointed him.[1380] Trump's outburst prompted Chief Justice John G. Roberts Jr. to issue a public rebuke to defend the independence of the judiciary, stating that the United States does not have "Obama judges or Trump judges, Bush judges or Clinton judges. What we have is an extraordinary group of dedicated judges doing their level best to do equal right to those appearing before them."[1381] Trump clapped back in a series of posts on Twitter:

> Sorry Chief Justice John Roberts, but you do indeed have "Obama judges," and they have a much different point of view than the people who are charged with the safety of our country. It would be great if the 9th Circuit was indeed an "independent judiciary," but if it is why . . . are so many opposing view (on Border and Safety) cases filed there, and why are a vast number of those cases overturned. Please study the numbers, they are shocking. We need protection and security—these rulings are making our country unsafe! Very dangerous and unwise!
>
> There are a lot of CRIMINALS in the Caravan. We will stop them. Catch and Detain! Judicial Activism, by people who know nothing about security and the safety of our citizens, is putting our country in great danger. Not good![1382]

Four days later, Trump continued his tirade online, calling the Ninth Circuit "a complete and total disaster" that was "out of control, has a horrible reputation, and is overturned more than any Court in the Country, 79%, and is used to get an almost guaranteed result."[1383] Trump suggested that the court was lawlessly interfering with law enforcement and national security. "Our great Law Enforcement professionals MUST BE ALLOWED TO DO THEIR JOB!" Trump tweeted.[1384] "If not there will be only bedlam, chaos, injury and death. We want the Constitution as written!"[1385]

Trump also blasted Judge Amy Berman Jackson, the jurist who presided over the 2020 trial of his ally Roger Stone and an earlier fraud case against Trump's former campaign chair, Paul Manafort. Trump falsely claimed in a tweet that Judge Jackson had placed Manafort in "SOLITARY CONFINEMENT, something that not even mobster Al Capone had to endure."[1386] After Stone was convicted at trial for lying to Congress, witness tampering, and obstruction of justice, Trump even singled out a juror for criticism.[1387] He tweeted, "There has rarely been a juror so tainted as the forewoman in the Roger Stone case. She never revealed her hatred of 'Trump' and Stone. She was totally biased, as is the judge. . . . Miscarriage of justice. Sad to watch!"[1388]

Trump's supporters often bolstered his false claims. On one occasion, Fox News showed a photo that had been altered to make it appear that the judge who had authorized the Mar-a-Lago search was having his foot massaged by Ghislaine Maxwell, a convicted sex trafficker of underage girls.[1389] Fox later explained that it had been simply "showing a meme in jest."[1390]

These attacks on the fairness and independence of the judiciary undermine the credibility of courts and judges in the eyes of the public, leading to erosion of respect for the rule of law. They also create a danger that someone will turn criticism into action and physically attack judges or even jurors, a very real threat in light of fatal attacks on judges and their families in recent years.[1391] In 2022, a man was charged with attempting to kill Supreme Court Justice Brett

Kavanaugh at the justice's home.[1392] That same year, John Roemer, a retired judge in Wisconsin, was shot and killed in his home by a man who had appeared before the judge years earlier in a criminal case.[1393] Two years earlier, a lawyer in New Jersey who had lost his case before Judge Esther Salas in federal court came to her home disguised as a package deliverer.[1394] When her son opened the door, the lawyer fired a gun, killing the teen and wounding Salas's husband.[1395] These murders appeared to be tied to the performance of the judges' official duties in court. In the long run, risk to their own safety or the lives of their family members may prevent good people from serving as judges or jurors, roles that are essential to the rule of law.

Disinformation from other sources is also contributing to the loss of public confidence in the Supreme Court. Gamesmanship in appointments to the Supreme Court was likely a factor in its diminishing share of public trust. When Barack Obama nominated Merrick Garland to the Court in March 2016, following the unexpected death of Justice Antonin Scalia, Senate Majority Leader Mitch McConnell refused to hold a confirmation hearing. Although the election was a full eight months away,[1396] McConnell said he was "following a long-standing tradition of not fulfilling a nomination in the middle of a presidential year."[1397] In fact, there was no such tradition.[1398] Trump was elected, and he appointed Neil Gorsuch to fill the vacancy. McConnell's lie became even more apparent four years later, when Justice Ruth Bader Ginsburg died in September, only *two* months before the 2020 election, and McConnell held a confirmation hearing for Amy Coney Barrett after she was nominated by Trump.[1399] McConnell's brazen hypocrisy created a conservative supermajority on the Court, which led to decisions such as *Dobbs v. Jackson Women's Health Organization* in 2022, overturning *Roe v. Wade*, the landmark case that had protected the right to an abortion during the first trimester of pregnancy.[1400] For some conservatives, overturning *Roe* was a dream come true, but it came at a great cost to the credibility of the court. In the minds of many members of the public, the court's decision to disregard almost fifty years of precedent and reverse *Roe* on the grounds that it was "egregiously wrong"[1401] undermined the court's fidelity to the rule of law. McConnell's lies had set the stage.

The following term, the court gutted affirmative action programs in higher education[1402] and prohibited enforcement of a Colorado antidiscrimination law, rulings that adversely affected people of color and the LGBTQ+ community.[1403] In the latter case, *303 Creative LLC v. Elenis*, the court sided with a website designer who challenged a state law that prohibited businesses from discriminating against customers on the basis of sexual orientation and other factors. The designer had alleged that the law would require her to accommodate requests for wedding websites for same-sex marriages, which she opposed on religious grounds. The court held that the law's antidiscrimination requirement violated the designer's First Amendment rights by compelling her to engage in creative speech she opposed. In dissent, Justice Sonia Sotomayor likened the outcome to segregated hotels in the Jim Crow South and signs outside businesses in another era stating, "No dogs or Jews allowed."[1404] Although the October 2022 term also saw the majority reject a conservative fringe election-law argument known as the "independent state legislature" theory, which would have given state legislatures free rein to set election rules without judicial review,[1405] the court in recent years has taken a sharp right turn. These recent rulings shed new light on the testimony of Chief Justice Roberts during his confirmation hearings in 2005, when he famously said that he had no agenda and that the role of a justice was like that of an umpire, to simply "call balls and strikes."[1406] Even though Roberts may have been calling them as he saw them, these particular cases came before the court only because the justices selected them for review. Roberts and the rest of the majority chose to decide cases that addressed pet conservative causes in ways that benefitted those causes, and which had profound negative consequences for women, minorities, lower-income students, and members of the LGBTQ+ community. Real umpires don't get to choose their pitchers.

On the last day of the term in June 2023, a clearly exasperated Justice Elena Kagan criticized her conservative colleagues in a scathing dissent in a case striking down student loan relief.[1407] "From the first page to the last," Kagan wrote, "today's opinion departs from the demands of judicial restraint."[1408] She argued that the court ignored the lack of standing by the challenging party to reach a question that should have been a matter of public policy left to the political branches of government. The court, Kagan wrote, "by deciding this case, exercises authority it does not have. It violates the Constitution."[1409] By overplaying their hand because they have the power to do so, the justices in the majority have diminished the court's credibility.

Normalizing Corruption

Disinformation about corruption also threatens to undermine the rule of law. Accepting bribes, extorting kickbacks, and defrauding victims are serious crimes that harm the public by putting politicians' personal enrichment over the best interests of the public they purport to serve. Corrupt government officials must be held accountable, to signal society's moral condemnation of their abuse of trust and to deter similar illegal conduct in the future.

But as president, Trump used his pardon power to grant clemency to corrupt public officials, loyalists, and even—over the objection of Pentagon officials—military members who had been court-martialed on charges of murder.[1410] Pardons are intended to show mercy to people who are deserving of forgiveness for their crimes. By handing out pardons to corrupt political operatives and public officials, Trump sent a false message about them and the seriousness of their conduct that corroded respect for the rule of law.

Defendants convicted of some form of public corruption made up a significant percentage of the recipients of Trump's grants of clemency, suggesting that their conduct was not criminal but just politics as usual. Trump granted clemency to former Illinois governor Rod Blagojevich, former Detroit mayor Kwame Kilpatrick, and four former members of Congress, Duncan Hunter, Chris Collins, Steve Stockman, and Rick Renzi,[1411] who were all convicted of bribery, extortion, fraud, theft, and/or insider trading. North Carolina GOP chair Robin Hayes and former California legislator Randy "Duke" Cunningham also received clemency from their bribery convictions.[1412]

In addition to normalizing the corruption of others, Trump also used his pardon power to reward loyalists, demonstrating that clemency was based not simply on an offender's conduct and remorse but also on fealty to Trump himself. Trump's recipients of clemency—either through pardons or commutations of their sentence—included his former aides and advisers Steve Bannon, Paul Manafort, Roger Stone, George Papadopoulos, and Michael Flynn.[1413] Charles Kushner, the father of Trump's son-in-law Jared Kushner, received a pardon, as did Elliott Broidy, a Trump fundraiser.[1414] In 2022, Trump said that if he were reelected, he would consider pardoning the defendants charged for attacking the Capitol on January 6, 2021.[1415]

Trump even corrupted the pardon process itself, bypassing DOJ's Office of the Pardon Attorney, which uses a rigorous protocol to ensure uniformity in decisions about who gets pardons and under what circumstances, and failing to follow the normal waiting period of five years after conviction or release from prison, whichever comes later.[1416] Instead, Trump appeared to dole out pardons to people to advance his political interests, pardoning some defendants before their cases went to trial. Trump's first pardon went to Sheriff Joe Arpaio, convicted of contempt of court for using his office to engage in racial profiling of undocumented immigrants even after a court ordered him to stop—a blatant violation of the rule of law.[1417] The move was sure to curry favor with immigration hard-liners. Trump even pardoned some defendants, but not others, charged with the same conduct in the very same case. Trump pardoned Bannon for alleged fraud in soliciting funds to build a wall on the border with Mexico, but not Bannon's codefendants, all of whom were later convicted by trial or guilty plea.[1418] By giving clemency to allies and corrupt public officials, Trump sent a message that corruption in politics is nothing unusual and that power and loyalty matter more than process. Lies about corruption in government provide license for bad behavior by public officials and undermines respect for the rule of law.

Terrorism by Another Name

When people lose trust in law enforcement and courts, they may become inclined to bypass the law completely. In the United States, disinformation about unaddressed criminal conduct is sparking some people to address perceived wrongs with violence.

Our nation has an ugly history of racial violence. Ku Klux Klan members used violence to intimidate communities of color following the Civil War, during the civil rights movement of the 1960s, and beyond. Lynch mobs terrorized and brutally murdered Black men who prospered in business, were active in politics, or associated with white women.[1419] Today, vigilante violence is being kindled by disinformation. While some people read fantastic claims and know them to be false, others are deceived or are pushed toward more extreme beliefs. When they see law enforcement authorities or courts failing to stop what they believe to be serious criminal conduct, some channel their outrage into action. Violence is perhaps the inevitable result of disinformation that stokes paranoid visions of a changing America overrun with sexual predators and dangerous criminals. Information warfare, as Renée DiResta writes, renders civilians into either combatants or targets.[1420]

For example, in 2016, an armed North Carolina man was arrested after he fired an assault rifle in a Washington, DC, pizza parlor.[1421] Armed with an AR-15, two other guns, and a knife, he had traveled from his home to "self-investigate" an alleged conspiracy that children were being held captive there by a sex ring led by Hillary Clinton,[1422] a virulent bit of disinformation that had been pushed online by both "fabricators and wide-eyed believers."[1423] The origin of the "Pizzagate" scandal is unknown, but it was discussed on social media by Russian accounts, bots, and right-wing extremists, including the son of Trump's former national security adviser Michael Flynn, propagandist Alex Jones, and members of the QAnon movement.[1424] While many people who read such claims laugh at their absurdity, the susceptible become indoctrinated. When the believer is someone inclined toward acts of aggression, the consequences can be deadly.

During the summer of 2020, as Trump and other politicians exploited tensions following the killing of George Floyd, some conservatives not only failed to condemn racialized violence against communities of color but celebrated it. For example, an Illinois teen became the poster child for the ideal of white gun enthusiasts defending their country against internal threats. In August, a Black man was shot and left paralyzed by police in Kenosha, Wisconsin, sparking protests and civil unrest.[1425] In the following days, peaceful protests turned violent, with rioters throwing objects at law enforcement officers, setting fires, and smashing windows to loot businesses.[1426] Right-wing media capitalized on the moment to discredit the Black Lives Matter movement by showing nonstop coverage of the mayhem. According to researcher Joan Donovan, who studies online extremism, video footage inspired vigilantes to "live out fantasies of taking justice into their own hands."[1427] A former city alderman called for "patriots" to defend Kenosha from "evil thugs."[1428] Seventeen-year-old Kyle Rittenhouse traveled from his Illinois home just across the state line to Kenosha as one of the "peacekeepers" who answered the call; he brought along an AR-15-style semi-automatic assault rifle.[1429] That night, he killed two men and wounded another,[1430] a foreseeable consequence of an untrained civilian responding to a volatile situation. Rittenhouse was charged criminally for the shootings but was acquitted at trial, becoming a hero to the far right in the process.[1431] Even before the verdict, he was glorified as an admirable defender of an American city against woke activism by exercising his Second Amendment rights. As Tucker Carlson said on air, "How shocked are we that seventeen-year-olds with rifles decided they had to maintain order when no one else would?"[1432] T-shirts appeared bearing images of Rittenhouse and his gun.[1433] J. D. Vance, as a candidate for the US Senate in Ohio, posted a series of tweets, including one that said, "Our leaders abandoned this kid's community to lawless thug rioters, and he did something about it, and now a lawless thug prosecutor is trying to destroy his life."[1434] In another tweet, Vance said, "We leave our boys without fathers. We let the wolves set fire to their communities. And when human nature tells them to go and defend what no one else is defending, we bring the full weight of the state and the global monopolists against them."[1435] Three conservative members of Congress jumped on the Rittenhouse bandwagon by offering him an internship, even though he had expressed no interest in one.[1436] Representative Marjorie Taylor Greene introduced a bill to award Rittenhouse a Congressional Gold Medal.[1437] Conservative commentator Michelle Malkin tweeted, "ALL THE BEST PEOPLE #Stand WithKyle. It's now or never . . . and yes, it's war."[1438] Their support for Rittenhouse's conduct was a shocking affront to the rule of law.

Information warfare also led to the 2020 kidnapping plot against Michigan governor Gretchen Whitmer. In that case, members of a militia group called the Wolverine Watchmen and some associates were charged in the scheme.[1439] As part of their plan, they wanted to take her to a "secure location" in Wisconsin and put her on "trial."[1440] The conspiracy was motivated by perceived violations of their constitutional rights caused by the governor's stay-home orders during the Covid-19 pandemic.[1441] Disinformation deepened a divide over the public health response to Covid. The seriousness of the pandemic was downplayed by Trump, who refused to wear a mask even during the days before vaccines, when the virus was raging,[1442] and claimed that Democrats were overstating the risk just to make him look bad.[1443] (It was no surprise that Trump himself contracted the virus in October 2020.[1444]) The indictment alleged that the kidnapping plot began in June 2020, two months after Trump had tweeted, "LIBERATE MICHIGAN!"[1445] Even after the arrest of the defendants, Trump called the charges "fake" during a speech at a conservative conference and told the audience, "Gretchen Whitmer was in less danger than the people in this room right now, it seems to me."[1446] Trump's failure in that moment to condemn political violence was another blow to the rule of law.

Of course, the most serious of these vigilante attacks occurred on January 6, 2021, when thousands of people stormed the Capitol to rectify what they had been led to believe was a stolen election. According to Representative Liz Cheney (R-WY), vice chair of the House Select Committee that investigated the attack, Trump "summoned the mob, assembled the mob and lit the flame of this attack."[1447] Indeed, during his speech that day, Trump stoked outrage with disinformation about a stolen election. He described a "rigged" and "corrupt" election, "an egregious assault on our democracy" that was enabled by biased news media: "All of us here today do not want to see our election victory stolen by emboldened radical-left Democrats, which is what they're doing. And stolen by the fake news media."[1448]

Trump tapped into the crowd's grievances and fears of replacement. He warned that "they" want to take down or rename the monuments to George Washington, Thomas Jefferson, and Abraham Lincoln.[1449] He told his supporters, "You're the real people, you're the people that built this nation." He said, "Our country has been under siege for a long time. Far longer than this four-year period." Trump referred to his predecessor as "Barack Hussein Obama," including the forty-fourth president's middle name to signal his "otherness." Trump further appealed to bigotry by saying, "They also want to indoctrinate your children in school by teaching them things that aren't so."[1450]

The speech included a call to action: "We will never give up, we will never concede. It doesn't happen. You don't concede when there's theft involved. . . . We will not let them silence your voices. We're not going to let it happen, I'm not going to let it happen. . . . Because you'll never take back our country with weakness. You have to show strength and you have to be strong. . . ." Otherwise, he warned, "You will have an illegitimate president. That's what you'll have. . . . We must stop the steal and then we must ensure that such outrageous election fraud never happens again, can never be allowed to happen again."[1451]

Many heard Trump's words as a command from the president and commander-in-chief to take the law into their own hands. The January 6 mob then stormed barricades, assaulted police officers, broke windows, and rammed doors to gain entry. Some carried weapons.[1452] Others brought zip ties.[1453] Dustin Thompson, an Ohio man who was convicted of a felony, among other changes, for his role in storming the Capitol that day, testified at his trial that he had gone down a rabbit hole of disinformation online that led him to believe that the election had been stolen.[1454] When Vice President Mike Pence refused to go along with Trump's public demands to stop the certification during the joint session of Congress, the mob at the Capitol chanted, "Hang Mike Pence!"[1455] A gallows had already been erected outside the Capitol.[1456] Even after the coup attempt, right-wing media outlets claimed the attack was a "false flag" operation, conducted by Trump's enemies to discredit him.[1457]

If an election really were stolen, of course, the lawful way to contest it would be with election audits and lawsuits. The rule of law demands that we resolve our differences through the legal system and not through violence. By January 6, Trump had already lost his legal challenges to the election.[1458] The attack on January 6 was an effort to use brute force to bypass the rule of law and accomplish regime change—the definition of a coup.

Political violence continued into the 2022 midterm elections, with armed men wearing camouflage fatigues "guarding" ballot boxes in Arizona.[1459] They apparently believed unproven claims about ballot-box stuffing and decided to take the matter into their own hands. The League of Women Voters brought a lawsuit against the group, known as Clean Elections USA, complaining that members of the group had recorded voters on video and followed them after they had cast their ballot.[1460] Following complaints of voter intimidation, a judge ordered members of the group to stay at least 250 feet away from ballot boxes,[1461] a minor triumph for the rule of law.

The Militia Menace

Among the attackers on January 6 were members of white nationalist militia groups—the Proud Boys, the Oath Keepers, and Three Percenters. According to the Anti-Defamation League, the militia movement reemerged in the United States following the election of Barack Obama in 2008.[1462] Indeed, when I served as US attorney, the FBI special agent in charge of the Detroit division, Andy Arena, frequently said in public remarks that the militia movement had roared back to life with the election of our nation's first Black president. The Three Percenter movement was founded in 2008, and proclaim themselves "patriots" who protect Americans from government tyranny.[1463] The Oath Keepers, formed in 2009, recruit former members of law enforcement and the military to build a network of state militias.[1464] According to Sam Jackson, a scholar on extremism, the Oath Keepers have transformed from a fringe group to a national movement.[1465] Their core beliefs are the right to bear arms and the freedom to decide which federal laws to obey,[1466] the antithesis of the rule of law. The Proud Boys were established in 2016 and describe themselves as "Western chauvinists" who reject "political correctness" and endorse "the anti-white guilt agenda."[1467]

During the House Select Committee's hearings on the January 6 attack, Jason Van Tatenhove, the Oath Keepers' former communications director, testified that the Oath Keepers are Holocaust-denying racists.[1468] According to Van Tatenhove, the Oath Keepers' strategy "doesn't necessarily include the rule of law . . . it includes violence. It includes trying to get their way through lies, through deceit, through intimidation and through the perpetration of violence."[1469]

The very existence of private militia groups is based on disinformation.[1470] Kathleen Belew, a history professor who studies violent far-right extremism, refers to the groups not as "militias" but as "extralegal, unregulated private armies."[1471] They operate outside the law, free from the oversight of the US military or any law enforcement agency. According to Belew, the word "militia" is a misnomer for these groups because it falsely suggests some constitutional foundation in the Bill of Rights. But the "militia" referred to in the Second Amendment is one that is "well-regulated." The militia referenced in the Constitution is now the National Guard, part of the government itself.[1472] According to the Institute for Constitutional Advocacy and Protection at Georgetown University Law Center, "All 50 states prohibit private, unauthorized groups from engaging in activities reserved for the state militia, including law enforcement activities.[1473]

Online disinformation is helping to fuel the militia movement and normalize their extreme views.[1474] As discussed earlier, research shows that algorithms are designed to amplify the loudest voices, and this applies equally to the militia movement. According to Karen Kornbluh, director of the Digital Innovation and Democracy Initiative at the German Marshall Fund, "The more incendiary the material, the more it keeps users engaged, the more it is boosted by the algorithm."[1475] In experiments, researchers found that when a user explored militant movements, they received suggestions to view videos about militia organizing, weapons, ammunition, and tactical gear.[1476]

According to Catrina Doxsee, a researcher at the Center for Strategic and International Studies, militia groups "justify violent action by the alleged existential threat from socialists and globalists believed to be associated with the Democratic Party."[1477] Citing a 2021 threat assessment of the Office of the Director of National Intelligence, Doxsee posits that the threat posed by militia extremists in the United States is escalating, driven by their belief in government overreach, conspiracy theories, and perceived legitimization from authority figures.[1478] International terrorism expert Arie Perliger, who has studied violent extremists in Israel and Germany, has said that these groups are emboldened when political leaders encourage or tolerate violence to support their party.[1479] Segments of the GOP increasingly embrace and legitimize militia groups. In 2018, the Metropolitan Republican Club in Manhattan hosted the founder of the Proud Boys for a speech.[1480] The chairman of the Wyoming Republican Party is an open member of the Oath Keepers, as is Mark Finchem, the former state representative and election denier in Arizona who ran unsuccessfully for secretary of state.[1481] Republican groups in Oregon and Colorado have hired militia groups for security.[1482] Members of the Oath Keepers provided private security on January 6, 2021, for Trump ally Roger Stone;[1483] Congresswoman Marjorie Taylor Greene used a militia member for security at a Georgia rally in 2021.[1484] During the hearings of the January 6 Committee, a video recording showed Stone reciting the Proud Boys' "fraternal creed": "I'm a Western chauvinist," he said, "and I refuse to apologize for the creation of the modern world."[1485]

In one 2020 presidential debate, Trump refused an invitation to condemn white supremacists and militia groups.[1486] Instead, he doubled down, saying, "Proud Boys—stand back and stand by."[1487] Members of the group celebrated Trump's words online as validation of their tactics, even using them as a recruiting tool.[1488] The Proud Boys appear to have answered Trump's call when they stormed the Capitol on January 6. Members of the Oath Keepers and Proud Boys were convicted of seditious conspiracy for their roles in the attack, found to have used force to oppose the authority of the United States government in the lawful transition of presidential power.[1489] Upon the conviction of the Oath Keepers, an FBI official appropriately noted that they had "flouted and trampled the rule of law."[1490]

In March 2023, Trump seemingly embraced members of the militia movement when he held the first political rally of his campaign for the 2024 presidential election. He chose to locate the rally in Waco, Texas, during the thirtieth anniversary of the confrontation between government agents and the paramilitary cult group known as the Branch Davidians.[1491] In 1993, federal agents had been investigating the group's leader, David Koresh, and others for manufacturing and possessing machine guns and destructive devices.[1492] When agents came to the cult's compound in late February to execute a search warrant, Koresh and his followers responded with gunfire, killing four agents and wounding twenty others.[1493] On April 19, after a fifty-one-day standoff, federal agents used tear gas in an attempt to force members to surrender.[1494] Instead, cult members set the compound on fire, and seventy members of the group, including children, died.[1495]

Some members of the militia movement saw that event as a call to action against government overreach. According to Belew, far-right extremists "understood Waco as a massacre carried out by a rampant superstate and its corrupt agents" against innocent martyrs.[1496] Among the people who would travel to Waco to bear witness to the siege was Timothy McVeigh.[1497] According to lawyer and writer Jeffrey Toobin, Waco became "a psychological obsession" for McVeigh.[1498] Two years after the siege, to the day, McVeigh bombed the Alfred P. Murrah Federal Building in Oklahoma City, killing 168 people, including 19 infants and toddlers in the building's day-care center.[1499] McVeigh called the children's deaths "collateral damage" of military action.[1500]

The government attack on the compound in Waco remains a rallying cry for the militia movement, including the Proud Boys and Oath Keepers.[1501] Stuart Wright, a sociology professor who is an expert on the standoff, calls Waco "a touchstone for the far right."[1502] Choosing Waco as the site for Trump's political rally, Wright said, would have "some deep symbolism."[1503] A Trump campaign spokesman denied that Waco was chosen for any reason other than its location in central Texas, but some of Trump's supporters said they saw parallels between what they perceived as government overreach against the Branch Davidians then and against Trump in 2023, when the former president was the focus of multiple criminal investigations.[1504] Whether the choice was a deliberate effort to connect with antigovernment extremists or a mere coincidence, the campaign's failure to acknowledge the sensitivity of the location demonstrated a recklessness in Trump's regard for national security and public safety.

The Insurrection Theory of the Second Amendment

A key tenet of the militia movement is the false claim that the Second Amendment protects the right of the people to take up arms against our government. At the rally in Washington on January 6, 2021, a man sold US flags emblazoned with words he attributed to George Washington: "A free people ought not only to be armed and disciplined but they should have sufficient arms and ammunition to maintain a status of independence from any who might attempt to abuse them, which would include their own government."[1505] There is no evidence that George Washington ever said any such thing.[1506] And yet, public officials parrot similar sentiments: Representative Chip Roy (R-TX) has said that the Second Amendment was "designed purposefully to empower the people to resist the force of tyranny used against them."[1507] In fact, of course, nothing could be further from the truth. As Representative Jamie Raskin (D-MD), a former constitutional law professor, has noted, the Constitution does not promote insurrection or rebellions.[1508] Instead, it recognizes them as dangerous crimes.[1509] In fact, the Constitution gives Congress the power to call up real militias, government-sponsored bodies, "to *suppress* insurrections."[1510] The Constitution also guarantees that the federal government will protect states against "domestic violence."[1511]

The Constitution makes it clear that insurrection is forbidden— the Fourteenth Amendment disqualifies anyone from serving in state or federal office who has previously taken an oath to serve the public and then engages in insurrection or rebellion.[1512] The idea that the Constitution promotes insurrection is dangerous disinformation. Oath Keepers leader Stewart Rhodes, one of those convicted in the attack, had called on Trump to invoke the Insurrection Act to call up his group and other private paramilitary groups to overturn the 2020 election by force.[1513] In fact, the Insurrection Act authorizes the president to use the National Guard—not private entities—to quell civil unrest.[1514] The militia movement conflates the Declaration of Independence, a notice of revolution, with the Constitution, our blueprint for governing. Using force against our own government would be, like the shot heard round the world, an act of war.

This disinformed view of the Second Amendment as authorizing citizen uprisings against the government is also used to promote the possession of assault weapons. While fair-minded people may disagree about the need for guns for protection or hunting, it is impossible for me to defend civilian possession of semiautomatic assault weapons, such as the AR-15, the weapon of choice for mass shooters.[1515] AR-15s were used in hate-fueled massacres in Buffalo, Pittsburgh, El Paso, and numerous other mass shootings.[1516] These weapons are designed for combat purposes of dispatching large numbers of enemy soldiers quickly and efficiently. What possible reason could justify civilian ownership of such lethal firearms? Under the twisted insurrection theory of the Constitution promoted by the far right, assault weapons are needed to match the firepower of the military.[1517] If the people have a right to overthrow their government, this warped thinking goes, then they need the most powerful weapons that exist. Politicians amplify these claims as part of the culture wars. Representative Matt Gaetz (R-FL) has said that the Second Amendment "is about maintaining within the citizenry the ability to maintain an armed rebellion against the government, if that becomes necessary."[1518] On the contrary, the Supreme Court has rejected the idea that the Constitution prohibits the government from regulating dangerous guns. Even the conservative Supreme Court justice Antonin Scalia wrote in 2008 in *District of Columbia v. Heller*, "the right secured by the

Second Amendment is not unlimited," and is "not a right to keep and carry any weapon whatsoever in any manner whatsoever and for whatever purpose."[1519] The idea that the people need assault weapons so that they can overthrow their own government is dangerous disinformation that negates the rule of law and threatens our national security.

Members of the far right use gun imagery to signal their membership in a club that embraces, in their estimation, Christianity and traditional values. Wrapping guns in religion is part of the campaign for the hearts and minds of conservative Christians. Weapons makers in Georgia, Colorado, Florida, and Missouri even advertise their commitment to their faith in their marketing materials:[1520] Daniel Defense, a gun company that manufactures assault rifles and other firearms, markets its products via online images depicting guns and crosses along with religious scripture.[1521] One post showed a toddler with a rifle above a Bible verse reading, "Train up your child in the way he should go, and when he is old, he will not depart from it."[1522] It is repugnant to many that a verse from the Book of Proverbs about learning to live a virtuous life could be appropriated to promote deadly weapons. Likewise, a gunmaker in Florida sells an assault rifle emblazoned with a passage from the Book of Psalms: "Blessed be the Lord, my Rock, who trains my hands for war and my fingers for battle."[1523] According to the company's Facebook page, the passage appears on the gun to ensure that "no Muslim terrorist can use [it] to murder innocent people."[1524]

Politicians have also used guns to demonstrate their bona fides as members of the far-right tribe. According to the BBC, guns dominated GOP campaign ads in 2022.[1525] One ad for Arizona Senate candidate Blake Masters showed him firing what he called "the James Bond gun" in the desert, proclaiming it "fun" and "pretty cool."[1526] In December 2021, Representative Thomas Massie (R-KY) posted a photo on Twitter showing him with his wife and children brandishing assault weapons with the caption, "Merry Christmas!

Ps. Santa, please bring ammo."[1527] The post came shortly after a mass shooting at a high school in Michigan.[1528] Congresswoman Lauren Boebert (R-CO) responded to the tweet by saying, "That's my kind of Christmas card!" She then posted a photo of her family members wielding assault weapons.[1529]

We saw a similar glamorization of guns by the far right to fight back against nationwide Black Lives Matter protesters in the summer of 2020. In addition to Kyle Rittenhouse in Kenosha, a white couple stood in their front yard in St. Louis, Missouri, and pointed guns at demonstrators who were marching down the street past their home.[1530] Mark McCloskey brandished an AR-15-style rifle, and his wife, Patricia McCloskey, pointed a semi-automatic pistol at protesters.[1531] Mark McCloskey later stated, "Any time the mob approaches me, I'll do what I can to put them in imminent threat of physical injury, because that's what kept them from destroying my house and my family."[1532] The couple became heroes to the far right, even after they were convicted of misdemeanor charges for their actions.[1533] Trump and other Republicans blasted the city prosecutor for filing charges.[1534] Missouri's Republican governor pardoned the couple.[1535] Later that summer, they were invited to speak at the Republican National Convention, where they warned of the dangers of "Marxist liberals." "Make no mistake," Patricia McCloskey said, "no matter where you live, your family will not be safe in the radical Democrats' America."[1536] High-powered guns have become a symbol of right-wing intolerance of equality in America.

Coups d'État

The insurrection theory of the Second Amendment distorts the rule of law by endorsing the use of physical force to overthrow the government, overriding the rules for forming and modifying our democratic institutions. Instead of using the constitutional methods to replace elected officials—elections and impeachment—

adherents of the insurrection theory believe in the right to remove leadership through violence. The Three Percenter movement, which draws its name from the false claim that the American Revolution was fought by only 3 percent of colonists,[1537] has a motto: "When tyranny becomes law, rebellion becomes duty."[1538] Under certain circumstances, the motto does not just permit a coup, it *demands* one.

Coups are not unknown in the United States. In 1898, white citizens in Wilmington, North Carolina, took up arms against their city government.[1539] Black Americans made up a majority of the population in Wilmington, where they thrived in businesses and held a number of elected offices.[1540] Following the election of 1898, avowed white supremacists, including members of the Democratic Party and its enforcers, known as the "Red Shirts," began a campaign to intimidate Black leaders and their white Republican allies.[1541] On November 10 of that year, white attackers swept through town, setting fires and shooting Black men.[1542] The mob forced the resignations of the mayor, police chief, and aldermen at gunpoint.[1543] They replaced the city council and ran prominent leaders out of town.[1544] The new mayor was a Confederate officer and former congressman who had led the violent overthrow of the city's government. To the white supremacy movement, their coup was a success.[1545] Coups and attempts have also occurred in Rhode Island,[1546] Texas,[1547] Arkansas,[1548] Louisiana,[1549] and McMinn County, Tennessee.[1550]

Coups are not a thing of the past, even in democracies. In February 2021, in Myanmar,[1551] military leaders used force to prevent the swearing-in of the party that had been elected by the people the prior November.[1552] On the day the newly elected parliament was scheduled to convene, the military commander in chief seized power, and the acting president invalidated the results of the election, detained elected leaders, and declared a state of emergency.[1553] In fact, elections had been cancelled in parts of the country engaged in conflict, and members of the Muslim Rohingya minority had been denied the right to vote in the majority Buddhist nation.[1554]

United Nations investigators had accused Myanmar's military of killing the Rohingya with "genocidal intent."[1555] The US State Department said that the military's claims of widespread voter fraud were false and called the election "flawed but legitimate."[1556] When the coup triggered mass demonstrations, peaceful protesters were killed and thousands of Myanmar's citizens were arrested and jailed in the upheaval that followed.[1557]

In Germany in 2022, police disrupted an alleged coup attempt by a far-right group called "citizens of the Reich," who reject the legitimacy of the post–World War II government, as do German QAnon adherents.[1558] The group allegedly planned to storm parliament, execute the chancellor, and overthrow the government.[1559] The effort in Germany was motivated by global conspiracy theories surrounding Jews and the coronavirus.[1560]

In January 2023, Brazilians stormed their capital in a scene eerily similar to the January 6 coup attempt in the United States.[1561] Following the election in October 2022 that ousted far-right president Jair Bolsonaro, his supporters demanded that the military overturn the results.[1562] Police arrested more than 1,200 protesters.[1563] The *New York Times* reported at the time that the attack was motivated by the belief that the election had been "rigged," despite "audits and analyses by experts finding nothing of the sort."[1564] The *Times* reported that for years Bolsonaro and his allies had spread conspiracy theories and made misleading statements claiming that Brazil's voting system was corrupt.[1565] As a result, millions of Brazilians became convinced that the claims were true.[1566]

In 2021, our institutions were tested and held. Since then, the far right—including a heavily armed militia movement[1567]—has continued to test our democracy on multiple fronts. Disinformation has indoctrinated many Americans to believe that their rights and privileges are under existential threat and that saving them justifies violating the rule of law, including with violence. Equal justice demands evenhanded policing, resolution of disputes in courts, punishment for corruption, and use of the ballot box to choose and remove our leaders. Without it, power and violence will increasingly control our fates and erode our sovereignty. As the English philosopher John Locke said, "Wherever law ends, tyranny begins."[1568]

9.

WE ALONE CAN FIX IT: PROPOSED SOLUTIONS

"We choose to go to the moon in this decade
and do the other things not because they are easy
but because they are hard."

—PRESIDENT JOHN F. KENNEDY

IN 1900, FOR EVERY 1,000 babies born in the United States, 100 of them would die before reaching their first birthdays.[1569] Each tragic death was a family's heartbreak. For many parents, childhood mortality was a sad reality of life. But by the end of the century, the rate dropped to less than 0.1 deaths per 1,000 births.[1570] It was not just one solution but many solutions that led to the sharp decline: innovations in medicine, clean water, and sewage disposal all contributed to the dramatic improvement.[1571] Human ingenuity had found ways to substantially mitigate a serious problem.

The tandem threats of authoritarianism and disinformation can seem overwhelming, but we as a nation have solved big problems before. The stakes for democracy are simply too high to ignore them or to surrender to despair. Unless we take action, democracy in the United States seems destined to fail, and our sovereignty as citizens will perish with it. Along the way, elections will be compromised. Authoritarian figures will come into power. Dissenters will face political intimidation and violence. Disinformation will hamper our ability to solve challenges like climate change, pandemics, and wealth disparities. Raw power will replace the rule of law. Discredited and weaponized, civilian law enforcement and courts will lose legitimacy, leading to more crime and corruption. In their place, private paramilitary groups will use violence to achieve their goals over those who are weaker. Political violence and assassination will become increasingly frequent. Advancing technology will increase surveillance and militarize policing. Disinformation and the threat of new forms of totalitarian control are unlikely to ever be completely eradicated, but given the stakes, we must take affirmative steps to diminish them to the maximum degree.

The good news is that most problems created by humans can be solved by humans. We have figured out how to prevent polio and, as John F. Kennedy promised, to send a person to the moon. We can invest resources and devote American ingenuity to researching the best ways to stop disinformation. But addressing problems requires consensus, which is difficult to achieve without agreeing to a shared set of facts. In fact, at the moment, America seems to be going in the exact opposite direction of solving problems of disinformation and hyperpartisan political rhetoric, and so we have to ask ourselves: What will it take for us to change? Americans are understandably skeptical of any efforts that could hamper free speech. As discussed earlier, when the Department of Homeland Security set up its Disinformation Governance Board to counter disinformation, it was immediately accused of engaging in propaganda and censorship, and the board was quickly disbanded.[1572] Earlier efforts by the FBI to create an interactive online game called "Don't Be a Puppet," to help educate young people about the recruiting tactics of terrorist organizations, were criticized over concerns about surveillance and profiling.[1573] It was a good-faith but clumsy effort that seemed, at least to me, unlikely to appeal to its target audience. Despite these setbacks, addressing disinformation is not an impossible task. For example, in September 2022, the Office of the Director of National Intelligence launched a Foreign Malign Influence Center to analyze information warfare and election interference efforts by actors outside the United States.[1574] Civil liberties concerns prevent a domestic counterpart, but perhaps this focus on the strategies of foreign adversaries can provide some valuable lessons for dealing with internal disinformers. In addition, a 2023 study concluded that people who had been exposed to extreme views on television news programs revised their own opinions when they turned to different news sources.[1575] Political scientists David E. Broockman and Joshua L. Kalla asked regular viewers of Fox News to watch CNN instead for a month. They concluded that the switch "caused substantial learning and moderated participants' attitudes."[1576] As former US attorney and current law professor Joyce Vance commented in her *Civil Discourse* Substack newsletter, the study "provides reason to be optimistic about the value of sustained engagement with people we care about on important issues, like holding onto the Republic."[1577] While one study may not be dispositive, it provides hope that minds can be changed. Like many complex problems, disinformation cannot be solved with a single solution, but we can take action to mitigate its harms.

Reduce Disinformation from the Supply Side

Ideas for reducing the flood of disinformation abound, and I include only some of them here. For example, Germany, with its particularly painful history of propaganda and genocide, controls online hate speech.[1578] Germany's Network Enforcement Act requires digital platforms to monitor and remove illegal content or face civil penalties.[1579] In the European Union, the Digital Services Act allows governments to remove "illegal" content, such as terrorist recruitment and harassment, and even allows users to challenge the content moderation decisions of social media platforms.[1580] Of course, solutions that work in foreign countries don't always work in the United States, in light of the First Amendment and the core values it protects. But even in America, free speech protections are not absolute. And solutions that look to regulating processes instead of banning content do not implicate censorship concerns.

Amend Section 230

One way to reduce the supply of online information would be to repeal or amend Section 230 of the Communications Decency Act of 1996, the law that gives internet service providers immunity from legal liability.[1581] Making online media companies legally responsible for the content on their platforms would force them to remove posts that endanger the public. The counterargument to this solution is that Section 230 fosters innovation and has made the United States a leader in digital technology. But we need not go so far as to make platforms subject to liability for everything posted there, an impossible task and a move that would drive them out of business. Instead, there are legal remedies that stop short of stripping platforms of their immunity. Amending Section 230 could accomplish some important reforms, according to a commission on disinformation organized by the Aspen Institute.[1582] The Supreme Court sidestepped a ruling on Section 230 immunity in a 2023 opinion, *Twitter, Inc. v. Taamneh*, deciding the case on narrower grounds and leaving it to Congress to take action to make changes to the law.[1583]

The Aspen Institute commission recommended that Congress modify Section 230 in two ways to combat disinformation. One change would be to remove immunity for publication of content that is promoted by social media platforms in exchange for a fee;[1584] this would include political ads and other paid content. According to the commission, paid content targeted toward particular audiences promotes questionable health cures, smears political opponents, and facilitates voter suppression.[1585] This change would give social media the same responsibility to moderate paid content as traditional media outlets, such as television, radio, and newspapers.[1586] By making platforms legally liable for promoted content, they would be incentivized to screen for and reject content that makes false claims.

The second change the commission proposed was to amend Section 230 such that immunity does not extend to algorithms, the digital instructions that social media companies use to amplify provocative content or to send users toward particular posts.[1587] As Facebook whistleblower Frances Haugen revealed in her congressional testimony, her former employer used algorithms to boost the posts that received the most engagement—those that provoked outrage, turning the platform into a sort of outrage machine, where "[m]isinformation, toxicity, and violent content are inordinately prevalent among reshares."[1588] Manipulative users learned to take advantage of this cycle of animosity and began producing content designed to maximize engagement and sharing. Algorithms are not content at all; they are the platform's own products. The commission proposes removing immunity to make internet service providers legally liable for harms caused by their algorithms, design elements over which they exercise complete control. By removing immunity in these limited ways, online media platforms would be deterred from posting false claims and pushing harmful content.

Regulate online publishers like other industries

Another way to address disinformation online would be to reimagine the business model of social media. Twitter founder and former CEO Jack Dorsey has expressed the view that social media should not be funded through advertising but should instead be run by nonprofit foundations.[1589] A more practical solution might be to treat online messaging platforms like utilities or natural monopolies—companies that serve a market with large barriers to entry that limit competition. Information technology scholar Dipayan Ghosh makes this argument in the *Harvard Business Review*.[1590] Utility companies that provide essential supplies like water, electricity, and natural gas are subject to rigorous government regulation to protect the public. So are natural monopolies, such as railroads and telecommunications companies. If unregulated, utilities and natural monopolies could potentially gouge consumers in these industries with high prices, requiring some people to overpay and leaving others without essential services they are unable to afford. Treating social media companies like utilities or natural monopolies would allow regulation to protect the public by government agencies, such as the Federal Trade Commission, the Federal Communications Commission, or even a new federal agency with expertise in digital communications networks. Regulators can set industry rules and standards and can impose penalties for noncompliance, such as fines or even debarment from the market. Or, we could think of information as a consumer good that is potentially dangerous. We regulate the marketing of certain products to protect health and safety: Lawn mowers are required to carry labels warning of the dangers of mowing while barefoot. Medicines bear labels warning of side effects, require prescriptions, or may be banned altogether. Regulation of online publication could help to reduce the spread of disinformation. Regulation would allow us to impose a variety of rules to legally abolish disinformation as a form of violence against life, liberty, and the pursuit of happiness.

Prohibit anonymous users and bots

One way we can use regulation is to stop anonymous users and bots.[591] As AI proliferates, preventing anonymity becomes more important than ever. As we have seen, online disinformation can be planted by people using false personas. We could enact legislation directing the Federal Trade Commission or another agency to enforce rules that require social media companies above a certain size to authenticate their users. Before Elon Musk's acquisition of Twitter, the platform verified users who submitted personal information to permit verification of their identity. Once they were verified, the user's profile featured a blue checkmark indicating that their identity had been authenticated. Musk later changed this feature to require users to pay for verification. Verifying the identity of all users should instead be a required service offered by all large online platforms. Transparency regarding who is posting content would prevent people from being fooled into thinking that the user was someone with a position of authority or credibility whose messages should be believed.

We should also require social media companies to prohibit bots from opening accounts. Bots are automated accounts that use artificial intelligence to make it appear that they belong to real people. In fact, they are part of an army of fake accounts that one account holder can use to amplify messages, extend their reach, and make their content appear more popular than it actually is. The use of bots is like having thousands of friends to help spread a rumor. Tech companies already use tools to block bots, such as CAPTCHA tests that bots are unable to perform. Online ticketing services use these tools, for example, to weed out brokers who would use bots to buy up all the tickets to a concert and resell them to fans at a profit. Social media companies could use similar tools to rid their sites of accounts that use artificial intelligence to fool the public into thinking they are real people. Of course, as AI becomes more sophisticated, the tools to detect bots will need to advance as well.

Require disclosure of funding sources

Another regulatory step to reduce disinformation online would be to require social media platforms to disclose the source of funding for paid online content. As the Aspen Institute commission noted, "paid posts, including political advertising, can be a powerful vector for misinformation."[1592] The Federal Communications Act and Federal Communications Commission rules already require disclosure for paid content on broadcast media, but not online communications.[1593] Greater transparency would allow users to assess the credibility of a particular message. It would also improve public trust in online content that is accurate, essential to combating the loss of faith in all news.[1594] Besides mandating disclosure of funding sources for ads, regulators could also require social media companies to reveal the types of data they collect from users, which would permit researchers, the media, and the public to understand efforts to influence particular demographic groups.[1595]

In addition, the Aspen Institute's commission recommended requiring social media companies to disclose which communities were being targeted for particular content.[1596] It is more difficult to manipulate groups when they know they are being targeted or even microtargeted. We should go one step further and require platforms to disclose the ways in which they permit researchers and marketing firms to access private data of users. When we use social media for free, *we* are the product. With more corporate transparency about how our data are used, Americans can make better decisions about their use of online media.

Regulate algorithms

In addition to removing immunity from legal liability for harms caused by algorithms, as discussed above, government agencies could require social media companies to disclose how they use algorithms to amplify content and microtarget users. Regulations could prohibit the use of certain algorithms altogether, such as those designed to generate outrage and keep users on a platform. Rules could even require social media platforms to affirmatively use algorithms directing readers to content that would combat disinformation, such as official websites of secretary of state offices containing accurate voting information.[1597]

End "sponcon"

Even legitimate publications use content that masquerades as news but is actually paid content generated at the behest of an advertiser. These are the "sponsored" stories that are difficult to separate from actual news stories,[1598] and the algorithms may cause sponsored content to look different to each user. While writing these words, I checked the mobile sites for the newspapers of record in my hometown, and among the news stories were those titled "Experts Have Warned against Cuddling Pets, and Here's

Why,"[1599] and "When You Eat Instant Oatmeal Every Day, Here's What Happens."[1600] Although both stories were marked "ad content," those words were small, and the print was faint. According to Richard Stengel, the journalist and former State Department official, "[t]he companies that produce such content are warehouses of misinformation, rumor, mistakes, and distortion, and they adhere to none of the policies that shape real news stories on the same page."[1601] By including actual news stories alongside paid ad content disguised to look like news stories, news organizations are creating two risks—that readers are likely to believe the sponsored stories, and that they will begin to question the accuracy of the real news on the same page.[1602] Both results compromise the public-interest contribution of journalism necessary for genuine democracy. Requiring prominent labels on ad content would help readers know the difference.

Subsidize Paywalls

By 2023, paywalls had grown increasingly ubiquitous. By requiring users to subscribe to a publication or pay a fee to read a particular news story, paywalls create revenue to compensate the kinds of gatekeepers and fact-checkers who can reduce misinformation. This infrastructure supports reliable news brands that consumers can trust. But paywalls are creating a knowledge gap between users who are willing and able to pay and those who are not. Online users who do not pay to access content are left to read only free content, which is far more likely to contain deceptive and misleading information.[1603] We risk a society where one class of citizens is far better informed than another.

One way to address this concern is to subsidize paywalls with government funds. To avoid government interference with content, users could receive a certain number of credits for content that could be used to access the paywalls of their choice. Using taxpayer funds to access news may seem to some like a wasteful allocation of resources, but an informed electorate is an essential component of democracy.

Strengthen local journalism

One factor that allows disinformation to go unchecked is the decline of local journalism. Small newspapers struggle to make ends meet. One way to address this is to fund local news outlets.[1604] Local journalism informs citizens about important issues in their communities and elections for public office at the state and municipal level. News outlets in small and midsize cities provide watchdog roles that can expose corruption and wasteful government spending. Not only can local journalism provide a set of shared facts about issues close to home, it can also create a sense of community.[1605] Stories about the success of the high school football team or the teen who won a science competition can create local pride and provide subjects of conversation for positive interactions. But local newspapers are declining as their business model becomes unsustainable in an era when ad revenue no longer meets the costs of printing and distribution. Family-owned newspapers are selling to large national chains, leading to less local news coverage.[1606]

To remedy this problem, we should fund local news outlets and coverage. If market forces alone are not enough to support local journalism, then government policy can fill the gaps. Free-speech concerns should preclude the government from involving itself in content decisions, but it can provide funding to cover the operational costs of news outlets. Harvard Law professor Martha Minow suggests government support for local news organizations through government tax policy, with exemptions, deductions, and credits.[1607] She notes that some news organizations, such as Pro Publica, the Texas Tribune, and the *Salt Lake Tribune* use grants, donations, and subscriptions. Their nonprofit status allows them to receive public subsidies. In addition, nonprofit collaboratives are training and supporting journalists to conduct investigative reporting.[1608] Some philanthropic foundations, such as the Knight Foundation, already support local journalism.[1609] The Knight Foundation uses revenue from their larger outlets and solicits donations to support local media and reporters; donations are deductible under the tax code. Philanthropic foundations also help news organizations learn to increase their own ability to generate revenue.[1610] We should conduct public service campaigns to persuade members of the public and organizations of the value of supporting local journalism. In the same way some people make charitable donations to fight diseases and other social ills, they should give money to fight disinformation and build communities by funding local news coverage.

Equal time and the Fairness Doctrine

Unlike broadcast media, online media and cable news are not bound by the "equal time rule." The FCC requires licensees to provide comparable time and placement of airtime devoted to opposing candidates.[1611] In light of amendments and exceptions, this rule translates mostly into opportunities for increased revenues from advertising. The purpose of the rule is to prevent broadcast media from giving undue exposure to one candidate over another and unduly influencing the outcome of elections; the equal time rule is the reason you see campaign ads for candidates from both parties during a local six o'clock news broadcast. Extending the equal time rule to modern media would expose audiences to more candidates and diverse viewpoints. While the equal time rule would be difficult to impose online, it is not impossible. Two information policy experts have proposed the facilitation of counter-speech online using technology:[1612] when a social media company publishes a political ad, an algorithm could promote ads from rival campaigns to the very same users.[1613] Such a tool would help users to escape the echo chambers on social media.

The equal time rule could also improve the content viewers see on cable television. As long as television success is measured by ratings, the networks are incentivized to give the viewers what they want. Fox News lost viewers when it correctly called Arizona for Biden in 2020 and, in response, chose to align itself with profit, not democracy.[1614] It fired the politics editor who made the call and quickly jumped onto the election-fraud bandwagon. The 2023 settlement with Dominion Voting Systems should have been a moment of reckoning for Fox; the $787.5 million payout reflected its liability for knowingly airing false claims about election fraud, which no doubt influenced the beliefs of at least some of its 3.5 million prime-time viewers.[1615] Instead, the settlement seems to have been no more than a blip on the network's radar. While the First Amendment protects the editorial decisions of news outlets, the equal time rule would at least expose viewers to candidates with opposing views.

The equal time rule is not to be confused with the Fairness Doctrine, the former FCC policy that required broadcast media to report on matters of public interest and to present contrasting views.[1616] The Fairness Doctrine ended in 1987, after President Ronald Reagan vetoed legislation to codify it into statute, and the FCC deemed it a violation of the First Amendment. Many media scholars have attributed the rise of misleading, one-sided news coverage to the end of the Fairness Doctrine, though it never applied to cable television.[1617] Restoring and updating the Fairness Doctrine might help address misleading newscasts, but it brings with it other problems, such as the risk of "both-sides-ing" a debate—that is, legitimizing a position that has no basis in fact, such as false claims of a stolen election. Instead, the equal time rule would expose people to news and opinions that would fill in gaps in their knowledge or prompt them to question inconsistent information and baseless arguments.

Perhaps cable news programs should reimagine their strategy altogether. All cable news networks have been losing viewers as they struggle to adapt to the changing nature of online media. As Americans increasingly engage in "cord-cutting"—turning to the internet for information and entertainment—cable news audiences shrink.[1618] Instead of succumbing to the temptation of chasing the "breaking" news that appears on social media, cable news outlets should focus more on analysis, to contribute to an informed citizenry. Networks could facilitate discussions among panelists offering various viewpoints to help audiences form their own opinions. In my own commentary on MSNBC, for example, I try to simply explain the law, allowing viewers to form their own opinions about the conclusions to draw. By providing an alternative to online information, cable news networks might be able to reclaim larger audiences. Sometimes what is good for business is also good for the public.

Create a code of ethics for social media platforms

Another solution, short of removing immunity and imposing regulations, is to encourage social media platforms to monitor themselves. In light of First Amendment concerns, content-based solutions are difficult for the US government to impose, but platforms could impose their own. The European Union has a voluntary Code of Practice on Disinformation, which commits participants to enforcing community standards, removing fake accounts and bots, and disclosing funding sources for ads.[1619] While voluntary compliance with industry standards lacks the teeth of government oversight, social media companies would comply if such a code affected profits. Consumers could drive market forces to pressure companies into adhering to ethics rules; platforms that fail to comply with standards would be seen as less desirable, pushing users toward platforms that do. Voluntary codes of ethics could include setting community standards that prohibit threats, harassment, and verifiably false claims. The code could also require the platform to enforce its own standards by suspending or deplatforming violators. Social media companies could agree to check facts and flag false claims, suggesting to users that they look at other sources for accurate information. They could even use algorithms to detect and delete false content.[1620]

Reduce Disinformation from the Demand Side

In addition to addressing the supply side of disinformation, we can also take steps to reduce disinformation by focusing on consumers of news. All of us are susceptible to disinformation online. As I did with the Patrick Mahomes story, we may believe a false claim and then unwittingly share it. One solution lies in public education. Finland, a country that has dealt with Soviet and then Russian disinformation, has invested in public education to equip its citizens to detect false claims by teaching them to assess information and understand the functioning of their own government.[1621] Italy has worked with broadcasters and the private sector to train students to recognize fake news and online conspiracy theories.[1622] Public school curricula in the United States should include media literacy, to teach students to become more discriminating consumers of online information.[1623] Students should be taught to recognize the telltale signs of a deceptive account, such as a non-name profile, like @PatriotGirl or @6283015, or an account with few or no followers. Lessons should include verifying news stories against other sources before sharing them online. If something truly remarkable has occurred, more than one media outlet will be reporting it. In addition, we should teach students to use existing fact-checking resources, such as FactCheck.org, PolitiFact, and Snopes. While evolving technology will make it impossible to teach students to spot every trick, education can help arm them against disinformation simply by raising their awareness of the problem.

Adults would also benefit from online media literacy, though this population is more difficult to capture than school-age children. Such education for adults could be offered by civic groups, faith-based groups, foundations, and nonprofit organizations, in person and online.

Adult education could include techniques for dealing with information overload, which may cause us to isolate our news consumption to a single outlet or tune out political news altogether.[1624] Those strategies may include helping people recognize credible news sources and encouraging occasional breaks from the virtual world to talk with real people in person about news, politics, and organizing.

In addition to media literacy, educational efforts should include civics and history. Currently, only nine states require a full year of civics or government in public schools, and ten states have no civics requirements at all.[1625] Understanding our government institutions can help people recognize the importance of political discourse based on a shared understanding of facts. A deeper appreciation for the institutions of democracy can also build resilience against appeals to divisive politics.[1626] According to political scientists, "When such civic-minded motivations are primed . . . people [are] more willing to adjust important attitudes (including partisan identification!) in response to new information."[1627]

We must also teach citizens about the history of disinformation as a tool for advancing political agendas that are ultimately harmful to the people. Schoolchildren and adults who are aware of the use of propaganda by authoritarians and fascists would be better equipped to recognize it and defeat it. When we say "never again" when discussing Native American removal, Jim Crow, or the Holocaust, we must take action to back our words.

Conduct public service campaigns

An effort to raise awareness could also help reduce disinformation online. Such a campaign could appeal to integrity or patriotism to persuade people to use diligence in posting and amplifying messages. Memes and insults that mock our political opponents contribute to the coarseness of public speech. It is tempting to make snarky comments at the expense of someone with whom we disagree. Making fun of Nancy Pelosi's husband after he was attacked in his home by an intruder with a hammer, or mocking Marjorie Taylor Greene over her divorce, may earn likes on social media, but these jabs contribute to the downward spiral of civil discourse that increases national divisiveness. In the same way Mothers Against Drunk Driving cast driving under the influence of alcohol as a harmful and irresponsible behavior deserving social condemnation, a government agency or nonprofit organization could lead public service messaging to raise awareness of the harms of sharing disinformation or trolling others. We should each be encouraged to refrain from taking the bait from trolls when we see a post that provokes our outrage.

Use and improve online tools

One way to combat the harms of technology is with technology. Existing resources already allow people to assess the accuracy of facts and the legitimacy of accounts. For example, one tool called "ClaimBuster" is an automated program that uses language processing and human coding to determine whether information is accurate.[1628] Another web-based tool known as a "botometer" uses artificial intelligence to score profiles to determine whether an account holder is a real person or fictitious, a product of AI.[1629] Botometer examines friends or followers, account activity, social network structure, language, and other factors to measure on a scale from zero to five the likelihood that the account holder is a bot. Researchers continue to develop tools that can be used to detect disinformation,[1630] and we should fund this work in light of the importance of information in a country that relies on self-governance. While it may seem like a naive aspiration today, perhaps one day we can even harness artificial intelligence to fact-check news reports and determine in an instant whether they have been corroborated by other sources.

Promote civic engagement

In addition to tackling disinformation head-on, we also need to focus on strengthening public resilience. As discussed earlier, increasing social alienation contributes to media users' susceptibility to manipulation. The phenomenon documented in *Bowling Alone* has only been exacerbated in the digital age. When we spend more time online and less time in the presence of other people, we become not only indifferent to them but more inclined to believe the worst about them. If you have never met a Muslim or a born-again Christian, you may not be aware of how much you have in common with them. Similarly, when we are bombarded by messages demonizing our political opponents, our divides deepen, and we become more polarized. We retreat to our affinity groups instead of considering what's best for our larger communities. Our time in seclusion during the Covid-19 pandemic likely made matters worse.

We can take steps to improve civic engagement that force us out of our preference bubbles and into real public squares where we can exchange ideas and test our understanding of facts. We should undertake a public campaign to join—*anything*. Organizations are especially valuable when they bring together people of different political affiliations.[163] Faith communities, labor unions, Rotary and Kiwanis clubs, student organizations, nonprofit boards, book clubs, trivia teams at the local bar and, of course, bowling leagues can all accomplish this. The more diverse perspectives to which we can expose ourselves, the better. Being part of a group that provides opportunities for conversations with real people forces us to defend our positions on issues and exposes us to different perspectives. Taking this step requires exercising individual responsibility and sacrificing disposable time but is a worthwhile investment in promoting a shared sense of ownership in our democracy.

Mitigate the Harms to Democracy

In addition to reducing the supply of disinformation, we can also blunt its impact. First and foremost, we must protect the right to vote. As discussed in chapter 6, lies about voter fraud are driving laws that suppress and interfere with voting access, particularly among communities of color. These laws restrict provisional ballots, ban mobile voting, reduce access to ballot drop boxes, and create other obstacles to voting, all under the pretext of preventing voter fraud. The effect of these laws is to exclude some members of society from the electorate, a result that is antithetical to democracy.

Among the steps that could reverse this trend would be passing federal legislation that would supersede state laws and protect the right to vote. Proposed bills have stalled in a gridlocked Congress. One such bill is the John R. Lewis Voting Rights Advancement Act,[1632] which, among other things, would protect voters from discrimination committed under the pretense of voter fraud.[1633] The act calls the bluff of election deniers by requiring states to *prove* voter fraud before they may enact rules that make it more difficult to vote.[1634] Another proposed bill, the For the People Act, would make it easier to vote, end partisan gerrymandering of congressional districts, and improve transparency in campaign finance.[1635] To facilitate voting, the bill would require all states to provide automatic voter registration, offer early voting for at least fifteen days, make election day a federal holiday, and take other steps to remove barriers to voting.[1636] Neither bill has mustered sufficient support from Senate Republicans, who called them a "power grab," arguing that election administration is a matter for the states.[1637] But as we saw when Congress passed the Help America Vote Act following the 2000 *Bush v. Gore* controversy, nothing prevents federal legislation that provides additional protections for voters. Finding common ground on federal legislation is one way to address voter suppression laws in the states.

Reform campaign finance

Another important reform would be to improve transparency in campaign financing, particularly in the use of dark money, a problem that seems to grow worse with each passing year. As discussed in chapter 5, the Supreme Court's 2010 decision in *Citizens United v. Federal Election Commission* opened the doors to dark money by holding that the First Amendment prohibits restrictions on corporations, unions, and other independent groups from spending unlimited amounts on political ads. The decision has led to the rise of super PACs, shadowy committees with misleading names that are not required to disclose the identities of their donors, allowing a small number of individuals or interest groups to provide unlimited financial support to candidates, often under the guise of a "grassroots organization." When super PACs use a misleading name that suggests support of ordinary citizens, the public can be left with the false impression that certain candidates are more popular than they are. The lack of transparency makes it impossible to identify the donors behind the ads to determine whether they may have a vested interest in the outcome of an election. Even if *Citizens United* forbids limits on campaign spending, it does not prohibit disclosure of who is spending it. One proposal has been the DISCLOSE Act,[1638] federal legislation first introduced in 2010 that would provide more transparency in campaign spending. The proposal would require organizations to disclose their donors, identify themselves on the ads they fund, and restrict the use of shell companies to conceal the sources of funds.[1639] The DISCLOSE Act failed to pass in September 2022, with all forty-nine Senate Republicans opposing it.[1640] It is difficult to combat well-funded political forces that seek to preserve the status quo, but anyone who truly cares about good government, regardless of party, would have to agree that disclosing the source of political funding is essential to good government.

Online campaign ads, in particular, would benefit from more transparency. A proposal for disclosure in political ads was made in a bill called the Honest Ads Act, first proposed in 2017 and not yet passed.[1641] The bill would subject campaign ads on social media to the same standards as ads on television and radio by requiring disclosure of the payment source and including disclaimers in the ads. Passing such legislation would be an important step toward reducing false and misleading claims online.

Protect election machinery

Protecting democracy from the harms of disinformation also requires efforts to safeguard the machinery of elections. Elections are currently administered by elected officials—politicians who are members of one party or another. Sometimes secretary of state candidates who are supervising an election are on the ballot themselves. In 2022, election deniers ran for secretary of state in ten states.[1642] They banded together as the America First SOS Coalition and solicited contributions nationally; two of them won their elections. It is reasonable to assert that it is a conflict of interest to allow a partisan actor with skin in the game to oversee elections. A coup-supporting election denier who is willing to go along with false claims of a stolen election would likely be catastrophic.

One way to avoid this scenario is to put election administration into the hands of independent actors. In other democracies where voter satisfaction is high, elections are run by government bodies that are designed to be nonpartisan.[1643] In Canada, for example, elections are controlled by an independent chief electoral officer who is appointed by the House of Commons.[1644] The chief electoral officer serves a ten-year term that is not renewable and cannot be removed from office except for cause.[1645] While elections in the United States are conducted by individual states, each could implement its own nonpartisan method for selecting an independent election administrator. One model could be the Independent Citizens Redistricting Commission that recently drew new voting district lines in Michigan.[1646] The thirteen commissioners include four who "affiliate" with the Democratic Party, four who affiliate with the GOP, and five who do not affiliate with either of the two major parties.[1647] A similar independent commission could select a qualified election administrator unaffiliated with either party to serve for a nonrenewable term at a competitive salary.

Another way to protect the machinery of voting from the harms of disinformation is to make a greater investment in the administration of elections. Providing funding for adequate staffing and training is essential to smooth voting processes. Well-trained poll workers can minimize disruptions and efforts to intimidate volunteers at polling places and vote counting centers when accusations of fraud arise. In the 2020 election, baseless claims of voter fraud brought protesters to Detroit's TCF Center, where absentee votes were being counted. Local press described the tense scene inside as comparable to "a sports stadium, complete with yelling, taunting, cheering, fists pounding on glass and unruly challengers being hauled off by cops."[1648] Similar raucous protests broke out at counting centers in Pennsylvania and Arizona.[1649] In Philadelphia, vote counters tallying the ballots received death threats.[1650] As the count continued, two days after the election, two armed men were arrested near the convention center where votes were being counted.[1651] They had driven from Virginia in a Hummer bearing QAnon stickers. Inside the vehicle, police had found an assault rifle and 160 rounds of ammunition.[1652] We should expend the funds needed to protect election workers from threats, harassment, and physical harm by providing security guards for them at polling places and counting centers.

Funding for election administration should also be used to educate the public, to help inoculate them against disinformation. Election officials can use their websites, mailings, posters, and public service announcements to provide voters with accurate information about the voting process and tips for spotting false claims.[1653] Election administrators could even "pre-bunk" falsehoods they can anticipate, such as claims that voting by mail is susceptible to fraud. In 2022, the National Association of State Election Directors shared what it called an elections communication "toolkit," which contained social media graphics, animated videos, and media literacy tip sheets, all in English and Spanish.[1654] The messaging directed consumers to go to state election officials for accurate information and urged them to think critically about what they might see and share online.[1655] In 2023, a group called the NewDEAL Forum published a "Democracy Playbook" containing suggestions to improve election transparency and trust, such as publicly testing voting machines and requiring mandatory post-election audits.[1656]

Ranked-choice voting

There will always be candidates who aim to incite outrage by making outrageous claims. At one time, we relied on party bosses in smoke-filled rooms to decide who would represent the party in general elections. They served as gatekeepers against outlier candidates, but it was hardly a democratic process. Allowing voters to choose the party's nominee from a crowded field in the primary process, on the other hand, permits fringe candidates to capture primary elections without winning a majority of the vote. One way to safeguard against extremist candidates is by using ranked-choice voting. Ranked-choice voting allows voters to rank candidates in order of preference rather than voting for only one.[1657] If a candidate wins a majority of the votes, he is proclaimed the winner. If not, the last-place finisher is eliminated, and the second-choice votes of those voters whose first choice was eliminated are counted. Rounds continue in this fashion until one candidate receives a majority of votes.[1658] Ranked-choice voting prevents two popular candidates from splitting the moderate vote and allowing a dangerous outlier to win an election by a plurality. It tends to favor moderate candidates—perhaps an unsatisfactory outcome for voters who grow tired of waiting for social progress—but choosing candidates through compromise would serve as a safeguard against candidates who are wholly ill-suited to governing.

Mitigate the Harms to Public Safety and National Security

Other harms of disinformation that require urgent attention are threats and violence. We can mitigate these threats through enforcement, prevention, and commonsense changes to laws. Wrongdoers must be held accountable through the legal system. Criminal prosecution and civil liability are effective tools not only because they punish bad actors for their past misconduct but because they send a message to people who might disobey the law in the future. By holding wrongdoers accountable, we can deter the same kind of conduct from occurring again.

Criminal prosecution is one way to protect democracy. After the January 6 attacks, the US Department of Justice prosecuted more than a thousand individuals who had participated in one way or another.[1659] Many expressed the view that they were following the instructions of the president and commander in chief.[1660] Convictions ranged from misdemeanor offenses for trespassing to seditious conspiracy—using force to oppose the authority of the United States government in administering the lawful transfer of presidential power. Following his conviction by guilty plea, one of the attackers testified at the trial of another that he felt "ashamed and embarrassed" for "acting like a traitor" on January 6.[1661] Others similarly expressed shame and remorse.[1662] Attorney General Merrick Garland promised to hold accountable all responsible for the attack, "whether they were present that day or were otherwise criminally responsible for the assault on our democracy,"[1663] and Special Counsel Jack Smith charged Donald Trump in August 2023 in an indictment for orchestrating the scheme. Two weeks later, Fulton County district attorney Fani T. Willis charged Trump and eighteen other defendants in Georgia in an indictment alleging racketeering and other crimes for attempting to overturn the election.[1664] In Michigan, Attorney General Dana Nessel charged sixteen Michigan residents for forgery and related offenses for submitting a document falsely claiming that they were the "duly elected" electors for the state and that Donald Trump had won the election there when, in fact, Biden had carried the state.[1665] Criminal convictions signal moral condemnation for violating the rules of society. To avoid normalizing an attempted coup, we must prosecute all those involved in aiding and abetting the effort, despite any reluctance we might feel about prosecuting public officials. The House committee that investigated the January 6 attack concluded, "The central cause of Jan. 6 was one man, former President

Donald Trump, who many others followed. None of the events of Jan. 6 would have happened without him."[1666]

Criminal prosecution must also be considered for individuals who threaten, harass, and attack public officials. The prosecution of the men who plotted to kidnap Michigan governor Gretchen Whitmer sent an important signal to others who might engage in political violence, even though some were acquitted. It is equally important to prosecute individuals who communicate threats to local public officials, such as election officials and poll workers, public health officials, school board members, and educators. Based on false claims and hot-button issues in the culture wars, threats and harassment are making it more difficult for public servants to do their jobs and are driving them from office. Holding accountable those who engage in threatening and harassing conduct is essential to signaling the moral repugnance of this behavior and its danger to our public institutions.

Hate crimes laws must also be enforced vigorously. While most acts of violence constitute serious crimes, hate crimes are especially egregious because they are intended to intimidate members of a particular group. Singling out victims for violence because of their race, religion, ethnicity, sexual orientation, or other demographic characteristic deepens divisions within society. Criminal prosecution sends the message that America views hate crimes as morally reprehensible in our pluralistic society.

In addition to criminal prosecution, civil liability can also be an effective deterrent to attacks on public safety. Following the violence occurring at the Unite the Right rally in 2017, residents of Charlottesville successfully sued the organizers under the Ku Klux Klan Act, alleging that they had interfered with their rights to be free from racial terrorism.[1667] A jury found the organizers liable and awarded the victims more than twenty-five million dollars in damages. That kind of penalty can get the attention of other would-be organizers of violence. Among the defendants in the civil case was James Fields Jr., who was also prosecuted criminally and convicted of killing counterprotester Heather Heyer by plowing his car into a crowd of people.[1668] An advantage of civil lawsuits over criminal prosecution is the lower burden of proof, establishing liability by a preponderance of the evidence (more than 50 percent) rather than proving guilt beyond a reasonable doubt. In addition, the award of money damages can drain defendants' resources and impair their ability to continue their activities.[1669]

A mechanism unique to insurrection can also be used to protect the country against attacks from within. As mentioned earlier, the Fourteenth Amendment contains a clause providing that no person may hold a federal or state office who, after taking an oath of office, "shall have engaged in insurrection or rebellion against the same, or given aid or comfort to the enemies thereof."[1670] The amendment was passed after the Civil War, to keep Confederate rebels out of office, but would seem to apply to the president or any member of Congress who participated in the January 6 attack. The clause has not been widely tested, and the language includes no enforcement mechanism, but pursuing enforcement would be an important way to protect the country from a future coup. Results so far have been mixed: In New Mexico, a judge ruled in 2022 that a county commissioner was disqualified from holding office under the Fourteenth Amendment following his conviction for entering a restricted area at the US Capitol on January 6.[1671] Similar efforts against members of Congress in North Carolina and Georgia failed.[1672] Preventing insurrectionists from holding office is essential to protecting our country from further insider attacks and sends an important message that attempting to overthrow our government bars people from the privilege of ever holding office again.

Prevent political violence

In addition to enforcing laws to hold accountable those who engage in political violence, we should also work diligently to prevent such violence from occurring in the first place. One contributing factor to the severity of the attack on January 6 was the failure of the intelligence community to recognize the danger of attack in advance. According to Frank Figliuzzi, a former assistant director for counterintelligence at the FBI, federal agencies possessed intelligence before January 6 that "screamed about coming violence."[1673] Even though the intelligence was "passed around," he wrote, "no one seemed to know what to do with it." The reason for the inaction remained unclear, and Figliuzzi criticized the House committee that investigated the attack for focusing myopically on Trump and failing to assess whether the intelligence failures were caused by "an inability to view fellow Americans as domestic threats, operating guidelines that need to be changed, orders from the White House to ignore threats—or all of the above."[1674] Even if the House committee failed to reach a conclusion about the intelligence failure, the FBI and other agencies could still conduct their own after-action assessments to determine how they can better assess risks and share actionable intelligence in the future, to disrupt attacks before they occur in any community in America.

Investing in physical security for elected officials by providing home security systems, police surveillance, and even armed guards in some instances would help to ward off attacks. School boards, city councils, and other local governmental bodies could enact codes of conduct to provide clear rules for audience behavior in public meetings and enforcement mechanisms for violations.[1675] Local officials should also be trained in de-escalation techniques to prevent unruly citizens from resorting to violence.[1676] Reduction of political violence, threats, harassment, and hate crimes can also be achieved through public messaging. Media coverage of prosecution for these crimes, billboards, and ad campaigns can all raise public awareness of the seriousness of these threats and their harms to public safety and national security.

Police violent content online

Another way to prevent threats and harassment from turning into violence is by refusing to normalize them. Speech that threatens to harm others is not protected by the First Amendment. Prosecuting threats not only deters others from engaging in the same conduct but also prevents the threat from escalating into a physical attack. People who engage in violence often have expressed aggressive views online.[1677] Expressions that amount to threats to harm others could be prosecuted; communications that fall short of that standard should be removed from platforms under community standards. While the First Amendment prevents the government from forcing private social media platforms to police content, market forces could be used to influence them to enforce responsible rules online to limit hate speech. For example, following the acquisition of Twitter by Musk, who pledged to loosen community standards to all speech within legal bounds, civil rights groups called for advertisers to pull out,[1678] and more than one third of the platform's top one hundred advertisers responded by leaving.[1679]

In addition, we should actively prosecute cases of doxxing— publicly disclosing a person's home address, workplace, and other personal information in attempt to prompt harassment and violence. Following the 2020 election, some Republicans who refused to go along with the coup attempt, like Arizona House Speaker Rusty Bowers and Pennsylvania House Speaker Brian Cutler, became victims of doxxing.[1680] The Trump campaign posted online the personal cell phone numbers for the Michigan House Speaker and Senate majority leader after they refused to decertify their state's election results.[1681] Federal statutes make it a crime to use the internet to publish personal information for the purpose of harassment or intimidation.[1682] Making enforcement of anti-doxxing laws a priority would signal the serious risk posed by the practice and would deter its use for terrorizing public officials. Combating doxxing would advance a substantial public interest in safeguarding democracy from threats by intimidation.

Change laws

In addition to enforcing existing laws, we must explore ways to use the law to deter and punish conduct that endangers public safety. One legal change that is needed to prevent political violence is the enactment of a domestic terrorism statute.[1683] Currently, federal law criminalizes international terrorism but not domestic terrorism. The international terrorism statute makes it a crime to engage in transnational acts of violence intended to intimidate the population or coerce government action. No similar statute exists for crimes that occur solely within the United States. Appropriate concerns about civil liberties from the left and the right have hampered efforts to enact a domestic terrorism law. Critics sometimes point to other statutes that can be used in cases of domestic terrorism, such as the Ku Klux Klan Act and laws prohibiting the use of weapons of mass destruction, or even state murder charges. While such laws are effective for holding accountable domestic terrorists *after* their attacks, they fail to achieve the primary law enforcement goal of disrupting an attack before it occurs. And, as former acting assistant attorney general for national security Mary McCord has noted, even after a deadly attack, if a domestic terrorist has used a gun or a vehicle instead of a bomb, federal law provides no recourse.[1684] Perhaps a domestic terrorism statute could have prevented the January 6 attack from occurring.

During my work in national security at the US attorney's office in Detroit, I learned that the FBI refers to the time before an attack as "left of boom." The phrase connotes a visual image of a timeline, on which "boom" is the attack itself; any point left of boom is a time before the attack. A domestic terrorism statute would allow the FBI to act left of boom by using the same tactics they use in international terrorism cases. Under the international terrorism statute, the FBI may open an investigation when it first learns of a possible plot. The bureau might use undercover agents to communicate with the subject online, to investigate the identities of any potential coconspirators and their plans. Federal agents might use a sting operation to feign selling weapons or ammunition to the people under investigation. These tactics are permissible once an investigation is open and allow the FBI to prevent a possible attack with international connections. But without a domestic terrorism statute on the books, the FBI lacks the same authority to conduct a proactive investigation that takes place exclusively within the United States. Sometimes agents get "lucky," and the particular facts of a case fit another statute on the books—such as kidnapping, in the Whitmer case—but without a law protecting the nation from acts of domestic terrorism, federal agents are sometimes left without recourse when a plot utilizes guns or vehicles as weapons. Murder is generally governed by state law, and so federal agents are sometimes left without the ability to open an investigation. State law enforcement agencies often lack the resources, investigative tools, and nationwide jurisdiction to conduct an effective preemptive investigation left of boom. A domestic terrorism statute that made it a crime to commit acts of violence for a political purpose could address this gap in the law and allow the FBI to stop future attacks like the one on January 6 before they occur. Legislation has been proposed that would do just that, and Congress should enact it.[1685]

Restore the ban on assault weapons

To protect public safety, Congress should also restore the assault weapons ban of the 1990s. Disinformation has fueled the rise of assault weapons in American society, leaving us all less safe. Assault rifles are the weapon of choice of mass shooters. When a trauma doctor and I cotaught a graduate-level course on reducing gun violence, he explained to me and our class that assault weapons are so lethal because they don't leave small holes for doctors to repair—they tear out entire vital organs and cause victims to bleed out quickly, often rendering medical care futile. AR-15-style rifles were used by shooters motivated by ethnic hate in Jacksonville, Pittsburgh, El Paso, and Buffalo[1686]—and all four shooters obtained their guns legally.[1687] In 1994, Congress passed a law prohibiting the manufacture, transfer, and possession of certain weapons and high-capacity magazines.[1688] The ban was allowed to lapse ten years later and has not been renewed, as attitudes about guns have been deeply influenced by lobbyists paid by profit-driven gunmakers. Far-right politicians now glorify guns. They use high-powered guns to signal their need and willingness to protect themselves from intruders, often portrayed as racial and religious minorities.

As mentioned earlier, people who espouse the insurrectionist theory of the Second Amendment believe that they have a right to possess guns that can match the firepower of the government so that they can overthrow tyrants. In fact, nothing in the Constitution protects their right to overthrow the government; instead, our nation's founding document condemns it. The Supreme Court has made it clear that the Second Amendment permits reasonable restrictions on guns and is "not a right to keep and carry any weapon whatsoever in any manner whatsoever and for whatever purpose."[1689] Because the 1994 law was allowed to expire after only ten years, evidence about its effect on public safety is incomplete.[1690] But common sense tells us that without a killing machine capable of firing off multiple shots per second, even if attacks became no less frequent, they would be far less lethal. One reason the ban lacked significant short-term effects is that people still possessed the assault weapons they obtained before the law went into effect. This problem could be addressed by banning ammunition for the assault weapons as well as the guns themselves. A ban on new assault weapons may seem futile in the light of the abundance of these guns already in the hands of the public, but the problem will become worse in the absence of action.

Counter Harms to the Rule of Law

Agreeing to comply with laws and to resolve our differences in courts is essential to a peaceful society. The rule of law requires all members of society to comply with laws because they express the will of the people. When people engage in corruption or take the law into their own hands, the rule of law is diminished. We must take steps to buttress it.

One way to reinforce the rule of law is to dispel the idea of "vigilante justice" and replace it with terms that describe it for what it is—terrorism. Most often, citizens who "take the law into their own hands" lack training and knowledge of the law, or even an awareness of all relevant facts. When three men ambushed and murdered Ahmaud Arbery while he was jogging on a street in Georgia in 2020, they claimed they suspected him of a crime and were acting under legal authority to conduct a citizen's arrest.[1691] The men who plotted to kidnap Michigan governor Gretchen Whitmer over her shutdown orders were engaging in vigilantism. In Michigan, an election-denying county sheriff suggested the Whitmer kidnap plotters may simply have been performing a citizen's arrest.[1692]

Laws permitting citizen's arrests are on the books in a number of states.[1693] And while the laws vary, they generally permit a member of the public to detain a suspect who has allegedly committed a crime in their presence. The laws were created with good intentions; for example, they allow a citizen to stop a thief caught in the act of stealing a wallet, or a security guard to temporarily detain a shoplifter. But these laws tend to do more harm than good, because they allow wrongdoers to rationalize their conduct to hold or even harm someone they believe has violated the law, even when they lack probable cause, a standard many lay people are unlikely to understand. According to Michael J. Moore, a former US attorney in Georgia, the danger of citizen's arrest laws is that "some people see the laws as license to become a cowboy, or that somehow it deputizes you to become a cop."[1694] Some people see citizen's arrest laws as permission to serve as judge, jury, and executioner—a gross distortion of the rule of law. Add disinformation to the mix, and citizens who believe that they are in a war of good against evil may be inclined to use citizen's arrests to defeat their perceived enemies. Removing these laws from the books would encourage people who believe they have identified a criminal suspect to call the police instead of taking the law into their own hands, a dangerous step with potentially deadly consequences.

Enforce laws against paramilitary activity

Another way to protect public safety would be to use the laws already on the books to address groups calling themselves militias.[1695] The 2021 US National Strategy for Countering Domestic Terrorism stated that "militia violent extremists" pose the greatest threat of domestic terrorism directed against government personnel and facilities.[1696] Enforcing laws already on the books would discourage private groups from performing military and law enforcement functions and signal that they operate outside the rule of law.

According to the Institute for Constitutional Advocacy and Protection at Georgetown Law Center, "All 50 states prohibit private, unauthorized groups from engaging in activities reserved for the state militia, including law enforcement activities."[1697] Some states restrict unauthorized private militias by forbidding groups of civilians from "parading" or "drilling" in public with firearms.[1698] Others prohibit individuals from training people in the use of firearms, explosives, or "techniques capable of causing injury or death."[1699] And still more prohibit civilians from assuming the uniform or duties of a peace officer.[1700] Civil liberties concerns about free speech, free assembly, and the right to bear arms may make law enforcement authorities reluctant to enforce existing laws, but arrests and prosecution would deter others from engaging in conduct that endangers the public.

Combat corruption

Public officials who take bribes, extort contractors, engage in fraud, or otherwise abuse their office allow powerful people to play by different rules. Ignoring corruption spreads the lie that some people are above the law. Declining to prosecute or pardoning offenders normalizes corruption, which degrades the rule of law.

We must vigorously enforce laws against even powerful politicians who engage in corruption. If leaders get a pass, then ordinary citizens can rightly question the fairness of the criminal justice system. In addition, presidents should take into consideration the counsel of the Department of Justice's Office of the Pardon Attorney, a norm Donald Trump violated.[1701] Relying on institutions to approve pardons lends uniformity to the process and the results, so that offenders under similar circumstances are treated alike, an important tenet of the rule of law.

No one of these proposed solutions will cure all ills of disinformation, but we must have the political courage and will to try some of them, or others. Our democracy is too precious to simply surrender to authoritarians, fascists, foreign influence operations, and scammers. But all the laws in the world cannot eradicate disinformation unless the citizenry wants to defeat it. We need to pass legislation that compels public servants—even the president and commander in chief—to adhere to facts and not deceptions. We must demand the truth from those who represent us rather than accept as true that which we want to believe. This is a battle for democracy that requires us to assert our nonnegotiable sovereignty and powers of self-governance.

10.

WE HOLD THESE TRUTHS TO BE SELF-EVIDENT: A WAY FORWARD

"We, the People, recognize that we have responsibilities as well as rights; that our destinies are bound together; that a freedom which only asks what's in it for me, a freedom without a commitment to others, a freedom without love or charity or duty or patriotism, is unworthy of our founding ideals, and those who died in their defense."

—PRESIDENT BARACK OBAMA

I WAS VISITING IRELAND in the spring of 2018, when the country was considering a referendum that would end the nation's prohibition on abortion. In a country with an official Catholic faith, I imagined that the debate would be raging with the passion of a blood feud. Instead, I was surprised to find that advocates on both sides of the issue stood on street corners, passing out literature and politely engaging passersby who expressed interest in learning more about the issue. To this day, I still keep on my desk a button that says "Tá," Irish Gaelic for "yes"—the choice that would change the law to permit abortion and the side that ultimately prevailed in the election by an overwhelming margin. Irish feminist Ailbhe Smyth observed that the country was able to conduct the vote without becoming split.[1702] She attributed that success to "creating an empathetic framework of discourse so that people are not at each other's throats."[1703]

Combating disinformation is a massive undertaking, and defeating it will require the kind of empathy I saw in Ireland. The Irish people were committed to preserving their national unity above all else. As I saw in Ireland, I do not expect us to find unity on the substance of issues—we will always have differences of opinion on issues such as criminal justice and government spending—but we must be united in the *process* of how we solve problems. The ability to solve any problem requires a shared understanding of facts and truth.

What is truth? Philosophers and religious scholars debate the meaning of the term. There are some truths that may be unknowable to the human mind, such as the meaning of life or whether intelligent beings exist elsewhere in the cosmos. But truth is different from fact. Facts can be verified, even if our perceptions of them may vary. The color of the traffic light at the time of a car accident is often a knowable fact. So is the number of votes a particular candidate received in an election. Finding facts requires investigation, discovery, documentation, and testing. Scientists find facts. Researchers find facts. Ordinary people find facts every day. *Are we out of milk? Did Dad take the car?* These are facts that are knowable. Our opinions about facts may vary: *Is the coffee hot? Do we need to fill the gas tank?* Reaching conclusions requires interpretation, and reasonable minds may disagree. What I deem "hot" may be different from the preferences of others; the fuel level at which I think a car requires a refill likely varies from the risk tolerance of others. We can tell the difference between opinion and facts. And while we are all free to form our own views, we must commit to debating them from a shared set of facts.

Overcoming Fear

How do we preserve our democracy when political opportunists are willing to grab power through lies instead of adhering to democratic norms? I think the answer lies in the same strategy basic to every relationship: we need to care more about maintaining the relationship than getting our way. In American government, that means needing to care more about ensuring democracy than about imposing our will.

In *How Democracies Die*, authors Steven Levitsky and Daniel Ziblatt examine not only the demise of democratic governments but the factors that permit them to survive. They conclude that democracies thrive when leaders abide by "unwritten democratic norms."[1704] In America, these norms have been "mutual toleration" and "forbearance."[1705] They define mutual toleration as the acceptance of the opposing party as a legitimate part of our political system. In the United States, political candidates engage in mutual toleration when they concede elections to the winning opponent. Forbearance is the use of restraint in exercising power.[1706] Presidents exercise forbearance when they refrain from using their veto power over measures enacted by other branches of government.[1707]

In American history, both parties have been guilty of failing to exercise forbearance at times. Legislatures engage in gerrymandering to create voting districts that will give advantages to their party.[1708] Both Republican and Democratic presidents have granted ill-advised pardons.[1709] But in recent years, the Republican Party seems to have abandoned forbearance, perhaps because its leaders see their political power dwindling. While losing the popular vote for the presidency in five of the six elections between 2000 and 2020, the GOP nonetheless managed to capture five of eight open seats on the Supreme Court during that same period, in part by violating norms. Senator Mitch McConnell was unabashedly duplicitous in holding a confirmation vote for President Trump's nominee Amy Coney Barrett following the death of a sitting justice in an election year, after refusing to provide a hearing for President Obama's nominee under similar circumstances.[1710]

And now, we have reached the point where some political opportunists have even sacrificed the democratic norm of mutual toleration, the acceptance of the legitimacy of political rivals. Is this the natural end of American democracy?

Sometimes democracies die. Perhaps ours has outlived its natural life. But the alternatives to democracy, as Churchill said, are inferior forms of government. Democracies protect the sovereign power of the people to choose who will serve and represent them. The people can hold leaders accountable and express their dissatisfaction by voting them out of office. Allowing decisions to be made in any way except by the will of the people risks creating preferences for one group of people over another, a far cry from the self-evident truth that all of us are created equal.

Demanding Leaders Who Speak the Truth

To preserve our democracy, we must commit to working together for the greater public good. That means choosing leaders who will reject the use of disinformation to achieve political gain. Democracy requires an informed electorate. While our pluralistic society will always contain differing opinions, we must start from common ground so that we may engage in meaningful debate and make decisions that are in the best interests of our country. The solutions suggested in the last chapter can help us reduce disinformation and blunt its impact, but defeating disinformation will require something more.

We have real problems to solve—climate change, persistent racial injustice, growing disparities in wealth distribution, a changing economy, public health challenges, global conflict, refugee crises, poverty, crime, cyber threats, and many more. To rise to the challenges we collectively face, we need leadership that can bring us together. Our abilities to solve problems have never been greater: Technology offers unimaginable advances in medicine, food distribution, and alternative energy. Distance learning presents opportunities for job retraining and access to higher education. Social media allow us to maintain relationships with family members and friends and to collaborate with people on the other side of the world. Certainly, we face significant challenges, but leaders who offer rational solutions give us our best chance to solve them. Navigating that world requires leaders who will bring out our best hopes rather than prey on our worst fears. As he took office during the Great Depression, President Franklin D. Roosevelt appealed to people's courage when he told them, "The only thing we have to fear is fear itself,"[171] assuring Americans that they could meet any threat that might come. At this moment,

America needs leaders who can unite us to face our challenges with courage and optimism.

We the People

But leaders in a democracy, of course, are simply a reflection of the voters who elect them—all of us. In a time when we spend inordinate amounts of time and money on spectator sports, movies, and reality television shows, it can be argued that we get the leaders we deserve. In a democracy, a government of the people, we need responsible leadership not just from our elected officials but from our citizenry. We the people need to recognize that the use of disinformation as a weapon to exercise political power is a threat to democracy, and we must work to abolish it. We must use our voting power to insist on leaders who use facts to solve problems instead of lies to divide us. Voters must accept reasonable compromise from our leaders rather than demanding ideological purity at any cost. We can hold candidates and leaders accountable by refusing to elect or reelect those who knowingly perpetuate false claims and engage in deliberately divisive rhetoric. We should call out those who stand with any political party over country, who allow political ends to justify unscrupulous means. We should condemn leaders who glorify violence and bigotry. If we do not, we will be opening the door wider to greedy hucksters and power-hungry opportunists.

We must also exercise mutual tolerance and forbearance in our own lives. We need to do the work to verify facts needed to make informed decisions about significant societal issues, such as health crises and climate stabilization. We must avoid the temptation to go along with the con when our own side uses disinformation to advance its goals. We need to exercise restraint when we see a snarky comment online. Sharing, liking, and adding a mocking comment for cheap, fleeting laughs to "own" our opponents just exacerbate divisions and fuel disinformers.

Lasting Peace among Ourselves

An essential way to begin to heal our divide is by offering olive branches to people with whom we disagree. We must see people with different views not just as our political opponents but as our fellow Americans. People who have been duped by constant lies, as we have seen, will be reluctant to change their minds. The way to persuade them of the facts is not by mocking their foolishness or judging their enabling behavior. According to Ruth Ben-Ghiat, those who have followed duplicitous leaders "may feel ashamed and unwilling to admit their errors in judgment unless they are approached with the right spirit of openness, at the right time."[1712] In a polarized society, people can "dig their trenches deeper, or they can reach across the lines to stop a new cycle of destruction, knowing that solidarity, love, and dialogue" can conquer political demagogues.[1713] Taking this approach requires grace.

According to journalist Anand Giridharadas, author of *The Persuaders*, a book on political reconciliation, we must meet people where they are.[1714] If we want to win over the hearts and minds of our fellow Americans, we can't insist that everyone share all of our views. "In a time of escalating and cynical right-wing attacks on so-called wokeness," he writes, we should all work to make space for "the still waking."[1715] While we may have strong commitments to certain values like fighting hate and respecting personal pronouns, we should express "gentleness toward people who haven't got it all figured out, who are confused or even unsettled by the onrushing future."[1716]

This model is not a fantasy. It was at work in Ireland in 2018. It has worked in our own history. As president, Abraham Lincoln understood the need to welcome fellow citizens back into the fold, even after a bloody civil war. As the war ended, he delivered his second inaugural address, which ended with a plea for reconciliation:

With malice toward none, with charity for all, with firmness in the right as God gives us to see the right, let us strive on to finish the work we are in, to bind up the nation's wounds, to care for him who shall have borne the battle and for his widow and his orphan, to do all which may achieve and cherish a just and lasting peace among ourselves and with all nations.[1717]

Respecting each other means telling each other the truth. While we can never rid politics of spin and advocacy, we can insist on facts and refuse to perpetuate assertions we know to be lies simply to make a buck or somehow get ahead. Allowing public leaders, media, businesses, and institutions to propagate falsehoods assaults the integrity of our democracy. If we want to protect our rights from tyrants and con men, we must fight disinformation as unpatriotic, a betrayal of the American people. We must denounce as traitors the liars who use members of the public as their unsuspecting political pawns. To love America is to love the truth. We must make truth in democracy our national purpose.

Only an unyielding commitment to the truth can save us from the fate that met Rosanne Boyland, Ashli Babbitt, and Brian Sicknick. We can best honor their memory, and the memories of the service members who have sacrificed their lives for our country, by working to save American democracy from death by disinformation.

ACKNOWLEDGMENTS

This book is the product of my work in national security, begun as a federal prosecutor after the attacks of September 11 and continuing as a law school professor. During that time, I have seen threats against America evolve from those posed by foreign terrorist organizations like al-Qaeda to violent domestic extremists radicalized by the demagogues the founders warned us would come. What I failed to see back in 2001 was that the most potent weapons would be not bombs or airplanes but words, images, and lies.

Completing the book would not have been possible without my husband, who is a continuous source of inspiration, encouragement, and support. Before embarking on this project, I had read that Toni Morrison managed to become an author by waking up before dawn each day to seize the quality time she needed to think and work. When I told him I was considering the same strategy, but had some reluctance in light of my lifelong aversion to early mornings, he gave me his typically blunt but valuable advice: "I think you just gotta do it." Each morning, when the alarm went off, his words became my mantra. My thanks to him for his love, devotion, and many sacrifices for me and our family. He makes me think, he makes me laugh, and he makes me a better person. You are everything to me, and I love you.

Other family members also provided inspiration. Our children bring us boundless joy. We love you and are very proud of the kind young adults you have become. My mother, Beverly, taught me the value of making lists. The kitchen table in my childhood home was blanketed with her penciled reminders of things to do, to buy, to pack. We teased her then, but the lists were her secret weapon for getting things done. Mom's lists bear a close resemblance to the Post-It notes that now adorn my computer screen and desk. Many thanks to my sister, Kim, for a lifetime of the kind of brutally honest opinions only a sister can give: "You're wearing *that?*" My father, Bob, would have loved to read this book. His praise, which was glowing often to the point of being embarrassing, made me feel like I could do anything. He passed on a love of baseball by teaching me to read the box scores in the newspaper. My maternal grandparents, Les and Sally Taylor, taught me the magic of storytelling. My mother- and father-in-law served as early role models for couples with demanding careers raising families as equal partners. My father-in-law is a testament to what a person can achieve through hard work and decency.

Greg Ruggiero, an extraordinary editor, was a key partner for this book. Our brainstorming sessions helped to mold a clump of ideas into the arguments presented here. I valued his cheerful check-ins, generous feedback, and deference to my sometimes strong opinions. Isabelle Gross, my research assistant, provided tremendous help, combining excellent work with a can-do attitude. I am grateful to everyone at Seven Stories Press, including Dan Simon and Ruth Weiner, for making this book a reality. I admire their fiercely independent spirit and commitment to publishing books about human rights and social justice. My literary agents, Philippa "Flip" Brophy and Jessica Friedman of Sterling Lord Literistic, held my hand as I navigated the mysterious world of publishing. Copy editors Molly Pisani and Tal Mancini used their meticulous eyes for detail to check facts carefully and express ideas accurately—an essential part of a book on disinformation! Thanks to the great Rodrigo Corral for designing the magnificent cover for this book. The image of a white fist punching through a blue map of the United States perfectly captures the willingness of the MAGA right to destroy the fundamental principles of democracy to retain power.

Thank you to my colleagues and students at the University of Michigan Law School. What a wonderful gift to return to my alma mater in 2017, after twenty-six years of practicing law. At Michigan Law School, I am privileged to engage every day with people who are bright, curious, and scrupulously ethical. During a time when political events could have made the world seem deeply depressing, these brilliant minds are continually finding new ways to use the law to solve problems. They make me optimistic for our future.

I am indebted to former FBI counterintelligence agents Asha Rangappa and Clint Watts, frequent guest speakers in my class on national security and civil liberties at the law school. They have both done important work in the field of disinformation, and they are cited extensively in this book. I have learned so much from both of them. I am thankful for the friends who shared wisdom from their own experiences in writing books—Michelle Adams, John U. Bacon, Preet Bharara, Scott Hershovitz, Don Herzog, Dahlia Lithwick, David Maraniss, Steve Vladeck, Jill Wine-Banks, and James B. White, among others.

Many thanks to the hardworking people at NBC News and MSNBC for giving me a platform to explain the news. I am grateful for the opportunity to help people understand how the legal system works, so that they can form their own opinions based on law and facts. And thank you to the viewers who watch and share words of support; I appreciate every one. Robert Palassou, whom I have never met, sent inspiring notes about the importance of truth to honoring the memories of people like his father, who fought for democracy in World War II.

I am honored to have worked with my former colleagues at the US Department of Justice and the US Attorney's Office for the

Eastern District of Michigan, where I learned what it means to seek justice. They are a special group of smart and honorable people who make countless personal sacrifices to serve the public. I am a better person for every minute I have spent with them. I can't name them all here, but I remain grateful to Saul Green, the US attorney who hired me in 1998, and I still draw inspiration from Stacey Harris, with her unyielding optimism and enthusiasm to take on whatever comes her way. Thanks to my fellow US attorneys from across the country for their encouragement in all my endeavors. I treasure their continuing friendship. Eric Holder, the former attorney general with whom I had the privilege to serve during the Obama administration, was a source of motivation. His book on voting rights, *Our Unfinished March*, helped kickstart this project. After we discussed the idea for this book, he would text me from time to time saying, simply, "Write your book."

Thank you to my career-long mentor, Judge Bernard Friedman, and every generation of his chambers family of law clerks and staff. I learned so much from all of you. Mountains never meet, but men do. I am grateful to my former colleagues at the law firm of Butzel Long, where I became a lawyer. Before law school, I had the good fortune to work as a sportswriter and copy editor at the *Democrat and Chronicle* in Rochester, New York. The buzz of the newsroom was thrilling. Journalists there taught me to edit words to say more with less. Jim and Mary Holleran and Craig and Laura Gordon gave me a family away from home when I was young and alone in a new city; I can never repay you for your friendship and wisdom. Thank you to my fellow writers and editors at my college newspaper, the *Michigan Daily*, where I learned to interview people who intimidated me and, most importantly, to understand the importance of accuracy in the news. My college degree may say otherwise, but I majored in the *Michigan Daily*. Thanks to all of the teachers, counselors, coaches, and faith leaders who helped me find my way, with a special shout-out to Mrs. Adrienne Allard, a high school counselor whose confidence in me helped me believe in myself.

I am fortunate to have friends who provided positive support during this project—my sisters in the law, Kimberly Atkins Stohr, Joyce Vance, and Jill Wine-Banks, and our producers at Politicon. They help me think about legal issues in the news, and they remind me to laugh sometimes at the absurdity of it all. Maureen (Mo-Jo) Murrett is always a source of positive motivation. She has found her true calling as a coach, and is an extraordinary one. Marissa Pollick is a friend and mentor who dares to combine law and justice. I appreciate my tennis friends, who always inquired about the book and offered words of encouragement between sets. Thank you to my childhood friends Maria Yencha, Sue Doherty, and Sandy Kronst—the neighborhood newspapers, plays, songs, and time capsule histories my sister and I created together with them inspired a lifelong love of writing. I am grateful for school friends who remind me still of the wonder of our youth and our dreams for the future: Kathy Nicholl, Tammy Olsztyn, Pam Williams, the Bursley crew, the Pi Phis, and the N-Mates.

And thanks to you, the reader, for choosing to learn more about how we can take our country back from the authoritarians who use lies to manipulate public opinion. An informed electorate has always been necessary for democracy. To solve the problems that face us and contribute to human advancement, we all have a responsibility to gather facts from reliable sources so that we can engage in meaningful debate. We must reject lies designed to maintain the dominance of some groups over others, an affront to the American ideal that we are all created equal. If we remember that we all have more in common than we have differences, if we respect human dignity, if we stride confidently together in our quest for the truth, we can continue to make progress in our journey toward a more perfect union.

—Barbara McQuade
Ann Arbor, Michigan

NOTES

Introduction: Disinformed to Death

1. Evan Hill, Arielle Ray, and Dahlia Kozlowsky, "Video Shows How Rioter Was Trampled in Stampede at Capitol," *New York Times,* May 31, 2021.
2. "It's Official: The Election Was Secure," Brennan Center for Justice, December 11, 2020, https://www.brennancenter.org/our-work/research-reports/its-official-election-was-secure.
3. Hill, Ray, and Kozlowsky, "Video Shows."
4. Hill, Ray, and Kozlowsky, "Video Shows."
5. Boyland's death certificate listed her official cause of death as an amphetamine overdose. "Facts First," Politics, CNN, https://www.cnn.com/factsfirst/politics/factcheck_be6205ad-ee31-42e8-843f-9fbeb156b25a.
6. Nicholas Bogel-Burroughs and Evan Hill, "Death of QAnon Follower at Capitol Leaves a Wake of Pain," *New York Times,* May 30, 2021.
7. Bogel-Burroughs and Hill, "Death of QAnon."
8. Bogel-Burroughs and Hill, "Death of QAnon."
9. Michael Waldman, "Focus on the Big Lie, Not the Big Liar," Brennan Center for Justice, June 14, 2022, https://www.brennancenter.org/our-work/analysis-opinion/focus-big-lie-not-big-liar.
10. Chris Cameron, "These Are the People Who Died in Connection with the Capitol Riot," *New York Times,* January 5, 2022; Jan Wolfe, "Four Officers Who Responded to US Capitol Attack Have Died by Suicide," Reuters, August 2, 2021, https://www.reuters.com/world/us/officer-who-responded-us-capitol-attack-is-third-die-by-suicide-2021-08-02/.
11. Nicholas Wu and Katherine Tully-McManus, "Capitol Police Lt. Michael Byrd Speaks Out on Fatal Shooting of Ashli Babbitt," Politico, August 26, 2021, https://www.politico.com/news/2021/08/26/capitol-police-officer-byrd-ashli-babbitt-506971.
12. Peter Hermann and Spencer S. Hsu, "Capitol Police Officer Brian Sicknick, Who Engaged Rioters, Suffered Two Strokes and Died of Natural Causes, Officials Say," *Washington Post,* April 19, 2021.
13. Luke Broadwater, "Capitol Police Officer's Suicide after Jan. 6 Qualifies for Line-of-Duty Death Benefit," *New York Times,* November 21, 2022.
14. Sarah Longwell, "Trump Supporters Explain Why They Believe the Big Lie," *The Atlantic,* April 18, 2022.
15. Barton Gellman, "Trump's Next Coup Has Already Begun," *The Atlantic,* December 6, 2021.
16. J. Michael Luttig, "Opinion: The Republican Blueprint to Steal the 2024 Election," CNN Opinion, April 27, 2022, https://www.cnn.com/2022/04/27/opinions/gop-blueprint-to-steal-the-2024-election-luttig/index.html.
17. David Rovella, "Your Evening Briefing: Conservative Legal Icon Calls Trump 'Clear and Present Danger,'" Bloomberg, June 16, 2022.
18. RealDonaldTrump, Truth Social, Sept. 3, 2023, 6:11 p.m., https://truthsocial.com/@realDonaldTrump/posts/111003506583743120
19. Gellmann, "Trump's Next."
20. Catie Edmondson and Nicholas Fandos, "Republicans Oust a Defiant Cheney, Confirming Trump's Grasp on the Party," *New York Times,* May 18, 2021.
21. US Department of Homeland Security, *Summary of Terrorism Threat to the US Homeland,* National Terrorism Advisory System Bulletin, February 7, 2022, https://www.dhs.gov/ntas/advisory/national-terrorism-advisory-system-bulletin-february-07-2022.
22. US Department of Homeland Security, *Summary of Terrorism.*
23. Jared Gans, "House GOP Leaders Defend Trump on Day of Arraignment: 'A Dark Day for Our Country,'" The Hill, June 13, 2023, https://thehill.com/homenews/house/4048322-house-gop-leaders-defend-trump-after-arraignment/.

24. Colin Woodard, *American Nations: A History of the Eleven Rival Regional Cultures of North America* (New York: Penguin Books, 2012), 2.

25. "Transcript: Barack Obama Speech on Technology and Democracy," Tech Policy Press, April 22, 2022, https://techpolicy.press/transcript-barack-obama-speech-on-technology-and -democracy/.

26. "Transcript: Barack Obama Speech."

27. Maggie Macdonald and Megan A. Brown, "Republicans Are Increasingly Sharing Misinformation, Research Finds," *Washington Post*, August 29, 2022.

28. "Posts Spread Edited Photo of Oz on Hollywood Walk of Fame," AP News, August 22, 2022, https://apnews.com/article/fact-check-dr-oz-hollywood-star-trump-080309769407.

29. "Posts Spread Edited Photo."

30. Hemant Kakkar and Asher Lawson, "We Found the One Group of Americans Who Are Most Likely to Spread Fake News," Politico, January 14, 2022, https://www.politico.com /news/magazine/2022/01/14/we-found-the-one-group-of-americans-who-are-most-likely-to -spread-fake-news-526973.

31. Oliver Darcy et al., "Fox Chairman Rupert Murdoch Rejected Election Conspiracy Theories, Dominion Lawsuit Documents Show," Business, CNN, March 8, 2023, https://www.cnn .com/2023/03/07/media/fox-news-dominion-lawsuit/index.html.

32. Jeremy W. Peters and Katie Robertson, "Fox News Settles Defamation Suit for $787.5 Million, Dominion Says," *New York Times*, April 19, 2023.

33. Jeremy Barr, "Fox News Shocks with 'Wannabe Dictator' Graphic during Biden Speech," *Washington Post*, June 14, 2023.

34. Final Report of the Select Committee to Investigate the January 6th Attack on the United States Capitol, H.R. Rep. No. 117-663, 2d. Sess., at 4 (Dec. 22, 2022).

35. David Ignatius, "Nearly Every American Has a Foreboding the Country They Love Is Losing Its Way," Opinion, *Washington Post*, July 3, 2022.

36. Quoctrung Bui, "The Rise and Fall of US Inequality in Two Graphs," NPR, February 11, 2015, https://www.npr.org/sections/money/2015/02/11/384988128/the-fall-and-rise-of-u-s -inequality-in-2-graphs.

37. Mark Kumleben, Samuel Woolley, and Katie Joseff, *Electoral Confusion: Contending with Structural Disinformation in Communities of Color* (Protect Democracy, June 2022), 13.

38. Kimberly Atkins Stohr, "Jan. 6 Committee Leaves Crucial Lessons about Race Unspoken," *Boston Globe*, December 20, 2022.

39. Stohr, "Jan. 6 Committee Leaves."

40. Stohr, "Jan. 6 Committee Leaves."

41. Catie Edmondson, "'So the Traitors Know the Stakes': The Meaning of the Jan. 6 Gallows," *New York Times*, June 16, 2022.

42. Nicole Narea, "Kari Lake's Lonely and Deeply Absurd Quest to Challenge the Arizona Election Results," Vox, November 30, 2022, https://www.vox.com/policy-and-politics /2022/11/30/23484972/kari-lake-election-denier-arizona-trump.

43. Associated Press, "Appeals Court Rejects Kari Lake's Challenge of Her Defeat in Arizona Governor's Race and Claims of Election Misconduct," February 16, 2023, https://apnews .com/article/ap-news-alert-kari-lake-arizona-634615cd005cec1d18abfcf1c95de4c7.

44. Alice Herman et al., "The Election-Denying Republicans Who Aided Trump's 'Big Lie' and Got Promoted," *The Guardian* (London), March 9, 2023.

45. Ben Jacobs, "Did George Santos Lie about Everything?" Vox, January 19, 2023, https://www.vox .com/policy-and-politics/23520848/george-santos-fake-resume; Timothy Bella, "George Santos Said 9/11 'Claimed My Mother's Life.' She Died in 2016." *Washington Post*, December 29, 2022.

46. Matthew Boyle, "George Santos's Defense That Everyone Lies on Their Resumes Has Truth to It," Bloomberg, January 13, 2023, https://www.bloomberg.com/news/articles/2023-01-13 /george-santos-says-everyone-lies-on-their-resume-he-s-telling-the-truth#xj4y7vzkg.

47. Grace Ashford, Michael Gold, William K. Rashbaum, and Annie Karni, "Santos Is Accused of Using Illicit Campaign Contributions for Personal Expenses," *New York Times*, May 10, 2023.

48. Greg Sargent, "New Fears about Ron DeSantis's Book Crackdowns Show His Odious Game," Opinion, *Washington Post*, January 27, 2023; Matt Dixon and Gary Fineout, "'Where Woke Goes to Die': DeSantis, with Eye Toward 2024, Launches Second Term," Politico,

January 3, 2023, https://www.politico.com/news/2023/01/03/desantis-2024-second
-term-00076160.

49. Luke Broadwater and Catie Edmondson, "Divided House Approves G.O.P. Inquiry into
'Weaponization' of Government," *New York Times*, January 10, 2023.

50. Katherine Pompilio, "Manhattan DA Sues Jim Jordan," *Lawfare*, April 11, 2023.

51. Greg Sargent, "Jim Jordan's Latest Antics Won't Save Trump from a Jury's Judgment," *Washington Post*, August 28, 2023.

52. Steven Lee Myers and Sheera Frenkel, "GOP Targets Researchers Who Study Disinformation
Ahead of 2024 Election," New York Times, June 19, 2023.

53. Naomi Nox, Cat Zakrzewski, and Joseph Menn, "Misinformation Research is Buckling
Under GOP Legal Attacks," *Washington Post*, September 23, 2023.

54. Nox, Zakrzewski, and Menn, "Misinformation Research

55. Monique Curet, "Claim about Schools Providing Litter Boxes for Students Debunked in
Several States," PolitiFact, April 8, 2022, https://www.politifact.com/factchecks/2022/apr/08
/facebook-posts/claim-about-schools-providing-litter-boxes-student/; Dana Hunsinger Benbow, "Tony Dungy Deletes Controversial Cat Litter Tweet after Backlash, Outrage,"
IndyStar, January 18, 2023, https://www.indystar.com/story/sports/nfl/colts/2023/01/19/ex
-indianapolis-colts-coach-tony-dungy-deletes-cat-litter-tweet/69820624007/.

56. Thomas Rid, *Active Measures: The Secret History of Disinformation and Political Warfare* (New
York: Farrar, Straus and Giroux, 2020), 25.

57. Rid, *Active Measures*, 26.

58. Rid, *Active Measures*, 27–28.

59. Alexander Hamilton or James Madison, *The Federalist*, no. 63, Library of Congress, https://guides
.loc.gov/federalist-papers/text-61-70#s-lg-box-wrapper-25493450.

60. Jack Mitchell, "20 Years Ago, the US Warned of Iraq's Alleged 'Weapons of Mass Destruction,'" NPR, February 3, 2023, https://www.npr.org/transcripts/1151160567.

61. "Psychological Operations," US Army, https://www.goarmy.com/careers-and-jobs/specialty
-careers/special-ops/psychological-operations.html.

62. "Psychological Operations," US Army.

63. US Department of the Army, *Psychological Operations*, Field Manual no. 3-05.30, April 15,
2005, 1–12.

64. "Three Men Are Convicted of Supporting a Plot to Kidnap Michigan Gov. Gretchen Whitmer," NPR, October 26, 2022, https://www.npr.org/2022/10/26/1131607112/michigan-governor
-gretchen-whitmer-kidnapping-convictions.

65. Annie Karni and Tim Arango, "Court Releases Video of Paul Pelosi Hammer Attack, Adding
Chilling Details," *New York Times*, January 27, 2023.

66. Ayana Archie and Bill Chappell, "A Losing Republican Candidate in N.M. Is Charged over
Shootings at Homes of Democrats," NPR, January 18, 2023, https://www.npr.org/2023
/01/17/1149464953/new-mexico-shooting-politicians-solomon-pena.

67. Marshall Cohen, "Mar-a-Lago Special Master Orders Trump Team to Back Up Any Claims
of FBI 'Planting' Evidence," Politics, CNN, September 23, 2022, https://www.cnn
.com/2022/09/22/politics/mar-a-lago-special-master-trump-fbi-planting-evidence/index.html.

68. Julie Bosman, "Kyle Rittenhouse Acquitted on All Counts," *New York Times*, January 27,
2022.

69. Alan Feuer, "In Capitol Attack, Over 900 People Have Been Criminally Charged," *New York
Times*, December 19, 2022.

70. Jamie Raskin, "The Second Amendment Gives No Comfort to Insurrectionists," Opinion,
New York Times, September 27, 2022.

71. "Democracy," US Department of State, https://2009-2017.state.gov/j/drl/democ
/#:~:text=Assist%20democracy%20advocates%20around%20the,free%2C%20fair%2C%20
and%20transparent, Jan. 20, 2017.

72. Steven Levitsky and Daniel Ziblatt, *How Democracies Die* (New York: Crown, 2018), 3.

73. Levitsky and Ziblatt, *How Democracies Die*, 3.

74. Levitsky and Ziblatt, *How Democracies Die*, 5.

75. David E. Sanger and Steve Lee Myers, "China Sows Disinformation about Hawaii Fires
Using New Techniques," *New York Times*, Sept. 11, 2023.

76. "People Are Entitled to Their Own Opinions but Not to Their Own Facts," Quote Investigator, March 17, 2020, https://quoteinvestigator.com/2020/03/17/own-facts/.

77. Timothy Bella, "Missouri Republicans Adopt Stricter House Dress Code—but Just for Women," *Washington Post*, January 12, 2023.

78. Barack Obama, "Remarks by the President at the 50th Anniversary of the Selma to Montgomery Marches," speech presented at Edmund Pettus Bridge, Selma, Alabama, March 7, 2015, The White House: President Barack Obama, Briefing Room, https://obamawhitehouse.archives.gov/the-press-office/2015/03/07/remarks-president-50th-anniversary-selma-montgomery-marches.

79. Monica Hesse, "Liz Cheney Understood the Assignment," *Washington Post*, July 22, 2022.

1. The Authoritarian Playbook: How Disinformers Gain Power

80. Keith Gessen, "How Stalin Became Stalinist," *New Yorker*, October 30, 2017.

81. Gessen, "How Stalin."

82. Will Englund, "Why Trump's 'Enemy of the People' Bluster Can't Be Compared to Stalin's Savage Rule," Retropolis, *Washington Post*, January 17, 2018.

83. Gessen, "How Stalin."

84. Gessen, "How Stalin."

85. Gessen, "How Stalin."

86. Gessen, "How Stalin."

87. Gessen, "How Stalin."

88. Englund, "Why Trump's."

89. Englund, "Why Trump's."

90. Jennifer Dresden, Aaron Baird, and Ben Raderstorf, *The Authoritarian Playbook* (Protect Democracy, June 2022).

91. Hannah Arendt, *The Origins of Totalitarianism* (New York: Mariner Books, 1968), 382.

92. "What Is the Difference between Totalitarianism and Authoritarianism?" Britannica, accessed August 2, 2023, https://www.britannica.com/question/What-is-the-difference-between-totalitarianism-and-authoritarianism.

93. "What Is the Difference," Britannica.

94. "Authoritarianism," Britannica, last updated June 20, 2023, https://www.britannica.com/topic/authoritarianism.

95. "Authoritarianism," Britannica.

96. "What Is the Difference," Britannica.

97. Britannica, "Learn about Benito Mussolini, His Rise to Power, and Role in World War II," Britannica Q&A video, 2:21, https://www.britannica.com/biography/Benito-Mussolini/images-videos.

98. "Learn about," Britannica.

99. Dresden, Baird, and Raderstorf, *Authoritarian Playbook*, 7; Ruth Ben-Ghiat, *Strongmen: Mussolini to the Present* (New York: W. W. Norton & Company, 2020).

100. Ben-Ghiat, *Strongmen*, 104–10.

101. The 1990s science-fiction series featured an iconic poster with those words beneath a picture of a UFO. Ella Morton, "The *X-Files* 'I Want to Believe' Poster's Origin Story," *New Republic*, December 29, 2015.

102. Donald A. Barclay, *Disinformation: The Nature of Facts and Lies in the Post-Truth Era* (Lanham, MD: Rowman & Littlefield, 2022), 40–41.

103. Barclay, *Disinformation*, 41.

104. Ben-Ghiat, *Strongmen*, 103.

105. "Full Text: 2017 Donald Trump Inauguration Speech Transcript," Politico, January 20, 2017, https://www.politico.com/story/2017/01/full-text-donald-trump-inauguration-speech-transcript-233907.

106. "Full Text: 2017 Donald Trump."

107. John Gramlich, "What the Data Says (and Doesn't Say) about Crime in the United States," Pew Research Center, November 20, 2020, https://www.pewresearch.org/short-reads/2020/11/20/facts-about-crime-in-the-u-s/.

108. "National Poverty in America Awareness Month: January 2023," Press Release Number CB23-SFS.003, United States Census Bureau, January 2023, https://www.census.gov/newsroom /stories/poverty-awareness-month.html.

109. Gopal K. Singh and Stella M. Yu, "Infant Mortality in the United States, 1915–2017: Large Social Inequalities Have Persisted for over a Century," *International Journal of Maternal and Child Health and AIDS* 8, no. 1 (2019): 19–31.

110. "College Enrollment in the United States from 1965 to 2020 and Projections up to 2031 for Public and Private Colleges," Statista, released December 2022, https://www.statista.com /statistics/183995/us-college-enrollment-and-projections-in-public-and-private-institutions/.

111. Ben-Ghiat, *Strongmen*, 93.

112. Ben-Ghiat, *Strongmen*, 102.

113. Ben-Ghiat, *Strongmen*, 104.

114. Alan Feuer and Maggie Haberman, "Trump Rally Plays Music Resembling QAnon Song, and Crowds React," *New York Times*, September 18, 2022.

115. Charles Homans, "How 'Stop the Steal' Captured the American Right," *New York Times*, July 19, 2022.

116. Homans, "How 'Stop.'"

117. United States Holocaust Memorial Museum, "Reichstag Speech," Holocaust Encyclopedia.

118. "Apartheid," History, last accessed November 2, 2022, https://www.history.com/topics/africa /apartheid.

119. David Hoffman, "Putin's Career Rooted in Russia's KGB," *Washington Post*, January 30, 2000.

120. US Department of Justice, *Report on the Investigation into Russian Interference in the 2016 Presidential Election*, by Robert S. Mueller III, March 2019, vol. I, 22.

121. US Department of Justice, *Report on the Investigation*, vol. I, 24.

122. US Department of Justice, *Report on the Investigation*, vol. I, 4.

123. David Klepper, "Thousands of Pro-Trump Bots Are Attacking DeSantis, Haley," Associated Press, March 6, 2023.

124. Barclay, *The Nature*, 39.

125. Homans, "How 'Stop.'"

126. Theda Skocpol and Vanessa Williamson, *The Tea Party and the Remaking of Republican Conservatism* (New York: Oxford University, 2016).

127. Homans, "How 'Stop.'"

128. Russell Muirhead and Nancy L. Rosenblum, *A Lot of People Are Saying: The New Conspiracism and the Assault on Democracy* (Princeton, NJ: Princeton University Press, 2019), 60.

129. Rich Lowry, "I'm a Uniter, Not a Divider," *Washington Post*, October 29, 2000.

130. The American Presidency Project, July 27, 2004, https://www.presidency.ucsb.edu/documents /keynote-address-the-2004-democratic-national-convention.

131. Marjorie Taylor Greene (@mtgreenee), "Thread: Why the left and right should consider a national divorce, not a civil war but a legal agreement to separate our ideological and political disagreements by states while maintaining our legal union. Definition of irreconcilable differences: inability to agree on most things or on important things. Tragically, I think we, the left and right, have reached irreconcilable differences. I'll speak for the right and say, we are absolutely disgusted and fed up with the left cramming and forcing their ways on us and our children with no respect for our religion/faith, traditional values, and economic & government policy beliefs." Twitter, February 21, 2023, 11:03 a.m., https://twitter.com/mtgreenee /status/1628062900345602048?lang=en.

132. Greene, "Thread: Why the left."

133. Greene, "Thread: Why the left."

134. Ashley Parker, "Donald Trump Says Hillary Clinton Doesn't Have 'a Presidential Look,'" *New York Times*, September 6, 2016.

135. Steve Wyche, "Colin Kaepernick Explains Why He Sat during National Anthem," NFL.com, updated August 27, 2016, available at http://web.archive.org/web/20160827220920/ http://www.nfl.com/news/story/0ap3000000691077/article/colin-kaepernick-explains-why -he-sat-during-national-anthem.

136. Jeremy Gottlieb and Mark Maske, "Roger Goodell Responds to Trump's Call to 'Fire' NFL Players Protesting during National Anthem," *Washington Post*, September 23, 2017.

137. Peter Baker, "A Long History of Language That Incites and Demonizes," *New York Times*, August 31, 2020.

138. Andrew Solender, "Trump Campaign Suggests Democrats Are Not Americans," *Forbes*, October 5, 2020.

139. Solender, "Trump Campaign."

140. Bryan Ke, "Trump Calls Elaine Chao 'Coco Chow' in Latest Attack on Mitch McConnell," NextShark, October 3, 2022, https://nextshark.com/trump-calls-elaine-chao-coco-chow-in -latest-attack-on-mitch-mcconnell.

141. Aris Folley, "Trump Supporters Whose Russia Shirts Went Viral: 'We're Not Traitors,'" The Hill, August 28, 2018, https://thehill.com/blogs/blog-briefing-room/news/404017-trump -supporters-whose-pro-russia-shirts-went-viral-were-not/.

142. Homans, "How 'Stop.'"

143. Anthony Izaguirre, "Florida Board of Education Expands 'Don't Say Gay' Classroom Ban to All Grades," PBS News Hour, April 19, 2023, https://www.pbs.org/newshour/politics/florida -board-of-education-expands-dont-say-gay-classroom-ban-to-all-grades.

144. Jesus Jiménez and Brooks Barnes, "What We Know about the DeSantis Disney Dispute," *New York Times*, May 19, 2023.

145. Amber Phillips, "'They're Rapists.' President Trump's Campaign Launch Speech Two Years Later, Annotated," *Washington Post*, June 16, 2017.

146. Maggie Haberman and Richard A. Oppel Jr., "Donald Trump Criticizes Muslim Family of Slain US Soldier, Drawing Ire," *New York Times*, July 30, 2016.

147. Alan Feuer, "Charlottesville Extremists Lose in Court, but Replacement Theory Lives On," *New York Times*, November 24, 2021; "You Will Not Replace Us," Hate on Display, Anti-Defamation League, accessed August 4, 2023, https://www.adl.org/resources/hate-symbol/you -will-not-replace-us.

148. "Great Replacement," Translate Hate, American Jewish Committee, accessed August 4, 2023, https://www.ajc.org/translatehate/great-replacement.

149. "Great Replacement," American Jewish Committee.

150. Angie Drobnic Holan, "In Context: Donald Trump's 'Very Fine People on Both Sides' Remarks (Transcript)," PolitiFact, April 26, 2019, https://www.politifact.com/article/2019 /apr/26/context-trumps-very-fine-people-both-sides-remarks/.

151. Isaac Stanley-Becker and Jacqueline Alemany, "Judge Asks Trump Not to Incite Violence amid Volley of Online Attacks," *Washington Post*, April 4, 2023.

152. Alejandra Marquez Janse, Patrick Jarenwattanon, and Mary Louise Kelly, "The Truth and Half-Truths of George Soros' Relationship to Manhattan DA Alvin Bragg," NPR, April 6, 2023, https://www.npr.org/2023/04/06/1168490400/soros-doesnt-have-power-over-the -trump-case-like-trump-supporters-think-author-s.

153. Janse, Jarenwattanon, and Kelly, "The Truth."

154. Janse, Jarenwattanon, and Kelly, "The Truth."

155. Janse, Jarenwattanon, and Kelly, "The Truth."

156. Harmeet Kaur, "What It Reveals When Senators Repeatedly Mispronounce the Names of Kamala Harris and Sundar Pichai," CNN, October 31, 2020, https://www.cnn.com/2020 /10/30/us/sundar-pichai-kamala-harris-names-mispronounced-trnd/index.html.

157. Kaur, "What It Reveals."

158. Erin Mansfield, "Rep. Lauren Boebert and the Politics of Outrage: Why Lawmakers Reap Rewards from Firebrand Tactics," *USA Today*, December 5, 2021.

159. Janse, Jarenwattanon, and Kelly, "The Truth."

160. Cailin O'Connor and James Owen Weatherall, *The Misinformation Age: How False Beliefs Spread* (New Haven, CT: Yale University Press, 2018), 126.

161. Ben-Ghiat, *Strongmen*, 67.

162. Ben-Ghiat, *Strongmen*, 67.

163. Sarah Pulliam Bailey, "Photo Surfaces of Evangelical Pastors Laying Hands on Trump in the Oval Office," *Washington Post*, July 12, 2017.

164. Daniel Politi, "Watch Trump Kiss and Caress an American Flag at CPAC: 'I Love You, Baby,'" *Slate*, March 1, 2020, https://slate.com/news-and-politics/2020/03/watch-trump-kiss-caress-american-flag-cpac-love-you-baby.html.

165. Eugene Scott, "Why Ted Cruz Was Making a Biblical Case for Gun Rights after the Odessa Shooting," *Washington Post*, September 4, 2019.

166. Renzo Downey, "'Portraits in Patriotism' Highlighted as Counter to Critical Race Theory," Florida Politics, June 22, 2021, https://floridapolitics.com/archives/437474-portraits-in-patriotism-highlighted-as-counter-to-critical-race-theory/.

167. Steve Benen, "Why Jim Jordan Should Avoid Fights over What's 'Un-American,'" *Maddow-Blog*, MSNBC, September 8, 2021, https://www.msnbc.com/rachel-maddow-show/maddowblog/why-jim-jordan-should-avoid-fights-over-what-s-un-n1278683.

168. William McCants, "How ISIS Got Its Flag," *The Atlantic*, September 22, 2015.

169. Katya Soldak, "This Is How Propaganda Works: A Look Inside a Soviet Childhood," *Forbes*, December 20, 2017.

170. Jack Jenkins, "Republicans Mostly Mum on Calls to Make GOP 'Party of Christian Nationalism,'" *Washington Post*, August 19, 2022.

171. Jenkins, "Republicans Mostly."

172. Tim Carman, "Rep. Lauren Boebert's Gun-Themed Shooters Grill Closes in Rifle, Colo.," *Washington Post*, July 14, 2022.

173. Carman, "Rep. Lauren."

174. Timothy Snyder, *On Tyranny: Twenty Lessons from the Twentieth Century* (New York: Tim Duggan Books, 2017), 73.

175. Emma Graham-Harrison, "'Enemy of the People': Trump's Phrase and Its Echoes of Totalitarianism," *The Guardian* (London), August 3, 2018.

176. "Augusto Pinochet," Britannica, last updated June 28, 2023, https://www.britannica.com/biography/Augusto-Pinochet.

177. Ben-Ghiat, *Strongmen*, 108.

178. Ben-Ghiat, *Strongmen*, 108.

179. "Sixty Years of News Media and Censorship," Reporters Without Borders.

180. "Sixty Years," Reporters Without Borders.

181. "Sixty Years," Reporters Without Borders.

182. Rick Noack, "The Ugly History of 'Lugenpresse,' a Nazi Slur Shouted at a Trump Rally," *Washington Post*, October 24, 2016.

183. Noack, "The Ugly."

184. Noack, "The Ugly."

185. Noack, "The Ugly."

186. Noack, "The Ugly."

187. Glenn Kessler, Salvador Rizzo, and Meg Kelly, "Trump's False or Misleading Claims Total 30,573 over 4 Years," *Washington Post*, January 24, 2021.

188. Jim Acosta, "How Trump's 'Fake News' Rhetoric Has Gotten out of Control," Politics, CNN, June 11, 2019, https://www.cnn.com/2019/06/11/politics/enemy-of-the-people-jim-acosta-donald-trump/index.html.

189. John Wagner, "Trump Renews Attacks on Media as 'the True Enemy of the People,'" *Washington Post*, October 29, 2018.

190. Muirhead and Rosenblum, *A Lot of People*, 114.

191. Muirhead and Rosenblum, *A Lot of People*, 113.

192. Muirhead and Rosenblum, *A Lot of People*, 113.

193. Ben-Ghiat, *Strongmen*, 115.

194. Eileen Sullivan, "Trump Attacks 'Failing New York Times' over Tax Scheme Reporting," *New York Times*, October 3, 2018.

195. Louis Nelson, "Trump Slams CNN's 'Crazy Jim Acosta' in Shutdown Victory Lap Tweet," Politico, January 23, 2018, https://www.politico.com/story/2018/01/23/trump-tweet-cnn-jim-acosta-358249.

196. Jack Share, "Trump Is Right. It Is the Amazon *Washington Post*," Politico, April 4, 2018, https://www.politico.com/magazine/story/2018/04/04/trump-amazon-washington-post-jeff-bezos-217774/.

197. Amanda Wills and Alysha Love, "All the President's Tweets," CNN, November 7, 2019, https://www.cnn.com/interactive/2017/politics/trump-tweets/.
198. Ben-Ghiat, *Strongmen*, 116–117.
199. Ben-Ghiat, *Strongmen*, 117.
200. Amie Parnes and Dominick Mastrangelo, "DeSantis Steps Up Attacks on the Media," The Hill, October 10, 2022, https://thehill.com/homenews/state-watch/3678541-desantis-steps-up-attacks-on-media/.
201. Parnes and Mastrangelo, "DeSantis Steps."
202. Arek Sarkissian, "DeSantis Continues Broadsides against the Media Ahead of Likely 2024 Run," Politico, February 7, 2023, https://www.politico.com/news/2023/02/07/desantis-media-attacks-2024-00081566.
203. Martin Pengelly, "Arizona's Kari Lake Vows to Be Media's 'Worst Fricking Nightmare' If She Wins," *The Guardian* (London), November 8, 2022.
204. Kari Lake (The Kari Lake), "Sledgehammer to Media Lies," video, 3:30, Facebook, July 22, 2021, https://www.facebook.com/watch/?v=322618936226365.
205. Kari Lake (The Kari Lake), "Sledgehammer to Media."
206. Acosta, "How Trump's."
207. Acosta, "How Trump's."
208. Chris Cillizza, "Donald Trump Just Accidentally Revealed Something Very Important about His 'Fake News' Attacks," Politics, CNN, May 9, 2018, https://www.cnn.com/2018/05/09/politics/donald-trump-media-tweet/index.html.
209. Quoted in Peter Stone, "Trump's Increasing Tirade against FBI and DoJ Endangering Lives of Officials," *The Guardian* (London), September 11, 2022.
210. Landon R. Y. Storrs, "The Ugly History behind Trump's Attacks on Civil Servants," Politico, March 26, 2017, https://www.politico.com/magazine/story/2017/03/history-trump-attacks-civil-service-federal-workers-mccarthy-214951/.
211. Rebecca Harrington, "Here's What Trump Means When He Says 'Drain the Swamp'—Even Though It's Not an Accurate Metaphor," Business Insider, November 11, 2016, https://www.businessinsider.com/what-does-drain-the-swamp-mean-was-dc-built-on-a-swamp-2016-11.
212. Charles S. Clark, "Deconstructing the Deep State," Government Executive, accessed August 8, 2023, https://www.govexec.com/feature/gov-exec-deconstructing-deep-state/.
213. Clark, "Deconstructing the Deep."
214. Clark, "Deconstructing the Deep."
215. Clark, "Deconstructing the Deep."
216. Martin Pengelly, "Stephen Miller Blamed Impeachment on Deep State—Bannon Says That's for 'Nut Cases,'" *The Guardian* (London), October 4, 2019.
217. Michael D. Shear and Alexander Burns, "Trump Calls Comey 'Untruthful Slime Ball' as Book Details Released," *New York Times*, April 13, 2018.
218. Jennifer Hansler, "Trump's Twitter Attacks on Sessions: An Annotated Timeline," Politics, CNN, August 25, 2018, https://www.cnn.com/2018/08/25/politics/trump-sessions-twitter-timeline/index.html.
219. Hansler, "Trump's Twitter."
220. "Trump Lashes out at 'Treasonous' Officials after McCabe Interview," BBC News, February 18, 2019, https://www.bbc.com/news/world-us-canada-47283737.
221. Quint Forgey, "Trump Goes on Twitter Tear after White House Official Condemns His Ukraine Call," Politico, October 29, 2019, https://www.politico.eu/article/twitter-white-house-official-ukraine-call-donald-trump/.
222. Forgey, "Trump Goes."
223. Forgey, "Trump Goes."
224. Forgey, "Trump Goes."
225. Sharon LaFraniere, Nicholas Fandos, and Andrew E. Kramer, "Ukraine Envoy Says She Was Told Trump Wanted Her Out over Lack of Trust," *New York Times*, October 11, 2019.
226. Mike Allen, "First Casualty of Impeachment War," Axios, last modified November 16, 2019.
227. Allen, "First Casualty."

228. Josephine Harvey, "William Barr Gives Blunt New Definition to Trump's Favorite Insult of Republicans," Yahoo! News, last updated September 7, 2022, https://news.yahoo.com /william-barr-gives-blunt-definition-012134512.html.

229. Karl de Vries, "Milley Says Trump Disrespected Military with Execution Comment," CNN Politics, September 28, 2023, https://www.cnn.com/2023/09/28/politics/milley-donald -trump-execution-comment/index.html.

230. de Vries,. "Milley Says."

231. "Executive Order on Creating Schedule F in the Excepted Service," Executive Orders, White House, October 21, 2020, https://trumpwhitehouse.archives.gov/presidential-actions /executive-order-creating-schedule-f-excepted-service/.

232. Ed Kilgore, "Trump World Plans to Take Over the Deep State," *New York*, July 22, 2022.

233. Kilgore, "Trump World."

234. Lisa Rein, Tom Hamburger, Juliet Eilperin, and Andrew Freedman, "How Trump Waged War on His Own Government," *Washington Post*, October 29, 2020.

235. Ed Kilgore, "Trump World."

236. Rein, Hamburger, Eilperin, and Freedman, "How Trump."

237. *An Inconvenient Truth*, directed by Davis Guggenheim (2006; Los Angeles: Paramount Home Entertainment, 2006), DVD.

238. James T. Andrews, "Warning Signs: Authoritarian Constraints on Scientific Inquiry in the Recent Past," *Items* (blog), Social Science Research Council, June 13, 2017, https://items.ssrc.org /insights/warning-signs-authoritarian-constraints-on-scientific-inquiry-in-the-recent-past/.

239. Andrews, "Warning Signs."

240. Andrews, "Warning Signs."

241. Andrews, "Warning Signs."

242. Coral Davenport, "Trump's Environmental Rollbacks Find Opposition Within: Staff Scientists," *New York Times*, March 27, 2020.

243. Dino Grandoni and Brady Dennis, "Biden Administration Revives EPA Web Page on Climate Change Deleted by Trump," *Washington Post*, March 18, 2021.

244. "White House Solar Panel," Behring Center, National Museum of American History, accessed August 8, 2023, https://americanhistory.si.edu/collections/search/object/nmah_1356218.

245. Muirhead and Rosenblum, *A Lot of People*, 107.

246. Rein, Hamburger, Eilperin, and Freedman, "How Trump."

247. Rein, Hamburger, Eilperin, and Freedman, "How Trump."

248. Daniel Wood and Geoff Brumfiel, "Pro-Trump Counties Continue to Suffer Far Higher COVID Death Tolls," NPR, March 19, 2022, https://www.npr.org/2022/05/19/1098543849 /pro-trump-counties-continue-to-suffer-far-higher-covid-death-tolls.

249. "Anthony S. Fauci, M.D., Former NIAID Director," National Institute of Allergy and Infectious Diseases, accessed August 8, 2023, https://www.niaid.nih.gov/about/director.

250. Benjamin Din, "Trump Lashes out at Fauci and Birx after CNN Documentary," Politico, March 29, 2021, https://www.politico.com/news/2021/03/29/trump-fauci-birx-cnn -documentary-478422.

251. "Deborah L. Birx, M.D.," George W. Bush Institute, accessed August 8, 2023, https://www .bushcenter.org/people/deborah-l-birx-m-d.

252. Benjamin Din, "Trump Lashes."

253. Z. Byron Wolf, "Trump's Attacks on Judge Curiel Are Still Jarring to Read," Politics, CNN, February 27, 2018, https://www.cnn.com/2018/02/27/politics/judge-curiel-trump-border-wall /index.html.

254. Wolf, "Trump's Attacks."

255. Wolf, "Trump's Attacks."

256. "Trump Lashes Out after Deposition Ordered in E. Jean Carroll Lawsuit," *The Guardian* (London), October 13, 2022.

257. Lauren del Valle, "Jury Finds Donald Trump Sexually Abused E. Jean Carroll in Civil Case, Awards Her $5 Million," Politics, CNN, May 9, 2023, https://www.cnn.com/2023/05/09 /politics/e-jean-carroll-trump-lawsuit-battery-defamation-verdict/index.html.

258. Jonathan Dienst, Rebecca Shabad, Ben Kamisar, and Laura Jarrett, "Trump Judge and His Family Receive Threats after New York Arrest," NBC News, April 5, 2023, https://www

.nbcnews.com/politics/donald-trump/judge-merchan-family-receive-threats-trumps-arrest-rcna78401.

259. Aaron, Blake, "Trump Ups the Ante on Going After Judges and Witnesses. Where's the Line?" *Washington Post*, August 14, 2023.

260. Blake, "Trump Ups."

261. Max Fisher, "Trump Tests a Role He's Long Admired: A Strongman Imposing Order," *New York Times*, June 4, 2020.

262. Fisher, "Trump Tests."

263. Fisher, "Trump Tests."

264. Fisher, "Trump Tests."

265. Fisher, "Trump Tests."

266. "Tiananmen Square: What Happened in the Protests of 1989?" BBC News, December 23, 2021, https://www.bbc.com/news/world-asia-48445934.

267. "Tiananmen Square," BBC News.

268. Jennifer Jett and Austin Ramzy, "From Protester to Prisoner: How Hong Kong Is Stifling Dissent," *New York Times*, May 28, 2021.

269. Marc Lynch, "How Arab Authoritarian Regimes Learned to Defeat Popular Protests," *Washington Post*, August 25, 2016 (citing Maria Josua, a research scholar who studies authoritarianism in the Middle East and North Africa).

270. Ivan Nechepurenko, "Moscow Police Arrest More than 1,300 at Election Protest," *New York Times*, June 27, 2019.

271. Valerie Hopkins, "At Least 745 People Are Detained in Protests across Russia," *New York Times*, September 24, 2022.

272. Hopkins, "At Least."

273. Andrew Higgins, "Russia Jumps on Floyd Killing as Proof of US Hypocrisy," *New York Times*, June 4, 2020.

274. "Protests Continue to Rage after Death of George Floyd," *New York Times*, May 28, 2020.

275. Stephen Tankel, "Trump's Moves Are Right out of the Authoritarian Playbook," Just Security, June 3, 2020, https://www.justsecurity.org/70544/trumps-moves-are-right-out-of-the-authoritarian-playbook/.

276. Tankel, "Trump's Moves."

277. Fisher, "Trump Tests."

278. Fisher, "Trump Tests."

279. Tankel, "Trump's Moves."

280. Fisher, "Trump Tests."

281. Katie Rogers, "Protesters Dispersed with Tear Gas so Trump Could Pose at Church," *New York Times*, June 1, 2020.

282. Fisher, "Trump Tests."

283. Fisher, "Trump Tests."

284. Fisher, "Trump Tests."

285. "Great Terror," History, last updated October 4, 2022, https://www.history.com/topics/european-history/great-purge.

286. "Great Terror," History.

287. "Nazi Political Violence in 1933," Holocaust Encyclopedia, United States Holocaust Memorial Museum, last edited June 18, 2019, https://encyclopedia.ushmm.org/content/en/article/nazi-political-violence-in-1933.

288. "The SA," Holocaust Encyclopedia, United States Holocaust Memorial Museum, last edited September 17, 2018, https://encyclopedia.ushmm.org/content/en/article/the-sa.

289. Ben-Ghiat, *Strongmen*, 168.

290. "Documenting Numbers of Victims of the Holocaust and Nazi Persecution," Holocaust Encyclopedia, United States Holocaust Memorial Museum, last edited December 8, 2020, https://encyclopedia.ushmm.org/content/en/article/documenting-numbers-of-victims-of-the-holocaust-and-nazi-persecution.

291. Dresden, Baird, and Raderstorf, *Authoritarian Playbook*, 17.

292. Robert Hart, "Putin's Poisonous Playbook—Before Abramovich, Russia Has a Dark History of Reportedly Poisoning Opponents," *Forbes*, March 29, 2022.

293. Ben-Ghiat, *Strongmen*, 167.
294. Michael M. Grynbaum, "Trump Tweets a Video of Him Wrestling 'CNN' to the Ground," *New York Times*, July 2, 2017.
295. Alayna Treene, "Trump Shares Meme of Train Running Over CNN," Axios, August 15, 2017, https://www.axios.com/2017/12/15/trump-shares-meme-of-train-running-over-cnn -1513304846.
296. Grynbaum, "Trump Tweets."
297. Emily Cochrane, "'That's My Kind of Guy,' Trump Says of Republican Lawmaker Who Body-Slammed a Reporter," *New York Times*, October 19, 2018.
298. David Smith, "Donald Trump Hints at Assassination of Hillary Clinton by Gun Rights Supporters," *The Guardian* (London), August 10, 2016.
299. Smith, "Donald Trump Hints."
300. Aaron Blake, "Trump Promoted N.M. Official's Comment That 'the Only Good Democrat Is a Dead Democrat.' Now the Man Is Arrested in the Capitol Riot," *Washington Post*, January 18, 2021.
301. Mathew S. Schwartz, "Trump Speaks Fondly of Supporters Surrounding Biden Bus in Texas," NPR, November 1, 2020, https://www.npr.org/2020/11/01/930083915/trump-speaks -fondly-of-supporters-protecting-biden-bus-in-texas.
302. Schwartz, "Trump Speaks."
303. Schwartz, "Trump Speaks."
304. Schwartz, "Trump Speaks."
305. Schwartz, "Trump Speaks."
306. Zach Everson, "Trump and J6 Prison Choir Track Sells 'Impressive' 22,500 Digital Downloads," *Forbes*, March 14, 2023.
307. Everson, "Trump and J6 Prison."
308. Everson, "Trump and J6 Prison."
309. Lisa Mascaro, "Marjorie Taylor Greene's Jail Visit Pulls GOP Closer to Jan. 6 Rioters," Associated Press, 2023.
310. Jenna Johnson and Mary Jordan, "Trump on Rally Protester: 'Maybe He Should Have Been Roughed Up,'" *Washington Post*, November 22, 2015.
311. Johnson and Jordan, "Trump on Rally."
312. Johnson and Jordan, "Trump on Rally."
313. Michael E. Miller, "Donald Trump on a Protester: 'I'd Like to Punch Him in the Face,'" *Washington Post*, February 23, 2016.
314. Justin Wm. Moyer, Jenny Starrs, and Sarah Larimer, "Trump Supporter Charged after Sucker-Punching at North Carolina Rally," *Washington Post*, March 11, 2016.
315. Moyer, Starrs, and Larimer, "Trump Supporter."
316. Barbara Sprunt, "The History behind 'When the Looting Starts, the Shooting Starts,'" NPR, May 29, 2020, https://www.npr.org/2020/05/29/864818368/the-history-behind-when-the-looting-starts-the-shooting-starts.
317. Sprunt, "The History."
318. Andrew Rafferty and Chelsea Bailey, "NYPD Calls Trump's Police Quip about Use of Force 'Irresponsible,'" *NBC News*, July 28, 2017.
319. Jess Bravin, "Acting DEA Chief Rebuts Trump's Remarks on Police Use of Force," *Wall Street Journal*, August 1, 2017.
320. Bravin, "Acting DEA Chief."
321. Stanley-Becker and Alemany, "Judge Asks."
322. Stanley-Becker and Alemany, "Judge Asks."
323. Alan Feuer, "In Ad, Shotgun-Toting Greitens Asks Voters to Go 'RINO Hunting,'" *New York Times*, June 20, 2022.
324. Feuer, "In Ad, Shotgun-Toting."
325. Feuer, "In Ad, Shotgun-Toting."
326. Felicia Sonmez, "Rep. Paul Gosar Tweets Altered Anime Video Showing Him Killing Rep. Ocasio Cortez and Attacking President Biden," *Washington Post*, November 8, 2021.
327. Sonmez, "Rep. Paul Gosar."
328. Sonmez, "Rep. Paul Gosar."

329. Sonmez, "Rep. Paul Gosar."
330. Craig Silverman, Jane Lytvynenko, and Pranav Dixit, "How 'The Women for America First' Bus Tour Led to the Capitol Coup Attempt," BuzzFeed News, January 25, 2021, https://www.buzzfeednews.com/article/craigsilverman/maga-bus-tour-coup.
331. Lisa Lerer and Astead W. Herndon, "Menace Enters the Republican Mainstream," *New York Times*, November 12, 2021.
332. Lerer and Herndon, "Menace Enters."
333. "Pushing Election Lies, TPUSA Audience Member Asks Charlie Kirk When They Can 'Use the Guns' and 'Kill These People,'" Media Matters for America, October 26, 2021, https://www.mediamatters.org/charlie-kirk/pushing-election-lies-tpusa-audience-member-asks-charlie-kirk-when-they-can-use-guns.
334. Ben Adams (@TheBenAdams3), "Our Republic would not exist without this kind of rhetoric. The question is fair, but Charlie Kirk probably isn't the person to ask," Twitter, November 1, 2021, 5:43 p.m., https://twitter.com/TheBenAdams3/status/1455289448447369216.
335. Kelly Kasulis Cho, "Pelosi Said She Wanted to Punch Trump as Jan. 6 Riot Began, Video Shows," *Washington Post*, October 14, 2022.
336. Cho, "Pelosi Said."
337. Feuer, "In Ad, Shotgun-Toting."
338. Moyer, Starrs, and Larimer, "Trump Supporter."
339. Dan Mangan, "'MAGA Bomber' Cesar Sayoc Sentenced to 20 Years in Prison for Trying to Kill Trump Critics, Including Obama, Clinton, Biden, Booker, Harris," CNBC, August 5, 2019, https://www.cnbc.com/2019/08/05/cesar-sayoc-sentenced-to-20-years-for-sending-bombs-to-trump-critics.html.
340. Mangan, "'MAGA Bomber.'"
341. Joanna Slater, "Three Men Convicted of Aiding Plot to Kidnap Michigan Gov. Whitmer," *Washington Post*, October 26, 2022.
342. Feuer, "In Ad, Shotgun-Toting"; Adam Kinzinger (@AdamKinzinger), "Here is the letter. Addressed to my wife, sent to my home, threatening the life of my family. The Darkness is spreading courtesy of cowardly leaders fearful of truth. Is the [*sic*] what you want @GOP? Pastors?" Twitter, June 19, 2022, 6:18 p.m., https://twitter.com/AdamKinzinger/status/1538647426348859393.
343. Molly Amman and J. Reid Meloy, "Stochastic Terrorism: A Linguistic and Psychological Analysis," *Perspectives on Terrorism* 15, no. 5 (October 2021): 3; Barbara McQuade, "Note from Barb: The Terrorism of the Spoken Word," *CAFE Insider*, May 24, 2022.
344. Edmondson, "House Republicans."
345. Ashley Parker, Hannah Allam, and Marianna Sotomayor, "Attack on Nancy Pelosi's Husband Follows Years of GOP Demonizing Her," *Washington Post*, October 29, 2022.
346. Kellen Browning, Tim Arango, Luke Broadwater, and Holly Secon, "Pelosi's Husband Is Gravely Injured in a Hammer Attack by an Intruder," *New York Times*, October 30, 2022.
347. Parker, Allam, and Sotomayor, "Attack on Nancy."
348. Parker, Allam, and Sotomayor, "Attack on Nancy."
349. Parker, Allam, and Sotomayor, "Attack on Nancy."
350. Parker, Allam, and Sotomayor, "Attack on Nancy."
351. Parker, Allam, and Sotomayor, "Attack on Nancy."
352. Daniella Diaz, Nicky Robertson, and Chandelis Duster, "McCarthy Says 'It Will Be Hard Not to Hit' Pelosi with Gavel If He Becomes House Speaker," Politics, CNN, August 2, 2021, https://www.cnn.com/2021/08/01/politics/kevin-mccarthy-nancy-pelosi-gavel/index.html.
353. Parker, Allam, and Sotomayor, "Attack on Nancy."
354. Eric Swalwell (@RepSwalwell), "Thank you to the @fbi, @CapitolPolice, @YonkersPD, and @DOJCrimDiv for stopping this violent threat to me and my staff. MAGA political violence is at peak level in America. Somebody is going to get killed. I urge GOP leaders to denounce the violence," Twitter, October 28, 2022, 3:40 p.m., https://twitter.com/RepSwalwell/status/1586080384676073477.
355. Brian Karem, "Donald Trump Has Gone off the Deep End for Real: He's a Danger to Humanity," *Salon*, August 10, 2023.
356. Grynbaum, "Trump Tweets."

357. Paul Egan, "Gretchen Whitmer's Husband, Marc Mallory, Retired Early from Dentistry Due to Threats," *Detroit Free Press*, January 5, 2023.
358. Ben-Ghiat, *Strongmen*, 252.
359. Ben-Ghiat, *Strongmen*, 252.
360. Ben-Ghiat, *Strongmen*, 8.
361. Ben-Ghiat, *Strongmen*, 6.
362. Ben-Ghiat, *Strongmen*, 7–8.
363. Ben-Ghiat, *Strongmen*, 8–9.
364. Ben-Ghiat, *Strongmen*, 9.
365. Ben-Ghiat, *Strongmen*, 8.
366. Ben-Ghiat, *Strongmen*, 8.
367. Ben-Ghiat, *Strongmen*, 120.
368. "'Show Them Our Pecs': G7 Leaders Mock Putin's Bare-Chested Horse-Riding," *The Guardian* (London), June 23, 2022.
369. "Vladimir Putin Scores at Least Eight Goals in Hockey Exhibition, Then Falls on Face," *The Guardian* (London), May 10, 2019.
370. Chris Cillizza and Brenna Williams, "15 Times Donald Trump Praised Authoritarian Rulers," Politics, CNN, July 2, 2019, https://www.cnn.com/2019/07/02/politics/donald-trump-dictators-kim-jong-un-vladimir-putin/index.html.
371. Ben-Ghiat, *Strongmen*, 139.
372. Ben-Ghiat, *Strongmen*, 139.
373. "NFT INT," Collect Trump Cards, accessed August 30, 2023, https://collecttrumpcards.com/.
374. Michael Kruse, "Exclusive: Madison Cawthorn Photos Reveal Him Wearing Women's Lingerie in Public Setting," Politico, April 22, 2022, https://www.politico.com/news/2022/04/22/madison-cawthorn-photos-00027286.
375. Josh Hawley, *Manhood: The Masculine Virtues America Needs* (Washington, DC: Regnery Publishing, 2023).
376. Luke Winkie, "A Governing Body," Slate, June 26, 2023, https://slate.com/human-interest/2023/06/rfk-jr-shirtless-bench-press-pushup-workout.html.
377. Ben-Ghiat, *Strongmen*, 104.
378. "Mobutu Sese Seko," Britannica, last updated December 23, 2022, https://www.britannica.com/biography/Mobutu-Sese-Seko.
379. Ben-Ghiat, *Strongmen*, 104.
380. Ben-Ghiat, *Strongmen*, 110.
381. Patrick Radden Keefe, "How Mark Burnett Resurrected Donald Trump as an Icon of American Success," *New Yorker*, December 27, 2018.
382. Michael Kruse, "The Escalator Ride That Changed America," Politico, June 14, 2019, https://www.politico.com/magazine/story/2019/06/14/donald-trump-campaign-announcement-tower-escalator-oral-history-227148/.
383. Kruse, "The Escalator."
384. Ellen Brait, "Donald Trump Would Be America's Healthiest President, Doctor's Letter Says," *The Guardian* (London), December 14, 2015.
385. Dan Balz, "In His Most Important Speech Ever, Trump Echoes Richard Nixon," *Washington Post*, July 21, 2016.
386. David Klepper, "Trump Article Prompts Jesus Comparisons: 'Spiritual Warfare,'" AP News, April 5, 2023, https://apnews.com/article/donald-trump-arraignment-jesus-christ-conspiracy-theory-670c45bd71b3466dcd6e8e188badcd1d.
387. Ben-Ghiat, *Strongmen*, 110.
388. Victor Klemperer, *The Language of the Third Reich*, trans. Martin Brady (New York: Continuum International Publishing Group, 2006), 113.
389. "Donald Trump: 'I Could Shoot Somebody and I Wouldn't Lose Any Voters,'" *The Guardian* (London), January 24, 2016.

2. From Gaslighting to the Liar's Dividend: Disinformation Tactics

390. Alissa Wilkinson, "What Is Gaslighting? The 1944 Film *Gaslight* Is the Best Explainer," Vox, January 21, 2017, https://www.vox.com/culture/2017/1/21/14315372/what-is-gaslighting -gaslight-movie-ingrid-bergman.
391. Wilkinson, "What Is Gaslighting?"
392. Patrick J. Kiger, "How Joseph Stalin Starved Millions in the Ukrainian Famine," History, April 16, 2019, https://www.history.com/news/ukrainian-famine-stalin.
393. Piers Brendon, "Death of Truth: When Propaganda and 'Alternative Facts' First Gripped the World," *The Guardian* (London), March 11, 2017.
394. Timothy Snyder, "How Hitler Pioneered 'Fake News,'" *New York Times*, October 16, 2019.
395. Ruth Ben-Ghiat, *Strongmen: Mussolini to the Present* (New York, NY: W. W. Norton & Company, 2020), 96–97.
396. Ben-Ghiat, *Strongmen*, 96–97.
397. Matt Pickles, "Did the Trojan Horse Exist? Classicists Tests Greek 'Myths,'" Oxford News Blog, Oxford University, July 25, 2014, https://www.ox.ac.uk/news/arts-blog/did-trojan -horse-exist-classicist-tests-greek-myths.
398. Sun Tzu, *The Art of War*, (New York: Basic Books, 1994), 15.
399. "The Story of Propaganda," in Ralph D. Casey, *What Is Propaganda?* pamphlet, GI Roundtable Series, American Historical Association, 1944, available at https://www.historians.org /about-aha-and-membership/aha-history-and-archives/gi-roundtable-series/pamphlets/em -2-what-is-propaganda-(1944)/the-story-of-propaganda.
400. Linda Villarosa, "Myths about Physical Racial Differences Were Used to Justify Slavery—and Are Still Believed by Doctors Today," *New York Times*, August 14, 2019.
401. Snyder, "How Hitler."
402. Snyder, "How Hitler."
403. Ben-Ghiat, *Strongmen*, 102.
404. Ben-Ghiat, *Strongmen*, 113.
405. Ben-Ghiat, *Strongmen*, 94.
406. "Cultural Revolution," History, last updated April 3, 2020, https://www.history.com/topics /asian-history/cultural-revolution.
407. "Cultural Revolution," History.
408. Ben-Ghiat, *Strongmen*, 113.
409. Miriam Berger, "Putin Says He Will 'Denazify' Ukraine. Here's the History behind That Claim," *Washington Post*, February 24, 2022.
410. Berger, "Putin Says."
411. "The USS *Maine* Explodes in Cuba's Havana Harbor," History, last updated March 29, 2023, https://www.history.com/this-day-in-history/the-maine-explodes.
412. "The USS *Maine*," History.
413. "The USS *Maine*," History.
414. "Pentagon Papers," History, last updated June 16, 2023, https://www.history.com/topics /vietnam-war/pentagon-papers.
415. "Pentagon Papers," History.
416. "Pentagon Papers," History.
417. New York Times Co. v. United States, 403 U.S. 724, 728 (1971).
418. Anne Godlasky, "21 Types of Political Spin You Should Know," National Press Foundation, last modified March 15, 2022, https://nationalpress.org/topic/21-types-of-political-spin-you -should-know/.
419. Andrew Glass, "Nixon Denies Role in Watergate Cover-Up, Aug. 15, 1973," Politico, August 15, 2018, https://www.politico.com/story/2018/08/15/nixon-denies-role-in-watergate-cover-up -aug-15-1973-773476.
420. Peter Baker, "Clinton Perjury Allegations," Clinton Accused Special Report, *Washington Post*, September 24, 1998.
421. Steven Nelson, "Bill Clinton 15 Years Ago: 'I Did Not Have Sexual Relations with That Woman,'" *US News*, January 25, 2013.

422. Kathryn Cramer Brownell, "Commentary: Trump's Voter Fraud 'Solution' Is Rooted in the Jim Crow South," Reuters, October 20, 2016, https://www.reuters.com/article/us-election -debate-voting-commentary/commentary-trumps-voter-fraud-solution-is-rooted-in-the -jim-crow-south-idUKKCN12K0AQ.

423. Justin Levitt, "The Truth about Voter Fraud," report, Brennan Center for Justice, November 9, 2007, https://www.brennancenter.org/our-work/research-reports/truth-about-voter-fraud.

424. Deidre McPhillips, "More than 1 Million People Have Died of COVID-19 in the US," Health, CNN, May 17, 2022, https://www.cnn.com/2022/05/17/health/us-reports-1 -million-covid-deaths/index.html.

425. Thomas Jefferson to Richard Price, January 8, 1789, manuscript/mixed material, Library of Congress, https://www.loc.gov/item/mtjbib004021/ .

426. "US Election 2016: Trump Says Election 'Rigged at Polling Places,'" BBC News, October 17, 2016, https://www.bbc.com/news/election-us-2016-37673797.

427. "US Election."

428. Office of the Director of National Intelligence, Assessing Russian Activities and Intentions in Recent US Elections, S. Rep. (Jan. 6, 2017), ii.

429. US Department of Justice, *Report on the Investigation into Russian Interference in the 2016 Presidential Election*, by Robert S. Mueller III, March 2019, vol. 1, 1.

430. US Department of Justice, *Report on the Investigation*, vol. 1, 1, 5.

431. US Department of Justice, *Report on the Investigation*, vol. 1, 14.

432. Michael D. Shear and Emmarie Huetteman, "Trump Repeats Lie about Popular Vote in Meeting with Lawmakers," *New York Times*, January 23, 2017.

433. "#StopTheSteal: Timeline of Social Media and Extremist Activities Leading to 1/6 Insurrec- tion," Just Security, February 10, 2021, https://www.justsecurity.org/74622/stopthesteal -timeline-of-social-media-and-extremist-activities-leading-to-1-6-insurrection/.

434. Cheryl Teh, "New Video Shows Roger Stone Telling Trump Supporters That 'The Key Thing to Do Is Claim Victory' after the Election, No Matter the Outcome," Yahoo! News, October 14, 2022, https://sports.yahoo.com/video-shows-roger-stone-telling-065216462.html.

435. Adam Gabbat and Hugo Lowell, "'Game Over': Steve Bannon Audio Reveals Trump Planned to Claim Early Victory," *The Guardian* (London), July 14, 2022.

436. "#StopTheSteal: Timeline," Just Security.

437. Jessica Guynn, "President Trump Permanently Banned from Twitter over Risk He Could Incite Violence," *USA Today*, January 13, 2021.

438. Tim Elfrink, "Trump Repeats Unfounded Election Fraud Claims in Late-Night Posts Flagged by Twitter," *Washington Post*, November 23, 2020.

439. William Cummings, Joey Garrison, and Jim Sergent, "By the Numbers: President Donald Trump's Failed Efforts to Overturn the Election," *USA Today*, January 6, 2021.

440. Brian Naylor, "Read Trump's Jan. 6 Speech, a Key Part of Impeachment Trial," NPR, February 10, 2021, https://www.npr.org/2021/02/10/966396848/read-trumps-jan-6-speech-a-key-part -of-impeachment-trial.

441. Naylor, "Read Trump's."

442. Kat Lonsdorf et al., "A Timeline of How the Jan. 6 Attack Unfolded—including Who Said What and When," NPR, June 9, 2022, https://www.npr.org/2022/01/05/1069977469/a -timeline-of-how-the-jan-6-attack-unfolded-including-who-said-what-and-when.

443. Zachary Snowdon Smith, "Capitol Riot Costs Go Up: Government Estimates $2.73 Million in Property Damage," *Forbes*, April 8, 2022.

444. Zach Montague, "Watch What the Committee Has Covered in Its Hearings So Far," *New York Times*, October 13, 2022.

445. Ron Elving, "Claims of Voter Fraud, Old as the Republic, Still Work as Weapons for Trump," NPR, September 4, 2022, https://www.npr.org/2022/09/04/1120904265/claims-voter -fraud-donald-trump.

446. Help America Vote Act of 2022, Pub. L. No. 107-252, 116 Stat. 1666, Sec. 301 (Oct. 29, 2002).

447. Help America Vote Act of 2022, Pub. L. No. 107-252, 116 Stat. 1666, Sec. 303 (Oct. 29, 2002).

448. "Debunking the Voter Fraud Myth," Brennan Center for Justice, January 31, 2017, https:// www.brennancenter.org/our-work/research-reports/debunking-voter-fraud-myth.

449. Thomas Rid, *Active Measures: The Secret History of Disinformation and Political Warfare* (New York: Farrar, Straus and Giroux, 2020), 7.

450. Donald A. Barclay, *Disinformation: The Nature of Facts and Lies in the Post-Truth Era* (Lanham, MD: Rowman & Littlefield, 2022), 43.

451. Barclay, *Disinformation*, 43.

452. Rid, *Active Measures*, 7.

453. Mike Mariani, "Is Trump's Chaos Tornado a Move from the Kremlin's Playbook?" *Vanity Fair*, March 28, 2017.

454. Clint Watts, *Messing with the Enemy: Surviving in a Social Media World of Hackers, Terrorists, Russians, and Fake News* (New York: Harper, 2018), 129.

455. Mariani, "Is Trump's."

456. Mariani, "Is Trump's."

457. Mariani, "Is Trump's."

458. Richard L. Hasen, *Cheap Speech: How Disinformation Poisons Our Politics—and How to Cure It* (New Haven, CT: Yale University Press, 2022), 64.

459. Mariani, "Is Trump's."

460. Charles Homans, "How 'Stop the Steal' Captured the American Right," *New York Times*, July 28, 2022.

461. Homans, "How 'Stop.'"

462. Homans, "How 'Stop.'"

463. Luke Broadwater and Catie Edmondson, "Divided House Approves G.O.P. Inquiry into 'Weaponization' of Government," *New York Times*, January 10, 2023.

464. Matthew Rozsa, "The Psychological Reason That So Many Fall for the 'Big Lie,'" Salon, February 3, 2022, https://www.salon.com/2022/02/03/the-psychological-reason-that-so-many -fall-for-the-big-lie/.

465. Rozsa, "The Psychological Reason."

466. Rozsa, "The Psychological Reason."

467. Rozsa, "The Psychological Reason."

468. Rozsa, "The Psychological Reason."

469. Homans, "How 'Stop.'"

470. Sarah Longwell, "Trump Supporters Explain Why They Believe the Big Lie," *The Atlantic*, April 18, 2022.

471. David Leonhardt, "Internal Inconsistencies," *New York Times*, July 7, 2022.

472. Leonhardt, "Internal Inconsistencies."

473. Leonhardt, "Internal Inconsistencies."

474. Leonhardt, "Internal Inconsistencies."

475. Robert Draper, "The Problem of Marjorie Taylor Greene," *New York Times*, October 17, 2022.

476. Mahita Gajanan, "'What You're Seeing . . . Is Not What's Happening.' People Are Comparing This Trump Quote to George Orwell," *Time*, July 24, 2018.

477. Watts, *Messing with the Enemy*, 247.

478. Snyder, "How Hitler."

479. Hasen, *Cheap Speech*, 163.

480. Barclay, *Disinformation*, 39.

481. Barclay, *Disinformation*, 39.

482. Mariani, "Is Trump's."

483. Mariani, "Is Trump's."

484. "Kim Kardashian Fined for Cryptocurrency Promotion, Here's What It Means for Crypto," *Forbes*, October 3, 2022.

485. Asha Rangappa (@AshaRangappa_), "The purpose of legitimizing propaganda is to have a seemingly independent third party claim something. Then HE points to that person and says, 'See? He's saying the same thing! It must be true!' You can see how, in the examples in OT, it would have been a 'story' if it worked 3/," Twitter, June 13, 2022, 10:47 p.m., https:// twitter.com/asharangappa_/status/1536540852469866499.

486. Asha Rangappa (@AshaRangappa_), "A great example of a successful op using legitimizing propaganda was the Soviet's Operation Infektion, claiming that U.S. created the AIDS virus. The story was originally placed in an Indian paper. Then THAT paper was cited as 'evidence.'

Rinse, repeat.," Twitter, June 13, 2022, 10:55 p.m., https://twitter.com/AshaRangappa_/status
/1536542697086980097.

487. David A. Graham, "Gordon Sondland Is Aiming Right at Trump's Achilles' Heel," *The Atlantic*, November 20, 2019.

488. Graham, "Gordon Sondland."

489. Luke Broadwater and Katie Benner, "Jan. 6 Panel Outlines Trump's Bid to Coerce Justice Dept. Officials," *New York Times*, June 23, 2022.

490. Ben-Ghiat, *Strongmen*, 101–109.

491. Ben-Ghiat, *Strongmen*, 112.

492. Steve Inskeep and Charles Maynes, "Russia Has Reasserted State Control over the Country's Major Media Companies," NPR, March 7, 2022, https://www.npr.org/2022/03/07 /1084870797/russia-has-reasserted-state-control-over-the-country-s-major-media-companies.

493. Nell Clark, "Trump's Social Media Site Hits the App Store a Year after He Was Banned from Twitter," NPR, February 22, 2022, https://www.npr.org/2022/02/22/1082243094/trumps -social-media-app-launches-year-after-twitter-ban.

494. Yochai Benkler, Robert Faris, Hal Roberts, and Ethan Zuckerman, "Study: Breitbart-Led Right-Wing Media Ecosystem Altered Broader Media Agenda," *Columbia Journalism Review*, March 3, 2017.

495. Benkler, Faris, Roberts, and Zuckerman, "Study: Breitbart-Led."

496. Shannon Bond, "How Alex Jones Helped Mainstream Conspiracy Theories Become Part of American Life," NPR, August 6, 2022, https://www.npr.org/2022/08/06/1115936712/how-alex -jones-helped-mainstream-conspiracy-theories-into-american-life.

497. Bond, "How Alex Jones."

498. Bond, "How Alex Jones."

499. Brett Edkins, "Fox News Ratings Hit Record High in Trump's First Few Months as President," *Forbes*, March 28, 2017.

500. Lloyd Green, "Hoax Review: Fox News, Donald Trump and Truth v Owning the Libs," *The Guardian* (London), August 24, 2020.

501. Green, "Hoax Review."

502. Olivia Nuzzi, "Donald Trump and Sean Hannity Like to Talk before Bedtime," *New York*, May 14, 2018.

503. Nuzzi, "Donald Trump."

504. Green, "Hoax Review."

505. Jeremy W. Peters, "In Testimony, Hannity and Other Fox Employees Said They Doubted Trump's Fraud Claims," *New York Times*, December 21, 2022.

506. Peters, "In Testimony."

507. Green, "Hoax Review."

508. "Highlights from New Fox News Documents Released in Dominion Lawsuit," *Washington Post*, March 7, 2023.

509. "Highlights from New Fox News Documents."

510. Charlotte Klein, "Tucker 'Just Asking Questions' Carlson Wants to Know What Putin Ever Did to You," *Vanity Fair*, February 23, 2022.

511. Derek Hawkins, Sarah Ellison, and Blair Guild, "What Tucker Carlson Said about Trump in Private Text vs. on Fox News," *Washington Post*, March 9, 2023.

512. David Folkenflik, "You Literally Can't Believe the Facts Tucker Carlson Tells You. So Say Fox's Lawyers," NPR, September 29, 2020, https://www.npr.org/2020/09/29/917747123/you -literally-cant-believe-the-facts-tucker-carlson-tells-you-so-say-fox-s-lawye.

513. Folkenflik, "You Literally."

514. Nicholas Confessore, "How Tucker Carlson Reshaped Fox News—and Became Trump's Heir," *New York Times*, April 30, 2022.

515. Jeremy W. Peters, Katie Robertson, and Michael M. Grynbaum, "Tucker Carlson, a Source of Repeated Controversies, Is Out at Fox News," *New York Times*, April 24, 2023.

516. Daniel Dale, "Steve Bannon's Popular Podcast Is a 'Dangerous' Fantasyland of Election Lies," Politics, CNN, November 7, 2021, https://www.cnn.com/2021/11/07/politics/bannon -podcast-war-room-election-lies/index.html.

517. Dale, "Steve Bannon's."

518. Rob Minto, "Steve Bannon's Trial Is Giving His Podcast a Boost," *Newsweek*, July 20, 2022.

519. Hasen, *Cheap Speech*, 59–60.

520. Annie Karni, "With Falsehoods and Ridicule about Pelosi Attack, Republicans Mimic Trump," *New York Times*, November 1, 2022.

521. Aaron Blake, "Trump Pitches a Pelosi Conspiracy Theory, Which Quickly Goes up in Flames," *Washington Post*, November 2, 2022.

522. Chris Cillizza, "Donald Trump Joins the Paul Pelosi Conspiracy Caucus," Politics, CNN, November 2, 2022, https://www.cnn.com/2022/11/01/politics/donald-trump-paul-pelosi -reaction/index.html.

523. Matt Stefon, "Fairness Doctrine," Britannica, last updated June 23, 2023, https://www.britannica .com/topic/Fairness-Doctrine.

524. Duncan J. Watts and David M. Rothschild, "Don't Blame the Election on Fake News. Blame It on the Media," *Columbia Journalism Review*, December 5, 2017.

525. Watts and Rothschild, "Don't Blame."

526. Marc Tracy, "Trump Is Gone, But the Media's Misinformation Challenge Is Still Here," *New York Times*, July 27, 2021.

527. Tracy, "Trump Is Gone."

528. Cailin O'Connor and James Owen Weatherall, *The Misinformation Age: How False Beliefs Spread* (New Haven, CT: Yale University Press, 2018), 167.

529. Mario Cacciottolo, "The Streisand Effect: When Censorship Backfires," BBC, June 15, 2012, https://www.bbc.com/news/uk-18458567.

530. Cacciottolo, "The Streisand Effect."

531. Cacciottolo, "The Streisand Effect."

532. Barclay, *Disinformation*, 141.

533. Russell Muirhead and Nancy L. Rosenblum, *A Lot of People Are Saying: The New Conspiracism and the Assault on Democracy* (Princeton, NJ: Princeton University Press, 2019), 3.

534. "President Trump Renews Attack on 'Disgraceful' FBI," BBC, December 15, 2017, https:// www.bbc.com/news/av/world-us-canada-42360540; Joseph Tanfani, "Trump Says Americans Are 'Very, Very Angry' at FBI before He Pledges His Support," *Los Angeles Times*, December 15, 2017.

535. Lauren Collins, "Who Is Trump's Friend Jim?" *New Yorker*, March 5, 2017.

536. Daniel Dale, "'Sir' Alert: This One Word Is a Telltale Sign Trump Is Being Dishonest," Politics, CNN, July 17, 2019, https://www.cnn.com/2019/07/16/politics/sir-trump-telltale-word -false/index.html.

537. Longwell, "Trump Supporters Explain."

538. Ben-Ghiat, *Strongmen*, 111.

539. Mariani, "Is Trump's."

540. Harry Bruinius, "With NFL Controversy, Did Media Play into Trump's Distraction Tactics?" *Christian Science Monitor*, September 28, 2017.

541. Bruinius, "With NFL Controversy."

542. Ben-Ghiat, *Strongmen*, 111.

543. Ben-Ghiat, *Strongmen*, 111.

544. Jack Schafer, "The New Rules for Covering Trump," Politico, November 28, 2016, https:// www.politico.com/magazine/story/2016/11/donald-trump-media-coverage-new-rules-214485/.

545. Watts, *Messing with the Enemy*, 229.

546. Emily Couch, "Why We Should Stop Portraying African Americans as Victims in the Soviet Propaganda Game," *The Russia File* (blog), Wilson Center, February 18, 2020, https://www .wilsoncenter.org/blog-post/why-we-should-stop-portraying-african-americans-victims -soviet-propaganda-game.

547. Sophie Tatum, "Trump Defends Putin: 'You Think Our Country's So Innocent?'" Politics, CNN, February 6, 2017, https://www.cnn.com/2017/02/04/politics/donald-trump-vladimir -putin/index.html.

548. Danielle Kurtzleben, "Trump Embraces One of Russia's Favorite Propaganda Tactics— Whataboutism," NPR, March 17, 2017, https://www.npr.org/2017/03/17/520435073/trump -embraces-one-of-russias-favorite-propaganda-tactics-whataboutism.

549. Graph Massara, "Obama Didn't Keep Millions of Classified White House Documents," AP News, August 12, 2022, https://apnews.com/article/fact-check-obama-million-documents -929954890662.
550. Massara, "Obama Didn't."
551. Massara, "Obama Didn't."
552. Carl Hulse, Luke Broadwater, and Annie Karni, "McCarthy, Facing and Ouster and a Shutdown, Orders Impeachment Inquiry," *New York Times*, September 12, 2023.
553. Kurtzleben, "Trump Embraces."
554. Watts, *Messing with the Enemy*, 229; "MH17: Four Charged with Shooting Down Plane over Ukraine," BBC News, June 19, 2019, https://www.bbc.com/news/world-europe-48691488.
555. Watts, *Messing with the Enemy*, 229.
556. Watts, *Messing with the Enemy*, 229.
557. "MH17 Ukraine Plane Crash: What We Know," BBC News, February 26, 2020, https://www .bbc.com/news/world-europe-28357880.
558. "MH17 Ukraine Plane Crash."
559. "MH17 Ukraine Plane Crash."
560. Tal Kopan, "Is Trump Right? Could a 400-Pound Couch Potato Have Hacked the DNC?" Politics, CNN, September 27, 2016, https://www.cnn.com/2016/09/27/politics/dnc -cyberattack-400-pound-hackers/index.html.
561. Kopan, "Is Trump Right?"
562. Barclay, *Disinformation*, 41.
563. Kevin Quealy, "The Complete List of Trump's Twitter Insults (2015–2021)," *New York Times*, January 19, 2021.
564. Asma Khalid, "Warren Apologizes to Cherokee Nation for DNA Test," NPR, February 1, 2019.
565. Tevi Troy, "From 'Huckleberry Capone' to 'Turd Blossom': A History of White House Nicknames," Politico, December 5, 2021, https://www.politico.com/news/magazine/2021/12/05 /huckleberry-capone-turd-blossom-white-house-nicknames-523723.
566. Kelsey Vlamis, "Trump Mocked Florida Gov. Ron DeSantis—Finally Debuting a Nickname, 'Ron DeSanctimonious'—as the 2 Popular Republicans Could Face Off in 2024," Yahoo! News, November 5, 2022, https://news.yahoo.com/trump-mocked-florida-gov-ron -022032581.html.
567. David Smith, "Midterm 'Mini-Me': Is Copying Trump a Winning Strategy for Rightwingers?" *The Guardian* (London), August 5, 2018.
568. Colin Jackson, "The Republican Nominee for Michigan Attorney General Is Under Investigation Himself," NPR, October 18, 2022, https://www.npr.org/2022/10/18/1129521692 /matthew-deperno-dana-nessel-michigan-attorney-general-voting-machines.
569. Alyssa Mertes, "The 50 Best Company Slogans of All Time," Quality Logo Products, July 3, 2020, https://www.qualitylogoproducts.com/promo-university/10-best-slogans-of-all-time.htm.
570. Barclay, *Disinformation*, 129.
571. Barclay, *Disinformation*, 129.
572. Piers Brendon, "Death of Truth: When Propaganda and 'Alternative Facts' First Gripped the World," *The Guardian* (London), March 11, 2017.
573. Joshua Green, "This Man Is the Most Dangerous Political Operative in America," *Bloomberg Businessweek*, October 8, 2015.
574. Green, "This Man Is the Most."
575. Watts, *Messing with the Enemy*, 221.
576. Asha Rangappa, "How Barr and Trump Use a Russian Disinformation Tactic," *New York Times*, April 19, 2019.
577. Rangappa, "How Barr and Trump."
578. Asha Rangappa, "Class 13: Reflexive Control," The Freedom Academy with Asha Rangappa, last modified April 7, 2023, https://asharangappa.substack.com/p/class-12-reflexive-control.
579. Rangappa, "Class 13," The Freedom Academy with Asha Rangappa.
580. Rangappa, "Class 13," The Freedom Academy with Asha Rangappa.
581. Rangappa, "Class 13," The Freedom Academy with Asha Rangappa.
582. Rangappa, "Class 13," The Freedom Academy with Asha Rangappa.

583. Rangappa, "Class 13," The Freedom Academy with Asha Rangappa.
584. Rangappa, "How Barr and Trump."
585. Charlie Savage, "Judge Calls Barr's Handling of Mueller Report 'Distorted' and 'Misleading,'" *New York Times*, March 5, 2020; US Department of Justice, *Report on the Investigation*, vol. 1, 5.
586. Jeremy Herb, Laura Jarrett, and Katelyn Polantz, "Mueller Did Not Find Trump or His Campaign Conspired with Russia, Also Did Not Exonerate Him on Obstruction," Politics, CNN, March 24, 2019, https://www.cnn.com/2019/03/24/politics/mueller-report-release /index.html.
587. Herb, "Mueller Did Not Find."
588. Richard Gonzales and Sasha Ingber, "Mueller's Letter to Barr Complained that Trump-Russia Report Summary Lacked 'Context,'" NPR, April 30, 2019, https://www.npr .org/2019/04/30/718883130/mueller-complained-that-barr-summary-of-trump-russia-probe -lacked-context.
589. Savage, "Judge Calls."
590. Savage, "Judge Calls."
591. Ben-Ghiat, *Strongmen*, 6.
592. Ben-Ghiat, *Strongmen*, 6.
593. Ben-Ghiat, *Strongmen*, 6.
594. Olivia B. Waxman, "Historian: Today's Authoritarian Leaders Aren't Fascists—but They Are Part of the Same Story," *Time*, November 10, 2020.
595. David Smith, "'I Am Your Retribution': Trump Rules Supreme at CPAC as He Relaunches Bid for White House," *The Guardian* (London), March 4, 2023.
596. Muirhead and Rosenblum, *A Lot of People*, 113; William P. Davis, "'Enemy of the People': Trump Breaks Out This Phrase During Moments of Peak Criticism," *New York Times*, July 19, 2018.
597. Brian Naylor, "Read Trump's Jan. 6 Speech, a Key Part of Impeachment Trial," NPR, February 10, 2021, https://www.npr.org/2021/02/10/966396848/read-trumps-jan-6-speech-a -key-part-of-impeachment-trial.
598. Philip Bump, "Trump's Career-Defining Sales Pitch: They're Targeting You, Not Me," *Washington Post*, August 16, 2022.
599. Jack Shafer, "This Criminal Indictment Is About to Bite Mr. Know-It-All in His Blind Spot," Politico, June 9, 2023.
600. "Pres. Trump: They Only Attack Me, Because I Fight for You," One America News, April 3, 2023, https://www.oann.com/video/oan-contribution/pres-trump-they-only-attack-me -because-i-fight-for-you/.
601. Matt Dixon, "Trump Delivers Fiery Post-Indictment Speech: 'They're Coming After You,'" NBC News, June 10, 2023, https://www.nbcnews.com/politics/donald-trump/trump -deliver-fiery-post-indictment-speech-georgia-rcna88561.
602. Bump, "Trump's Career-Defining Sales Pitch."
603. Kaia Hubbard, "Trump Boasts about Investigation Record Ahead of Jan. 6 Committee Hearing, Continued Mar-A-Lago Probe," *US News*, October 10, 2022.
604. Rebecca Shabad, Ryan J. Reilly, and Ken Dilanian, "FBI Found 184 Classified Documents in Boxes Returned by Trump, Redacted Affidavit Says, Prompting Search," NBC News, August 26, 2022, https://www.nbcnews.com/politics/donald-trump/redacted-fbi-affidavit-used-justify -search-mar-lago-released-rcna44959.
605. Brianne Pfannenstiel and Tyler Jett, "Donald Trump Teases Iowa Crowd: 'I Will Very, Very, Very Probably' Run for President," *Des Moines Register*, November 3, 2022.
606. Myah Ward and Andrew Desiderio, "Trump Warns of 'Problems' Like 'We've Never Seen' If He's Indicted," Politico, September 15, 2022, https://www.politico.com/news/2022/09/15 /trump-warns-of-problems-like-weve-never-seen-if-hes-indicted-00056911.
607. Daniel Dale and Marshall Cohen, "Fact Check: Trump Makes Numerous False Claims in Speech after Court Appearance," Facts First, CNN, June 14, 2023, https://www.cnn.com /2023/06/14/politics/fact-check-trump-bedminster-speech/index.html.
608. Nick Visser, "Trump Furious on Social Media after Fourth Indictment, This Time in Georgia," Huffington Post, August 15, 2023, https://www.huffpost.com/entry/trump-truth-social-georgia -indictment_n_64d47fd4e4b0d52beea23efe.

609. John Wagner, "Trump Claims Political Persecution after FBI Search of Mar-a-Lago Residence," *Washington Post*, August 9, 2022.

610. Morgan Winsor, "Republicans Speak Out against FBI Raid of Trump's Mar-a-Lago Estate," ABC News, August 9, 2022, https://abcnews.go.com/Politics/republicans-speak-fbi -raid-trumps-mar-lago-estate/story?id=88134193; Laurie Roberts, "Kari Lake Is Melting Down over FBI's Mar-a-Lago Raid. Can Someone Pass Her Smelling Salts?," *Arizona Republic* (Phoenix), August 9, 2022.

611. Domenico Montanaro, "Hillary Clinton's 'Basket of Deplorables,' in Full Context of This Ugly Campaign," NPR, September 10, 2016, https://www.npr.org/2016/09/10/493427601 /hillary-clintons-basket-of-deplorables-in-full-context-of-this-ugly-campaign.

612. Montanaro, "Hillary Clinton's 'Basket.'"

613. Montanaro, "Hillary Clinton's 'Basket.'"

614. Montanaro, "Hillary Clinton's 'Basket.'"

3. Hearts Are Bigger Than Minds: Why Disinformation Works

615. "Detroit Area Doctor Sentenced to 45 Years in Prison for Providing Medically Unnecessary Chemotherapy to Patients," press release, United States Department of Justice, July 10, 2015, https://www.justice.gov/opa/pr/detroit-area-doctor-sentenced-45-years-prison-providing -medically-unnecessary-chemotherapy.

616. "Detroit Area Doctor Sentenced," United States Department of Justice.

617. Rylan Vanacore, "Sensationalism in Media," *Reporter*, November 12, 2021.

618. Megan McArdle, "We Finally Know for Sure That Lies Spread Faster than the Truth. This Might Be Why," Opinion, *Washington Post*, March 14, 2018.

619. Marc Fisher, "Leaders of Democracies Increasingly Echo Putin in Authoritarian Tilt," *Washington Post*, October 16, 2022.

620. Fisher, "Leaders of Democracies."

621. Fisher, "Leaders of Democracies."

622. Adam Grant, "Doris Kearns Goodwin Knows What Presidential Leadership Looks like," *Fast Company*, August 14, 2018.

623. David Axelrod, "Doris Kearns Goodwin," podcast audio, 65:00, episode 426, *The Axe Files*, January 21, 2021.

624. Olivia B. Waxman, "Historian: Today's Authoritarian Leaders Aren't Fascists—but They Are Part of the Same Story," Time, November 10, 2020.

625. Constant Méheut, "The Far Right Wins a Record Number of Seats," *New York Times*, June 19, 2022.

626. Frances D'Emilio, "Far-Right Leader Giorgia Meloni Sworn in as Italy's Prime Minister," PBS, October 22, 2022, https://www.pbs.org/newshour/world/far-right-leader-giorgia-meloni -sworn-in-as-italys-prime-minister.

627. Tim Bale, "Tories Have Been Lurching Further Right for Years. Boris Johnson Was Just the Latest," *The Guardian* (London), July 10, 2022.

628. Christina Anderson and Isabella Kwai, "In Dramatic Shift, Right-Wing Bloc Wins Slim Majority in Sweden," *New York Times*, September 14, 2022.

629. Ishaan Tharoor, "Sweden's Election Marks a New Far-Right Surge in Europe," *Washington Post*, September 16, 2022.

630. Anderson and Kwai, "In Dramatic Shift."

631. Tharoor, "Sweden's Election."

632. Thomas Mallon, "A View from the Fringe," *New Yorker*, January 3, 2016.

633. Charles Homans, "How 'Stop the Steal' Captured the American Right," *New York Times*, July 19, 2022.

634. Dudley L. Poston, Jr., "3 Ways That the US Population Will Change over the Next Decade," PBS, January 2, 2020.

635. Russell Muirhead and Nancy L. Rosenblum, *A Lot of People Are Saying: The New Conspiracism and the Assault on Democracy* (Princeton, NJ: Princeton University Press, 2019), 90.

636. Lilliana Mason, Julie Wronski, and John V. Kane, "Activating Animus: The Uniquely Social Roots of Trump Support," *American Political Science Review* 115, no. 4 (June 30, 2021): 1508.

637. Michael H. Keller and David D. Kirkpatrick, "Their America Is Vanishing. Like Trump, They Insist They Were Cheated," *New York Times*, October 23, 2022.

638. Keller and Kirkpatrick, "Their America"; Diana C. Mutz, "Status Threat, Not Economic Hardship, Explains the 2016 Presidential Vote," *Proceedings of the National Academy of Sciences* 115, no. 19 (May 8, 2018).

639. Patricia Mazzei and Anemona Hartocollis, "Florida Rejects A.P. African American Studies Class," *New York Times*, January 19, 2023.

640. Mazzei and Hartocollis, "Florida Rejects."

641. Ganny Belloni, "Transgender Youth Care Targeted in Culture Battle Sweeping US," Bloomberg Law, February 21, 2023, https://news.bloomberglaw.com/health-law-and-business /transgender-youth-care-targeted-in-culture-battle-sweeping-us.

642. Alexandra Alter and Elizabeth A. Harris, "Attempts to Ban Books Doubled in 2022," *New York Times*, March 23, 2023.

643. Alter and Harris, "Attempts to Ban Books."

644. Ezra Klein, "Three Theories That Explain This Strange Movement," *New York Times*, November 12, 2022.

645. Waxman, "Historian: Today's Authoritarian Leaders."

646. Sahil Kapur (@sahilkapur), "'Does anybody need DC and Puerto Rico to be a state?' Sen. Lindsey Graham says in Georgia. 'No!' Crowd yells. 'That dilutes our power,' Graham says," Twitter, November 7, 2022, 7:57 p.m., https://twitter.com/sahilkapur/status/158978421179145 0112?lang=en.

647. Mike DeBonis, "Ted Cruz Once Called Trump 'Utterly Amoral' and a 'Sniveling Coward.' Then He Worked to Save His Presidency," *Washington Post*, February 15, 2020.

648. DeBonis, "Ted Cruz."

649. DeBonis, "Ted Cruz."

650. Matt Flegenheimer, "JD Vance Gets What He Came for in Ohio, No Elegy Necessary," *New York Times*, November 9, 2022.

651. Josh McLaurin (@JoshforGeorgia), "The screenshot below is @JDVancer's unfiltered explanation from 2016 of the breakdown in Republican politics that he now personally is trying to exploit. The 'America's Hitler' bit is at the end. The public deserves to know the magnitude of this guy's bad faith," Twitter, April 18, 2022, 12:36 p.m., https://twitter.com/JoshforGeorgia/status/1516093390378741763.

652. Dan Barry, "JD Vance's Ambition Comes at a Price in 'Hillbilly' Terms," *New York Times*, October 27, 2022.

653. Frank Bruni, "Ron DeSantis's God Complex," Opinion, *New York Times*, November 9, 2022.

654. J. D. Vance, *Hillbilly Elegy: A Memoir* (New York: Harper Collins, 2018).

655. "How the Left and JD Vance Learnt to Despise Each Other," *The Economist*, September 15, 2022.

656. Sydney Combs, "Why Two Million People Signed up to Storm Area 51," *National Geographic*, September 20, 2019.

657. Joe Phelan, "Why Do People Believe in Conspiracy Theories?" Live Science, July 3, 2022, https://www.livescience.com/why-people-believe-conspiracy-theories.

658. Muirhead and Rosenblum, *A Lot of People*, 45–46.

659. Phelan, "Why Do People."

660. Saul Mcleod, "Maslow's Hierarchy of Needs," Simply Psychology, last modified April 4, 2022, https://www.simplypsychology.org/maslow.html.

661. Phelan, "Why Do People."

662. "Why Do Our Brains Love Conspiracy Theories?" BBC, accessed August 30, 2023, https:// www.bbc.co.uk/programmes/articles/4JwGwwclsXGvxl2LfQPqk58/why-do-our-brains-love -conspiracy-theories.

663. Phelan, "Why Do People."

664. "Why Do Our Brains," BBC.

665. Phelan, "Why Do People."

666. Sarah Longwell, "Trump Supporters Explain Why They Believe the Big Lie," *The Atlantic*, April 18, 2022.

667. Elizabeth Kolbert, "Why Facts Don't Change Our Minds," *New Yorker*, February 19, 2017.

668. Donald A. Barclay, *Disinformation: The Nature of Facts and Lies in the Post-Truth Era* (Lanham, MD: Rowman & Littlefield, 2022), 50.
669. Barclay, *Disinformation*, 50.
670. Kolbert, "Why Facts."
671. Barclay, *Disinformation*, 50.
672. Barclay, *Disinformation*, 50.
673. Eric Simons, "The Psychology of Why Sports Fans See Their Teams as Extensions of Themselves," *Washington Post*, January 30, 2015.
674. Kolbert, "Why Facts."
675. Kolbert, "Why Facts."
676. Kolbert, "Why Facts."
677. US Department of Justice, "Financial Fraud Crime Victims," United States Attorney's Office, Western District of Washington, last updated February 10, 2015, https://www.justice.gov/usao-wdwa/victim-witness/victim-info/financial-fraud.
678. Cailin O'Connor and James Owen Weatherall, *The Misinformation Age: How False Beliefs Spread* (New Haven, CT: Yale University Press, 2018), 79–80.
679. O'Connor and Weatherall, *The Misinformation Age*, 79–80.
680. Barclay, *Disinformation*, 40; O'Connor and Weatherall, *The Misinformation Age*, 75.
681. Preet Bharara, *Doing Justice: A Prosecutor's Thoughts on Crime, Punishment, and the Rule of Law* (New York: Vintage Books, 2020), 34.
682. Bharara, *Doing Justice*, 34.
683. Bharara, *Doing Justice*, 37.
684. Bharara, *Doing Justice*, 42.
685. Bharara, *Doing Justice*, 42–43.
686. Bharara, *Doing Justice*, 43.
687. Zawn Villines, "Cognitive Dissonance: What to Know," Medical News Today, September 9, 2022, https://www.medicalnewstoday.com/articles/326738#articleHistory-mnt-1893109.
688. Villines, "Cognitive Dissonance."
689. Stephanie A. Sarkis, "Cognitive Dissonance," *Psychology Today*, September 28, 2017.
690. Sarah Ellison, Paul Farhi, and Jeremy Barr, "Fox News Feared Losing Viewers by Airing Truth about Election, Documents Show," *Washington Post*, February 17, 2023.
691. Barclay, *Disinformation*, 39.
692. Barclay, *Disinformation*, 39.
693. William Shakespeare, *The Tragedy of Hamlet, Prince of Denmark*, ed. Barbara A. Mowat and Paul Werstine (New York: Simon & Schuster Paperbacks, 2012), 151.
694. Longwell, "Trump Supporters."
695. Longwell, "Trump Supporters."
696. Barclay, *Disinformation*, 50.
697. Julie Carr Smyth, "Why Do Opponents of the Democrats Keep Calling It 'the Democrat Party'?" *Chicago Tribune*, February 27, 2021.
698. Smyth, "Why Do Opponents."
699. Smyth, "Why Do Opponents."
700. Elise Stefanik (@EliseStefanik), "The Republican Party is the party of parents, babies, grandparents, families, and patriotic Americans. Today's Democrat Party is the party of Socialists, illegals, criminals, Communist Truth Ministers, & media stenographers. This is why there will be a #RedTsunami in November," Twitter, May 13, 2022, 3:34 p.m., https://twitter.com/EliseStefanik/status/1525197906864746496.
701. Marjorie Taylor Greene (@RepMTG), "The Democrat Party has officially destroyed women's rights. Our nation's daughters are in grave danger from the Democrat's [*sic*] war on women. I will never stop fighting this evil. We will win and we will throw the boys out," Twitter, October 1, 2022, 8:41 a.m., https://twitter.com/RepMTG/status/1576190675703726080.
702. Lauren Boebert (@laurenboebert), "The Democrat Party spends more time defending criminals than they do in trying to fight the crime in their cities," Twitter, February 19, 2022, 2:19 p.m., https://twitter.com/laurenboebert/status/1495115879532699648.
703. Smyth, "Why Do Opponents."

704. Clint Watts, *Messing with the Enemy: Surviving in a Social Media World of Hackers, Terrorists, Russians, and Fake News* (New York: Harper, 2018), 127.

705. Longwell, "Trump Supporters."

706. Muirhead and Rosenblum, *A Lot of People*, 55–56.

707. O'Connor and Weatherall, *The Misinformation Age*, 154.

708. Brad Dress, "Donald Trump Jr. Mocks Paul Pelosi Attack," The Hill, October 31, 2022, https://thehill.com/blogs/blog-briefing-room/3712538-donald-trump-jr-mocks-paul-pelosi-attack/.

709. Joan Donovan, Emily Dreyfuss, and Brian Friedberg, "How Memes Led to an Insurrection," *The Atlantic*, September 13, 2022.

710. Barclay, *Disinformation*, 198–199.

711. Muirhead and Rosenblum, *A Lot of People*, 51.

712. Muirhead and Rosenblum, *A Lot of People*, 105–106.

713. Barbara Sprunt, "Here Are the Republicans Who Objected to the Electoral College Count," NPR, January 7, 2021, https://www.npr.org/sections/insurrection-at-the-capitol/2021/01/07/954380156/here-are-the-republicans-who-objected-to-the-electoral-college-count.

714. Sprunt, "Here Are the Republicans."

715. Richard L. Hasen, *Cheap Speech: How Disinformation Poisons Our Politics—and How to Cure It* (New Haven, CT: Yale University Press, 2022), 136.

716. Jason Lemon, "Ron Johnson Insists Capitol Attack 'By and Large' a Peaceful Protest after House OKs Jan. 6 Commission," *Newsweek*, May 20, 2021.

717. Jonathan Weisman and Reid J. Epstein, "G.O.P Declares Jan. 6 Attack 'Legitimate Political Discourse,'" *New York Times*, February 4, 2022.

718. Sahil Kupar, "Tucker Carlson, with Video Provided by Speaker McCarthy, Falsely Depicts Jan. 6 Riot as a Peaceful Gathering," NBC News, March 6, 2023, https://www.nbcnews.com/politics/justice-department/tucker-carlson-new-video-provided-speaker-mccarthy-falsely-depicts-jan-rcna73673.

719. Aaron Blake, "Stolen Elections Live On at Fox News, via Tucker Carlson," *Washington Post*, March 7, 2023.

720. Blake, "Stolen Elections."

721. Jonathan Allen and Henry J. Gomez, "Rep. Liz Cheney Loses Her Primary in Wyoming to Trump-Backed Challenger," NBC News, August 16, 2022, https://www.nbcnews.com/politics/2022-election/rep-liz-cheney-loses-primary-wyoming-trump-backed-challenger-rcna43379.

722. Brian Naylor, "GOP Rep. Adam Kinzinger, Who Voted to Impeach Trump, Won't Run for Reelection," NPR, October 29, 2021, https://www.npr.org/2021/10/29/1050454729/gop-rep-adam-kinzinger-who-voted-to-impeach-trump-wont-run-for-reelection.

4. The New Engines of Disinformation: The Danger of Emerging Technology

723. OpenAI, "GPT-4 System Card," at 11, March 23, 2023, https://cdn.openai.com/papers/gpt-4-system-card.pdf.

724. "GPT-4 System Card" at 11.

725. Thomas Rid, *Active Measures: The Secret History of Disinformation and Political Warfare* (New York: Farrar, Straus and Giroux, 2020), 7.

726. Megan McArdle, "We Finally Know for Sure That Lies Spread Faster than the Truth. This Might Be Why," Opinion, *Washington Post*, March 14, 2018.

727. "My Lai Massacre," History, last modified October 4, 2022, https://www.history.com/topics/vietnam-war/my-lai-massacre-1.

728. Gene Demby and Shereen Marisol Meraji, "A Decade of Watching Black People Die," podcast audio, 22:34, *Code Switch*, May 31, 2020.

729. Craig LeMoult, "For Many Black People, George Floyd's Death Has Triggered a Wave of Trauma," GBH News, May 26, 2021, https://www.wgbh.org/news/local/2021-05-26/for-many-black-people-george-floyds-death-has-triggered-a-wave-of-trauma.

730. Annie Karni, Maggie Haberman, and Sydney Ember, "Trump Plays on Racist Fears of Terrorized Suburbs to Court White Voters," *New York Times*, July 29, 2020.

731. Patrice Taddonio, "Life Underground: Inside a Kharkiv Metro Station, Home to Hundreds Amid Russia's Attack on Ukraine," *PBS*, August 2, 2022; Lynsey Addario and Andrew E. Kramer, "Ukrainian Family's Dash for Safety Ends in Death," *New York Times*, March 6, 2022.

732. Mstyslav Chernov, "Pregnant Woman, Baby Die after Russian Bombing in Mariupol," AP News, March 14, 2022, https://apnews.com/article/russia-ukraine-war-maternity-hospital -pregnant-woman-dead-c0f2f859296f9f02be24fc9edfca1085.

733. LeMoult, "For Many."

734. Alvin Toffler, *Future Shock* (New York: Bantam Books, 1970), 2.

735. Toffler, *Future Shock*, 11.

736. Melinda Wenner Moyer, "People Drawn to Conspiracy Theories Share a Cluster of Psychological Features," *Scientific American*, March 1, 2019.

737. Michael Cavna, "'Nobody Knows You're a Dog': As Iconic Internet Cartoon Turns 20, Creator Peter Steiner Knows the Joke Rings as Relevant as Ever," *Washington Post*, July 31, 2013.

738. "CAPTCHA" stands for "Completely Automated Public Turing test to tell Computers and Humans Apart." Deb Amlen, "The Crossword Stumper," *New York Times*, February 26, 2018.

739. Kevin Roose, "GPT-4 Is Exciting and Scary," *New York Times*, March 15, 2023.

740. Roose, "GPT-4 Is Exciting."

741. Roose, "GPT-4 Is Exciting."

742. Kelly Weill, "People Are Already Making Deepfake Videos of Trump's Arrest," *Daily Beast*, March 20, 2023, https://www.thedailybeast.com/people-are-already-making-deepfake-videos -of-trumps-arrest.

743. Weill, "People Are Already."

744. Lee Moran, "Donald Trump Trolls Joe Biden in Pettiest Possible Way," *Huffington Post*, August 29, 2023.

745. Clint Watts, *Messing with the Enemy: Surviving in a Social Media World of Hackers, Terrorists, Russians, and Fake News* (New York: Harper, 2018), 155.

746. Jon Bateman, Natalie Thompson, and Victoria Smith, "How Social Media Platforms' Community Standards Address Influence Operations," Carnegie Endowment for International Peace, April 1, 2021, https://carnegieendowment.org/2021/04/01/how-social-media-platforms -community-standards-address-influence-operations-pub-84201.

747. Bateman, Thompson, and Smith, "How Social Media Platforms."

748. Bateman, Thompson, and Smith, "How Social Media Platforms."

749. Watts, *Messing with the Enemy*, 246–47.

750. Steven Lee Myers, "Letters, Tweets, TV: How Midterm Disinformation Has Washed over Pennsylvania," *New York Times*, October 31, 2022.

751. Rachel Lerman and Cat Zakrzewski, "Elon Musk's First Big Twitter Product Paused after Fake Accounts Spread," *Washington Post*, November 11, 2022.

752. Donie O'Sullivan, "Kathy Griffin Suspended from Twitter for Impersonating Elon Musk," Business, CNN, November 7, 2022.

753. Bruce Y. Lee, "Fake Eli Lilly Twitter Account Claims Insulin Is Free, Stock Falls 4.37%," *Forbes*, November 12, 2022.

754. @itsdougthepug, "Doug the Pug," Instagram, accessed August 15, 2023, https://www.instagram .com/itsdougthepug/?hl=en.

755. @jiffpom, "Jiff Pom," Instagram, accessed August 15, 2023, https://www.instagram.com /jiffpom/?hl=en; https://www.tiktok.com/@jiffpom?lang=en.

756. United States v. Internet Research Agency, No. 1:18-cr-32, slip op. (D.D.C. February 16, 2018).

757. Richard Stengel, *Information Wars: How We Lost the Global Battle against Disinformation and What We Can Do about It* (New York: Atlantic Monthly Press, 2019), 198.

758. Stengel, *Information Wars*, 199.

759. Stengel, *Information Wars*, 199.

760. United States v. Internet Research Agency, slip op. at 3, 14.

761. United States v. Internet Research Agency, p 15, https://www.justice.gov/file/1035477/download.

762. Annie Kowaleski, "Disinformation and Reflexive Control: The New Cold War," *Georgetown Security Studies Review*, February 1, 2017.

763. United States v. Internet Research Agency, slip op. at 21–23 .

764. United States v. Internet Research Agency, No. 1:18-cr-32, slip op. at 23.
765. Jon Swaine, "Russian Propagandists Targeted African Americans to Influence 2016 US Election," *The Guardian* (London), December 17, 2018.
766. Swaine, "Russian Propagandists."
767. Swaine, "Russian Propagandists."
768. Swaine, "Russian Propagandists."
769. Barclay, *Disinformation*, 155.
770. Barclay, *Disinformation*, 155.
771. Barclay, *Disinformation*, 155.
772. Geoff Brumfiel, "Doubting Mainstream Medicine, COVID Patients Find Dangerous Advice and Pills Online," NPR, July 19, 2022, https://www.npr.org/sections/health-shots/2022/07/19/1111794832/doubting-mainstream-medicine-covid-patients-find-dangerous-advice-and-pills-onli.
773. Emma Grey Ellis, "The *Wired* Guide to Online Conspiracy Theories," *Wired*, October 5, 2018.
774. Kevin Roose, "What Is QAnon, the Viral Pro-Trump Conspiracy Theory?" *New York Times*, September 3, 2021.
775. Watts, *Messing with the Enemy*, 131–32.
776. Stengel, *Information Wars*, 289.
777. Watts, *Messing with the Enemy*, 216.
778. Watts, *Messing with the Enemy*, 247.
779. "Fact Check—Kansas City Chiefs Quarterback Did Not Demand His Team Change Its Name," Reuters Fact Check, July 27, 2021, https://www.reuters.com/article/factcheck-kansas-city-chiefs/fact-check-kansas-city-chiefs-quarterback-did-not-demand-his-team-change-its-name-idUSL1N2P324G.
780. Watts, *Messing with the Enemy*, 89.
781. Stengel, *Information Wars*, 199.
782. Barclay, *Disinformation*, 99.
783. Barclay, *Disinformation*, 99.
784. Stengel, *Information Wars*, 198.
785. Stengel, *Information Wars*, 198.
786. Stengel, *Information Wars*, 202.
787. Stengel, *Information Wars*, 202.
788. United States v. Internet Research Agency, slip op. at 20.
789. Bobby Allyn, "Here Are Four Key Points from the Facebook Whistleblower's Testimony on Capitol Hill," NPR, October 5, 2021, https://www.npr.org/2021/10/05/1043377310/facebook-whistleblower-frances-haugen-congress.
790. Allyn, "Here Are Four Key Points."
791. Keach Hagey and Jeff Horwitz, "Facebook Tried to Make Its Platform a Healthier Place. It Got Angrier Instead," *Wall Street Journal*, September 15, 2021.
792. Hagey and Horwitz, "Facebook Tried."
793. Hagey and Horwitz, "Facebook Tried."
794. Barclay, *Disinformation*, 83.
795. Asha Rangappa, "Disinformation, Democracy, and the Rule of Law" (speech, Connecticut Legal Conference, Connecticut Bar Association, Hartford, CT, June 10, 2019).
796. Rangappa, "Disinformation, Democracy, and the Rule of Law."
797. Rangappa, "Disinformation, Democracy, and the Rule of Law."
798. Rangappa, "Disinformation, Democracy, and the Rule of Law."
799. Watts, *Messing with the Enemy*, 18.
800. "People More Likely to Be Rude on Social Media; Affects Friendships in Real Life," *Daily News* (New York), April 10, 2013.
801. *Civility in America 2019: Solutions for Tomorrow*, Weber Shandwick, June 26, 2019, https://webershandwick.com/news/civility-in-america-2019-solutions-for-tomorrow.
802. Michael Pittaro, "Exposure to Media Violence and Emotional Desensitization," *Psychology Today*, May 6, 2019.
803. Watts, *Messing with the Enemy*, 227.

804. Watts, *Messing with the Enemy*, 214.

805. Cailin O'Connor and James Owen Weatherall, *The Misinformation Age: How False Beliefs Spread* (New Haven, CT: Yale University Press, 2018), 173.

806. Watts, *Messing with the Enemy*, 217.

807. Philip Bump, "The Platform Where the Right-Wing Bubble Is Least Likely to Pop," *Washington Post*, April 23, 2022.

808. Watts, *Messing with the Enemy*, 214.

809. O'Connor and Weatherall, *The Misinformation Age*, 172.

810. Watts, *Messing with the Enemy*, 218.

811. United States v. Internet Research Agency, slip op. at 20.

812. Teo Armus, "Texas Secession Was a Key Theme in Russian Disinformation Campaign During 2016 Elections, Report Says," Texas Tribune, December 17, 2018, https://www.texastribune.org/2018/12/17/texas-secession-russia-disinformation-2016-social-media-new-knowledge/.

813. The platform stated: "Texas retains the right to secede from the United States, and the Texas Legislature should be called upon to pass a referendum consistent thereto." Platform and Resolutions as amended and adopted by the 2022 State Convention of the Republican Party of Texas, at 6, https://texasgop.org/wp-content/uploads/2022/07/2022-RPT-Platform.pdf.

814. Watts, *Messing with the Enemy*, 218.

815. Barclay, *Disinformation*, 137.

816. Hannah Ritchie, "Read All about It: The Biggest Fake News Stories of 2016," CNBC, December 30, 2016, https://www.cnbc.com/2016/12/30/read-all-about-it-the-biggest-fake-news-stories-of-2016.html.

817. Merriam-Webster.com Dictionary, "microtarget," accessed August 15, 2023, https://www.merriam-webster.com/dictionary/microtarget.

818. Barclay, *Disinformation*, 108.

819. Matthew Rosenberg, Nicholas Confessore, and Carole Cadwalladr, "How Trump Consultants Exploited the Facebook Data of Millions," *New York Times*, March 17, 2018.

820. Rosenberg, Confessore, and Cadwalladr, "How Trump Consultants."

821. Rosenberg, Confessore, and Cadwalladr, "How Trump Consultants."

822. Rosenberg, Confessore, and Cadwalladr, "How Trump Consultants."

823. Rosenberg, Confessore, and Cadwalladr, "How Trump Consultants."

824. Rosenberg, Confessore, and Cadwalladr, "How Trump Consultants."

825. Rosenberg, Confessore, and Cadwalladr, "How Trump Consultants."

826. Jacob Gursky and Samuel Woolley, "The Trump 2020 App Is a Voter Surveillance Tool of Extraordinary Power," *MIT Technology Review*, June 21, 2020.

827. Gursky and Woolley, "The Trump 2020 App."

828. Gursky and Woolley, "The Trump 2020 App."

829. Gursky and Woolley, "The Trump 2020 App."

830. Gursky and Woolley, "The Trump 2020 App."

831. Gursky and Woolley, "The Trump 2020 App."

832. Gursky and Woolley, "The Trump 2020 App."

833. Gursky and Woolley, "The Trump 2020 App."

834. Watts, *Messing with the Enemy*, 230.

835. Gursky and Woolley, "The Trump 2020 App."

836. Watts, *Messing with the Enemy*, 163.

837. Barclay, *Disinformation*, 106–107.

838. "Newspapers Fact Sheet," Pew Research Center, https://www.pewresearch.org/journalism/fact-sheet/newspapers/.

839. "Newspapers Fact Sheet," Pew Research Center.

840. Barclay, *Disinformation*, 106.

841. Barclay, *Disinformation*, 106.

842. Christina A. Cassidy, "It's Normal Not to Know the Official Results on Election Night. Here's Why," PBS, October 27, 2022, https://www.pbs.org/newshour/politics/its-normal-not-to-know-the-official-results-on-election-night-heres-why.

843. Hope Yen and Jill Colvin, "AP Fact Check: Trump Clings to Bevy of Bogus Election Claims," AP News, November 29, 2020, https://apnews.com/article/fact-check-trump-bogus -election-claims-3d34646b34316d2f96f9ae5a267a3303.
844. Yen and Colvin, "AP Fact Check: Trump Clings."
845. Cassidy, "It's Normal."
846. Oliver Darcy et al., "Fox Chairman Rupert Murdoch Rejected Election Conspiracy Theories, Dominion Lawsuit Documents Show," Business, CNN, March 8, 2023, https://www.cnn .com/2023/03/07/media/fox-news-dominion-lawsuit/index.html.
847. Paul Farhi and Jeremy Barr, "CNN Leadership Under Fire after 'Disastrous' Trump Town Hall," *Washington Post*, May 11, 2023.
848. Farhi and Barr, "CNN Leadership."
849. Farhi and Barr, "CNN Leadership."
850. Farhi and Barr, "CNN Leadership."
851. Farhi and Barr, "CNN Leadership."
852. Farhi and Barr, "CNN Leadership."
853. Lynette Clemetson, "Embracing Local Empowerment," in "Is the Media Doomed?" Magazine, Politico, January 21, 2021.
854. Martha Minow, *Saving the News: Why the Constitution Calls for Government Action to Preserve Freedom of Speech*, (New York: Oxford University Press, 2021), 2.
855. Minow, *Saving the News*, 2.
856. Clemetson, "Embracing Local Empowerment."
857. "Is the Media Doomed?" Politico, January 21, 2021.
858. Emily Stewart, "Watch: Dozens of Local TV Anchors Read the Same Anti-'False News' Script in Unison," Vox, April 2, 2018, https://www.vox.com/policy-and-politics/2018/4/2 /17189302/sinclair-broadcast-fake-news-biased-trump-viral-video.
859. Stewart, "Watch: Dozens."
860. Stewart, "Watch: Dozens."
861. Watts, *Messing with the Enemy*, 158.
862. "Who Are We?" PinkNews, accessed August 15, 2023, https://careers.thepinknews.com/.
863. Hat tip to Joyce Vance, former US attorney in Alabama and a prominent member of the knitting community. "About Us," Knitting News, accessed August 15, 2023, https://knitting -news.com/about-us/.
864. "About Us," Crochet News, accessed August 15, 2023, https://crochet-news.com/about/.
865. Steve Vladeck, "One First with Steve Vladeck," accessed August 15, 2023, https://stevevladeck .substack.com/.
866. BowTiedEel's Real Estate and Home Improvement Rag, accessed August 15, 2023, https:// bowtiedeel.substack.com.
867. Stengel, *Information Wars*, 289.
868. Stengel, *Information Wars*, 289.
869. Martin Armstrong, "How Many Websites Are There?" Statista, August 6, 2021, https://www .statista.com/chart/19058/number-of-websites-online/.
870. Barclay, *Disinformation*, 106.
871. Watts, *Messing with the Enemy*, 219.
872. Tara Golshan, "Republicans' Successful Campaign to Protect Trump from Mueller's Report, in One Quote," Vox, May 30, 2019, https://www.vox.com/2019/5/30/18646048/republican -protect-trump-mueller-report-amash.
873. Golshan, "Republicans' Successful Campaign."
874. Golshan, "Republicans' Successful Campaign."
875. Quint Forgey, "Amash Indicates He Won't Seek Reelection to Congress," Politico, July 17, 2020, https://www.politico.com/news/2020/07/17/justin-amash-reelection-congress-367183.
876. Barclay, *Disinformation*, 107.
877. Barclay, *Disinformation*, 107.
878. Maria Konnikova, "How Headlines Change the Way We Think," *New Yorker*, December 17, 2014.
879. Konnikova, "How Headlines."
880. Konnikova, "How Headlines."

881. Caitlin Dewey, "6 in 10 of You Will Share This Link without Reading It, a New, Depressing Study Says," *Washington Post*, June 16, 2016.
882. Barclay, *Disinformation*, 107.
883. Muirhead and Rosenblum, *A Lot of People*, 173.
884. "The Year's Most Read," *New York Times*, December 29, 2021.
885. "GPT-4 System Card," at 10.
886. "GPT-4 System Card," at 10.
887. "GPT-4 System Card," at 10.
888. Adam Arnold, "Artificial Intelligence: Powerful AI Systems 'Can't Be Controlled' and 'Are Causing Harm,' Says UK Expert," Sky News, April 30, 2023, https://news.sky.com/story/artificial-intelligence-powerful-ai-systems-cant-be-controlled-and-are-causing-harm-says-uk-expert-12870035.
889. Amanda Holpuch, "German Magazine Editor Is Fired Over A.I. Michael Schumacher Interview," *New York Times*, April 24, 2023.
890. "GPT-4 System Card," at 11.
891. "GPT-4 System Card," at 11.
892. "GPT-4 System Card," at 11.

5. The Land of the Free: Why America Is Particularly Vulnerable to Disinformation

893. Jon Schuppe et al., "Ian Was One of the Most Lethal Hurricanes in Decades. Many of the Deaths Were Preventable," NBC News, November 22, 2022, https://www.nbcnews.com/news/us-news/hurricane-ian-florida-death-toll-rcna54069.
894. Schuppe et al., "Ian Was One of the Most."
895. David Leonhardt, Claire Moses, and Ian Prasad Philbrick, "Ian Moves North," *New York Times*, September 29, 2022.
896. James Bickerton, "Marjorie Taylor Greene's 10 Most Outrageous Quotes This Year," *Newsweek*, December 23, 2022.
897. Richard Stengel, *Information Wars: How We Lost the Global Battle against Disinformation and What We Can Do about It* (New York: Atlantic Monthly Press, 2019), 4.
898. The First Amendment also prevents Congress from establishing religion and protects the rights to free exercise of religion, peaceable assembly, and petition for redress. US Const. amend. I.
899. "Frederick Douglass's 'Plea for Freedom of Speech in Boston,'" introduction by Kurt Lash, *Law & Liberty*, August 21, 2019.
900. Abrams v. United States (Holmes, dissenting), 250 US 616, 630 (1919).
901. Hannah Ritchie, "Read All About It: The Biggest Fake News Stories of 2016," CNBC, December 30, 2016, https://www.cnbc.com/2016/12/30/read-all-about-it-the-biggest-fake-news-stories-of-2016.html.
902. Karena Phan and Ali Swenson, "Article Misrepresents CDC Data, Falsely Links Deaths to COVID Vaccines," AP News, December 15, 2022, https://apnews.com/article/fact-check-excess-deaths-covid-died-suddenly-793316776380.
903. Tom LoBianco, "Trump Falsely Claims 'Millions of People Who Voted Illegally' Cost Him Popular Vote," Politics, CNN, November 28, 2016, https://www.cnn.com/2016/11/27/politics/donald-trump-voter-fraud-popular-vote/index.html.
904. John Gramlich, "Violent Crime Is a Key Midterm Voting Issue, but What Does the Data Say?," Pew Research Center, October 31, 2022, https://www.pewresearch.org/short-reads/2022/10/31/violent-crime-is-a-key-midterm-voting-issue-but-what-does-the-data-say/.
905. Gramlich, "Violent Crime."
906. Gramlich, "Violent Crime."
907. David McCabe, "A Federal Court Clears the Way for a Texas Social Media Law," *New York Times*, September 16, 2022.
908. Adam Gabbatt, "Claims of Anti-Conservative Bias by Social Media Firms Is Baseless, Report Finds," *The Guardian*, February 1, 2021.
909. McCabe, "A Federal Court."

910. Mike Masnick, "Texas Legislature Sees Florida's Social Media Bill Go Down in Unconstitutional Flames; Decides 'We Can Do That Too!'" Techdirt, July 8, 2021, https://www.techdirt .com/2021/07/08/texas-legislature-sees-floridas-social-media-bill-go-down-unconstitutional -flames-decides-we-can-do-that-too/.

911. McCabe, "A Federal Court."

912. Rebecca Kern, "5th Circuit Upholds Texas Law Forbidding Social Media 'Censorship'— Again," Politico, September 16, 2022, https://www.politico.com/news/2022/09/16/5th-circuit -upholds-texas-law-forbidding-social-media-censorship-again-00057316.

913. Kern, "5th Circuit Upholds."

914. Eli Pariser, "Musk's Twitter Will Not Be the Town Square the World Needs," *Wired*, October 28, 2022.

915. US Department of Justice, *Report on the Investigation into Russian Interference in the 2016 Presidential Election*, by Robert S. Mueller III, March 2019, vol. I, 24.

916. Will Oremus, Chris Alcantara, Jeremy B. Merrill, and Artur Galocha, "How Facebook Shapes Your Feed," *Washington Post*, October 26, 2021.

917. Oremus, Alcantara, Merrill, and Galocha, "How Facebook Shapes."

918. Ryan Mac and Kellen Browning, "Elon Musk Reinstates Trump's Twitter Account," *New York Times*, November 19, 2022.

919. Mac and Browning, "Elon Musk Reinstates."

920. New York Times Co. v. Sullivan, 376 US 254, 279–80 (Mar. 9, 1964).

921. New York Times Co. v. Sullivan, 376 US 254, 280 (Mar. 9, 1964).

922. Ritchie, "Read All About It."

923. Ari Shapiro, "On Libel and the Law, U.S. and U.K. Go Separate Ways," NPR, March 21, 2015, https://www.npr.org/sections/parallels/2015/03/21/394273902/on-libel-and-the-law-u-s -and-u-k-go-separate-ways.

924. Caroline Kelly, "Lewandowski: 'I Have No Obligation to Be Honest with the Media,'" Politics, CNN, September 18, 2019, https://www.cnn.com/2019/09/17/politics/corey-lewandowski-the -media/index.html.

925. Buckley v. Valeo, 424 US 1, 143 (Jan. 30, 1976).

926. Citizens United v. Federal Election Commission, 558 US 310 (Jan. 21, 2010).

927. Tim Lau, "Citizens United Explained," Brennan Center for Justice, December 12, 2019, https://www.brennancenter.org/our-work/research-reports/citizens-united-explained.

928. *Citizens United*, 365.

929. *Citizens United*, 360.

930. "2022 Outside Spending, by Super PAC," Open Secrets, accessed August 30, 2023, https:// www.opensecrets.org/outside-spending/super_pacs.

931. "Citizens for a Better America PAC," Bloomberg, accessed August 15, 2023, https://www .bloomberg.com/profile/company/0577347D:US#xj4y7vzkg.

932. "2022 Outside Spending."

933. Lau, "Citizens United Explained."

934. Lau, "Citizens United Explained."

935. "Advertising and Disclaimers," Federal Elections Commission, accessed August 30, 2023, https://www.fec.gov/help-candidates-and-committees/advertising-and-disclaimers/; Tim Lau, "The Honest Ads Act Explained," Brennan Center for Justice, January 17, 2020, https://www .brennancenter.org/our-work/research-reports/honest-ads-act-explained.

936. "Registering as a Super PAC," Federal Election Commission, accessed August 30, 2023, https:// www.fec.gov/help-candidates-and-committees/filing-pac-reports/registering-super-pac/

937. Kevin Roose, "We Asked for Examples of Election Misinformation. You Delivered," *New York Times*, November 4, 2018.

938. Brandenburg v. Ohio, 395 US 444, 447 (June 9, 1969).

939. Vanessa Romo, "Charlottesville Jury Convicts 'Unite the Right' Protester Who Killed Woman," NPR, December 7, 2018, https://www.npr.org/2018/12/07/674672922/james-alex -fields-unite-the-right-protester-who-killed-heather-heyer-found-guilt.

940. Roberts v. United States Jaycees, 104 S. Ct. 3244, 3252 (July 3, 1984).

941. I have written on this topic previously. Barbara L. McQuade, "Not a Suicide Pact: Urgent Strategic Recommendations for Reducing Domestic Terrorism in the United States," *Texas National*

Security Review 5, no. 2 (Spring 2022); Barbara McQuade, "We Have Met the Enemy and They Are Us," podcast audio, 47:09, *Horns of a Dilemma*, June 17, 2022.

942. Intelligence Activities and the Rights of Americans, S. Rep. No. 94-755, 2d. Session, at 14 (April 26, 1976).

943. Intelligence Activities, 65–66 (Apr. 26, 1976).

944. Intelligence Activities, 70.

945. Intelligence Activities, 71.

946. Intelligence Activities, 66.

947. Intelligence Activities, 87.

948. Intelligence Activities, 89.

949. *The Attorney General's Guidelines for Domestic FBI Operations*, US Department of Justice, September 29, 2008, https://www.justice.gov/archive/opa/docs/guidelines.pdf.

950. *Domestic Investigations and Operations Guide*, last updated September 17, 2021, FBI Records: The Vault, US Federal Bureau of Investigation, https://vault.fbi.gov/FBI%20Domestic%20 Investigations%20and%20Operations%20Guide%20%28DIOG%29/fbi-domestic-investigations -and-operations-guide-diog-2021-version.

951. *Domestic Investigations and Operations Guide*, 1-2.

952. *Domestic Investigations and Operations Guide*, 3-3.

953. Quinta Jurecic, "Why Didn't the FBI Review Social Media Posts Announcing Plans for the Capitol Riot?" *Lawfare* (blog), June 29, 2021, https://www.lawfaremedia.org/article/why -didnt-fbi-review-social-media-posts-announcing-plans-capitol-riot.

954. Jurecic, "Why Didn't."

955. Jurecic, "Why Didn't."

956. Jurecic, "Why Didn't."

957. Charlie Savage, "F.B.I. Focusing on Security over Ordinary Crime," *New York Times*, August 23, 2011.

958. *The Attorney General's Guidelines*, 16.

959. Jurecic, "Why Didn't" (quoting *The Attorney General's Guidelines*, 17.

960. Marsha Blackburn to Alejandro Mayorkas, February 15, 2022.

961. Steven Lee Myers, "A Panel to Combat Disinformation Becomes a Victim of It," *New York Times*, May 18, 2022.

962. Myers, "A Panel."

963. Myers, "A Panel."

964. Myers, "A Panel."

965. Cat Zakrzewski, "Judge Blocks U.S. Officials from Tech Contacts in First Amendment Case," *Washington Post*, July 4, 2023.

966. Alexis de Tocqueville, *Democracy in America*, ed. and trans. Harvey C. Manfield and Delba Winthrop (Chicago, IL: University of Chicago Press, 2002), 50.

967. Protection for Private Blocking and Screening of Offensive Material, 47 USC. § 230.

968. Protection for Private Blocking and Screening of Offensive Material.

969. Stengel, *Information Wars*, 5.

970. Jordan Liles, "Did Mark Zuckerberg Say, 'Move Fast and Break Things'?" Snopes, July 29, 2022, https://www.snopes.com/fact-check/move-fast-break-things-facebook-motto/.

971. Protection for Private Blocking and Screening of Offensive Material.

972. Ryan Mac, Mike Isaac, and Kellen Browning, "Elon Musk's Twitter Teeters on the Edge after Another 1,200 Leave," *New York Times*, November 18, 2022.

973. Pariser, "Musk's Twitter."

974. Pariser, "Musk's Twitter."

975. Protection for Private Blocking and Screening of Offensive Material.

976. Pariser, "Musk's Twitter."

977. US Const. art. I § 2; "The Impact of the Three-fifths Clause on Representation in US House of Representatives, 1793," Center for the Study of the American Constitution, University of Wisconsin-Madison, February 12, 2021, https://csac.history.wisc.edu/2021/02/12/the-impact -of-the-three-fifths-clause-on-representation-in-u-s-house-of-representatives-1793/.

978. "The Impact of the Three-fifths Clause."

979. Deborah Turner, "Make Women's History: Add the ERA to the Constitution," *League of Women Voters* (blog), March 1, 2021, https://www.lwv.org/blog/make-womens-history-add -era-constitution.

980. Joseph Wiinikka-Lydon, "Dangerous Devotion: Congressional Hearing Examines Threat of White Christian Nationalism," Southern Poverty Law Center, December 28, 2022, https:// www.splcenter.org/news/2022/12/28/dangerous-devotion-congressional-hearing-examines -threat-white-christian-nationalism.

981. *Hearing on Confronting White Supremacy (Part 7): The Evolution of Anti-democratic Extremist Groups and the Ongoing Threat to Democracy: Hearings before the House Oversight Committee's Subcommittee on Civil Rights and Civil Liberties* (2022) (statement of Amanda Tyler, on Behalf of Baptist Joint Committee for Religious Liberty).

982. *Hearing on Confronting White Supremacy (Part 7)*, (statement of Amanda Tyler).

983. *Hearing on Confronting White Supremacy (Part 7)*, (statement of Amanda Tyler).

984. *Hearing on Confronting White Supremacy (Part 7)*, (statement of Amanda Tyler).

985. Stella Rouse and Shibley Telhami, "Most Republicans Support Declaring the United States a Christian Nation," Politico, September 21, 2022, https://www.politico.com/news/magazine /2022/09/21/most-republicans-support-declaring-the-united-states-a-christian-nation-00057736.

986. Rouse and Telhami, "Most Republicans."

987. Rouse and Telhami, "Most Republicans."

988. An Act Relating to Individual Freedom, H.R. 760, 2022d Leg. § 10 (Fla.).

989. "Trust in Public Institutions: Trends and Implications for Economic Security," Department of Economic and Social Affairs, United Nations, July 20, 2021, https://www.un.org /development/desa/dspd/2021/07/trust-public-institutions/.

990. "Public Trust in Government: 1958–2022," *Pew Research Center*, June 6, 2022, https://www .pewresearch.org/politics/2022/06/06/public-trust-in-government-1958-2022/.

991. "Public Trust."

992. Ronald Reagan, "Inaugural Address," speech delivered in Washington, DC, January 20, 1981, video excerpt, 00:36, Ronald Reagan Presidential Foundation and Institute, accessed August 16, 2023, https://www.reaganfoundation.org/ronald-reagan/reagan-quotes-speeches/inaugural -address-2/.

993. Michael Rezendes, "'Spotlight' Journalists Didn't Foresee Impact of Church Abuse Investiga-tion," *Boston Globe*, November 20, 2015, https://www.bostonglobe.com/metro/2015/11/20 /journalists-who-broke-church-sex-abuse-scandal-could-not-have-foreseen-impact /iIMZJD8RfLZXxKBVqh8h4K/story.html.

994. Eric Levenson, "How Minneapolis Police First Described the Murder of George Floyd, and What We Know Now," CNN, April 21, 2021.

995. Cailin O'Connor and James Owen Weatherall, *The Misinformation Age: How False Beliefs Spread* (New Haven, CT: Yale University Press, 2018), 155–56.

996. O'Connor and Weatherall, *The Misinformation Age*, 155–56.

997. Philip Rucker and Robert Costa, "Bannon Vows a Daily Fight for 'Deconstruction of the Administrative State,'" *Washington Post*, February 23, 2017.

998. "Public Trust in Government."

999. Harry Enten, "How Long-Standing Mistrust of Government Is Hurting Our Vaccination Efforts," Politics, CNN, July 10, 2021, https://www.cnn.com/2021/07/10/politics/vaccinations -government-mistrust-analysis/index.html.

6. "Stop the Steal": Disinformation Is Destroying Democracy

1000. Letitia James, "Attorney General James Takes Legal Action against Conspiracy Theorists for Threatening Robocalls to Suppress Black Voters," press release, Office of the New York State Attorney General, May 6, 2021, https://ag.ny.gov/press-release/2021/attorney-general-james -takes-legal-action-against-conspiracy-theorists.

1001. Daniel Wu, "Judge Sentences Men behind Election Robocall Scam to Register New Voters," *Washington Post*, December 1, 2022.

1002. "Attorney General James Takes Legal Action."

1003. Wu, "Judge Sentences Men."

1004. "Social Media Influencer Douglass Mackey Convicted of Election Interference in 2016 Presidential Race," press release, United States Attorney's Office, Eastern District of New York, March 31, 2023, https://www.justice.gov/usao-edny/pr/social-media-influencer-douglass -mackey-convicted-election-interference-2016; Colin Moynihan and Alan Feuer, "Trial of 2016 Twitter Troll to Test Limits of Online Speech," *New York Times*, March 20, 2023; "Social Media Influencer Charged with Election Interference Stemming from Voter Disinformation Campaign," press release, United States Department of Justice, January 27, 2021, https:// www.justice.gov/opa/pr/social-media-influencer-charged-election-interference-stemming -voter-disinformation-campaign.

1005. "Social Media Influencer Charged."

1006. "Social Media Influencer Charged."

1007. Renée DiResta, "The Digital Maginot Line," *Ribbonfarm* (blog), November 28, 2018, https:// www.ribbonfarm.com/2018/11/28/the-digital-maginot-line/.

1008. DiResta, "The Digital Maginot Line."

1009. John Villasenor, "How to Deal with AI-Enabled Disinformation," Brookings, November 23, 2020, https://www.brookings.edu/articles/how-to-deal-with-ai-enabled-disinformation/.

1010. Russell Muirhead and Nancy L. Rosenblum, *A Lot of People Are Saying: The New Conspiracism and the Assault on Democracy* (Princeton, NJ: Princeton University Press, 2019), 3.

1011. Ja'han Jones, "Right-Wing Group Behind '2000 Mules' Could Face Federal Scrutiny," MSNBC, October 17, 2022, https://www.msnbc.com/the-reidout/reidout-blog/arizona-fraud-investigation -2000-mules-rcna52549.

1012. Bill McCarthy and Amy Sherman, "The Faulty Premise of the '*2,000 Mules*' Trailer about Voting by Mail in the 2020 Election," PolitiFact, May 4, 2022, https://www.politifact.com /article/2022/may/04/faulty-premise-2000-mules-trailer-about-voting-mai/.

1013. McCarthy and Sherman, "The Faulty Premise."

1014. Jones, "Right-Wing Group."

1015. Ali Swenson, "Fact Focus: Gaping Holes in the Claim of 2K Ballot 'Mules,'" AP News, May 3, 2022, https://apnews.com/article/2022-midterm-elections-covid-technology-health-arizona -e1b49d2311bf900f44fa5c6dac406762.

1016. "2000 Mules," Dinesh D'Souza, accessed August 30, 2023, https://www.imdb.com/title/tt8924506/.

1017. Charles Homans, "How 'Stop the Steal' Captured the American Right," *New York Times*, July 19, 2022.

1018. Ben Rhodes, *After the Fall: Being American in the World We've Made* (New York: Random House, 2021), 103.

1019. Rhodes, *After the Fall*, 104.

1020. Rhodes, *After the Fall*, 104.

1021. Rhodes, *After the Fall*, 8.

1022. Heather Cox Richardson, "February 27, 2023," *Letters from an American* (blog), February 28, 2023, https://heathercoxrichardson.substack.com/p/february-27-2023.

1023. Ronald Reagan, "Remarks at a Ceremony Commemorating the 40th Anniversary of the Normandy Invasion, D-day," speech delivered June 6, 1984, Ronald Reagan Presidential Library and Museum, accesed August 16, 2023, https://www.reaganlibrary.gov/archives/speech /remarks-ceremony-commemorating-40th-anniversary-normandy-invasion-d-day.

1024. Eric Holder and Sam Koppelman, *Our Unfinished March: The Violent Past and Imperiled Future of the Vote—A History, a Crisis, a Plan* (New York: One World, 2022), 23–25.

1025. "Susan B. Anthony Quotes," National Susan B. Anthony Museum & House, accessed August 16, 2023, https://susanb.org/susan-b-anthony-quotes/.

1026. Holder and Koppelman, *Our Unfinished March*, 23.

1027. Jason Stanley, *How Propaganda Works* (Princeton, NJ: Princeton University Press, 2015), 34.

1028. Stanley, *How Propaganda Works*, 41.

1029. Steven Levitsky and Daniel Ziblatt, *How Democracies Die* (New York: Crown, 2018).

1030. Levitsky and Ziblatt, *How Democracies Die*, 3.

1031. Rachel Weiner, "Four Other Oath Keepers Found Guilty of Jan. 6 Seditious Conspiracy," *Washington Post*, January 23, 2023.

1032. Levitsky and Ziblatt, *How Democracies Die*, 3, 5.

1033. Levitsky and Ziblatt, *How Democracies Die*, 3.

1034. Levitsky and Ziblatt, *How Democracies Die*, 5–6.
1035. Levitsky and Ziblatt, *How Democracies Die*, 95.
1036. William L. Shirer, *The Rise and Fall of the Third Reich: A History of Nazi Germany* (New York: Simon & Shuster, 1959), 198.
1037. Levitsky and Ziblatt, *How Democracies Die*, 5.
1038. "Netanyahu Delays Plan to Overhaul Top Court," *New York Times*, March 28, 2023.
1039. Levitsky and Ziblatt, *How Democracies Die*, 21.
1040. Levitsky and Ziblatt, *How Democracies Die*, 21.
1041. Levitsky and Ziblatt, *How Democracies Die*, 79.
1042. Levitsky and Ziblatt, *How Democracies Die*, 88.
1043. Levitsky and Ziblatt, *How Democracies Die*, 88–89.
1044. David Leonhardt, "The G.O.P.'s 'Putin Wing,'" *New York Times*, August 7, 2022.
1045. Leonhardt, "The G.O.P.'s Putin Wing"; Arwa Mahdawi, "Why Does Putin Have Superfans among the US Right Wing?" *The Guardian* (London), March 1, 2022.
1046. Elisabeth Zerofsky, "How the American Right Fell in Love with Hungary," *New York Times*, October 19, 2021.
1047. Natalie Allison and Lamar Johnson, "Orbán Gets Warm CPAC Reception after 'Mixed Race' Speech Blowback," Politico, August 4, 2022, https://www.politico.com/news/2022/08/04/viktor-orban-cpac-00049935.
1048. Zerofsky, "How the American Right."
1049. Nate Barksdale, "What Is the World's Oldest Democracy?" History, last updated October 29, 2018, https://www.history.com/news/what-is-the-worlds-oldest-democracy.
1050. Holder and Koppelman, *Our Unfinished March*, 31.
1051. "Alexis de Tocqueville," History, last updated June 7, 2019, https://www.history.com/topics/european-history/alexis-de-tocqueville.
1052. Levitsky and Ziblatt, *How Democracies Die*, 89.
1053. Levitsky and Ziblatt, *How Democracies Die*, 90.
1054. Levitsky and Ziblatt, *How Democracies Die*, 90.
1055. Alan Greenblatt, "The Racial History of the 'Grandfather Clause,'" *NPR*, October 22, 2013, https://www.npr.org/sections/codeswitch/2013/10/21/239081586/the-racial-history-of-the-grandfather-clause.
1056. National Historic Landmarks Program, *Civil Rights in America: Racial Voting Rights*, (Washington, DC: US Department of the Interior, 2009), 9.
1057. Holder and Koppelman, *Our Unfinished March*, 97–99.
1058. Holder and Koppelman, *Our Unfinished March*, 95.
1059. "The Great Switch: How the Republican and Democratic Parties Flipped Ideologies," Students of History, accessed October 25, 2023, https://www.studentsofhistory.com/ideologies-flip-Democratic-Republican-parties.
1060. "The Great Switch."
1061. Natalie Wolchover, "When Did Democrats and Republicans Switch Platforms?" Live Science, October 17, 2022, https://www.livescience.com/34241-democratic-republican-parties-switch-platforms.html.
1062. Levitsky and Ziblatt, *How Democracies Die*, 168.
1063. Levitsky and Ziblatt, *How Democracies Die*, 169; Angie Maxwell, "What We Get Wrong About the Southern Strategy," *Washington Post*, July 26, 2019.
1064. Levitsky and Ziblatt, *How Democracies Die*, 158.
1065. Tamara Keith, "Why Biden Is Reviving His 'Soul of the Nation' Argument for the Midterm Elections," NPR, September 1, 2022, https://www.npr.org/2022/09/01/1120479578/why-biden-is-reviving-his-soul-of-the-nation-argument-for-the-midterm-elections.
1066. Zerofsky, "How the American Right."
1067. Tom Wheeler, "The 2020 Republican Party Platform: 'L'état, c'est moi,'" Brookings, August 25, 2020, https://www.brookings.edu/articles/the-2020-republican-party-platform-letat-cest-moi/.
1068. Wheeler, "The 2020 Republican Party Platform."
1069. Katherine Miller, "Considering the Post-Trump Era in a Tucson Sports Bar," *New York Times*, October 27, 2022.

1070. Mike Pompeo (@mikepompeo), "The 1619 project is a slander on the American people. It's a false narrative, and it has no place in our schools," Twitter, January 27, 2023, 10:45 a.m., https://twitter.com/mikepompeo/status/1618998542902726657.
1071. The messages were obtained by the *Washington Post.* Bob Woodward and Robert Costa, "Virginia Thomas Urged White House Chief to Pursue Unrelenting Efforts to Overturn the 2020 Election, Texts Show," *Washington Post,* March 24, 2022.
1072. Woodward and Costa, "Virginia Thomas."
1073. Woodward and Costa, "Virginia Thomas."
1074. Mike Lee (@SenMikeLee), "We're not a democracy," Twitter, October 7, 2020, 9:34 p.m., https://twitter.com/SenMikeLee/status/1314016169993670656; Zack Beauchamp, "Sen. Mike Lee's Tweets against 'Democracy,' Explained," Vox, October 8, 2020, https://www.vox.com/policy-and-politics/21507713/mike-lee-democracy-republic-trump-2020.
1075. Mike Lee (@SenMikeLee), "Democracy isn't the objective; liberty, peace, and prospefity [*sic*] are. We want the human condition to flourish. Rank democracy can thwart that," Twitter, October 8, 2020, 2:24 a.m., https://twitter.com/SenMikeLee/status/1314089207875371008.
1076. Homans, "How 'Stop.'"
1077. Ron Elving, "Is America a Democracy or a Republic? Yes, It Is," NPR, September 10, 2022, https://www.npr.org/2022/09/10/1122089076/is-america-a-democracy-or-a-republic-yes-it-is.
1078. Homans, "How 'Stop.'"
1079. Levitsky and Ziblatt, *How Democracies Die,* 74.
1080. Levitsky and Ziblatt, *How Democracies Die,* 75.
1081. Michael Tackett and Michael Wines, "Trump Disbands Commission on Voter Fraud," *New York Times,* January 3, 2018.
1082. Tackett and Wines, "Trump Disbands."
1083. Marina Villeneuve, "Report: Trump Commission Did Not Find Widespread Voter Fraud," AP News, August 3, 2018, https://apnews.com/article/f5f6a73b2af546ee97816bb35e82c18d.
1084. John Wagner, "Trump Abolishes Controversial Commission Studying Alleged Voter Fraud," *Washington Post,* January 4, 2018.
1085. William Cummings, Joey Garrison, and Jim Sergent, "By the Numbers: President Donald Trump's Failed Efforts to Overturn the Election," *USA Today,* January 6, 2021. In Trump's lone victory, a Pennsylvania judge ruled that voters who failed to produce ID had only three days to "cure" their ballots.
1086. Ariane de Vogue and Maegan Vazquez, "Supreme Court Rejects Texas' and Trump's Bid to Overturn Election," Politics, CNN, December 12, 2020, https://www.cnn.com/2020/12/11/politics/supreme-court-texas-trump-biden/index.html.
1087. Jacqueline Thomsen, "'Historic and Profound Abuse': In Blistering Opinion, Judge Sanctions Kraken Lawyers over Election Lawsuit," Law.com, August 25, 2021, https://www.law.com/nationallawjournal/2021/08/25/historic-and-profound-abuse-in-blistering-opinion-judge-sanctions-kraken-lawyers-over-election-lawsuit/?slreturn=20230716233244. The Sixth Circuit Court of Appeals later upheld the sanctions against seven of the nine Trump campaign lawyers involved in the case, including Powell. Timothy King, et al. v. Gretchen Whitmer, No. 21-1785 (Sixth Circuit Jun. 23, 2023).
1088. *Timothy King,* No. 20-13134, slip op. (E.D. Mich. Aug. 25, 2021).
1089. Mark Kumleben, Samuel Woolley, and Katie Joseff, *Electoral Confusion: Contending with Structural Disinformation in Communities of Color* (Protect Democracy, June 2022), 13.
1090. Kumleben, Woolley, and Joseff, *Electoral Confusion,* 14.
1091. Kumleben, Woolley, and Joseff, *Electoral Confusion,* 9.
1092. Kumleben, Woolley, and Joseff, *Electoral Confusion,* 13.
1093. Kumleben, Woolley, and Joseff, *Electoral Confusion,* 24.
1094. Kumleben, Woolley, and Joseff, *Electoral Confusion,* 24.
1095. Kumleben, Woolley, and Joseff, *Electoral Confusion,* 25.
1096. Andrew Garber, "Election Denial Rhetoric from Sponsors of State Voter Suppression Legislation," Brennan Center for Justice, April 13, 2022, https://www.brennancenter.org/our-work/research-reports/election-denial-rhetoric-sponsors-state-voter-suppression-legislation.
1097. Garber, "Election Denial Rhetoric."
1098. Garber, "Election Denial Rhetoric."

1099. Jane C. Timm, "In Supreme Court, GOP Attorney Defends Voting Restrictions by Saying They Help Republicans Win," NBC News, March 2, 2021, https://www.nbcnews.com /politics/elections/supreme-court-gop-attorney-defends-voting-restrictions-saying-they -help-n1259305.

1100. Timm, "In Supreme Court."

1101. Josh Dawsey and Amy Gardner, "Top GOP Lawyer Decries Ease of Campus Voting in Private Pitch to RNC," *Washington Post*, April 20, 2023.

1102. Shelby County v. Holder, 570 US 529 (Feb. 27, 2013).

1103. *Holder.*

1104. "Voting Laws Roundup: December 2021," Brennan Center for Justice, last updated January 12, 2022, https://www.brennancenter.org/our-work/research-reports/voting-laws-roundup -december-2021.

1105. Nick Corasaniti, "Georgia G.O.P. Passes Major Law to Limit Voting amid Nationwide Push," *New York Times*, March 25, 2021.

1106. Josh Dawsey, "Trump-Commissioned Report Undercut His Claims of Dead and Double Voters," *Washington Post*, March 17, 2023.

1107. Corasaniti, "Georgia G.O.P."

1108. Corasaniti, "Georgia G.O.P."

1109. Greg Sargent, "A Scorching Reply to Georgia's Vile New Voting Law Unmasks a Big GOP Lie," *Washington Post*, March 26, 2021.

1110. Sargent, "A Scorching Reply."

1111. United States v. The State of Georgia; The Georgia State Election; and Brad Raffensperger, No. 02575, slip op. (June 25, 2021).

1112. United States v. The State of Georgia; The Georgia State Election; and Brad Raffensperger.

1113. "Voters Pass Measure to Make Voting Easier, Including No-Reason Absentee Voting," Michigan Radio, November 7, 2018, https://www.michiganradio.org/news/2018-11-07/voters -pass-measure-to-make-voting-easier-including-no-reason-absentee-voting.

1114. "Voting Laws Roundup: October 2022," Brennan Center for Justice, October 6, 2022, https:// www.brennancenter.org/our-work/research-reports/voting-laws-roundup-october-2022.

1115. Tara Subramaniam, "Fact Checking Barr's Claim That It's 'Common Sense' That Foreign Countries Will Counterfeit Mail-In Ballots," Politics, CNN, July 29, 2020, https://www.cnn .com/2020/07/29/politics/barr-voter-fraud-fact-check-foreign-countries/index.html.

1116. Hope Yen, Ali Swenson, and Amanda Seitz, "AP Fact Check: Trump's Claims of Vote Rigging Are All Wrong," AP News, December 3, 2020, accessed August 30, 2023, https://apnews.com /article/election-2020-ap-fact-check-joe-biden-donald-trump-technology -49a24edd6d10888dbad61689c24b05a5.

1117. "The Impact of Voter Suppression on Communities of Color," Brennan Center for Justice, January 10, 2022, https://www.brennancenter.org/our-work/research-reports/impact-voter -suppression-communities-color.

1118. Hannah Klain, Kevin Morris, Max Feldman, and Rebecca Ayala, *Waiting to Vote: Racial Disparities in Election Day Experiences* (New York: Brennan Center for Justice, June 3, 2020), 8.

1119. Klain, Morris, Feldman, and Ayala, *Waiting to Vote*, 8.

1120. Klain, Morris, Feldman, and Ayala, *Waiting to Vote*, 9.

1121. Lorie Konish, "'50-plus Voters Were the Deciders.' How Seniors Influenced Key Congressional Districts in the Midterm Elections," CNBC, November 22, 2022, https://www.cnbc.com /2022/11/22/how-older-voters-impacted-midterms-vote-in-key-congressional-districts.html.

1122. Carol Anderson, *One Person, No Vote: How Voter Suppression Is Destroying Our Democracy* (New York: Bloomsbury Publishing, 2018), 66.

1123. Anderson, *One Person, No Vote*, 68.

1124. Anderson, *One Person, No Vote*, 67.

1125. Anderson, *One Person, No Vote*, 70.

1126. Anderson, *One Person, No Vote*, 68.

1127. "Voting Laws Roundup: October 2022."

1128. "Voting Laws Roundup: October 2022."

1129. Alexa Ura, "Texas Will End Its Botched Voter Citizenship Review and Rescind Its List of Flagged Voters," Texas Tribune, April 26, 2019, https://www.texastribune.org/2019/04/26 /texas-voting-rights-groups-win-settlement-secretary-of-state/.

1130. Sophia Lin Lakin, "Written Statement for a Hearing on Voting in America: The Potential for Voter List Purges to Interfere with Free and Fair Access to Ballot," May 4, 2021, https:// docs.house.gov/meetings/HA/HA08/20210506/112572/HHRG-117-HA08-Wstate-LakinS -20210506.pdf.

1131. "Voting Laws Roundup: October 2022."

1132. "Voting Laws Roundup: October 2022."

1133. "Voting Laws Roundup: October 2022."

1134. Wilder and Friel, "5 State Laws Based on Voter Fraud Myths That Will Hamper Future Elections," Brennan Center for Justice, July 7, 2022, https://www.brennancenter.org/our-work/ analysis-opinion/5-state-laws-based-voter-fraud-myths-will-hamper-future-elections.

1135. Nick Corasaniti and Reid J. Epstein, "What Georgia's Voting Law Really Does," New York Times, April 2, 2021.

1136. Corasaniti and Epstein, "What Georgia's Voting Law."

1137. Jonathan J. Cooper, "Cyber Ninjas Faces Fine over Arizona Election Review Records," AP News, January 6, 2022, https://apnews.com/article/elections-lawsuits-arizona-phoenix -8417d871de10db020ee11e26ab28d03b.

1138. Maggie Astor, "Arizona Attorney General Debunks Trump Supporters' Election Fraud Claims," New York Times, August 1, 2022.

1139. Cooper, "Cyber Ninjas Faces Fine."

1140. Cooper, "Cyber Ninjas Faces Fine."

1141. Cooper, "Cyber Ninjas Faces Fine."

1142. Astor, "Arizona Attorney General Debunks."

1143. Ciara Torres-Spelliscy, "Dominion Voting's Libel Suits, the First Amendment, and Actual Malice," Brennan Center for Justice, March 28, 2022, https://www.brennancenter.org/our -work/analysis-opinion/dominion-votings-libel-suits-first-amendment-and-actual-malice.

1144. Torres-Spelliscy, "Dominion Voting's Libel Suits."

1145. Clara Hendrickson, "Former AG Candidate DePerno, State Rep Rendon Charged with Violating Michigan Election Law," Detroit Free Press, August 1, 2023.

1146. Ali Swenson, "Posts Distort Reason for Pennsylvania Voting Machine Decertification," AP News, July 23, 2021, https://apnews.com/article/fact-checking-258630944294.

1147. Kate Brumback and Christina A. Cassidy, "Trump Election Probe in Georgia Cites Voting System Breach," AP News, August 26, 2022, https://apnews.com/article/2022-midterm -elections-voting-donald-trump-georgia-6c5483c82b47cf402136b39e72326309.

1148. Brumback and Cassidy, "Trump Election."

1149. Adrian Blanco, Daniel Wolfe, and Amy Gardner, "Tracking Which 2022 Election Deniers Are Winning, Losing in the Midterms," Washington Post, December 18, 2022.

1150. Amy Gardner, "Brad Raffensperger Stood Up to Trump. Now He's Courting Trump's Base," Washington Post, May 20, 2022.

1151. Allan Smith, "Rusty Bowers, a Jan. 6 Committee Star Witness, Loses GOP Primary in Arizona," CNBC, August 3, 2022, https://www.cnbc.com/2022/08/03/rusty-bowers-a-jan-6-committee-star -witness-loses-gop-primary-in-arizona.html.

1152. "Florida Secretary of State Katherine Harris, a Staunch Republican," CNN, November 14, 2000, https://www.cnn.com/2000/ALLPOLITICS/stories/11/14/harris.profile/index.html.

1153. "Hand Recounts Denied in Florida," New York Times, November 15, 2000.

1154. Tim Hains, "Trump: 'Sometimes the Vote-Counter Is More Important than the Candidate,'" Real Clear Politics, January 16, 2022, https://www.realclearpolitics.com/video/2022 /01/16/trump_sometimes_the_vote_counter_is_more_important_than_the_candidate.html.

1155. Adrian Blanco and Amy Gardner, "Where Republican Election Deniers Are on the Ballot near You," Washington Post, October 6, 2022.

1156. Blanco and Gardner, "Where Republican Election Deniers."

1157. Home page, America First Secretary of State Coalition, accessed August 17, 2023, https:// americafirstsos.com/.

1158. "Indiana Secretary of State Election, 2022," Ballotpedia, accessed August 17, 2023, https://ballotpedia.org/Indiana_Secretary_of_State_election,_2022.

1159. "Wyoming Secretary of State Election, 2022," Ballotpedia, accessed August 17, 2023, https://ballotpedia.org/Wyoming_Secretary_of_State_election,_2022.

1160. Jessica Boehm, "Arizona Election Deniers Kari Lake and Mark Finchem Have Not Conceded," Axios Phoenix, November 16, 2022, https://www.axios.com/local/phoenix/2022/11/16/kari-lake-mark-finchem-arizona-refuse-concede.

1161. Lawrence Norden and Derek Tisler, "Addressing Insider Threats in Elections," Brennan Center for Justice, December 8, 2021, https://www.brennancenter.org/our-work/analysis-opinion/addressing-insider-threats-elections.

1162. Nick Corasaniti and Alexandra Berzon, "The Strange Tale of Tina Peters," New York Times, June 26, 2022.

1163. Corasaniti and Berzon, "The Strange Tale"; People of the State of Colorado v. Tina Peters, No. 21CR100, (Mar. 8, 2022).

1164. Corasaniti and Berzon, "The Strange Tale."

1165. "Recount Confirms That Indicted Colorado Clerk Tina Peters Lost Election," NBC News, August 4, 2022, https://www.nbcnews.com/politics/2022-election/recount-confirms-indicted-colorado-clerk-tina-peters-lost-election-rcna41670.

1166. "Election-Denying Former Colorado Clerk Guilty of Obstruction," AP News, March 3, 2023, https://apnews.com/article/colorado-clerk-tina-peters-election-conspiracy-obstruction-927167c8d3739ad40cfb5c7057f0f412.

1167. Kathleen Foody, "Why an Obscure Michigan Board Has the Power to Reject a Ballot Initiative on Abortion Rights," PBS, August 31, 2022, https://www.pbs.org/newshour/politics/why-an-obscure-michigan-board-has-the-power-to-reject-a-ballot-initiative-on-abortion-rights.

1168. Foody, "Why an Obscure Michigan Board."

1169. Foody, "Why an Obscure Michigan Board."

1170. DiResta, "The Digital Maginot Line."

7. "Somebody Is Going to Get Killed": Disinformation Is Endangering Public Safety and National Security

1171. David Eggert and John Flesher, "Michigan Certifies Biden Win, Trump Challenge Thwarted Again," AP News, November 23, 2020, https://apnews.com/article/election-2020-joe-biden-donald-trump-senate-elections-gary-peters-19decf3108373883409fae7e6e810ac6, accessed August 30, 2023.

1172. "Statement from Secretary of State Jocelyn Benson concerning Threats against Her and Her Family," Michigan Department of State, accessed August 17, 2023, https://www.michigan.gov/sos/resources/news/2020/12/06/statement-from-secretary-of-state-jocelyn-benson-concerning-threats-against-her-and-her-family.

1173. "Statement from Secretary of State."

1174. "Statement from Secretary of State."

1175. US Federal Bureau of Investigation and Department of Homeland Security, Strategic Intelligence Assessment and Data on Domestic Terrorism, May 2021, 2. Available at https://www.fbi.gov/file-repository/fbi-dhs-domestic-terrorism-strategic-report.pdf/view.

1176. Strategic Intelligence Assessment, 6.

1177. "Foreign Terrorist Organizations," US Department of State, accessed August 17, 2023, https://www.state.gov/foreign-terrorist-organizations.

1178. Scott Shane, "The Lessons of Anwar al-Awlaki," New York Times, August 27, 2015; United States v. Yahya Farooq Mohammad, No. 00358, (N.D. Ohio Sept. 30, 2015).

1179. Clint Watts, Messing with the Enemy: Surviving in a Social Media World of Hackers, Terrorists, Russians, and Fake News (New York: Harper, 2018), 31.

1180. Watts, Messing with the Enemy, 31.

1181. Watts, Messing with the Enemy, 32.

1182. Azmat Khan, "The Magazine that 'Inspired' the Boston Bombers," PBS, April 30, 2013, https://www.pbs.org/wgbh/frontline/article/the-magazine-that-inspired-the-boston-bombers/.

1183. Khan, "The Magazine."

1184. Shane, "The Lessons of Anwar al-Awlaki."
1185. Watts, *Messing with the Enemy*, 45.
1186. Richard Stengel, *Information Wars: How We Lost the Global Battle against Disinformation and What We Can Do about It* (New York: Atlantic Monthly Press, 2019), 146–47.
1187. Watts, *Messing with the Enemy*, 46; "Transcript of Assistant Attorney General John P. Carlin's Briefing at the Foreign Press Center on the Foreign Terrorist Threat and Other National Security Issues," speech, New York, NY, September 28, 2015, Office of Public Affairs, United States Department of Justice, https://www.justice.gov/opa/pr/transcript-assistant-attorney -general-john-p-carlin-s-briefing-foreign-press-center-foreign-0.
1188. Watts, *Messing with the Enemy*, 46.
1189. Watts, *Messing with the Enemy*, 46.
1190. "Terrorist Attacks by Vehicle Fast Facts," CNN, March 3, 2023, https://www.cnn.com/2017 /05/03/world/terrorist-attacks-by-vehicle-fast-facts/index.html.
1191. Molly Amman and J. Reid Meloy, "Stochastic Terrorism: A Linguistic and Psychological Analysis," Perspectives on Terrorism 15, no. 5 (October 2021): 3; Barbara McQuade, "Note from Barb: The Terrorism of the Spoken Word," CAFE Insider, May 24, 2022.
1192. Juliette Kayyem, "How MAGA Extremism Ends," *The Atlantic*, January 12, 2021.
1193. Amman and Meloy, "Stochastic Terrorism," 2.
1194. Brian Naylor, "Read Trump's Jan. 6 Speech, a Key Part of Impeachment Trial," NPR, February 10, 2021, https://www.npr.org/2021/02/10/966396848/read-trumps-jan-6-speech-a-key -part-of-impeachment-trial.
1195. Alan Feuer, "Blaming Trump, Jan. 6 Suspect Says He Fell Down a 'Rabbit Hole' of Lies," *New York Times*, April 13, 2022.
1196. Editorial Board, "The Jan. 6 Hearing Showed How Lies Can Kill," Opinion, *Washington Post*, July 12, 2022.
1197. Travis Caldwell, "Trump's 'We Love You' to Capitol Rioters Is More of the Same," Politics, CNN, January 7, 2021, https://www.cnn.com/2021/01/07/politics/trump-history-comments -trnd/index.html.
1198. Aaron Blake, "More Republicans Now Call Jan. 6 a 'Legitimate Protest' than a 'Riot,'" *Washington Post*, July 7, 2022.
1199. Blake, "More Republicans."
1200. Blake, "More Republicans."
1201. Karsten Müller and Carlo Schwarz, "From Hashtag to Hate Crime: Twitter and Antiminority Sentiment," *American Economic Journal: Applied Economics* 15, no. 3 (July 24, 2020): 270–312.
1202. Daniel L. Byman, "How Hateful Rhetoric Connects to Real-World Violence," Brookings, April 9, 2021, https://www.brookings.edu/articles/how-hateful-rhetoric-connects-to-real -world-violence/.
1203. Byman, "How Hateful Rhetoric."
1204. Robert Steinback, "Muslim Basher Terry Jones Stirs Angry Demonstration in Dearborn," Southern Poverty Law Center, May 2, 2011, https://www.splcenter.org/hatewatch/2011/05/02 /muslim-basher-terry-jones-stirs-angry-demonstration-dearborn; Tresa Baldas, "Court: Anti-Muslim Slurs Get Legal Protection," *Detroit Free Press*, October 28, 2015.
1205. Emma Graham-Harrison, "'Enemy of the People': Trump's Phrase and Its Echoes of Totalitarianism," *The Guardian* (London), August 3, 2018.
1206. Dakin Andone and Gisela Crespo, "Suspect's Van—Plastered with Trump, Pence Stickers—a Focus of Bomb Investigation," Politics, CNN, October 27, 2018, https://www.cnn.com /2018/10/26/politics/cesar-sayoc-white-van-stickers/index.html.
1207. Alayna Treene, "Trump Shares Meme of Train Running Over CNN," Axios, August 15, 2017, https://www.axios.com/2017/12/15/trump-shares-meme-of-train-running-over-cnn-1513304846.
1208. "The 155 Craziest Things Trump Said This Election," Politico, November 5, 2016, https://www .politico.com/magazine/story/2016/11/the-155-craziest-things-trump-said-this-cycle-214420/.
1209. Andone and Crespo, "Suspect's Van."
1210. Alan Feuer, "As Right-Wing Rhetoric Escalates, So Do Threats and Violence," *New York Times*, August 15, 2022.
1211. "Armed Man Killed after Trying to Breach FBI Office, Standoff," NPR, August 11, 2022, https://www.npr.org/2022/08/11/1116986362/fbi-office-armed-man-cincinnati; Peter Stone,

"Trump's Increasing Tirade against FBI and DOJ Endangering Lives of Officials," *The Guardian* (London), September 11, 2022, https://www.theguardian.com/us-news/2022/sep/11/trump-mar -a-lago-witch-hunt-fbi-doj-safety.

1212. "Armed Man Killed."

1213. Robert Pengelly, "Kari Lake's Vow to Defend Trump with Guns Threatens Democracy, Democrat Says," *The Guardian* (London), June 12, 2023.

1214. "Texas Woman Charged with Threatening to Kill Judge Overseeing Trump's Federal Election Interference Case," CNN, August 17, 2023.

1215. Beth Reinhard and Jacqueline Alemany, "In Georgia, Grand Jurors' Names Are Public—Even in Trump Indictment," *Washington Post*, August 15, 2023.

1216. Ben Protess, Jonah E. Bromwich, and Kate Christobek, "Trump's Fraud Trial Starts with Attacks on Attorney General and Judge," *New York Times*, October 2, 2023.

1217. Elizabeth Williamson, "Sandy Hook Parents Tie Years of Threats and Vitriol to Alex Jones," *New York Times*, September 29, 2022.

1218. David Weigel, "On the Campaign Trail, Many Republicans Talk of Violence," *Washington Post*, July 23, 2022.

1219. Eugene Scott, "White House Condemns Greene over Claim She Would Have 'Won' Jan. 6 Insurrection," *Washington Post*, December 12, 2022.

1220. "Hate Crime Statistics," Federal Bureau of Investigation, accessed August 17, 2023, https:// www.fbi.gov/how-we-can-help-you/more-fbi-services-and-information/ucr/hate-crime.

1221. "Hate Crime in the United States Incident Analysis," Crime Data Explorer, Federal Bureau of Investigation, accessed August 17, 2023, https://cde.ucr.cjis.gov/LATEST/webapp/#/pages /explorer/crime/hate-crime.

1222. David Nakamura, "Ohio Submits Updated Hate-Crime Figures to FBI That Would Make 2020 US Tally Highest since 2001," *Washington Post*, September 10, 2021.

1223. Vanessa Williamson and Isabella Gelfand, "Trump and Racism: What Do the Data Say?" Brookings, https://www.brookings.edu/articles/trump-and-racism-what-do-the-data-say/.

1224. Williamson and Gelfand, "Trump and Racism."

1225. Edwin D. Rios, "Hate Incidents against Asian Americans Continue to Surge, Study Finds," *The Guardian*, July 21, 2022.

1226. Colby Itkowitz, "Trump Again Uses Racially Insensitive Term to Describe Coronavirus," *Washington Post*, June 23, 2020.

1227. "8 Dead in Atlanta Spa Shootings, with Fears of Anti-Asian Bias," *New York Times*, March 17, 2021.

1228. "What Is 'Grooming?' The Truth behind the Dangerous, Bigoted Lie Targeting the LGBTQ+ Community," Anti-Defamation League, September 16, 2022, https://www.adl.org/resources /blog/what-grooming-truth-behind-dangerous-bigoted-lie-targeting-lgbtq-community.

1229. Hannah Natanson and Moriah Balingit, "Teachers Who Mention Sexuality Are 'Grooming' Kids, Conservatives Say," *Washington Post*, April 5, 2022.

1230. Kelly Rissman, "'Disgusting and Appalling': Rep. Marjorie Taylor Greene Introduced Bill That Criminalizes Performing Transgender Medical Care," *Vanity Fair*, August 20, 2022.

1231. Jo Yurcaba, "Club Q Survivors Blame 'Hateful Rhetoric' for Colorado Springs Shooting," NBC News, December 14, 2022, https://www.nbcnews.com/nbc-out/out-politics-and-policy/club-q -survivors-blame-hateful-rhetoric-colorado-springs-shooting-rcna61720.

1232. Yurcaba, "Club Q Survivors."

1233. Caitlyn Kim, "Lauren Boebert Defends Her Past Anti-LGBTQ and Anti-Trans Tweets during KOA Radio Interview in Wake of Club Q Shooting," CPR News, November 22, 2022, https://www.cpr.org/2022/11/22/lauren-boebert-defends-anti-lgbtq-anti-trans-tweets -club-q-shooting/.

1234. Kim, "Lauren Boebert Defends."

1235. Kim, "Lauren Boebert Defends."

1236. "Buffalo Shooting Suspect Says His Motive Was to Prevent 'Eliminating the White Race,'" NPR, June 16, 2022, https://www.npr.org/2022/06/16/1105776617/buffalo-shooting -suspect-says-his-motive-was-to-prevent-eliminating-the-white-ra.

1237. Cindy Ramirez, "'I Think of Them Always,' Survivor of El Paso Walmart Shooting Says of Those Who Were Killed Three Years Ago," Texas Tribune, August 3, 2022, https://www.texastribune.org/2022/08/03/el-paso-walmart-shooting-survivor/.
1238. Ramirez, "'I Think of Them.'"
1239. Campbell Robertson, Christopher Mele, and Sabrina Tavernise, "11 Killed in Synagogue Massacre; Suspect Charged with 29 Counts," New York Times, October 27, 2018.
1240. Nicole Chavez, Emanuella Grinberg, and Eliott C. McLaughlin, "Pittsburgh Synagogue Gunman Said He Wanted All Jews to Die, Criminal Complaint Says," CNN, October 31, 2018, https://www.cnn.com/2018/10/28/us/pittsburgh-synagogue-shooting/index.html.
1241. Chavez, Grinberg, and McLaughlin, "Pittsburgh Synagogue Gunman."
1242. "You Will Not Replace Us," Hate on Display, Anti-Defamation League, https://www.adl.org/resources/hate-symbol/you-will-not-replace-us.
1243. Alan Feuer, "Charlottesville Extremists Lose in Court, but Replacement Theory Lives On," New York Times, November 24, 2021.
1244. Feuer, "Charlottesville Extremists."
1245. Feuer, "Charlottesville Extremists."
1246. Audit of Antisemitic Incidents 2022 (New York: Anti-Defamation League, March 2023).
1247. Jonathan Weisman, "Jewish Allies Call Trump's Dinner with Antisemites a Breaking Point," New York Times, November 28, 2022.
1248. Weisman, "Jewish Allies."
1249. Weisman, "Jewish Allies."
1250. "New Report: Harassment, Threats and Violence Directed at Local Elected Officials Rising at an Alarming Rate," press release, National League of Cities, November 10, 2021, https://www.nlc.org/post/2021/11/10/new-report-harassment-threats-and-violence-directed-at-local-elected-officials-rising-at-an-alarming-rate/.
1251. "New Report: Harassment, Threats and Violence."
1252. "New Report: Harassment, Threats and Violence."
1253. "On the Frontlines of Today's Cities: Trauma, Challenges and Solutions," National League of Cities, accessed August 25, 2023, https://www.nlc.org/resource/on-the-frontlines-of-todays-cities-trauma-challenges-and-solutions.
1254. "Remarks by President Biden on Standing up for Democracy," speech presented at Columbus Club, Union Station, Washington, DC, November 2, 2022, Briefing Room, The White House, https://www.whitehouse.gov/briefing-room/speeches-remarks/2022/11/03/remarks-by-president-biden-on-standing-up-for-democracy/.
1255. Election Officials Under Attack: How to Protect Administrators and Safeguard Democracy, Brennan Center for Justice and Bipartisan Policy Center, June 16, 2021, 4.
1256. Paul LeBlanc, "Threats Against Public Servants Define Chilling Jan. 6 Hearing," Politics, CNN, June 21, 2022, https://www.cnn.com/2022/06/21/politics/jan-6-hearings-election-threats-what-matters/index.html.
1257. LeBlanc, "Threats Against."
1258. LeBlanc, "Threats Against."
1259. LeBlanc, "Threats Against."
1260. James Verini, "He Wanted to Count Every Vote in Philadelphia. His Party Had Other Ideas," New York Times, December 16, 2020.
1261. Verini, "He Wanted."
1262. Election Officials Under Attack, 3.
1263. Election Officials Under Attack, 3.
1264. Verini, "He Wanted."
1265. Election Officials Under Attack, 3.
1266. LeBlanc, "Threats Against."
1267. LeBlanc, "Threats Against."
1268. LeBlanc, "Threats Against."
1269. Amy Gardner, "Election Workers Describe 'Hateful' Threats after Trump's False Claims," Washington Post, June 21, 2022.
1270. Gardner, "Election Workers."
1271. LeBlanc, "Threats Against."

1272. Gardner, "Election Workers."
1273. Gardner, "Election Workers."
1274. Gardner, "Election Workers."
1275. Gardner, "Election Workers."
1276. LeBlanc, "Threats Against."
1277. LeBlanc, "Threats Against."
1278. Perry Stein and Tom Hamburger, "Over 1,000 Election-Worker Threats Reported in Past Year, Official Says," *Washington Post*, August 3, 2022.
1279. *Local Officials Survey*, Brennan Center for Justice, March 10, 2022.
1280. Stein and Hamburger, "Over 1,000."
1281. Anna King, "Embattled Public Health Workers Leaving at 'Steady and Alarming' Rate," NPR, November 25, 2020, https://www.npr.org/2020/11/25/938873547/embattled -public-health-workers-leaving-at-steady-and-alarming-rate.
1282. King, "Embattled Public Health Workers."
1283. King, "Embattled Public Health Workers."
1284. Farah Yousry, "Back to School: Combating Misinformation on How to Keep Children Safe," WYFI Indianapolis, August 12, 2021, https://www.wfyi.org/news/articles/back-to -school--combating-misinformation-on-how-to-keep-children-safe.
1285. Leslie Gray Streeter, "'A Dog Whistle and a Lie': Black Parents on the Critical Race Theory Debate," *Washington Post*, December 7, 2021.
1286. Streeter, "'A Dog Whistle."
1287. Karin Brulliard, "Free Speech or Out of Order? As Meetings Grow Wild, Officials Try to Tame Public Comment," *Washington Post*, January 17, 2023.
1288. "Justice Department Addresses Violent Threats against School Officials and Teachers," press release, United States Department of Justice, October 4, 2021, https://www.justice.gov/opa /pr/justice-department-addresses-violent-threats-against-school-officials-and-teachers.
1289. Bart Jansen and Alia Wong, "'We Did Not Sic the FBI on Parents': Attorney General Merrick Garland Defends School Memo," *USA Today*, October 27, 2021.
1290. Jansen and Wong, "'We Did Not Sic the FBI on Parents.'"
1291. Kurtis Lee, "Elon Musk, in a Tweet, Shares Link from Site Known to Publish False News," *New York Times*, October 30, 2022.
1292. Isaac Stanley-Becker, "Elon Musk, Right-Wing Figures Push Misinformation about Pelosi Attack," *Washington Post*, October 30, 2022.
1293. Annie Karni, Malika Khurana, and Stuart A. Thompson, "How Republicans Fed a Misinformation Loop about the Pelosi Attack," *New York Times*, November 5, 2022.
1294. Stephanie Lai, "Lawmakers Consider More Security for Offices Following Connolly Staff Attack," *New York Times*, May 18, 2023.
1295. Cailin O'Connor and James Owen Weatherall, *The Misinformation Age: How False Beliefs Spread* (New Haven, CT: Yale University Press, 2018), 68.
1296. Eugene Scott, "Kinzinger, on Jan. 6 Panel, Shares Profane Threats Sent to His Office," *Washington Post*, July 5, 2022.
1297. Scott, "Kinzinger, on Jan. 6 Panel."
1298. Emily Hencken Ritter and Brett V. Benson, "An Insurrection and a New President Make the US Vulnerable to Foreign Policy Crises," *Political Violence at a Glance*, February 17, 2021, https://politicalviolenceataglance.org/2021/02/17/an-insurrection-and-a-new-president-make -the-us-vulnerable-to-foreign-policy-crises/.
1299. Ritter and Benson, "An Insurrection and a New President."
1300. Bill Chappell, Greg Myre, and Laurel Wamsley, "What We Know about Russia's Alleged Hack of the U.S. Government and Tech Companies," NPR, December 21, 2020, https://www.npr.org /2020/12/15/946776718/u-s-scrambles-to-understand-major-computer-hack-but-says-little.
1301. Ritter and Benson, "An Insurrection and a New President"; Harper Neidig, "Bannon Predicted 'All Hell Is Going to Break Loose Tomorrow' after Jan. 5 Call with Trump," *The Hill*, July 12, 2022, https://thehill.com/homenews/house/3556166-bannon-predicted-all-hell-is-going-to-break -loose-tomorrow-after-jan-5-call-with-trump/.
1302. Ritter and Benson, "An Insurrection and a New President."

1303. Maureen Breslin, "Kamala Harris Says Threat from Within US Makes US 'Weaker,'" The Hill, September 11, 2022, https://thehill.com/policy/national-security/domestic-terrorism /3637957-kamala-harris-says-threat-from-within-us-makes-us-weaker/.

1304. Michael Mainville, "Russia Sees U.S. Democracy 'Limping' after Capitol Stormed," The Moscow Times, January 7, 2021, https://www.themoscowtimes.com/2021/01/07/russia-sees-us -democracy-limping-after-capitol-stormed-a72551.

1305. Mainville, "Russia Sees."

1306. Mainville, "Russia Sees."

1307. Maria Repnikova, "The Balance of Soft Power," Foreign Affairs, July/August 2022.

1308. Bret Schafer, "Race, Lies and Social Media: How Russia Manipulated Race in America and Interfered in the 2016 Elections," in Under Siege: The Plot to Destroy Democracy (State of Black America) (New York: National Urban League, 2022), available at http://soba.iamempowered.com/race-lies -and-social-media-how-russia-manipulated-race-america-and-interfered-2016-elections.

1309. Zack Beauchamp, "Trump's Republican Party, Explained in One Photo," Vox, August 6, 2018, https://www.vox.com/policy-and-politics/2018/8/6/17656996/trump-republican-party -russia-rather-democrat-ohio.

1310. "NATO's Purpose," North Atlantic Treaty Organization, last modified July 4, 2023, https:// www.nato.int/cps/en/natohq/topics_68144.htm.

1311. Sean M. Lynn-Jones, "Why the United States Should Spread Democracy" (unpublished paper, Belfer Center for Science and International Affairs, John F. Kennedy School of Government, Harvard University, March 1998), https://www.belfercenter.org/publication/why -united-states-should-spread-democracy.

1312. Ben Rhodes, After the Fall: Being American in the World We've Made (New York, NY: Random House, 2021), 184.

1313. Rhodes, After the Fall, 184.

1314. Lynn-Jones, "Why the United States"; "Democracy," Archive, US Department of State, accessed August 17, 2023, https://2001-2009.state.gov/g/drl/democ/index.htm.

1315. Kyle Smith, "Why the Right Hates Fauci," National Review, May 20, 2021.

1316. Olivia B. Waxman, "Historian: Today's Authoritarian Leaders Aren't Fascists—but They Are Part of the Same Story," Time, November 10, 2020.

1317. Waxman, "Historian: Today's Authoritarian Leaders."

1318. Jonathan Swan, "Trump's Revenge," Axios, July 23, 2022, https://www.axios.com/2022/07/23 /donald-trump-news-schedule-f-executive-order.

1319. Michael Lewis, The Fifth Risk (New York: W. W. Norton & Company, 2018), 75.

1320. Lewis, The Fifth Risk, 76.

8. Trial by Combat: Disinformation Is Eroding the Rule of Law

1321. Maham Javaid, "N.Y. Prosecutor's Office Pushes Back on GOP Demands on Trump Probe," Washington Post, March 20, 2023.

1322. Javaid, "N.Y. Prosecutor's Office."

1323. Mark Berman and Shayna Jacobs, "With Trump Indictment Possible, Officials on Watch for Protests," Washington Post, March 20, 2023.

1324. Azi Paybarah, "What Republicans Have Said about a Possible Trump Indictment," Washington Post, March 20, 2023.

1325. Paybarah, "What Republicans Have Said."

1326. Javaid, "N.Y. Prosecutor's Office."

1327. "Overview—Rule of Law," United States Courts, accessed August 17, 2023, https://www .uscourts.gov/educational-resources/educational-activities/overview-rule-law.

1328. Steven Levitsky and Daniel Ziblatt, How Democracies Die (New York: Crown, 2018), 92.

1329. Jonathan Swan, Charlie Savage, and Maggie Haberman, "The Radical Strategy Behind Trump's Promise to 'Go After' Biden, New York Times, June 15, 2023.

1330. "May 25: President Lincoln Suspends the Writ of Habeas Corpus during the Civil War," History, accessed August 30, 2023, https://www.history.com/this-day-in-history/lincolns -suspension-of-habeas-corpus-is-challenged.

1331. Korematsu v. United States, 65 S. Ct. 193 (Dec. 18, 1944); "Proclamation 2527 and the Internment of Italian Americans," National WWII Museum, December 13, 2021, https://www .nationalww2museum.org/war/articles/proclamation-2527-internment-italian-americans.

1332. Levitsky and Ziblatt, *How Democracies Die*, 95, 98.

1333. Levitsky and Ziblatt, *How Democracies Die*, 95, 98.

1334. Kristen Holmes, "Trump Calls for the Termination of the Constitution in Truth Social Post," Politics, CNN, December 4, 2022, https://www.cnn.com/2022/12/03/politics/trump -constitution-truth-social/index.html.

1335. Holmes, "Trump Calls."

1336. Emily Ekins, *Policing in America: Understanding Public Attitudes toward the Police. Results from a National Survey* (Washington, DC: Cato Institute, December 7, 2016).

1337. Olivia B. Waxman, "Historian: Today's Authoritarian Leaders Aren't Fascists—but They Are Part of the Same Story," *Time*, November 10, 2020.

1338. David Leonhardt, "Why Isn't the 'Southern Strategy' Working?" *New York Times*, July 7, 2020. Bush's ad described felon Willie Horton, an African American man who raped a white woman and stabbed her boyfriend while on furlough from a Massachusetts prison. The ad suggested that Bush's opponent, former Massachusetts governor Michael Dukakis, was soft on crime. See Peter Baker, "Bush Made Willie Horton an Issue in 1988, and the Racial Scars Are Still Fresh," *New York Times*, December 3, 2018.

1339. Andrew Kaczynski, "Biden in 1993 Speech Pushing Crime Bill Warned of 'Predators on Our Streets' Who Were 'Beyond the Pale,'" Politics, CNN, March 7, 2019, https://www.cnn.com /2019/03/07/politics/biden-1993-speech-predators/index.html.

1340. "Fact Check: Hillary Clinton, Not Joe Biden, Used the Term Super Predator in 1990s," Reuters, October 26, 2020, https://www.reuters.com/article/uk-factcheck-hillary-clinton-biden-super /fact-checkhillary-clinton-not-joe-biden-used-thetermsuperpredatorin1990s-idUSKBN27B1PQ.

1341. Maanvi Singh and Nina Lakhani, "George Floyd Killing: Peaceful Protests Sweep America as Calls for Racial Justice Reach New Heights," *The Guardian* (London), June 7, 2020.

1342. Weihua Li, "The Truth about Violent Crime in American Cities, Explained in 11 Charts," Vox, September 25, 2020, https://www.vox.com/21454844/murder-crime-us-cities-protests.

1343. Tom Gjelten, "Peaceful Protesters Tear-Gassed to Clear Way for Trump Church Photo-Op," NPR, June 1, 2020, https://www.npr.org/2020/06/01/867532070/trumps-unannounced-church-visit -angers-church-officials.

1344. Laura Barron-Lopez and Alex Thompson, "Facing Bleak November, Republicans Look to Stoke BLM Backlash," Politico, August 10, 2020, https://www.politico.com/news/2020 /08/10/elections-republicans-black-lives-matterbacklash-389906.

1345. "Analysis of US Anti-Protest Bills," International Center for Not-for-Profit Law, accessed August 30, 2023, https://www.icnl.org/post/news/analysis-of-anti-protest-bills?location=& status=&issue=&date=.

1346. "Analysis of US Anti-Protest Bills."

1347. Philip Bump, "Trump's Defense against Federal Investigation: The 'Russia Hoax' Hoax," *Washington Post*, August 17, 2022.

1348. Eli Watkins, "Some of the Times Trump Has Called Russia Probe a 'Witch Hunt,'" Politics, CNN, January 11, 2018, https://www.cnn.com/2018/01/10/politics/donald-trump-witch-hunt -justice-department/index.html.

1349. Julie Hirschfeld Davis, "Trump Calls Justice Department and F.B.I. Conduct 'a Disgrace,'" *New York Times*, February 2, 2018.

1350. Davis, "Trump Calls Justice Department."

1351. *Review of Four FISA Applications and Other Aspects of the FBI's Crossfire Hurricane Investigation* (Washington, DC: Office of the Inspector General, December 2019), https://www .justice.gov/storage/120919-examination.pdf.

1352. Alan Feuer, "Trump Is Baselessly Suggesting That the FBI May Have Planted Evidence during Its Search," *New York Times*, August 10, 2022; David Klepper, "Trump's Angry Words Spur Warnings of Real Violence," AP News, August 16, 2022, https://apnews.com/article/ghislaine -maxwell-social-media-donald-trump-mar-a-lago-31741bb13f708ee68b52359262334eb.

1353. Klepper, "Trump's Angry Words."

1354. Klepper, "Trump's Angry Words."

1355. Klepper, "Trump's Angry Words."
1356. Klepper, "Trump's Angry Words."
1357. Linda Qiu, "Fact-Checking the Misleading Claim about 87,000 Tax Agents," *New York Times*, November 6, 2022.
1358. Qiu, "Fact-Checking the Misleading."
1359. Qiu, "Fact-Checking the Misleading."
1360. Qiu, "Fact-Checking the Misleading."
1361. Qiu, "Fact-Checking the Misleading."
1362. Qiu, "Fact-Checking the Misleading."
1363. Qiu, "Fact-Checking the Misleading."
1364. "Houston Attorney Sentenced to Prison for Offshore Tax Evasion Scheme," press release, United States Department of Justice, August 6, 2020, https://www.justice.gov/opa/pr/houston-attorney -sentenced-prison-offshore-tax-evasion-scheme.
1365. Luke Broadwater and Catie Edmondson, "Divided House Approves G.O.P. Inquiry into 'Weaponization' of Government," *New York Times*, January 10, 2023.
1366. Leigh Ann Caldwell and Theodoric Meyer, "The Most Contentious Committee in the New Congress," *Washington Post*, January 11, 2023.
1367. Broadwater and Edmondson, "Divided House Approves G.O.P. Inquiry."
1368. Jacqueline Alemany and Devlin Barrett, "House Republicans Form Committee to Investigate the Government," *Washington Post*, January 10, 2023.
1369. Jeffrey M. Jones, "Supreme Court Approval Holds at Record Low," Gallup, August 2, 2023, https://news.gallup.com/poll/509234/supreme-court-approval-holds-record -low.aspx#:~:text=62%25%20of%20Republicans%2C%2041%25,74%25%20rating %20in%20July%202022.
1370. Asha Rangappa, "Disinformation, Democracy, and the Rule of Law" (speech, Connecticut Legal Conference, Connecticut Bar Association, Hartford, CT, June 10, 2019).
1371. Rangappa, "Disinformation, Democracy, and the Rule of Law."
1372. Robert L. Tsai, "Trump's Travel Ban Faces Fresh Legal Jeopardy," Magazine, Politico, March 27, 2019, https://www.politico.com/magazine/story/2019/03/27/trump-travel-ban-lawsuit -supreme-court-unconstitutional-226103/.
1373. Tsai, "Trump's Travel Ban."
1374. "In His Own Words: The President's Attacks on the Courts," Brennan Center for Justice, last updated February 14, 2020, https://www.brennancenter.org/our-work/research-reports/his-own -words-presidents-attacks-courts.
1375. "In His Own Words."
1376. "In His Own Words."
1377. "In His Own Words."
1378. "In His Own Words."
1379. "In His Own Words."
1380. "In His Own Words."
1381. "In His Own Words."
1382. "In His Own Words."
1383. "In His Own Words."
1384. "In His Own Words."
1385. "In His Own Words."
1386. "In His Own Words."
1387. "In His Own Words."
1388. "In His Own Words."
1389. Myah Ward, "Fox News' Brian Kilmeade Clarifies That Image of Judge at Center of Trump Search Warrant Was a Fake," Politico, August 12, 2022, https://www.politico.com /news/2022/08/12/brian-kilmeade-judge-trump-warrant-00051527.
1390. Ward, "Fox News."
1391. Jodi Wilgoren, "Electrician Says in Suicide Note That He Killed Judge's Family," *New York Times*, March 11, 2005; William K. Rashbaum, "Misogynistic Lawyer Who Killed Judge's Son Had List of Possible Targets," *New York Times*, July 25, 2020.

1392. Holmes Lybrand and Tierney Sneed, "FBI Says Man Accused of Attempting to Kill Brett Kavanaugh Said He Was 'Shooting For 3' Justices," Politics, CNN, July 27, 2022, https://www.cnn.com/2022/07/27/politics/kavanaugh-roske-arrest-warrant/index.html.

1393. Whitney Wild, "A Former Judge Was Killed in His Wisconsin Home in a Targeted Attack, Officials Say," CNN, June 4, 2022, https://www.cnn.com/2022/06/04/us/wisconsin-judge-killed-targeted-attack/index.html.

1394. Eric Levenson and Boris Sanchez, "Federal Judge Whose Son Was Killed Two Years Ago Calls for Greater Judicial Protections after Former Wisconsin Judge Killed," CNN, June 5, 2022, https://www.cnn.com/2022/06/05/us/wisconsin-judge-killed-attack/index.html.

1395. Levenson and Sanchez, "Federal Judge."

1396. Russell Wheeler, "McConnell's Fabricated History to Justify a 2020 Supreme Court Vote," Brookings, September 24, 2020, https://www.brookings.edu/articles/mcconnells-fabricated-history-to-justify-a-2020-supreme-court-vote/.

1397. Wheeler, "McConnell's Fabricated History."

1398. Wheeler, "McConnell's Fabricated History."

1399. Carl Hulse, "How Mitch McConnell Delivered Justice Amy Coney Barrett's Rapid Confirmation," New York Times, October 27, 2020.

1400. Dobbs v. Jackson Women's Health Organization, 213 S. Ct. 545 (June 24, 2022).

1401. Dobbs.

1402. Students for Fair Admissions v. Harvard College, Students for Fair Admissions v. University of North Carolina, 600 U.S. ___ (June 29, 2023).

1403. 303 Creative v. Elenis, 600 U.S. ___ (June 30, 2023).

1404. 303 Creative (Sotomayor dissenting).

1405. Moore v. Harper, 600 U.S. ___ (June 27, 2023).

1406. Transcript, Confirmation Hearing of John G. Roberts Jr.; "Roberts: 'My Job is To Call Balls and Strikes and Not to Pitch or Bat,'" Politics, CNN, September 12, 2005, https://www.cnn.com/2005/POLITICS/09/12/roberts.statement/.

1407. Biden v. Nebraska, 600 U.S. ___ (June 30, 2023) (Kagan dissenting).

1408. Biden (Kagan dissenting).

1409. Biden (Kagan dissenting).

1410. Beth Reinhard and Anne Gearan, "Most Trump Clemency Grants Bypass Justice Dept. and Go to Well-Connected Offenders," Washington Post, February 3, 2020.

1411. "Here Are Some of the People Trump Pardoned," New York Times, January 26, 2021; Tresa Baldas, "Judge Frees Kwame Kilpatrick Pal Bobby Ferguson from Prison 10 Years Early," Detroit Free Press, April 29, 2021. As US Attorney for the Eastern District of Michigan, I supervised the prosecution of Kilpatrick, who was originally sentenced to twenty-eight years in prison following his conviction at trial for yearslong schemes involving bribery, fraud, and tax offenses. Trump commuted Kilpatrick's sentence after seven years, but not the sentence of his less culpable codefendant Bobby Ferguson, who was sentenced to twenty-one years in prison. The sentencing judge later granted Ferguson's request for compassionate release. Even my Trump-appointed successor as US attorney in Detroit called Kilpatrick's grant of clemency "unjustified."

1412. "Here Are Some of the People."

1413. Reinhard and Gearan, "Most Trump Clemency Grants."

1414. "Here Are Some of the People."

1415. Caroline Vakil, "Trump Says He Would Look 'Very, Very Seriously' at Pardons for Jan 6 Defendants If Reelected," The Hill, June 17, 2022, https://thehill.com/homenews/administration/3528189-trump-says-he-would-look-very-very-seriously-at-pardons-for-jan-6-defendants-if-reelected/.

1416. Reinhard and Gearan, "Most Trump Clemency Grants."

1417. Reinhard and Gearan, "Most Trump Clemency Grants."

1418. "Statement of U.S. Attorney Damian Williams on the Conviction of Timothy Shea," press release, United States Attorney's Office for the Southern District of New York, October 28, 2022, https://www.justice.gov/usao-sdny/pr/statement-us-attorney-damian-williams-conviction-timothy-shea; Rebecca Davis O'Brien and Jonah E. Bromwich, "In Bannon Case, Manhattan D.A. Takes on Another Pardoned Trump Ally," New York Times, September 7, 2022.

1419. "Lynching in America," American Experience, PBS, accessed August 17, 2023, https://www
.pbs.org/wgbh/americanexperience/features/emmett-lynching-america/.

1420. Renée DiResta, "The Digital Maginot Line," Ribbonfarm (blog), last modified November 28,
2018, https://www.ribbonfarm.com/2018/11/28/the-digital-maginot-line/.

1421. Faiz Siddiqui and Susan Svrluga, "N.C. Man Told Police He Went to D.C. Pizzeria with
Gun to Investigate Conspiracy Theory," *Washington Post*, December 5, 2016.

1422. Siddiqui and Svrluga, "N.C. Man Told Police"; Amy Davidson Sorkin, "The Age of Donald
Trump and Pizzagate," *New Yorker*, December 5, 2016.

1423. Sorkin, "The Age of Donald Trump."

1424. Amanda Robb, "Anatomy of a Fake News Scandal," *Rolling Stone*, November 16, 2017.

1425. Charles Homans, "Kyle Rittenhouse and the New Era of Political Violence," *New York Times*,
October 26, 2021.

1426. Homans, "Kyle Rittenhouse."

1427. Paige Williams, "Kyle Rittenhouse, American Vigilante," *New Yorker*, June 28, 2021.

1428. Williams, "Kyle Rittenhouse, American Vigilante."

1429. Neil Vigdor, "Rifle Used by Kyle Rittenhouse in Kenosha Shootings Will Be Destroyed,"
New York Times, January 28, 2022.

1430. Homans, "Kyle Rittenhouse."

1431. Homans, "Kyle Rittenhouse."

1432. Williams, "Kyle Rittenhouse, American Vigilante."

1433. Williams, "Kyle Rittenhouse, American Vigilante."

1434. J. D. Vance (@JDVance1), "I am not a criminal lawyer. I am sure people are right that it's
risky for him to testify. But our leaders abandoned this kid's community to lawless thug
rioters, and he did something about it, and now a lawless thug prosecutor is trying to destroy
his life," Twitter, November 10, 2021, 11:21 a.m., https://twitter.com/JDVance1/status
/1458469989426601988.

1435. J. D. Vance (@JDVance1), "We leave our boys without fathers. We let the wolves set fire to
their communities. And when human nature tells them to go and defend what no one else
is defending, we bring the full weight of the state and the global monopolists against them,"
Twitter, November 10, 2021, 11:26 a.m., https://twitter.com/JDVance1/status
/1458471055446659072.

1436. Zack Stanton, "POLITICO Playbook: Rittenhouse Verdict Pushes BBB out of the Headlines," Politico, November 20, 2021, https://www.politico.com/newsletters/playbook/2021
/11/20/rittenhouse-verdict-pushes-bbb-out-of-the-headlines-495177.

1437. Sam Tanenhaus, "Jan. 6 Wasn't an Insurrection. It Was Vigilantism. And More Is Coming,"
Washington Post, December 10, 2021.

1438. Homans, "Kyle Rittenhouse"; Michelle Malkin (@michellemalkin), "ALL THE BEST PEOPLE
#StandWithKyle. It's now or never . . . and, yes, it's war ==> Ann Coulter, Michelle Malkin Under
Fire for Supporting Accused Kenosha Shooter https://yahoo.com/entertainment/ann-coulter
-michelle-malkin-under-180012227.html?soc_src=social-sh&soc_trk=tw via @YahooEnt @
LLinWood @CaliKidJMP @MarinaMedvin #FightBack," Twitter, August 29, 2020, 8:26 p.m.,
https://twitter.com/michellemalkin/status/1299865972518481920.

1439. United States v. Adam Dean Fox, et al., No. 1:20-cr-00183-RJJ (Dec. 16, 2020). While most
of the defendants were convicted, two were acquitted by a conservative west Michigan jury
after they claimed they were entrapped by undercover government agents. Tresa Baldas and
Arpan Lobo, "2 Whitmer Kidnap Plot Suspects Found Not Guilty; Mistrial Declared for Other
2," *Detroit Free Press*, April 8, 2022; Ed White, "3 Men Convicted of Supporting Plot to Kidnap
Gov. Whitmer," AP News, October 26, 2022, https://apnews.com/article/michigan-gretchen
-whitmer-jackson-adam-fox-kidnap-plot-trial-0a5a930cf86e74f8a1365040b783deod.

1440. Nicholas Bogel-Burroughs, Shaila Dewan, and Kathleen Gray, "F.B.I. Says Michigan Anti-
Government Group Plotted to Kidnap Gov. Gretchen Whitmer," *New York Times*, October 8, 2020.

1441. White, "3 Men Convicted."

1442. Juana Summers, "Timeline: How Trump Has Downplayed the Coronavirus Pandemic,"
NPR, October 2, 2020, https://www.npr.org/sections/latest-updates-trump-covid-19
-results/2020/10/02/919432383/how-trump-has-downplayed-the-coronavirus-pandemic.

1443. Angie Drobnic Holan, "Ask PolitiFact: Are You Sure Donald Trump Didn't Call the Coronavirus a Hoax?" PolitiFact, October 8, 2020, https://www.politifact.com/article/2020/oct/08/ask-politifact-are-you-sure-donald-trump-didnt-cal/.

1444. Peter Baker and Maggie Haberman, "Trump Tests Positive for the Coronavirus," *New York Times*, October 2, 2020.

1445. Mary McCord, "Trump's 'LIBERATE MICHIGAN!' Tweets Incite Insurrection. That's Illegal," *Washington Post*, April 17, 2020.

1446. Mitch Smith, "Two Men Convicted in Plot to Kidnap Michigan's Governor," *New York Times*, August 23, 2022.

1447. Mychael Schnell, "Cheney: Trump 'Summoned the Mob, Assembled the Mob and Lit the Flame of This Attack,'" The Hill, June 9, 2022, https://thehill.com/policy/national-security/3518354-cheney-trump-summoned-the-mob-assembled-the-mob-and-lit-the-flame-of-this-attack/.

1448. "Transcript of Trump's Speech at Rally before Riot at US Capitol," Associated Press, January 13, 2021, https://apnews.com/article/election-2020-joe-biden-donald-trump-capitol-siege-media-e79eb5164613d6718e9f4502eb471f27.

1449. "Transcript of Trump's Speech."

1450. "Transcript of Trump's Speech."

1451. "Transcript of Trump's Speech."

1452. Tom Dreisbach and Tim Mak, "Yes, Capitol Rioters Were Armed. Here Are the Weapons Prosecutors Say They Used," NPR, March 19, 2021, https://www.npr.org/2021/03/19/977879589/yes-capitol-rioters-were-armed-here-are-the-weapons-prosecutors-say-they-used.

1453. Ryan J. Reilly, "Armed Jan. 6 Rioter Had Zip Ties during Capitol Attack, Friend Testifies at Trial," NBC News, March 4, 2022, https://www.nbcnews.com/politics/justice-department/armed-jan-6-rioter-zip-ties-capitol-attack-friend-testifies-trial-rcna18733.

1454. Alan Feuer, "Blaming Trump, Jan. 6 Suspect Says He Fell Down a 'Rabbit Hole' of Lies," *New York Times*, April 13, 2022.

1455. Betsy Woodruff Swan and Kyle Cheney, "Trump Expressed Support for Hanging Pence during Capitol Riot, Jan. 6 Panel Told," Politico, May 25, 2022, https://www.politico.com/news/2022/05/25/trump-expressed-support-hanging-pence-capitol-riot-jan-6-00035117.

1456. Catie Edmondson, "'So the Traitors Know the Stakes': The Meaning of the Jan. 6 Gallows," *New York Times*, June 16, 2022.

1457. Spencer S. Hsu and Hannah Allam, "Landmark Oath Keepers Verdict Hobbles Group, but the Movement Lives On," *Washington Post*, December 3, 2022.

1458. Russell Wheeler, "Trump's Judicial Campaign to Upend the 2020 Election: A Failure, but Not a Wipe-Out," Brookings, November 30, 2021, https://www.brookings.edu/articles/trumps-judicial-campaign-to-upend-the-2020-election-a-failure-but-not-a-wipe-out/.

1459. Terry Tang, "Judge Orders Armed Group Away from Arizona Ballot Drop Boxes," AP News, November 2, 2022, https://apnews.com/article/2022-midterm-elections-arizona-phoenix-5353cfd0774727e6dd03bdbf48c12211.

1460. Tang, "Judge Orders Armed Group."

1461. Tang, "Judge Orders Armed Group."

1462. Rachael Levy, "What Are Militias and Are They Legal?" *Wall Street Journal*, October 10, 2020; "The Militia Movement (2020)," Anti-Defamation League, October 19, 2020, https://www.adl.org/resources/backgrounder/militia-movement-2020.

1463. "Three Percenters," Southern Poverty Law Center, accessed August 17, 2023, https://www.splcenter.org/fighting-hate/extremist-files/group/three-percenters.

1464. "Antigovernment General," Southern Poverty Law Center, accessed August 17, 2023, https://www.splcenter.org/fighting-hate/extremist-files/ideology/antigovernment-general.

1465. Hsu and Allam, "Landmark Oath Keepers Verdict."

1466. Hsu and Allam, "Landmark Oath Keepers Verdict."

1467. "Proud Boys," Southern Poverty Law Center, accessed August 17, 2023, https://www.splcenter.org/fighting-hate/extremist-files/group/proud-boys.

1468. Hannah Allam, "Ex-Oath Keeper Outlines Dark Worldview behind US Capitol Attack," *Washington Post*, July 12, 2022.

1469. Gustaf Kilander, "Ex-Oath Keeper Gives Jan 6 Committee Sinister Warning If Trump Re-elected," *Independent*, July 12, 2022.

1470. Barbara McQuade, "We Have Met the Enemy and They Are Us," podcast audio, 47:09, *Horns of a Dilemma*, June 17, 2022.
1471. Kathleen Belew, "Militia Groups Were Hiding in Plain Sight on Jan. 6. They're Still Dangerous," *Washington Post*, January 6, 2022.
1472. Belew, "Militia Groups Were Hiding."
1473. "Fact Sheets on Unlawful Militias for All 50 States Now Available from Georgetown Law's Institute for Constitutional Advocacy and Protection," press release, September 22, 2020, Institute for Constitutional Advocacy and Protection, Georgetown Law, https://www.law .georgetown.edu/icap/our-press-releases/fact-sheets-on-unlawful-militias-for-all-50-states -now-available-from-georgetown-laws-institute-for-constitutional-advocacy-and-protection/.
1474. Seth G. Jones, "Violent Domestic Extremist Groups and the Recruitment of Veterans," statement before the House Committee on Veterans' Affairs, Capitol Building, October 13, 2021, Washington, DC, https://www.congress.gov/117/meeting/house/113968/witnesses/HHRG -117-VR00-Wstate-JonesS-20211013.pdf.
1475. Karen Kornbluh, "Disinformation, Radicalization, and Algorithmic Amplification: What Steps Can Congress Take?" *Just Security*, February 7, 2022, https://www.justsecurity.org /79995/disinformation-radicalization-and-algorithmic-amplification-what-steps-can -congress-take/.
1476. Kornbluh, "Disinformation, Radicalization and Algorithmic Amplification."
1477. Catrina Doxsee, "Examining Extremism: The Militia Movement," *CSIS* (blog), Center for Strategic and International Studies, August 12, 2021, https://www.csis.org/blogs/examining -extremism/examining-extremism-militia-movement.
1478. Doxsee, "Examining Extremism," *Domestic Violent Extremism Poses Heightened Threat in 2021* (Washington, DC: Office of the Director of National Intelligence, March 1, 2021).
1479. Rachel Kleinfeld, "The GOP's Militia Problem: Proud Boys, Oath Keepers and Lessons from Abroad," *Just Security*, July 6, 2022, https://www.justsecurity.org/81898/the-gops-militia -problem-proud-boys-oath-keepers-and-lessons-from-abroad/.
1480. Editorial Board, "How a Faction of the Republican Party Enables Political Violence," Opinion, *New York Times*, November 26, 2022.
1481. Kleinfeld, "The GOP's Militia Problem."
1482. Kleinfeld, "The GOP's Militia Problem."
1483. Alan Feuer, "Jan. 6 Panel Explores Links between Trump Allies and Extremist Groups," *New York Times*, June 29, 2022.
1484. Chris Joyner, "Militia Alliance in Georgia Signals New Phase for Extremist Paramilitaries," *Atlanta Journal-Constitution*, February 4, 2021.
1485. Laura Italiano, "The January 6 Investigators Obtained a Video of Roger Stone Reciting the Proud Boys' 'Fraternity Creed,' the First Step for Initiation to the Extremist Group," Business Insider, July 12, 2022, https://www.businessinsider.com/roger-stone-proud-boys-fraternity -creed-video-january-6-committee-2022-7.
1486. Sheera Frenkel and Annie Karni, "Proud Boys Celebrate Trump's 'Stand By' Remark about Them at the Debate," *New York Times*, September 29, 2020.
1487. Frenkel and Karni, "Proud Boys Celebrate."
1488. Frenkel and Karni, "Proud Boys Celebrate."
1489. "Leader of Oath Keepers and Oath Keepers Member Found Guilty of Seditious Conspiracy and Other Charges Related to the US Capitol Breach," press release, United States Department of Justice, November 29, 2022, https://www.justice.gov/opa/pr/leader-oath-keepers -and-oath-keepers-member-found-guilty-seditious-conspiracy-and-other; Alan Feuer and Zach Montague, "Four Proud Boys Convicted of Sedition in Key Jan. 6 Case," *New York Times*, May 4, 2023.
1490. "Leader of Oath Keepers."
1491. Kathleen Belew, *Bring the War Home: The White Power Movement and Paramilitary America* (Cambridge, MA: Harvard University Press, 2018).
1492. "Remembering Waco," Bureau of Alcohol, Tobacco, Firearms and Explosives, accessed August 18, 2023, https://www.atf.gov/our-history/remembering-waco.
1493. "Remembering Waco."
1494. "Remembering Waco."

1495. Charles Homans, "A Trump Rally, a Right-Wing Cause and the Enduring Legacy of Waco," *New York Times*, March 24, 2023.
1496. Belew, *Bring the War Home*, 206.
1497. Belew, *Bring the War Home*, 206.
1498. Jeffrey Toobin, *Homegrown: Timothy McVeigh and the Rise of Right-Wing Extremism* (New York: Simon & Schuster, 2023), 84.
1499. Belew, *Bring the War Home*, 210.
1500. Belew, *Bring the War Home*, 210.
1501. Homans, "A Trump Rally."
1502. Homans, "A Trump Rally."
1503. Homans, "A Trump Rally."
1504. Homans, "A Trump Rally."
1505. Barton Gellman, "Trump's Next Coup Has Already Begun," *The Atlantic*, December 6, 2021.
1506. Gellman, "Trump's Next Coup."
1507. Jamie Raskin, "The Second Amendment Gives No Comfort to Insurrectionists," Opinion, *New York Times*, September 27, 2022.
1508. Raskin, "The Second Amendment."
1509. Raskin, "The Second Amendment."
1510. US Const. art. I § 8, cl. 15.
1511. US Const. art. IV § 4.
1512. US Const. amend. XIV.
1513. Hsu and Allam, "Landmark Oath Keepers Verdict."
1514. Rebellion or Insurrection, 18 USC. § 2383 (Sept. 13, 1994).
1515. Glenn Thrush, "What Do Most Mass Shooters Have in Common? They Bought Their Guns Legally," *New York Times*, May 16, 2022.
1516. Thrush, "What Do Most."
1517. Raskin, "The Second Amendment."
1518. Raskin, "The Second Amendment."
1519. 554 US 570, 626.
1520. Peter Manseau, "The Myth of the 'Good Guy with a Gun' Has Religious Roots," *New York Times*, June 23, 2022.
1521. Manseau, "The Myth."
1522. Manseau, "The Myth."
1523. Spike's Tactical, "The New Spike's Tactical Crusader rifle is officially available . . ." video, 1:54, Facebook, September 1, 2015, https://www.facebook.com/watch/?v=10153567267228664.
1524. Spike's Tactical, "The New Spike's Tactical Crusader."
1525. "Why are there so many guns in US campaign ads?—BBC News," BBC News, YouTube video, 3:11, https://www.youtube.com/watch?v=xMSxt4dlfpQ.
1526. Shannon Watts (@shannonrwatts), "This 'campaign ad' put out by Blake Masters does a great job of illustrating: 1) Why gun extremism turns off voters, 2) Why deregulating silencers - a GOP/NRA priority - is insanely dangerous, 3) Why the FBI should keep tabs on Masters now that he's lost," Twitter, November 12, 2022, 11:18 a.m., https://twitter.com/shannonrwatts /status/1591465462420090887?lang=en.
1527. Paulina Villegas, "GOP Congressman's Gun-Toting Family Christmas Photo Sparks Outrage Days after School Shooting," *Washington Post*, December 5, 2021.
1528. Villegas, "GOP Congressman's."
1529. Christina Wyman, "A Christmas Card with Guns? Lauren Boebert and Thomas Massie Start a New Culture War," Think, NBC News, December 10, 2021, https://www.nbcnews.com /think/opinion/christmas-card-guns-lauren-boebert-thomas-massie-start-new-culture -ncna1285709.
1530. "Missouri Couple Who Pointed Guns at BLM Protesters Seek Return of Firearms," *The Guardian* (London), January 5, 2022.
1531. Adela Sulliman, "Missouri Couple Who Pointed Guns at BLM Protesters Face Possible Law License Suspension," *Washington Post*, September 21, 2021.
1532. Sulliman, "Missouri Couple."
1533. "Missouri Couple."

1534. Tom Jackman, "67 Current, Former Prosecutors Defend St. Louis Prosecutor from Attacks in McCloskey Gun Case," *Washington Post*, July 22, 2020.
1535. Jackman, "67 Current, Former Prosecutors."
1536. Caitlyn Oprysko, "In Grievance-Filled Speech, St. Louis Couple Warn of Chaos in the Suburbs If Democrats Elected," Politico, August 24, 2020, https://www.politico.com/news/2020/08/24/mccloskey-convention-speech-guns-suburbs-401297.
1537. "Three Percenters."
1538. Gellman, "Trump's Next Coup."
1539. David Zucchino, "By Bullet or Ballot: One of the Only Successful Coups in American History," *Literary Hub*, January 9, 2020.
1540. Zucchino, "By Bullet or Ballot."
1541. Timothy B. Tyson, "The Ghosts of 1898," special report, *News and Observer* (NC), November 17, 2006, https://media2.newsobserver.com/content/media/2010/5/3/ghostsof1898.pdf.
1542. Zucchino, "By Bullet or Ballot."
1543. Tyson, "The Ghosts of 1898."
1544. Tyson, "The Ghosts of 1898."
1545. Tyson, "The Ghosts of 1898."
1546. "The Dorr Rebellion," Phillips Memorial Library, Providence College, accessed August 18, 2023, https://library.providence.edu/dorr/.
1547. Gillian Brockell, "The Texas Governor Who Refused to Concede after Losing a Bitter Election," *Washington Post*, November 16, 2020.
1548. "Grant Ends the Brooks-Baxter War in Arkansas," The History Engine, University of Richmond, accessed August 18, 2023, https://historyengine.richmond.edu/episodes/view/1395.
1549. Gordon Chadwick, "Battle of Liberty Place," New Orleans Historical, accessed August 18, 2023, https://neworleanshistorical.org/tours/show/8.
1550. Lones Seiber, "The Battle of Athens," *American Heritage* 36, no. 2 (February/March 1985).
1551. According to the US State Department website, the "military government changed the country's name to 'Myanmar' in 1989. The United States government continues to use the name 'Burma.'" "US Relations with Burma," US Department of State, June 3, 2021, https://www.state.gov/u-s-relations-with-burma/.
1552. Richard C. Paddock, "Myanmar's Coup and Its Aftermath, Explained," *New York Times*, December 9, 2022.
1553. Paddock, "Myanmar's Coup."
1554. "Myanmar: Aung San Suu Kyi's Party Wins Majority in Election," BBC News, November 13, 2020, https://www.bbc.com/news/world-asia-54899170.
1555. "Myanmar Rohingya: What You Need to Know about the Crisis," BBC News, January 23, 2020, https://www.bbc.com/news/world-asia-41566561.
1556. "US Relations with Burma."
1557. "US Relations with Burma."
1558. Sam Denney, "A Foiled Coup Attempt in Germany and the Danger of Conspiracy Theories," *Lawfare* (blog), December 12, 2022, https://www.lawfaremedia.org/article/foiled-coup-attempt-germany-and-danger-conspiracy-theories.
1559. Katrin Bennhold and Erika Solomon, "Germany Arrests 25 Suspected of Planning to Overthrow Government," *New York Times*, December 7, 2022.
1560. Denney, "A Foiled Coup Attempt."
1561. Jack Nicas, "What Drove a Mass Attack on Brazil's Capital? Mass Delusion," *New York Times.*, January 9, 2023.
1562. Nicas, "What Drove a Mass Attack."
1563. Nicas, "What Drove a Mass Attack."
1564. Nicas, "What Drove a Mass Attack."
1565. Nicas, "What Drove a Mass Attack."
1566. Nicas, "What Drove a Mass Attack."
1567. Jennifer Steinhauer, "Veterans Fortify the Ranks of Militias Aligned with Trump's Views," *New York Times*, September 11, 2020.

1568. Jennifer Szalai, "A Prosecutor's Backstage Tour of the Mueller Investigation," review of *Where Law Ends: Inside the Mueller Investigation*, by Andrew Weissmann, *New York Times*, September 21, 2020.

9. We Alone Can Fix It: Proposed Solutions

1569. "Achievements in Public Health, 1900-1999: Healthier Mothers and Babies," Centers for Disease Control and Prevention, October 1, 1999, https://www.cdc.gov/mmwr/preview /mmwrhtml/mm4838a2.htm.
1570. "Achievements in Public Health."
1571. "Achievements in Public Health."
1572. Steven Lee Myers and Eileen Sullivan, "Disinformation Has Become Another Untouchable Problem in Washington," *New York Times*, July 6, 2022.
1573. "Why Countering Violent Extremism Programs Are Bad Policy," Brennan Center for Justice, September 9, 2019, https://www.brennancenter.org/our-work/research-reports/why-countering -violent-extremism-programs-are-bad-policy.
1574. "Organization," National Counterterrorism Center, Office of the Director of National Intelligence, accessed August 18, 2023, https://www.dni.gov/index.php/nctc-who-we-are /organization/340-about/organization/foreign-malign-influence-center.
1575. David. E. Broockman and Joshua L. Kalla, "Consuming Cross-Cutting Media Causes Learning and Moderates Attitudes: A Field Experiment with Fox News Viewers," OSF Preprints, April 14, 2023, https://osf.io/jrw26.
1576. Broockman and Kalla, "Consuming Cross-Cutting Media."
1577. Joyce Vance, "An Encouraging Study: Fox News Viewers Can Change Their Minds," *Civil Discourse* (Substack), May 31, 2023, https://joycevance.substack.com/p/an-encouraging-study -fox-news-viewers.
1578. Cailin O'Connor and James Owen Weatherall, *The Misinformation Age: How False Beliefs Spread* (New Haven, CT: Yale University Press, 2018), 183.
1579. Act to Improve Enforcement of the Law in Social Networks, 2017, accessed August 30, 2023, https://www.article19.org/wp-content/uploads/2017/09/170901-Legal-Analysis-German -NetzDG-Act.pdf
1580. "The Digital Services Act: Ensuring a Safe and Accountable Online Environment," European Commission, accessed August 18, 2023, https://commission.europa.eu/strategy-and-policy /priorities-2019-2024/europe-fit-digital-age/digital-services-act-ensuring-safe-and-accountable -online-environment_en; Jillian Deutsch, "The EU's Fight Over Fake News," Bloomberg, April 29, 2022, https://www.bloomberg.com/news/newsletters/2022-04-29/the-eu-s-fight-over-fake-news.
1581. Protection for Private Blocking and Screening of Offensive Material, 47 USC. § 230 (Oct. 21, 1998).
1582. *The Commission on Information Disorder Final Report* (Aspen Institute, November 2021), 18, accessed August 30, 2023, https://www.aspeninstitute.org/wp-content/uploads/2021/11/Aspen -Institute_Commission-on-Information-Disorder_Final-Report.pdf.
1583. Twitter v. Taamneh, 598 U.S. ___ (2023).
1584. *The Commission on Information Disorder*, 72–75.
1585. *The Commission on Information Disorder*, 74.
1586. *The Commission on Information Disorder*, 74.
1587. *The Commission on Information Disorder*, 73.
1588. Keach Hagey and Jeff Horwitz, "Facebook Tried to Make Its Platform a Healthier Place. It Got Angrier Instead," *Wall Street Journal*, September 15, 2021.
1589. Eli Pariser, "Musk's Twitter Will Not Be the Town Square the World Needs," *Wired*, October 28, 2022.
1590. Dipayan Ghosh, "Don't Break Up Facebook—Treat It Like a Utility," *Harvard Business Review*, May 30, 2019, https://hbr.org/2019/05/dont-break-up-facebook-treat-it-like-a-utility.
1591. Clint Watts, "Terrorism and Social Media: Is Big Tech Doing Enough?" speech delivered to US Senate Committee on Commerce, Science, and Transportation, Capitol Building, January 17, 2018, Washington, DC, US Senate Committee on Commerce, Science, and

Transportation, https://www.commerce.senate.gov/2018/1/terrorism-and-social-media-is
bigtechdoingenough.

1592. *The Commission on Information Disorder*, 40.

1593. "Sponsorship Identification Rules," Federal Communications Commission, accessed August 18, 2023, https://www.fcc.gov/consumers/guides/sponsorship-identification-rules.

1594. "Sponsorship Identification Rules."

1595. "Sponsorship Identification Rules."

1596. *The Commission on Information Disorder*, 40.

1597. Mekela Panditharatne et al., "Information Gaps and Misinformation in the 2022 Elections," Brennan Center for Justice, August 2, 2022, https://www.brennancenter.org/our-work/research-reports/information-gaps-and-misinformation-2022-elections.

1598. Richard Stengel, *Information Wars: How We Lost the Global Battle against Disinformation and What We Can Do about It* (New York: Atlantic Monthly Press, 2019), 303.

1599. This article was highlighted in the *Detroit Free Press* on January 1, 2023: "According to Experts, Here's the Real Reason Why You Should Stop Hugging Your Pets," Greedy Finance, November 16, 2021, https://greedyfinance.com/index.php/en/2021/11/16/according-to-experts-heres-the-real-reason-why-you-should-stop-hugging-your-pets/.

1600. This article was highlighted in the *Detroit News* on January 1, 2023: "Doctor Tells: If You Have Too Much Belly Fat? (Eat This before Bed)," Gundry MD, May 19, 2021.

1601. Stengel, *Information Wars*, 303.

1602. Stengel, *Information Wars*, 303.

1603. Stengel, *Information Wars*, 306.

1604. Richard L. Hasen, *Cheap Speech: How Disinformation Poisons Our Politics—and How to Cure It* (New Haven, CT: Yale University Press, 2022), 138.

1605. William McKenzie, "Combating Disinformation through Local News Ecosystems," George W. Bush Presidential Center, July 28, 2021, https://www.bushcenter.org/publications/combating-disinformation-through-local-news-ecosystems.

1606. Sara Fischer, "Cities Are Turning into News Deserts," Axios, July 10, 2019, https://www.axios.com/2019/07/10/cities-are-turning-into-news-deserts.

1607. Martha Minow, *Saving the News: Why the Constitution Calls for Government Action to Preserve Freedom of Speech* (New York: Oxford University Press, 2021), 139.

1608. Mark Glaser, "How Local Foundations Can Support Local News," Knight Foundation, accessed August 18, 2023, https://knightfoundation.org/how-local-foundations-can-support-local-news-full/.

1609. Glaser, "How Local Foundations."

1610. Glaser, "How Local Foundations."

1611. Fact Sheet: FCC Political Programming Rules, accessed August 30, 2023, https://www.fcc.gov/sites/default/files/political_programming_fact_sheet.pdf.

1612. Daniel Kreiss and Matt Perault, "Four Ways to Fix Social Media's Political Ads Problem—without Banning Them," Opinion, *New York Times*, November 16, 2019.

1613. Kreiss and Perault, "Four Ways."

1614. Tom Brueggemann, "The Fired Fox News Political Editor Just Testified at the January 6 Hearing—and Is Still Right," IndieWire, June 13, 2022, https://www.indiewire.com/features/general/fox-news-ratings-drop-election-night-call-1234615188/.

1615. Lindsey Ellefson, "February Cable News Ratings: Fox News Posts Best Primetime Numbers Ever," The Wrap, February 25, 2020, https://www.thewrap.com/february-cable-news-ratings-fox-news-posts-best-primetime-numbers-ever/.

1616. Camille Caldera, "Fact Check: Fairness Doctrine Only Applied to Broadcast Licenses, Not Cable TV Like Fox News," *USA Today*, November 28, 2020.

1617. Caldera, "Fact Check: Fairness Doctrine."

1618. Brad Adgate, "2022 Was Another Gloomy Years for Many Cable Networks," *Forbes*, January 3, 2023.

1619. "10 Ways the EU Is Fighting Disinformation," European Commission, September 18, 2019, https://europeancommission.medium.com/10-ways-the-eu-is-fighting-disinformation-f07fca60e918.

1620. Stengel, *Information Wars*, 300.

1621. Clint Watts, *Messing with the Enemy: Surviving in a Social Media World of Hackers, Terrorists, Russians, and Fake News* (New York: Harper, 2018), 254; Jenny Gross, "How Finland Is Teaching a Generation to Spot Misinformation," *New York Times*, January 10, 2023.

1622. Jason Horowitz, "In Italian Schools, Reading, Writing and Recognizing Fake News," *New York Times*, 2017.

1623. Stengel, *Information Wars*, 301.

1624. Donald A. Barclay, *Disinformation: The Nature of Facts and Lies in the Post-Truth Era* (Lanham, MD: Rowman & Littlefield, 2022), 107.

1625. Asha Rangappa, "Disinformation, Democracy, and the Rule of Law" (speech, Connecticut Legal Conference, Connecticut Bar Association, Hartford, CT, June 10, 2019).

1626. Rangappa, "Disinformation, Democracy and the Rule of Law."

1627. Rangappa, "Disinformation, Democracy and the Rule of Law."

1628. "ClaimBuster," RAND Corporation, accessed August 18, 2023, https://www.rand.org/research/projects/truth-decay/fighting-disinformation/search/items/claimbuster.html.

1629. "Tools That Fight Disinformation Online," RAND Corporation, accessed August 18, 2023, https://www.rand.org/research/projects/truth-decay/fighting-disinformation/search.html.

1630. "Tools That Fight Disinformation Online."

1631. Rangappa, "Disinformation, Democracy and the Rule of Law."

1632. John R. Lewis Voting Rights Advancement Act, H.R. 4, 117th Cong. (September 14, 2021).

1633. John R. Lewis Voting Rights Advancement Act.

1634. John R. Lewis Voting Rights Advancement Act.

1635. "Annotated Guide to the For the People Act of 2021," Brennan Center for Justice, last updated March 18, 2021, https://www.brennancenter.org/our-work/policy-solutions/annotated-guide-people-act-2021.

1636. "Annotated Guide to the For the People Act of 2021."

1637. Mariana Alfaro, "Republicans Who Supported Voting Rights Act Now Oppose Bill Democrats Say Would Strengthen Its Provisions," *Washington Post*, January 19, 2022; Jacob Pramuk, "Senate Republicans Block Democrats' Sweeping Voting, Ethics Bill," CNBC, June 22, 2021, https://www.cnbc.com/2021/06/22/senate-to-vote-on-s1-for-the-people-act-bill.html.

1638. Disclose Act of 2021, S. 443, 117th Cong. (July 19, 2022).

1639. Disclose Act of 2021, S. 443, 117th Cong. (July 19, 2022).

1640. Amy B. Wang, "Senate Republicans Block Bill to Require Disclosure of 'Dark Money' Donors," *Washington Post*, September 22, 2022.

1641. Tim Lau, "The Honest Ads Act Explained," Brennan Center for Justice, January 17, 2020, https://www.brennancenter.org/our-work/research-reports/honest-ads-act-explained; Honest Ads Act, S. 1356, 116th Cong. (May 7, 2019).

1642. Adrian Blanco and Amy Gardner, "Where Republican Election Deniers Are on the Ballot near You," *Washington Post*, October 6, 2022.

1643. Damien Cave, "The World's Democracies Ask: Why Can't America Fix Itself?" *New York Times*, November 8, 2022.

1644. "The Role and Structure of Elections Canada," Elections Canada, accessed August 18, 2023. https://www.elections.ca/content.aspx?section=abo&dir=role&document=index&lang=e.

1645. "The Role and Structure of Elections Canada."

1646. Home page, Michigan Independent Citizens Redistricting Commission, accessed August 18, 2023, https://www.michigan.gov/micrc.

1647. "FAQ," Michigan Independent Citizens Redistricting Commission, accessed August 18, 2023, https://www.michigan.gov/micrc/about/faq.

1648. Tresa Baldas et al., "'Get to TCF': What Really Happened inside Detroit's Ballot Counting Center," *Detroit Free Press*, November 6, 2020.

1649. James Verini, "He Wanted to Count Every Vote in Philadelphia. His Party Had Other Ideas," *New York Times*, December 16, 2021; Katie Shepherd and Hannah Knowles, "Driven by Unfounded 'SharpieGate' Rumor, Pro-Trump Protesters Mass outside Arizona Vote-Counting Center," *Washington Post*, November 5, 2020.

1650. Verini, "He Wanted to Count."

1651. Verini, "He Wanted to Count."

1652. Verini, "He Wanted to Count."

1653. Karim Doumar and Cynthia Gordy Giwa, "How to Outsmart Election Disinformation," ProPublica, October 21, 2022, https://www.propublica.org/article/misinformvation-vs -disinformation-midterm-election-guide.

1654. "Election Communications Toolkit," National Association of State Election Directors, accessed August 18, 2023, https://www.nased.org/electioncommstoolkit.

1655. "Election Communications Toolkit."

1656. *Democracy Playbook* (Washington, DC: NewDEAL Forum, February 2023), https://newdealforum .org/wp-content/uploads/2023/02/Democracy-Playbook-Final.pdf.

1657. Kaitlyn Radde and Connie Hanzhang Jin, "The Next Round of Counting Begins in Alaska. Here's How Ranked-Choice Voting Works," NPR, November 22, 2022, https://www.npr .org/2022/11/22/1138422560/the-next-round-of-counting-begins-in-alaska-heres-how-ranked -choice-voting-works.

1658. Radde and Jin, "The Next Round."

1659. "Capitol Breach Cases," United States Attorney's Office District of Columbia, accessed August 18, 2023, https://www.justice.gov/usao-dc/capitol-breach-cases.

1660. Final Report of the Select Committee to Investigate the January 6th Attack on the United States Capitol, H.R. Doc. No. 117-663, 2d Sess. (Dec. 22, 2022).

1661. Final Report of the Select Committee.

1662. Final Report of the Select Committee.

1663. Matt Zapotosky and Devlin Barrett, "Garland: DOJ Will Hold Those Responsible for Jan. 6 Riot Accountable, Whether They Were Present or Committed Other Crimes," *Washington Post*, January 5, 2022.

1664. Richard Fausset and Danny Hakim, "With Racketeering Charges, Georgia Prosecutor Aims to 'Tell the Whole Story,'" *New York Times*, August 15. 2023.

1665. Clara Hendrickson, "Trumps' Fake Electors Charged by Michigan AG in Alleged 2020 Election Scheme," *Detroit Free Press*, July 18, 2023.

1666. "Jan. 6 Committee Refers Former President Trump for Criminal Prosecution," *New York Times*, December 19, 2022; Final Report of the Select Committee.

1667. James Doubek and Vanessa Romo, "Jury Finds Rally Organizers Liable for the Violence That Broke Out in Charlottesville," NPR, November 23, 2021, https://www.npr.org/2021/11/23 /1058024314/charlottesville-unite-the-right-trial-verdict.

1668. Doubek and Romo, "Jury Finds."

1669. Doubek and Romo, "Jury Finds."

1670. US Const. amend. XIV.

1671. Ashley Lopez, "A New Mexico Judge Cites Insurrection in Barring a County Commissioner from Office," NPR, September 6, 2022, https://www.wnyc.org/story/a-new-mexico-judge -cites-insurrection-in-barring-a-county-commissioner-from-office.

1672. Lopez, "A New Mexico Judge."

1673. Frank Figliuzzi, "Why the Jan. 6 Committee's 845-Page Report Wasn't Long Enough," Opinion, MSNBC, December 31, 2022, https://www.msnbc.com/opinion/msnbc-opinion /jan-6-committee-report-was-frustratingly-incomplete-rcna63555.

1674. Figliuzzi, "Why the Jan. 6 Committee."

1675. Clarence E. Anthony, Tina Lee, Jacob Gottlieb, and Brooks Rainwater, *On the Frontlines of Today's Cities: Trauma, Challenges and Solutions* (Washington, DC: National League of Cities, 2021), 33.

1676. Anthony, Lee, Gottlieb, and Rainwater, *On the Frontlines*, 32.

1677. *The Use of Social Media by United States Extremists*, National Consortium for the Study of Terrorism and Responses to Terrorism, accessed August 30, 2023. https://www.start.umd.edu /pubs/START_PIRUS_UseOfSocialMediaByUSExtremists_ResearchBrief_July2018.pdf.

1678. Cat Zakrzewski, Faiz Siddiqui, and Joseph Menn, "Musk's 'Free Speech' Agenda Dismantles Safety Work at Twitter, Insiders Say," *Washington Post*, November 22, 2022.

1679. Naomi Nix and Jeremy B. Merrill, "Advertisers Are Dropping Twitter. Musk Can't Afford to Lose Any More," *Washington Post*, November 22, 2022.

1680. Paul LeBlanc, "Threats Against Public Servants Define Chilling Jan. 6 Hearing," Politics, CNN, June 21, 2022, https://www.cnn.com/2022/06/21/politics/jan-6-hearings-election -threats-what-matters/index.html.

1681. The Trump campaign posted the wrong number for the House Speaker, resulting in a random citizen being bombarded with calls and text messages. Beth LeBlanc, "Trump Campaign Lists Lawmakers' Cells, Misdirects Calls for Chatfield to Former Petoskey Resident," *Detroit News*, January 4, 2021.

1682. Title 18, US Code, Section 2261A.

1683. Mary B. McCord and Jason M. Blazakis, "A Road Map for Congress to Address Domestic Terrorism," *Lawfare* (blog), February 27, 2019, https://www.lawfaremedia.org/article/road -map-congress-address-domestic-terrorism; Barbara McQuade, "Proposed Bills Would Help Combat Domestic Terrorism," *Lawfare* (blog), August 20, 2019, https://www.lawfaremedia .org/article/proposed-bills-would-help-combat-domestic-terrorism.

1684. Mary B. McCord, "It's Time for Congress to Make Domestic Terrorism a Federal Crime," *Lawfare* (blog), December 5, 2018, https://www.lawfaremedia.org/article/its-time-congress -make-domestic-terrorism-federal-crime.

1685. Hadley Baker, "Sen. McSally Proposes Domestic Terrorism Bill," *Lawfare* (blog), August 14, 2019, https://www.lawfaremedia.org/article/sen-mcsally-proposes-domestic-terrorism-bill.

1686. Glenn Thrush, "What Do Most Mass Shooters Have in Common? They Bought Their Guns Legally," *New York Times*, May 16, 2022; Barbara L. McQuade, "Not a Suicide Pact: Urgent Strategic Recommendations for Reducing Domestic Terrorism in the United States," *Texas National Security Review* 5, no. 2 (Spring 2022).

1687. Thrush, "What Do Most"; Eric Levinson, Sara Smart, Nouran Salaheih, Isabel Rosales, and Andy Rose, "Jacksonville Gunman in Racially Motivated Attack Legally Bought Two Weapons Earlier This Year, Sheriff Says," CNN, August 27, 2023.

1688. An Act to Control and Prevent Crime, Pub. L. No. 103-322, 108 Stat. (Sept. 13, 1994).

1689. District of Columbia v. Heller, 554 US 570, 626 (2008).

1690. Jeremy Travis, *Impacts of the 1994 Assault Weapons Ban: 1994–96* (Washington, DC: National Institute of Justice, March 1999).

1691. "Federal Judge Sentences Three Men Convicted of Racially Motivated Hate Crimes in Connection with the Killing of Ahmaud Arbery in Georgia," press release, United States Department of Justice, August 8, 2022, https://www.justice.gov/opa/pr/federal-jury-finds -three-men-guilty-hate-crimes-connection-pursuit-and-killing-ahmaud-arbery.

1692. Paul Egan, "Sheriff Who Suggested Whitmer Kidnapping Could Be 'Citizen's Arrest' Sues over Election," *Detroit Free Press*, December 7, 2020.

1693. AJ Willingham, "Citizen's Arrest Laws Aren't Cut and Dry. Here's What You Need to Know," CNN, November 10, 2021, https://www.cnn.com/2021/11/10/us/citizens-arrest-what -is-explained-trnd/index.html.

1694. Willingham, "Citizen's Arrest Laws."

1695. Barbara McQuade, "We Have Met the Enemy and They Are Us," podcast audio, 47:09, *Horns of a Dilemma*, June 17, 2022.

1696. *National Strategy for Countering Domestic Terrorism* (Washington, DC: National Security Council, June 2021), 10–11; McQuade, "We Have Met the Enemy."

1697. "Fact Sheets on Unlawful Militias for All 50 States Now Available from Georgetown Law's Institute for Constitutional Advocacy and Protection," press release, September 22, 2020, Institute for Constitutional Advocacy and Protection, Georgetown Law, https://www.law .georgetown.edu/our-press-releases/fact-sheets-on-unlawful-militias-for-all-50-states -now-available-from-georgetown-laws-institute-for-constitutional-advocacy-and-protection/.

1698. *Prohibiting Private Armies at Public Rallies* (Washington, DC: Institute for Constitutional Advocacy and Protection, September 2020), 5.

1699. *Prohibiting Private Armies*, 6.

1700. *Prohibiting Private Armies*, 7.

1701. Beth Reinhard and Anne Gearan, "Most Trump Clemency Grants Bypass Justice Dept. and Go to Well-Connected Offenders," *Washington Post*, February 3, 2020.

10. We Hold These Truths to Be Self-Evident: A Way Forward

1702. Maureen Dowd, "Irish Eyes Aren't Smiling," *New York Times*, July 16, 2022.

1703. Dowd, "Irish Eyes."

1704. Steven Levitsky and Daniel Ziblatt, *How Democracies Die* (New York, NY: Crown, 2018), 8.

1705. Levistsky and Ziblatt, *How Democracies Die*, 9.

1706. Levitsky and Ziblatt, *How Democracies Die*, 9.

1707. Levitsky and Ziblatt, *How Democracies Die*, 128–29.

1708. Chris Leaverton, "Who Controlled Redistricting in Every State," Brennan Center for Justice, October 5, 2022, https://www.brennancenter.org/our-work/research-reports/who-controlled -redistricting-every-state.

1709. I would include here President Bill Clinton's pardon of hedge fund manager Marc Rich, whose ex-wife had donated to Clinton's presidential library and Hillary Clinton's Senate campaign, and President Donald Trump's pardon of political allies and politicians convicted of public corruption. Jessica Taylor, "More Surprises: FBI Releases Files on Bill Clinton's Pardon of Marc Rich," NPR, November 1, 2016, https://www.wgbh.org/news/2016-11-01/more -surprises-fbi-releases-files-on-bill-clintons-pardon-of-marc-rich.

1710. Russell Wheeler, "McConnell's Fabricated History to Justify a 2020 Supreme Court Vote," Brookings, September 24, 2020, https://www.brookings.edu/articles/mcconnells-fabricated -history-to-justify-a-2020-supreme-court-vote/.

1711. "1933 Inaugural Address Curriculum Hub," Franklin D. Roosevelt Presidential Library and Museum, accessed August 18, 2023, https://www.fdrlibrary.org/first-inaugural-curriculum -hub.

1712. Ruth Ben-Ghiat, *Strongmen: Mussolini to the Present* (New York, NY: W. W. Norton & Company, 2020), 260.

1713. Ben-Ghiat, *Strongmen*, 260–61.

1714. Anand Giridharadas, "The Uncomfortable Truths That Could Yet Defeat Fascism," *New York Times*, October 17, 2022.

1715. Giridharadas, "The Uncomfortable Truths."

1716. Giridharadas, "The Uncomfortable Truths."

1717. Abraham Lincoln, "Second Inaugural Address," speech, March 4, 1865, Washington, DC, National Park Service, https://www.nps.gov/linc/learn/historyculture/lincoln-second-inaugural .htm.

INDEX

accountability, 71
Acosta, Jim, 40
active measures, 69–91
Active Measures (Rid), 70
advertising
  nostalgia and, 36
  political, 149
  on social media, 149
  television, 36
Affordable Health Care Act, 82
Afrikaner National Party, 30
AG Guidelines. *See Attorney General's*
  Guidelines for Domestic FBI Operations
AI. *See* artificial intelligence
AIDS epidemic, 13
Åkesson, Jimmie, 97–98
alternate truths, 65
Amash, Justin, 136
America First, 173, 185–86
  Trump on, 27
American Nations (Woodard), 7
Amman, Molly, 193–94
anonymity
  free speech and, 145–46
  Internet Research Agency and, 119
  prohibiting, 254–55
  social media and, 118–20, 145–46
Anthony, Susan B., 168
anticipatory disinformation, 117
Antifa, 49
antipathy, 125
apartheid South Africa, 30
The Apprentice, 59
Arab Spring, 48
Arbery, Ahmaud, 279
Arena, Andy, 235
Arendt, Hannah, 24
Arpaio, Joe, 229–30
artificial intelligence (AI), 137–38. *see also*
  bots; ChatGPT
  Hawaii wildfires and, 17–18

The Art of War (Sun Tzu), 64
Asian Americans, 198
Aspen Institute, 252
assault weapons, 240. *See also* Second
  Amendment
  banning, 277–78
  glamorization of, 15–16, 242
  images, 241–42
  promotion of, 16
  religion and, 241
  tribe signaling and, 242
asymmetry of information, 86
Attorney General's Guidelines for Domestic FBI
  Operations (AG Guidelines), 152–53
Atwood, Margaret, 99
authoritarianism
  attraction of, 169–70
  Ben-Ghiat on, 99, 218
  branding and, 37
  civil servants and, 41–46
  critics and, 37–49
  defined, 24
  demonization and, 30–35
  elitism and, 38
  emotions and, 25–29
  examples of, 24
  experts and, 38, 44–46
  fear and, 25–26
  image and, 58–60
  insults and, 84–85
  judicial system and, 46–47
  media and, 38–41
  nostalgia seduction and, 35–36
  Orbán and, 169
  Pepinsky on, 47
  playbook, 24, 25
  protesters and, 47–49
  scapegoating and, 30–35
  simplicity and, 85
  societal divisions and, 29–37
  in Sweden, 97–98

ABOUT THE AUTHOR

Barbara McQuade is a professor from practice at the University of Michigan Law School, her alma mater, where she teaches courses in criminal law, criminal procedure, national security, and data privacy. She is also a legal analyst for NBC News and MSNBC, and co-host of the #SistersInLaw podcast.

From 2010 to 2017, McQuade served as the US Attorney for the Eastern District of Michigan. She was appointed by President Barack Obama and was the first woman to serve in her position. Earlier in her career, she worked as a sportswriter and copy editor, a judicial law clerk, an associate in private practice, and an assistant US attorney. She and her husband have four children and live in Ann Arbor.